The Short Fiction of
AMBROSE BIERCE

The Short Fiction of
AMBROSE BIERCE

A Comprehensive Edition

Edited by
S. T. Joshi
Lawrence I. Berkove
David E. Schultz

III

The University of Tennessee Press / Knoxville

LIBRARY OF CONGRESS CATALOGING-IN-PUBLICATION DATA

Bierce, Ambrose, 1842–1914?
[Short stories]
The short fiction of Ambrose Bierce : a comprehensive edition / edited by S.T. Joshi,
Lawrence I. Berkove, and David E. Schultz.— 1st ed.
    p. cm.
Includes bibliographical references and index.
ISBN 1-57233-475-4 (set : acid-free paper) — ISBN 1-57233-538-6 (v. 3 : acid-free paper)
I. Joshi, S. T., 1958 – II. Berkove, Lawrence I. III. Schultz, David E., 1952– IV. Title.
PS1097.A1 2006
813'.4— dc22

                    2006001036

CONTENTS
VOLUME 1

Part 1. 1868–1876

Some Fiction: From *The Fiend's Delight*

Part 2. 1878–1886

VOLUME 2
Part 3. 1887–1893

VOLUME 3

Part 4. 1895–1904

Part 5. 1905–1910

One of the last photographs of Ambrose Bierce. University of Virginia Library, Manuscript Division.

PART 4

1895–1904

INTRODUCTION

In 1894, as if at last exhausted by grappling with the agonizing moral and philosophical enigmas that had increasingly engaged him from the time he left the
army, AB almost abruptly ceased composing his nightmarish tales of desperate
humans driven to, and past, their limits of endurance. He published no tales
at all during the year, and when he returned to fiction in 1895 he fell back, as
it were, either on tales of the supernatural, which he had earlier turned out easily because to him they were only entertainment and did not require tightly
woven plots, or on extended social satires, such as the sketches that he would
soon combine into "The Land Beyond the Blow." Although these constituted
the bulk of his fiction from 1895 to 1904, he quickly regained his strength and
wrote some few tales that prove his fire was not out.

The satires, moreover, with their strange names and even stranger customs, although inferior to their model of *Gulliver's Travels*, are not negligible.
Bizarre though they may seem at first glance, they share the common underlying enterprise of challenging what society accepted as self-evident standards.
Repeatedly, the satires invert accepted values and either show that the inver-
sions are not as revolutionary as they might appear or that, if really new, they
also have merit. This, therefore, is a continuation of Bierce's long-standing
practice of demonstrating that conventional wisdom is not only not absolute
but is even not necessarily as sound as society believes it to be.

For the most part, the satires expose social hypocrisy by making explicit
through exaggeration features of American culture whose practices are at odds
with its ideals. In "The Great Strike of 1895," for instance, despite the official
American position in favor of free trade, competition, and open markets, publishers are depicted as having conspired with each other to set the percentages

they would allow to authors. That this is regarded as standard business practice can only mean that the claims to competition and free markets are just words. The organization of authors into unions, although understandable, is, however, another violation of free market theory and a reduction of the rights of individuals. "Industrial Discontent in Ancient America" concentrates on criticizing unions, but Bierce's main objection to them in this piece is that they encourage and use violence. Unless readers are familiar with American history of this period, they are unlikely to know that unions then indulged more in violence—bombings, sabotage, riots, and even murders—than happens today. Bierce rejects the extremes of the "ruling" classes and the mobs but is left in a lonely position, maintaining the stated ideals of the early republic.

The first satire on Ug continues to demonstrate that those ideals are mainly honored in the breach. The narrator is an American patriot, but when he attempts to criticize the open conflicts of interest which characterize Uggard jurisprudence he either encounters rational arguments that he cannot best or has to fall back on the theoretical—and embarrassing because obviously untrue—position that American jurisprudence is beyond corruption and operates routinely in a state of purity.

In "The War with Wug," Bierce satirizes governments so fundamentally dedicated to holding costs down that they repay the devoted service of its veterans by killing them off when they are no longer needed. On the other hand, governments that do support their veterans incur heavy and long-lasting financial obligations, and these can cause national financial distress down the road. Inasmuch as the piece was written as the Spanish-American War ended, there is a possibility of its having topical value as a commentary. Readers can decide for themselves how close or distant those policies may be to reality.

Bierce was an active and outspoken opponent of big businesses and monopolies like the railroads that used their power and influence to control government and cheat the populace. But he was also definitely not a sentimental believer in the wisdom or virtue of the common man, nor did he align himself automatically with the underdog. "Trustland" had to have been an infuriating dissent from the popular hue and cry against trusts in 1899, all the more so because it is so rational. The fear of bigness is still a live issue in twenty-first-century America, and Bierce's response to it has not lost any of its validity. As a way of criticizing organized Christianity, the religion of the classes and the masses, "The Dog in Ganegwag" sarcastically makes the point that the sincerity, warmth, and tolerance that should be central to Christianity is absent from its formal branches but alive and well in the true religion of the population, caniolatry—dog worship.

Bierce's criticism of his society was based in profound pessimism, a feature of his late period. It should be noted, however, that he was far from being alone

897

in deep pessimism, or even the most extreme pessimist of the early twentieth century. Mark Twain considered the whole human race literally damned. Henry Adams lost a sense of coherence and direction for modern civilization and regarded the world with a shudder. Even Lincoln Steffens, the once-hopeful muckraking reformer, and John Reed, the idealistic journalist, came to believe that Russia represented the hope of the future and that America was opposed to progress. Other famous pessimists of the period include the English writers Thomas Hardy and A. E. Housman. It is too easy to look back on Bierce and these contemporaries with condescension and depreciate their writings as being morbid or moody. It would be more profitable to respect their intelligence and sincerity and ponder the reasons for their pessimism. In Bierce's case, it is that he considered America so rotten with fraud and folly that it was doomed.

"The Alternative Proposal" supplies some specific examples. Bierce had been an outspoken critic of the way the Spanish-American War was conducted. Although he commented on the war from San Francisco he understood more about military matters than any of the many correspondents who were sent to Cuba to cover the battles. From thousands of miles away Bierce concluded that the dispatches the military gave to the press and the jingoistic press to the credulous public were not accurate; he recognized exaggerated claims, bad planning, and inept execution from afar and quickly figured out that America was beating Spain because the Spanish military leaders were even more incompetent than the American. "The Alternative Proposal" satirizes the selfsame American military leaders as pompous diplomats, self-blinded to their arrogant errors. Bierce's fears for the future were reasonable.

A device Bierce invented in his late period to comment gloomily on current trends as well as current events was the persona of the Future Historian. A literary ancestor of this device was Shelley's "Ozymandias" (1817), a famous poem that pictured an utter desolation except for a broken statue of a king with an inscription arrogantly proclaiming his greatness. Similarly, the Future Historian sketches all share the assumptions that the American civilization of the moment will one day be so obliterated that historians of the future will have to attempt to reconstruct it from surviving fragments of documents, and so few will be those fragments that those future historians, like those of today with surviving artifacts of the past, will make ingenious but erroneous interpretations about them. Each separate sketch, moreover, concentrates on some separate topic of major interest to contemporary society: yachting as a sport, the temperance reformer Carry Nation, and President Theodore Roosevelt. By the implication of the Future Historian context, these topics are only of accidental and ephemeral importance to the history of the America of their day. In "The Extinction of the Smugwumps," however, the Future Historian has substantiated evidence that misunderstood Nature, through the agencies of murderous weather and geological cataclysm, doomed America.

Bierce projected these fears into a future when the folly and willful blindness of Europe brought the downfall of the West. "A Chronicle of the Time to Be" astutely recognized that presently backward but potentially powerful countries would sooner rather than later realize their potential and seek vengeance on the West, which had humiliated them. They would accomplish this by deception on their part and by taking advantage of Western nations' internal vying with each other for profit and commercial advantage and of their short-sighted indisposition to maintaining their strength and unity. Here again, Bierce was not alone. Admonitions against the "yellow peril" were commonplace in Europe and America, a mixed chorus of voices of arrogant imperialism, gross racism, and empirical prudence. For decades, England had quietly engaged in "the Great Game" in India, an undeclared war against Russian influence. Kipling's poem "The Truce of the Bear" (1898) warned against believing Russian overtures of peace: "When he shows as seeking quarter, with paws like hands in prayer, / *That* is the time of peril—the time of the Truce of the Bear!" A few years earlier, in his poem "Tommy," a defense against militant pacifism on behalf of the eponymous British soldier Tommy Atkins, Kipling observed "Yes, makin' mock o' uniforms that guard you while you sleep / Is cheaper than them uniforms, an' they're starvation cheap." Bierce, who hated war, also understood that peace has a price, and that remaining vigilant and prepared and willing to fight is paradoxically part of that price in a world where war is the norm and peace is only the temporary interludes between wars.

Bierce did not completely forgo the writing of conventional fiction during these years, nor did his pen forget its cunning. "An Affair of Outposts" is excellent, second only to Bierce's best Civil War stories. "At Old Man Eckart's," while typical of the supernatural sketches of inexplicable disappearances he had been writing since the late 1880s, is still better than the average tale of that kind in the general market. "A Diagnosis of Death," with its challenge of reason, is a better tale of the uncanny. "The Eyes of the Panther" is an even more effective story in its audacity, sureness of touch, and build up of suspense. In "A Letter from a Btrugumian," Bierce ventures lightly into the relatively new territory of science fiction. "Moxon's Master," subtle, deft, and straight-faced in its weaving of an attractive web of deliberately hopeless complexity, is one of the best hoaxes Bierce ever wrote, and one of the best ever written. He was at the top of his form in it, showing not only a command of ghost stories and the genres of the detective story and science fiction, but also an anticipation of styles of literary interpretation, probably including the brand-new one of Freudian psychology. Clearly, the master still had surprises for his readers.

THE GREAT STRIKE OF 1895

NEW YORK, July 2, 1895.—The strike of the American Authors' Guild continues to hold public attention. No event in the history of trades-unionism since the great railroad strike of last year has equaled it in interest. Nothing else is talked of here. In some parts of the city all business is suspended and the excitement grows more intense hourly.

At about 10 o'clock this morning a non-union author attempting to enter the premises of D. Appleton & Co. with a roll of manuscript was set upon by a mob of strikers and beaten into insensibility. The strikers were driven from their victim by the police, but only after a fight in which both sides suffered severely.

NEW YORK, July 3.—Rioting was renewed last night in front of the boycotted publishing house of Charles Scribner's Sons, 153–157 Fifth avenue. Though frequently driven back by charges of the police, who used their clubs freely, the striking authors succeeded in demolishing all the front windows by stone-throwing. One shot was fired into the interior, narrowly missing a young lady typewriter. Mr. William D. Howells,[1] a member of the Guild's board of managers, declares that he has irrefragable proof that this outrage was committed by some one connected with the Publishers' Protective League for the purpose of creating public sympathy.

It has been learned that the non-union author so severely beaten yesterday died of his injuries last night. His name is said to have been Richard Henry (or Hengist) Stoddard,[2] formerly a member of the Guild, but expelled for denouncing the action of President Brander Matthews[3] in ordering the strike.

LATER.—Matters look more and more threatening. A crowd of ten thousand authors, headed by Col. Thomas Wentworth Higginson,[4] is reported to be marching upon the Astor Library,[5] which is strongly guarded by police, heavily armed. Many book-stores have been wrecked and their contents destroyed.

Mrs. Julia Ward Howe, who was shot last night while setting fire to the establishment of Harper & Bros., cannot recover. She is delirious, and lies on her cot in the Bellevue Hospital singing "The Battle Hymn of the Republic."[6]

BOSTON, July 3.—Industrial discontent has broken out here. The members of the local branch of the American Authors' Guild threw down their pens this morning and declared that until satisfactory settlement of novelists' percentages should be arrived at not a hero and heroine should live happily ever afterward in Boston. The publishing house of Houghton, Mifflin & Co. is guarded by a detachment of Pinkerton men[7] armed with Winchester rifles and a Gatling gun. The publishers say that they are getting all the manuscripts that they are able to reject, and profess to have no apprehension as to the future. Mr. Joaquin Miller, a non-union poet from Nevada, visiting some Indian relatives here, was terribly beaten by a mob of strikers to-day. Mr. Miller was the aggressor; he was calling them "sea-doves"—by which he is said to have meant "gulls."[8]

CHICAGO, July 3.—The authors' strike is assuming alarming dimensions and is almost beyond control by the police. The Mayor is strongly urged to ask for assistance from the militia, but the strikers profess to have no fear of his doing so. They say that he was once an author himself, and is in sympathy with them. He wrote "The Beautiful Snow."[9] In the mean time a mob of strikers numbering not fewer than one thousand men, women and children, headed by such determined labor leaders as Percival Pollard and Hamlin Garland,[10] are parading the streets and defying the authorities. A striker named Opie Reed,[11] arrested yesterday for complicity in the assassination of Mr. Stone, of the publishing firm of Stone & Kimball,[12] was released by this mob from the officers that had in him custody. Mr. Pollard publishes a letter in the *Herald* this morning saying that Mr. Stone was assassinated by an emissary of the Publishers' Protective League to create public sympathy, and strongly hints that the assassin is the head of the house of McClurg & Co.

NEW YORK, July 4.—All arrangements for celebrating the birthday of American independence are "off." The city is fearfully excited, and scenes of violence occur hourly. Macmillan & Co.'s establishment was burned last night, and four lives were lost in the flames. The loss of property is variously estimated. All the publishing houses are guarded by the militia, and it is said that Government troops will land this afternoon to protect the United States mails carrying the manuscripts of strike-breaking authors, in transit to publishers. The destruction of the Astor Library and the Cooper Union[13] and the closing of all the book-stores that escaped demolition in yesterday's rioting have caused sharp public distress. No similar book-famine has ever been known in this city. Novel-readers particularly, their needs being so imperative, are suffering severely, and unless relieved soon will leave the metropolis. While beating a noisy person named E. W. Townsend[14] last night, one Richard Harding Davis[15] had the misfortune to break two of his fingers. He said Townsend was a strike-breaker and had given information to the police, but it turns out that he is a zealous striker, and was haranguing the mob at the time of the assault. His audience of rioting authors, all of whom belonged to the War Story branch of the Guild, mistook Mr. Davis for an officer of the peace and ran away. Mr. Townsend, who cannot recover and apparently does not wish to, is said to be the author of a popular book called *The Chimney Fadder*. Advices from Boston relate the death of a Pinkerton spy named T. B. Aldrich,[16] who attempted to run the gauntlet of union pickets and enter the premises of The Arena Publishing Company, escorting Walter Blackburn Harte.[17] Mr. Harte was rescued by the police and sailed at once for England.

PHILADELPHIA, July 5.—A mob of striking authors attacked the publishing house of J. B. Lippincott & Co. this morning and were fired on by the militia. Twenty are known to have been killed outright—the largest number of writers ever immortalized at one time.

NEW YORK, July 5.—In an interview yesterday Mrs. Louise Chandler Moulton,[18] treasurer of the Guild, said that notwithstanding the heavy expense of maintaining needy strikers with dependent families, there would be no lack of funds to carry on the fight. Contributions are received daily from sympathetic trades. Sixty dollars have been sent in by the Confederated Undertakers and forty-five by the Association of Opium-Workers. President Brander Matthews has telegraphed to all the Guild's branches in other cities that they can beat the game if they will stand pat.

NEW YORK, July 6.—Sympathy strikes are the order of the day, and "risings" are reported everywhere. In this city the entire East Side is up and out. Shantytown, Ballyspalpeen, Goatville and Niggernest are in line. Among those killed in yesterday's conflict with the United States troops at Madison-square was Mark Twain,[19] who fell while cheering on a large force of women of the town. He was shot all to rags, so as to be hardly distinguishable from a human being.

CHICAGO, July 7.—John Vance Cheney[20] was arrested at 3 o'clock this morning while placing a dynamite bomb on the Clark-street bridge. He is believed to have entertained the design, also, of setting the river on fire. Two publishers were shot this morning by General Lew Wallace,[21] who escaped in the confusion of the incident. The victims were employed as accountants in the Methodist Book Concern.

THE GREAT STRIKE OF 1895

NEW YORK, July 8.—The authors' strike has collapsed, and the strikers are seeking employment as waiters in the places made vacant by the lockout of the Restaurant Trust. The Publishers' Protective League declares that no author concerned in the strike will ever again see his name upon a title-page. The American Authors' Guild is a thing of the past. Arrests are being made every hour. As soon as he can procure bail, President Brander Matthews will go upon the vaudeville stage.

E (5 May 1895): 26 (as "The Strike of 1899"); *CW* 12.297–304.

NOTES

The 1890s in America were years of financial and labor unrest. AB was critical of both the high-handedness and inclination of business and industry toward monopolies or trusts, and the demagogic practices of labor unions and their tendency to unleash lawbreaking and violence. He believed that one extreme represented the worst features of American democracy and its capitalistic orientation, and the other a reaction in the direction of socialism and anarchy, and that both extremes endangered the republic. In imagining this strike, therefore, AB satirized publishers for their complicity in setting agreed-upon authorial percentages and for the commercial arrogance suggested by their claim that despite the strike they were "getting all the manuscripts that they are able to *reject*" (emphasis added). On the other hand, he satirized authors not only for their willingness to pervert by stretching what AB believed should be a pure impulse to create individual works of literature into an ongoing commercial arrangement of literary production for sustainable income, and also for their base willingness to enforce their financial ambitions upon all authors and thereby warp artistic individualism into conformity. In other words, he took the position of "a plague on both your houses." No pattern is readily apparent in AB's political positioning of friends and enemies except, possibly, that despite their professions of artistic high-mindedness, authors at bottom are shown as mercenary and self-serving as everybody else. The tale, however, ends ominously but realistically with business ultimately winning and former authors worse off than they were before. In *CW* 12, AB retitled the work and dated its composition to 1894.

1. William Dean Howells (1837–1920) was one of the most respected authors and critics of his day, but AB did not think much of him or his work: "Men of letters manufacture one another. The two finest products of the mill are [Henry] James and Howells. Neither can think and the latter cannot write. He can not write at all. The other day . . . I took a random page of this man's work and in twenty minutes had marked forty solecisms—instances of the use of words without a sense of their importance or a knowledge of their meaning—the substitution of a word that he did not want for a word that he did not think of" ("Prattle," *W,* no. 342 [17 Feb. 1883]: 5). Howells's chief publisher was Harper & Brothers. AB was outspokenly critical of Howells for advocating that American literature should reflect the "smiling aspects" of life and not make female readers uncomfortable. AB called Howells "Miss Nancy," implying that he was effeminitely prissy.

2. A deliberate confusion of two authors, the American poet and editor Richard Henry Stoddard (1825–1903) and the British poet Richard Henry (or Hengist) Horne (1803–84).

3. Brander Matthews (1852–1929), leading American critic and editor of the period. In late 1892 AB had written Matthews thanking him for his favorable notice of *Tales of Soldiers and Civilians* in "More American Stories," *Co* 13, no. 5 (Sept. 1892): 629–30 (see AB to Brander Matthews, 28 Nov. 1892, MS, Columbia University).

4. Thomas Wentworth Higginson (1823–1911), American essayist and first editor of the poems of Emily Dickinson. He commanded a regiment of African Americans during the Civil War, attaining the rank of colonel.

5. The first free library in New York, founded in 1854 and located at 425 Lafayette Street. In 1911 its holdings were merged with two other collections to form the New York Public Library.

6. The American author Julia Ward Howe (1819–1910) composed "The Battle Hymn of the Republic" in 1861; it was published the next year. Bellevue Hospital opened in 1736, eventually securing a large tract of land for its various branches on First Avenue and Twenty-sixth Street on the East Side of Manhattan; its current name was adopted in 1825. A ward for the insane was added in the late 1870s.

7. The Pinkertons, a private detective agency founded in 1850, were frequently used in the later nineteenth century by owners of factories and other businesses to protect property and, in some cases, to intimidate striking workers. In a notorious incident in July 1892, a battle between Pinkertons and strikers at the steel plant in Homestead, Pennsylvania, owned by Andrew Carnegie, resulted in the deaths of ten strikers and three Pinkertons.

8. Joaquin Miller was born in Indiana but moved to California and achieved celebrity both for his poetry and his flamboyant personality. For a time he lived with a tribe of Digger Indians. He was a longtime friend of AB, who nevertheless often satirized him.

9. John Hopkins was the mayor of Chicago in 1893–95, George Swift in 1895–97, and Carter Harrison II in 1897–1905. None were known for their literary skills. "The Beautiful Snow" (*Harper's Weekly*, 27 Nov. 1858) was published anonymously and became widely popular. Many conjectures were made as to its authorship until John Whitaker Watson (1824–90) came forward as the author, reprinting the poem in *The Beautiful Snow and Other Poems* (1869). AB joked often about the numerous claimants to authorship.

10. Percival Pollard (1869–1911), critic, playwright, and friend of AB. He had reprinted portions of AB's journalism in his magazine, *Figaro* (Chicago), in 1893 and wrote a substantial chapter on him in *Their Day in Court* (1909). Hamlin Garland (1860–1940), novelist and memoirist.

11. Opie Read (1852–1939), novelist, journalist, and editor. AB's misspelling of his last name is probably inadvertent.

12. AB submitted several works to the Chicago firm of Stone & Kimball in the period 1893–96, including *The Fall of the Republic and Other Satires*, a collection of his political satires (probably the four included in *CW* 1).

13. The Cooper Union for the Advancement of Science and Art, at Astor Place and East 7th Street, was founded by Peter Cooper in 1859 as an institution offering free education to the sons and daughters of working-class families. It is now associated with New York University.

14. E. W. Townsend (1855–1942), author of *"Chimmie Fadden"; Major Max; and Other Stories* (1895), was a friend of AB, although AB did not care for Townsend's use of dialect in his stories.

15. Richard Harding Davis (1864–1916), popular novelist and journalist.

THE GREAT STRIKE OF 1895

16. Thomas Bailey Aldrich (1836–1907), once-celebrated poet, novelist, and dramatist.
17. Walter Blackburn Harte (1867–98), essayist, editor of the *New England Magazine*, and friend of AB. His book *Meditations in Motley* (1894) was published by the Arena Publishing Co.
18. Louise Chandler Moulton (1835–1908), poet, journalist, and children's writer.
19. Pseudonym of Samuel Langhorne Clemens (1835–1910). He and AB had been sporadically acquainted since the 1870s, and they disliked each other.
20. John Vance Cheney (1848–1922), California poet and friend of AB.
21. Gen. Lew Wallace (1827–1905), author of the immensely popular novel *Ben-Hur: A Tale of the Christ* (1880).

THE GREAT STRIKE OF 1895

THE EYES OF THE PANTHER

ONE DOES NOT ALWAYS MARRY WHEN INSANE[1]

A man and a woman—Nature had done the grouping—sat on a rustic seat, in the late afternoon. The man was middle-aged, slender, swarthy, with the expression of a poet and the complexion of a pirate—a man at whom one would look again. The woman was young, blonde, graceful, with something in her figure and movements suggesting the word "lithe." She was habited in a gray gown with odd brown markings in the texture. She may have been beautiful; one could not readily say, for her eyes denied attention to all else. They were gray-green, long and narrow, with an expression defying analysis. One could only know that they were disquieting. Cleopatra may have had such eyes.

The man and the woman talked.

"Yes," said the woman, "I love you, God knows! But marry you, no. I cannot, will not."

"Irene, you have said that many times, yet always have denied me a reason. I've a right to know, to understand, to feel and prove my fortitude if I have it. Give me a reason."

"For loving you?"

The woman was smiling through her tears and her pallor. That did not stir any sense of humor in the man.

"No; there is no reason for that. A reason for not marrying me. I've a right to know. I must know. I will know!"

He had risen and was standing before her with clenched hands, on his face a frown—it might have been called a scowl. He looked as if he might attempt to learn by strangling her. She smiled no more—merely sat looking up into his face with a fixed, set regard that was utterly without emotion or sentiment. Yet it had something in it that tamed his resentment and made him shiver.

"You are determined to have my reason?" she asked in a tone that was entirely mechanical—a tone that might have been her look made audible.

"If you please—if I'm not asking too much."

Apparently this lord of creation was yielding some part of his dominion over his co-creature.

"Very well, you shall know: I am insane."

The man started, then looked incredulous and was conscious that he ought to be amused. But, again, the sense of humor failed him in his need and despite his disbelief he was profoundly disturbed by that which he did not believe. Between our convictions and our feelings there is no good understanding.

"That is what the physicians would say," the woman continued—"if they knew. I might myself prefer to call it a case of 'possession.' Sit down and hear what I have to say."

The man silently resumed his seat beside her on the rustic bench by the wayside. Over-against them on the eastern side of the valley the hills were already sunset-flushed and the stillness all about was of that peculiar quality that foretells the twilight. Something of its mysterious and significant solemnity had imparted itself to the man's mood. In the spiritual, as in the material world, are signs and presages of night. Rarely meeting her look, and whenever he did so conscious of the indefinable dread with which, despite their feline beauty, her eyes always affected him, Jenner Brading listened in silence to the story told by Irene Marlowe. In deference to the reader's possible prejudice against the artless method of an unpracticed historian the author ventures to substitute his own version for hers.

II
A ROOM MAY BE TOO NARROW FOR THREE, THOUGH ONE IS OUTSIDE

In a little log house containing a single room sparsely and rudely furnished, crouching on the floor against one of the walls, was a woman clasping to her breast a child. Outside, a dense unbroken forest extended for many miles in every direction. This was at night and the room was black dark: no human eye could have discerned the woman and the child. Yet they were observed, narrowly, vigilantly, with never even a momentary slackening of attention; and that is the pivotal fact upon which this narrative turns.

Charles Marlowe was of the class, now extinct in this country, of woodmen pioneers—men who found their most acceptable surroundings in sylvan solitudes that stretched along the eastern slope of the Mississippi Valley, from the Great Lakes to the Gulf of Mexico. For more than a hundred years these men pushed ever westward, generation after generation, with rifle and ax, reclaiming from Nature and her savage children here and there an isolated acreage for the plow, no sooner reclaimed than surrendered to their less venturesome but more thrifty successors. At last they burst through the edge of the forest into the open country and vanished as if they had fallen over a cliff. The woodman pioneer is no more; the pioneer of the plains—he whose easy task it was to subdue for occupancy two-thirds of the country in a single generation—is another and inferior creation. With Charles Marlowe in the wilderness, sharing the dangers, hardships and privations of that strange, unprofitable life, were his wife and child, to whom, in the manner of his class, in which the domestic virtues were a religion, he was passionately attached. The woman was still young enough to be comely, new enough to the awful isolation of her lot to be cheerful. By withholding the large capacity for happiness which the simple satisfactions of the forest life could not have filled, Heaven had dealt honorably with her. In her light household tasks, her child, her husband and her few foolish books, she found abundant provision for her needs.

One morning in midsummer Marlowe took down his rifle from the wooden hooks on the wall and signified his intention of getting game.

"We've meat enough," said the wife; "please don't go out to-day. I dreamed last night, O, such a dreadful thing! I cannot recollect it, but I'm almost sure that it will come to pass if you go out."

It is painful to confess that Marlowe received this solemn statement with less of gravity than was due to the mysterious nature of the calamity foreshadowed. In truth, he laughed.

"Try to remember," he said. "Maybe you dreamed that Baby had lost the power of speech."

The conjecture was obviously suggested by the fact that Baby, clinging to the fringe of his hunting-coat with all her ten pudgy thumbs, was at that moment uttering her sense of the situation in a series of exultant goo-goos inspired by sight of her father's raccoon-skin cap.

The woman yielded: lacking the gift of humor she could not hold out against his kindly badinage. So, with a kiss for the mother and a kiss for the child, he left the house and closed the door upon his happiness forever.

At nightfall he had not returned. The woman prepared supper and waited. Then she put Baby to bed and sang softly to her until she slept. By this time the fire on the hearth, at which she had cooked supper, had burned out and the room was lighted by a single candle. This she afterward placed in the open window as a sign and welcome to the hunter if he should approach from that side. She had thoughtfully closed and barred the door against such wild animals as might prefer it to an open window—of the habits of beasts of prey in entering a house uninvited she was not advised, though with true female prevision she may have considered the possibility of their entrance by way of the chimney. As the night wore on she became not less anxious, but more drowsy, and at last rested her arms upon the bed by the child and her head upon the arms. The candle in the window burned down to the socket, sputtered and flared a moment and went out unobserved; for the woman slept and dreamed.

THE EYES OF THE PANTHER

In her dreams she sat beside the cradle of a second child. The first one was dead. The father was dead. The home in the forest was lost and the dwelling in which she lived was unfamiliar. There were heavy oaken doors, always closed, and outside the windows, fastened into the thick stone walls, were iron bars, obviously (so she thought) a provision against Indians. All this she noted with an infinite self-pity, but without surprise—an emotion unknown in dreams. The child in the cradle was invisible under its coverlet which something impelled her to remove. She did so, disclosing the face of a wild animal! In the shock of this dreadful revelation the dreamer awoke, trembling in the darkness of her cabin in the wood.

As a sense of her actual surroundings came slowly back to her she felt for the child that was not a dream, and assured herself by its breathing that all was well with it; nor could she forbear to pass a hand lightly across its face. Then, moved by some impulse for which she probably could not have accounted, she rose and took the sleeping babe in her arms, holding it close against her breast. The head of the child's cot was against the wall to which the woman now turned her back as she stood. Lifting her eyes she saw two bright objects starring the darkness with a reddish-green glow. She took them to be two coals on the hearth, but with her returning sense of direction came the disquieting consciousness that they were not in that quarter of the room, moreover were too high, being nearly at the level of the eyes—of her own eyes. For these were the eyes of a panther.[2]

The beast was at the open window directly opposite and not five paces away. Nothing but those terrible eyes was visible, but in the dreadful tumult of her feelings as the situation disclosed itself to her understanding she somehow knew that the animal was standing on its hinder feet, supporting itself with its paws on the window-ledge. That signified a malign interest—not the mere gratification of an indolent curiosity. The consciousness of the attitude was an added horror, accentuating the menace of those awful eyes, in whose steadfast fire her strength and courage were alike consumed. Under their silent questioning she shuddered and turned sick. Her knees failed her, and by degrees, instinctively striving to avoid a sudden movement that might bring the beast upon her, she sank to the floor, crouched against the wall and tried to shield the babe with her trembling body without withdrawing her gaze from the luminous orbs that were killing her. No thought of her husband came to her in her agony—no hope nor suggestion of rescue or escape. Her capacity for thought and feeling had narrowed to the dimensions of a single emotion—fear of the animal's spring, of the impact of its body, the buffeting of its great arms, the feel of its teeth in her throat, the mangling of her babe. Motionless now and in absolute silence, she awaited her doom, the moments growing to hours, to years, to ages; and still those devilish eyes maintained their watch.

Returning to his cabin late at night with a deer on his shoulders Charles Marlowe tried the door. It did not yield. He knocked; there was no answer. He laid down his deer and

THE EYES OF THE PANTHER

went round to the window. As he turned the angle of the building he fancied he heard a sound as of stealthy footfalls and a rustling in the undergrowth of the forest, but they were too slight for certainty, even to his practiced ear. Approaching the window, and to his surprise finding it open, he threw his leg over the sill and entered. All was darkness and silence. He groped his way to the fire-place, struck a match and lit a candle. Then he looked about. Cowering on the floor against a wall was his wife, clasping his child. As he sprang toward her she rose and broke into laughter, long, loud and mechanical, devoid of gladness and devoid of sense—the laughter that is not out of keeping with the clanking of a chain. Hardly knowing what he did he extended his arms. She laid the babe in them. It was dead—pressed to death in its mother's embrace.

III
THE THEORY OF THE DEFENSE

That is what occurred during a night in a forest, but not all of it did Irene Marlowe relate to Jenner Brading; not all of it was known to her. When she had concluded the sun was below the horizon and the long summer twilight had begun to deepen in the hollows of the land. For some moments Brading was silent, expecting the narrative to be carried forward to some definite connection with the conversation introducing it; but the narrator was as silent as he, her face averted, her hands clasping and unclasping themselves as they lay in her lap, with a singular suggestion of an activity independent of her will.

"It is a sad, a terrible story," said Brading at last, "but I do not understand. You call Charles Marlowe father; that I know. That he is old before his time, broken by some great sorrow, I have seen, or thought I saw. But, pardon me, you said that you—that you—"

"That I am insane," said the girl, without a movement of head or body.

"But, Irene, you say—please, dear, do not look away from me—you say that the child was dead, not demented."

"Yes, that one—I am the second. I was born three months after that night, my mother being mercifully permitted to lay down her life in giving me mine."

Brading was again silent; he was a trifle dazed and could not at once think of the right thing to say. Her face was still turned away. In his embarrassment he reached impulsively toward the hands that lay closing and unclosing in her lap, but something—he could not have said what—restrained him. He then remembered, vaguely, that he had never altogether cared to take her hand.

"Is it likely," she resumed, "that a person born under such circumstances is like others—is what you call sane?"

Brading did not reply; he was preoccupied with a new thought that was taking shape in his mind—what a scientist would have called an hypothesis; a detective, a theory. It might throw an added light, albeit a lurid one, upon such doubt of her sanity as her own assertion had not dispelled.

THE EYES OF THE PANTHER

The country was still new and, outside the villages, sparsely populated. The professional hunter was still a familiar figure, and among his trophies were heads and pelts of the larger kinds of game. Tales variously credible of nocturnal meetings with savage animals in lonely roads were sometimes current, passed through the customary stages of growth and decay, and were forgotten. A recent addition to these popular apocrypha, originating, apparently, by spontaneous generation in several households, was of a panther which had frightened some of their members by looking in at windows by night. The yarn had caused its little ripple of excitement—had even attained to the distinction of a place in the local newspaper; but Brading had given it no attention. Its likeness to the story to which he had just listened now impressed him as perhaps more than accidental. Was it not possible that the one story had suggested the other—that finding congenial conditions in a morbid mind and a fertile fancy, it had grown to the tragic tale that he had heard?

Brading recalled certain circumstances of the girl's history and disposition, of which, with love's incuriosity, he had hitherto been heedless—such as her solitary life with her father, at whose house no one, apparently, was an acceptable visitor and her strange fear of the night, by which those who knew her best accounted for her never being seen after dark. Surely in such a mind imagination once kindled might burn with a lawless flame, penetrating and enveloping the entire structure. That she was mad, though the conviction gave him the acutest pain, he could no longer doubt; she had only mistaken an effect of her mental disorder for its cause, bringing into imaginary relation with her own personality the vagaries of the local myth-makers. With some vague intention of testing his new "theory," and no very definite notion of how to set about it he said, gravely, but with hesitation:

"Irene, dear, tell me—I beg you will not take offense, but tell me—"

"I have told you," she interrupted, speaking with a passionate earnestness that he had not known her to show—"I have already told you that we cannot marry; is anything else worth saying?"

Before he could stop her she had sprung from her seat and without another word or look was gliding away among the trees toward her father's house. Brading had risen to detain her; he stood watching her in silence until she had vanished in the gloom. Suddenly he started as if he had been shot; his face took on an expression of amazement and alarm: in one of the black shadows into which she had disappeared he had caught a quick, brief glimpse of shining eyes! For an instant he was dazed and irresolute; then he dashed into the wood after her, shouting: "Irene, Irene, look out! The panther! The panther!"

In a moment he had passed through the fringe of forest into open ground and saw the girl's gray skirt vanishing into her father's door. No panther was visible.

THE EYES OF THE PANTHER

IV
AN APPEAL TO THE CONSCIENCE OF GOD

Jenner Brading, attorney-at-law, lived in a cottage at the edge of the town. Directly behind the dwelling was the forest. Being a bachelor, and therefore, by the Draconian moral code of the time and place denied the services of the only species of domestic servant known thereabout, the "hired girl," he boarded at the village hotel, where also was his office. The woodside cottage was merely a lodging maintained—at no great cost, to be sure—as an evidence of prosperity and respectability. It would hardly do for one to whom the local newspaper had pointed with pride as "the foremost jurist of his time" to be "homeless," albeit he may sometimes have suspected that the words "home" and "house" were not strictly synonymous. Indeed, his consciousness of the disparity and his will to harmonize it were matters of logical inference, for it was generally reported that soon after the cottage was built its owner had made a futile venture in the direction of marriage—had, in truth, gone so far as to be rejected by the beautiful but eccentric daughter of Old Man Marlowe, the recluse. This was publicly believed because he had told it himself and she had not—a reversal of the usual order of things which could hardly fail to carry conviction.

Brading's bedroom was at the rear of the house, with a single window facing the forest. One night he was awakened by a noise at that window; he could hardly have said what it was like. With a little thrill of the nerves he sat up in bed and laid hold of the revolver which, with a forethought most commendable in one addicted to the habit of sleeping on the ground floor with an open window, he had put under his pillow. The room was in absolute darkness, but being unterrified he knew where to direct his eyes, and there he held them, awaiting in silence what further might occur. He could now dimly discern the aperture—a square of lighter black. Presently there appeared at its lower edge two gleaming eyes that burned with a malignant lustre inexpressibly terrible! Brading's heart gave a great jump, then seemed to stand still. A chill passed along his spine and through his hair; he felt the blood forsake his cheeks. He could not have cried out—not to save his life; but being a man of courage he would not, to save his life, have done so if he had been able. Some trepidation his coward body might feel, but his spirit was of sterner stuff. Slowly the shining eyes rose with a steady motion that seemed an approach, and slowly rose Brading's right hand, holding the pistol. He fired!

Blinded by the flash and stunned by the report, Brading nevertheless heard, or fancied that he heard, the wild, high scream of the panther, so human in sound, so devilish in suggestion. Leaping from the bed he hastily clothed himself and, pistol in hand, sprang from the door, meeting two or three men who came running up from the road. A brief explanation was followed by a cautious search of the house. The grass was wet with dew; beneath the window it had been trodden and partly leveled for a wide space, from which a devious trail, visible in the light of a lantern, led away into the bushes. One of the men stumbled and fell upon his hands, which as he rose and rubbed them together were slippery. On examination they were seen to be red with blood.

THE EYES OF THE PANTHER

An encounter, unarmed, with a wounded panther was not agreeable to their taste; all but Brading turned back. He, with lantern and pistol, pushed courageously forward into the wood. Passing through a difficult undergrowth he came into a small opening, and there his courage had its reward, for there he found the body of his victim. But it was no panther. What it was is told, even to this day, upon a weather-worn headstone in the village churchyard, and for many years was attested daily at the graveside by the bent figure and sorrow-seamed face of Old Man Marlowe, to whose soul, and to the soul of his strange, unhappy child, peace. Peace and reparation.

E (17 Oct. 1897): 3; *IML* 343–62; ***CW* 2.385–403**.

NOTES

This gripping story skirts the border between plausibility and the supernatural. In a letter to C. W. Doyle (ca. Oct. 1897, transcript, BL), AB said of it: "My story is not a 'wonder-story,' and does not, I think, even pass the bounds of probability—merely an instance of pre-natal influence. The girl can see in the dark—which means gleaming eyes—and has a mania for looking into windows o' nights. Transformation into an animal is another matter. So I dismiss my fears." This comment may suggest that the story is to be interpreted nonsupernaturally—i.e., that Irene Marlowe does not actually transform herself, at times, into a panther—but AB's comment is as ambivalent and inconclusive as the story itself.

1. Cf. TC, *NL*, 18, no. 52 (23 Jan. 1869): 9: "A man in England recently became insane just as he was about to be married. Whom the gods wish to destroy they first make mad." And TC, *NL*, 9, no. 12 (17 Apr. 1869): 9: "An attempt is making in the Fourth District Court to set aside a marriage, upon the ground that the man was insane at the time of its consummation. Nonsense; this would invalidate half the marriages in the State; and the only evidence required would be the production of the wife in Court." See also "The Suitable Surroundings," p. 683 note 4.

2. Cf. "Little Johnny on Babies," *F* 21 (30 Jan. 1875): 53 (unsigned): "There was a man and his wife and their little baby, and they lived by their selfs in the woods, ten hundred thousand miles from any other house. The man he hunted deers with a gun, and the woman she stade to home to mind baby and cuke the meat. And one offle dark nite the man haddent come home, and the woman she new he had got lost, and was kil by sabbages, and et by a wile beest, and she was a frade. Bime by, way in the nite, she herd some thing like a little chile a cryin, and a cryin, out side in the dark, some times on one side of the house, and some times not, and she said it was a spirrit wich had come for her baby, so she set in the middel of the room and hugged her baby, and was friten mose to deth. And the Thing kep a cryin, and a cryin, til her blud run cole, but her baby was a sleep in her arms, poor thing. At last she herd a nois at the windo, and she luked up and hollered, for she see two grate eyes a lukin in thru the glas, like coles of fire, and Ime that friten I cant rite any more, cos its nite, and Ime a lone, weres my mother?" A variation appears in "Little Johnny's Menagerie—V" under the heading "The Baby," *Ar* 2, no. 5 (9 Feb. 1878): 11 (unsigned).

AN AFFAIR OF OUTPOSTS

I

CONCERNING THE WISH TO BE DEAD

Two men sat in conversation. One was the Governor of the State. The year was 1861; the war was on and the Governor already famous for the intelligence and zeal with which he directed all the powers and resources of his State to the service of the Union.

"What! *you?*" the Governor was saying in evident surprise—"you too want a military commission? Really, the fifing and drumming must have effected a profound alteration in your convictions. In my character of recruiting sergeant I suppose I ought not to be fastidious, but"—there was a touch of irony in his manner—"well, have you forgotten that an oath of allegiance is required?"

"I have altered neither my convictions nor my sympathies," said the other, tranquilly. "While my sympathies are with the South, as you do me the honor to recollect, I have never doubted that the North was in the right. I am a Southerner in fact and in feeling, but it is my habit in matters of importance to act as I think, not as I feel."

The Governor was absently tapping his desk with a pencil; he did not immediately reply. After a while he said: "I have heard that there are all kinds of men in the world, so I suppose there are some like that, and doubtless you think yourself one. I've known you a long time and—pardon me—I don't think so."

"Then I am to understand that my application is denied?"

"Unless you can remove my belief that your Southern sympathies are in some degree a disqualification, yes. I do not doubt your good faith, and I know you to be abundantly fitted by intelligence and special training for the duties of an officer. Your convictions, you say, favor the Union cause, but I prefer a man with his heart in it. The heart is what men fight with."

"Look here, Governor," said the younger man, with a smile that had more light than warmth: "I have something up my sleeve—a qualification which I had hoped it would not be necessary to mention. A great military authority has given a simple recipe for being a good soldier: 'Try always to get yourself killed.'[1] It is with that purpose that I wish to enter the service. I am not, perhaps, much of a patriot, but I wish to be dead."

The Governor looked at him rather sharply, then a little coldly. "There is a simpler and franker way," he said.

"In my family, sir," was the reply, "we do not do that—no Armisted has ever done that."

A long silence ensued and neither man looked at the other. Presently the Governor lifted his eyes from the pencil, which had resumed its tapping, and said:

"Who is she?"

"My wife."

The Governor tossed the pencil into the desk, rose and walked two or three times across the room. Then he turned to Armisted, who also had risen, looked at him more coldly than before and said: "But the man—would it not be better that he—could not the country spare him better than it can spare you? Or are the Armisteds opposed to 'the unwritten law'?"[2]

The Armisteds, apparently, could feel an insult: the face of the younger man flushed, then paled, but he subdued himself to the service of his purpose.

"The man's identity is unknown to me," he said, calmly enough.

"Pardon me," said the Governor, with even less of visible contrition than commonly underlies those words. After a moment's reflection he added: "I shall send you to-morrow a captain's commission in the Tenth Infantry, now at Nashville, Tennessee. Good night."

"Good night, sir. I thank you."

Left alone, the Governor remained for a time motionless, leaning against his desk. Presently he shrugged his shoulders as if throwing off a burden. "This is a bad business," he said.

Seating himself at a reading-table before the fire, he took up the book nearest his hand, absently opening it. His eyes fell upon this sentence:

"When God made it necessary for an unfaithful wife to lie about her husband in justification of her own sins He had the tenderness to endow men with the folly to believe her."

He looked at the title of the book; it was, *His Excellency the Fool.*

He flung the volume into the fire.

II
HOW TO SAY WHAT IS WORTH HEARING

The enemy, defeated in two days of battle at Pittsburg Landing, had sullenly retired to Corinth, whence he had come. For manifest incompetence Grant, whose beaten army had been saved from destruction and capture by Buell's soldierly activity and skill, had been relieved of his command, which nevertheless had not been given to Buell, but to Halleck, a man of unproved powers, a theorist, sluggish, irresolute.[3] Foot by foot his troops, always deployed in line-of-battle to resist the enemy's bickering skirmishers, always entrenching against the columns that never came, advanced across the thirty miles of forest and swamp toward an antagonist prepared to vanish at contact, like a ghost at cock-crow. It was a campaign of "excursions and alarums,"[4] of reconnoissances and counter-marches, of cross-purposes and countermanded orders. For weeks the solemn farce held attention, luring distinguished civilians from fields of political ambition to see what they safely could of the horrors of war. Among these was our friend the Governor. At the headquarters of the army and in the camps of the troops from his State he was a familiar figure, attended by the several members of his personal staff, showily horsed, faultlessly betailored and bravely silk-hatted. Things of charm they were, rich in suggestions of peaceful lands beyond a sea of strife. The bedraggled soldier looked up from his trench as they passed, leaned upon his spade and audibly damned them to signify his sense of their ornamental irrelevance to the austerities of his trade.

"I think, Governor," said General Masterson[5] one day, going into informal session atop of his horse and throwing one leg across the pommel of his saddle, his favorite posture—"I think I would not ride any farther in that direction if I were you. We've nothing out there but a line of skirmishers. That, I presume, is why I was directed to put these siege guns here: if the skirmishers are driven in the enemy will die of dejection at being unable to haul them away—they're a trifle heavy."

There is reason to fear that the unstrained quality of this military humor dropped not as the gentle rain from Heaven[6] upon the place beneath the civilian's silk hat. Anyhow he abated none of his dignity in recognition.

"I understand," he said, gravely, "that some of my men are out there—a company of the Tenth, commanded by Captain Armisted. I should like to meet him if you do not mind."

"He is worth meeting. But there's a bad bit of jungle out there, and I should advise that you leave your horse and"—with a look at the Governor's retinue—"your other impedimenta."

The Governor went forward alone and on foot. In a half-hour he had pushed through a tangled undergrowth covering a boggy soil and entered upon firm and more open ground. Here he found a half-company of infantry lounging behind a line of stacked rifles. The men wore their accouterments—their belts, cartridge-boxes, haversacks and canteens. Some lying at full length on the dry leaves were fast asleep; others in small groups gossiped idly of this and that; a few played at cards; none was far from the line of stacked arms. To the civilian's eye the scene was one of carelessness, confusion, indifference; a soldier would have observed expectancy and readiness.

AN AFFAIR OF OUTPOSTS

At a little distance apart an officer in fatigue uniform, armed, sat on a fallen tree noting the approach of the visitor, to whom a sergeant, rising from one of the groups, now came forward.

"I wish to see Captain Armisted," said the Governor.

The sergeant eyed him narrowly, saying nothing, pointed to the officer, and taking a rifle from one of the stacks, accompanied him.

"This man wants to see you, sir," said the sergeant, saluting. The officer rose.

It would have been a sharp eye that would have recognized him. His hair, which but a few months before had been brown, was streaked with gray. His face, tanned by exposure, was seamed as with age. A long livid scar across the forehead marked the stroke of a saber; one cheek was drawn and puckered by the work of a bullet. Only a woman of the loyal North would have thought the man handsome.

"Armisted—Captain," said the Governor, extending his hand, "do you not know me?"

"I know you, sir, and I salute you—as the Governor of my State."

Lifting his right hand to the level of his eyes he threw it outward and downward. In the code of military etiquette there is no provision for shaking hands. That of the civilian was withdrawn. If he felt either surprise or chagrin his face did not betray it.

"It is the hand that signed your commission," he said.

"And it is the hand—"

The sentence remains unfinished. The sharp report of a rifle came from the front, followed by another and another. A bullet hissed through the forest and struck a tree near by. The men sprang from the ground and even before the captain's high, clear voice was done intoning the command "At-ten-tion!" had fallen into line in rear of the stacked arms. Again—and now through the din of a crackling fusillade—sounded the strong, deliberate sing-song of authority: "Take . . . arms!" followed by the rattle of unlocking bayonets.

Bullets from the unseen enemy were now flying thick and fast, though mostly well spent and emitting the humming sound which signified interference by twigs and rotation in the plane of flight. Two or three of the men in the line were already struck and down. A few wounded men came limping awkwardly out of the undergrowth from the skirmish line in front; most of them did not pause, but held their way with white faces and set teeth to the rear.

Suddenly there was a deep, jarring report in front, followed by the startling rush of a shell, which passing overhead exploded in the edge of a thicket, setting afire the fallen leaves. Penetrating the din—seeming to float above it like the melody of a soaring bird—rang the slow, aspirated monotones of the captain's several commands, without emphasis, without accent, musical and restful as an evensong under the harvest moon. Familiar with this tranquilizing chant in moments of imminent peril, these raw soldiers of less than a year's training yielded themselves to the spell, executing its mandates with the composure and precision of veterans. Even the distinguished civilian behind his tree, hesitating between pride and terror, was accessible to its charm and suasion. He was conscious of a fortified resolution and ran away only when the skirmishers, under orders to rally on the reserve, came out of the woods like hunted hares and formed on the left of the stiff little line, breathing hard and thankful for the boon of breath.

III
THE FIGHTING OF ONE WHOSE HEART
WAS NOT IN THE QUARREL

Guided in his retreat by that of the fugitive wounded, the Governor struggled bravely to the rear through the "bad bit of jungle." He was well winded and a trifle confused. Excepting a single rifle-shot now and again, there was no sound of strife behind him; the enemy was pulling himself together for a new onset against an antagonist of whose numbers and tactical disposition he was in doubt. The fugitive felt that he would probably be spared to his country, and inly commended the arrangements of Providence to that end, but in leaping a small brook in more open ground one of the arrangements incurred the mischance of a disabling sprain at the ankle. He was unable to continue his flight, for he was too fat to hop, and after several vain attempts, causing intolerable pain, seated himself on the earth to nurse his ignoble disability and deprecate the military situation.

A brisk renewal of the firing broke out and stray bullets came flitting and droning by. Then came the crash of two clean, definite volleys, followed by a continuous rattle, through which he heard the yells and cheers of the combatants, punctuated by thunderclaps of cannon. All this told him that Armisted's little command was bitterly beset and fighting at close quarters. The wounded men whom he had distanced began to straggle by on either hand, their numbers visibly augmented by new levies from the line. Singly and by twos and threes, some supporting comrades more desperately hurt than themselves, but all deaf to his appeals for assistance, they sifted through the underbrush and disappeared. The firing was increasingly louder and more distinct, and presently the ailing fugitives were succeeded by men who strode with a firmer tread, occasionally facing about and discharging their pieces, then doggedly resuming their retreat, reloading as they walked. Two or three fell as he looked, and lay motionless. One had enough of life left in him to make a pitiful attempt to drag himself to cover. A passing comrade paused beside him long enough to fire, appraised the poor devil's disability with a look and moved austerely on, inserting a cartridge in his weapon.

In all this was none of the pomp of war—no hint of glory. Even in his distress and peril the helpless civilian could not forbear to contrast it with the gorgeous parades and reviews held in honor of himself—with the brilliant uniforms, the music, the banners and the marching. It was an ugly and sickening business: to all that was artistic in his nature, revolting, brutal, in bad taste.

"Ugh!" he grunted, shuddering—"this is beastly! Where is the charm of it all? Where are the elevated sentiments, the devotion, the heroism, the—"

From a point somewhere near, in the direction of the pursuing enemy, rose the clear, deliberate sing-song of Captain Armisted.

"Stead-y, men—stead-y. Halt! Com-mence fir-ing."

The rattle of fewer than a score of rifles could be distinguished through the general uproar, and again that penetrating falsetto:

"Cease fir-ing. In re-treat . . . maaarch!"

In a few moments this remnant had drifted slowly past the Governor, all to the right of him as they faced in retiring, the men deployed at intervals of a half-dozen paces. At the extreme left and a few yards behind came the captain. The civilian called out his name, but he did not hear. A swarm of men in gray now broke out of cover in pursuit, making directly for the spot where the Governor lay—some accident of the ground had caused them to converge upon that point: their line had become a crowd. In a last struggle for life and liberty the Governor attempted to rise, and looking back the captain saw him. Promptly, but with the same slow precision as before, he sang his commands.

"Skirm-ish-ers, halt!" The men stopped and according to rule turned to face the enemy.

"Ral-ly on the right!"—and they came in at a run, fixing bayonets and forming loosely on the man at that end of the line.

"Forward . . . to save the Gov-ern-or of your State . . . doub-le quick . . . maaarch!"

Only one man disobeyed this astonishing command! He was dead. With a cheer they sprang forward over the twenty or thirty paces between them and their task. The captain having a shorter distance to go arrived first—simultaneously with the enemy. A half-dozen hasty shots were fired at him, and the foremost man—a fellow of heroic stature, hatless and bare-breasted—made a vicious sweep at his head with a clubbed rifle. The officer parried the blow at the cost of a broken arm and drove his sword to the hilt into the giant's breast. As the body fell the weapon was wrenched from his hand and before he could pluck his revolver from the scabbard at his belt another man leaped upon him like a tiger, fastening both hands upon his throat and bearing him backward upon the prostrate Governor, still struggling to rise. This man was promptly spitted upon the bayonet of a Federal sergeant and his death-gripe on the captain's throat loosened by a kick upon each wrist. When the captain had risen he was at the rear of his men, who had all passed over and around him and were thrusting fiercely at their more numerous but less coherent antagonists. Nearly all the rifles on both sides were empty and in the crush there was neither time nor room to reload. The Confederates were at a disadvantage in that most of them lacked bayonets; they fought by bludgeoning—and a clubbed rifle is a formidable arm. The sound of the conflict was a clatter like that of the interlocking horns of battling bulls—now and then the pash of a crushed skull, an oath, or a grunt caused by the impact of a rifle's muzzle against the abdomen transfixed by its bayonet. Through an opening made by the fall of one of his men Captain Armisted sprang, with his dangling left arm; in his right hand a full-charged revolver, which he fired with rapidity and terrible effect into the thick of the gray crowd: but across the bodies of the slain the survivors in the front were pushed forward by their comrades in the rear till again they breasted the tireless bayonets. There were fewer bayonets now to breast—a beggarly half-dozen, all told. A few minutes more of this rough work—a little fighting back to back—and all would be over.

Suddenly a lively firing was heard on the right and the left: a fresh line of Federal skirmishers came forward at a run, driving before them those parts of the Confederate line that had been separated by staying the advance of the center. And behind these new and noisy combatants, at a distance of two or three hundred yards, could be seen, indistinct among the trees, a line-of-battle!

Instinctively before retiring, the crowd in gray made a tremendous rush upon its handful of antagonists, overwhelming them by mere momentum and, unable to use weapons in the crush, trampled them, stamped savagely on their limbs, their bodies, their necks, their faces; then retiring with bloody feet across its own dead it joined the general rout and the incident was at an end.

IV
THE GREAT HONOR THE GREAT

The Governor, who had been unconscious, opened his eyes and stared about him, slowly recalling the day's events. A man in the uniform of a major was kneeling beside him; he was a surgeon. Grouped about were the civilian members of the Governor's staff, their faces expressing a natural solicitude regarding their offices. A little apart stood General Masterson addressing another officer and gesticulating with a cigar. He was saying: "It was the beautifulest fight ever made—by God, sir, it was great!"

The beauty and greatness were attested by a row of dead, trimly disposed, and another of wounded, less formally placed, restless, half-naked, but bravely bebandaged.

"How do you feel, sir?" said the surgeon. "I find no wound."

"I think I am all right," the patient replied, sitting up. "It is that ankle."

The surgeon transferred his attention to the ankle, cutting away the boot. All eyes followed the knife.

In moving the leg a folded paper was uncovered. The patient picked it up and carelessly opened it. It was a letter three months old, signed "Julia." Catching sight of his name in it he read it. It was nothing very remarkable—merely a weak woman's confession of unprofitable sin—the penitence of a faithless wife deserted by her betrayer. The letter had fallen from the pocket of Captain Armisted; the reader quietly transferred it to his own.

An aide-de-camp rode up and dismounted. Advancing to the Governor he saluted.

"Sir," he said, "I am sorry to find you wounded—the Commanding General has not been informed. He presents his compliments and I am directed to say that he has ordered for to-morrow a grand review of the reserve corps in your honor. I venture to add that the General's carriage is at your service if you are able to attend."

"Be pleased to say to the Commanding General that I am deeply touched by his kindness. If you have the patience to wait a few moments you shall convey a more definite reply."

He smiled brightly and glancing at the surgeon and his assistants added: "At present—if you will permit an allusion to the horrors of peace—I am 'in the hands of my friends.'"

The humor of the great is infectious; all laughed who heard.

"Where is Captain Armisted?" the Governor asked, not altogether carelessly.

The surgeon looked up from his work, pointing silently to the nearest body in the row of dead, the features discreetly covered with a handkerchief. It was so near that the great man could have laid his hand upon it, but he did not. He may have feared that it would bleed.

E (19 Dec. 1897): 20; *IML* 161–80; *CW* 2.146–64.

NOTES

A study of what may underlie bravery and duty, this tale is aggressively antiromantic both in its brutally vivid description of combat and in its debunking of conventional views of women and authority. It resembles "Killed at Resaca" in its recognition of the powerful influence a "weak" woman may have on a man's motives. The tale is also iconoclastic in its harsh treatment of the governor, who governs a state but cannot govern himself, who ably leads his state to support the Union but destroys the union of a marriage and drives the husband to volunteer out of despair, and whose patriotism is partly founded on the naive notion that war is somehow charming and that it elicits from soldiers "elevated sentiments . . . devotion . . . heroism." Roy Morris Jr. believes that AB might have loosely based the portrait of the governor on a historical event: in 1862 Indiana Gov. Oliver P. Morton visited the Union front lines at Corinth (*Ambrose Bierce: Alone in Bad Company*, 40, 42).

1. Possibly a reference to an aphorism attributed to Napoleon: "Soldiers are made on purpose to be killed" (spoken in conversation with Gaspard Gourgard, 1818).

2. "The unwritten law" is the "right" of a husband to kill a man who commits adultery with his wife.

3. AB refers to the battle of Shiloh (6–7 April 1862), taking place near Pittsburg Landing, Tennessee. Gen. Ulysses S. Grant's army had invaded the area in March, and Confederate forces hoped to attack it before reinforcements led by Gen. Don Carlos Buell (1818–98) could reach the area. Although the Confederates seem to have caught Grant off-guard on the first day of the battle, they were unable to follow up their momentum, allowing Grant to reorganize his troops and, with Buell's forces having arrived, to mount an offensive of his own. The Confederates at last retreated to Corinth. Grant's apparent incompetence was criticized for months afterward. Gen. Henry Wager Halleck (1815–72), who had ordered Buell into the area, assumed command of Grant's forces on 11 April, Grant being humiliatingly

demoted to second in command. For AB's celebrated account of his participation in the battle, see "What I Saw of Shiloh" (*SS* 10–25) and "Prattle," *E* (4 Dec. 1898): 12 (rpt. *SS* 25–26).

4. The sounds of war or warlike activity, used as a stage direction for the moving of soldiers across stage in Elizabethan drama.

5. This fictitious general was first cited in "One Kind of Officer" (p. 833).

6. Shakespeare, *The Merchant of Venice,* 4.1.182–84: "The quality of mercy is not strained; / It droppeth as the gentle rain from heaven / Upon the place beneath."

MAROONED ON UG

When consciousness returned I found myself lying on the strand a short remove from the margin of the sea. The sun was high in the heavens, and an insupportable itching pervaded my entire frame, that being the effect of sunshine in that country, as heat is in ours. Having observed that the discomfort was abated by the passing of a light cloud between me and the sun, I dragged myself with some difficulty to a clump of trees near by and found permanent relief in their shade. As soon as I was comfortable enough to examine my surroundings I saw that the trees were of metal, apparently bronze, with leaves of what resembled pure silver, but may have contained alloy. Some of the trees bore burnished flowers shaped like bells, and in a breeze the tinkling as they clashed together was exceedingly sweet. The grass with which the open country was covered as far as I could see amongst the patches of forest was of a bright scarlet hue, excepting along the water-courses, where it was white. Lazily cropping it at some little distance away, or lying in it, indolently chewing the cud and attended by a man half-clad in skins and bearing a crook, was a flock of tigers. My travels in New Jersey having made me proof against surprise, I contemplated these several visible phenomena without emotion, and with a merely expectant interest in what might be revealed by further observation.

The tigerherd having perceived me, now came striding forward, brandishing his crook and shaking his fists with great vehemence, gestures which I soon learned were, in that country, signs of amity and good-will. But before knowing that fact I had risen to my feet and thrown myself into a posture of defense, and as he approached I led for his head with my left, following with a stiff right upon his solar plexus, which sent him rolling on the grass in great pain. After learning something of the social customs of the country I experienced extreme mortification in recollecting this breach of etiquette, and even to this day I cannot think upon it without a blush.

Such was my first meeting with Jogogle-Zadester, Pastor King of Ug, the wisest and best of men. Later in our acquaintance, when I had for a long time been an honored guest at his court, where a thousand fists were ceremoniously shaken under my nose daily, he explained that my lukewarm reception of his hospitable advances gave him, for the moment, an unfavorable impression of my breeding and culture.

The island of Ug, upon which I was marooned in the year 1872, and from which I escaped only last summer, lies in the South Pacific, but has neither latitude nor longitude. It has an area of nearly seven hundred square samtains and is peculiar in shape, its width being considerably greater than its length. Politically it is a limited monarchy, the right of succession to the throne being vested in the sovereign's father, if he have one; if not in his grandfather, and so on upward in the line of ascent. (As a matter of fact there has not within historic times been a legitimate succession, even the great and good Jogogle-Zadester being a usurper chosen by popular vote.) To assist him in governing, the King is given a Parliament, the Uggard word for which is Gabagab, but its usefulness is greatly circumscribed by the Blubosh, or Constitution, which requires that every measure, in order to become a law, shall have an affirmative majority of the actual members, yet forbids any member to vote who has not a distinct pecuniary interest in the result. I was once greatly entertained by a spirited contest over a matter of harbor improvement, each of two proposed harbors having its advocates. One of these gentlemen, a most eloquent patriot, held the floor for hours in advocacy of the port where he had an interest in a projected mill for making dead kittens into cauliflower pickles; while other members were being vigorously buttonholed by one Japy-Djones, who at the other place had a clam ranch. In a debate in the Uggard Gabagab no one can have a "standing" except a party in interest; and as a consequence of this enlightened policy every bill that is passed is found to be most intelligently adapted to its purpose.

The original intent of this requirement was that members having no pecuniary interest in a proposed law at the time of its inception should not embarrass the proceedings and pervert the result; but the inhibition is now thought to be sufficiently observed by formal public acceptance of a nominal bribe to vote one way or the other. It is of course understood that behind the nominal bribe is commonly a more substantial one of which there is no record. To an American accustomed to the incorrupt methods of legislation in his own country the spectacle of every member of the Uggard Gabagab qualifying himself to vote by marching up, each in his turn as his name is called, to the proponent of the bill, or to its leading antagonist, and solemnly receiving a tonusi (the smallest coin of the realm) is exceedingly novel. When I ventured to mention to the King my lack of faith in the principle upon which this custom is founded, he replied:

"Guest of my country and heart of my soul, if you and your compatriots distrust the honesty and intelligence of an interested motive why is it that in your own courts of law, as you describe them, no private citizen can institute a civil action to right the wrongs of anybody but himself?"

I had nothing to say and the King proceeded: "And why is it that your Judges will listen to no argument from any one who has not acquired a selfish concern in the result?"

MAROONED ON UG

"O, your Majesty," I answered with animation, "they listen to attorneys-general, district attorneys and salaried officers of the law generally, whose prosperity depends in no degree upon their success; who prosecute none but those whom they believe to be guilty; who are careful to present no false or misleading testimony and argument; who are solicitous that even the humblest accused person shall be accorded every legal right and every advantage to which he is entitled; who, in brief, are animated by the most humane sentiments and actuated by the purest and most unselfish motives."

The King's discomfiture was pitiful: he retired at once from the capital and passed a whole year pasturing his flock of tigers in the solitudes beyond the River of Wine. Seeing that I would henceforth be persona non grata at the palace, I disguised myself as a native and sought obscurity in the writing and publication of books. In this vocation I was greatly assisted by a few standard works that had been put ashore with me in my sea-chest.

The literature of Ug is copious and of high merit, but consists altogether of fiction, mainly history, biography, theology and novels. Authors of exceptional excellence receive from the State marks of signal favor, being appointed to the positions of laborers in the Department of Highways and Cemeteries. Having been so fortunate as to win public favor and attract official attention by my now famous works, "The Decline and Fall of the Roman Empire," "David Copperfield," "Pilgrim's Progress," and "Ben Hur," I was myself that way distinguished and my future assured. Unhappily, through ignorance of the duties and dignities of the position I had the mischance to accept a tip for sweeping a street crossing and was compelled to fly for my life. After incredible hardships, privations and perils I arrived at Dyea, and am about to restore exhausted Nature by a trip to Dawson via the Chilcoot Pass.[1]

E (20 Feb. 1898): 18. Incorporated into "The Land Beyond the Blow."

NOTES

A tale in the Gulliverian tradition, this story displays Cynic tendencies in its reversal of conventional thinking. The narrator, like Gulliver, is extremely naive in his patriotic belief in the "incorrupt" superiority of the legislative and judicial practices of his native land but can find nothing to say when loopholes in his assumptions are exposed. The conclusion of this story is broadly ridiculous and obviously ironic. Having situated Ug in the South Seas (but without latitude or longitude), the narrator winds up in Dyea, a town in the Alaskan panhandle, and proposes refreshing himself by a trip up the notoriously difficult Chilcoot Pass to the Yukon gold-mining town of Dawson.

1. Dawson is a major city on the east bank of the Yukon River in west-central Yukon Territory. It became important during the Klondike gold rush of the 1890s. The Chilcoot (more properly, Chilkoot) Pass lies on the border between Alaska and northern British Columbia and was one of the two routes from Skagway, on the Alaskan coast, to Dawson. This route went through the now deserted town of Dyea.

THE WAR WITH WUG

TRANSCRIBED FROM THE MANUSCRIPT NARRATIVE OF A MARINER

It is now ten months since I escaped from the island of Ug, upon which I had been marooned by my crew, but, notwithstanding the hardships and privations endured in getting away, my memory of the country, its inhabitants and their wonderful manners and customs is exceedingly vivid. Some small part of what most interested me I shall here set down.

The Uggards are, or fancy themselves, a warlike race: nowhere in those distant seas are there any islanders so vain of their military power, the consciousness of which they acquired chiefly by fighting one another. Two years ago, however, they had a war with the people of another island kingdom, called Wug. The Wuggards held dominion over a third island, Scumadumclitchclitch, whose people had tried to throw off the yoke. In order to subdue them—at least to tears—it was decided to deprive them of garlic, the sole article of diet known to either them or the Wuggards, and in that country dug out of the ground like coal. So the Wuggards stopped up all the garlic mines, supplying their own needs by purchase from foreign trading proas. Having little money, or rather cowrie shells, with which to purchase, the poor Scumadumclitchclitchians suffered a great distress, which so touched the hearts of the compassionate Uggards—a most humane and conscientious people—that they declared war against the Wuggards and sent a fleet of proas to the relief of the sufferers. The fleet established a strict blockade of every port in Wug, and not a clove of garlic could enter the island. That compelled the Wuggard army of occupation to reopen the mines for its own subsistence.

All this was told to me by the great and good and wise Jogogle-Zadester, King of Ug.

"But, your Majesty," I said, "what became of the poor Scumadumclitchclitchians?"

"They all died," he answered with royal simplicity.

"Then your Majesty's humane intervention," I said, "was not entirely—well, fattening?"

"The fortune of war," said the King, gravely, looking over my head to signify that the interview was at an end; and sticking out my tongue in token of respect, I retired from the Presence on hands and feet, as is the etiquette in that country.

As soon as I was out of hearing I threw a stone in the direction of the palace and said: "I never in my life heard of such a cold blooded scoundrel!"

In conversation with the King's Prime Minister, the famous Grumsquutzy, I asked him how it was that Ug, being a great military power, was apparently without soldiers.

"Guest of my sovereign," he replied, courteously shaking his fist under my nose in sign of amity, "know that when Ug needs soldiers she enlists them. At the end of the war they are put to death."

"Visible embodiment of a great nation's wisdom," I said, "far be it from me to doubt the expediency of that military method; but merely as a matter of economy would it not be better to keep an army in time of peace than to be compelled to create one in time of war?"

"Ug is rich," he replied; "we do not have to consider matters of economy. There is among our people a strong and instinctive distrust of a standing army."

"What are they afraid of," I asked—"what do they fear that it will do?"

"It is not what the army may do," answered the great man, "but what it may prevent themselves from doing. You must know that we have in this land a thing known as Industrial Discontent."

"Ah, I see," I exclaimed, interrupting—"the industrial classes fear that the army may destroy, or at least subdue, their discontent."

The Prime Minister reflected profoundly, standing the while, in order that he might assist his faculties by scratching himself, even as we, when thinking, scratch our heads.

"No," he said presently; "I don't think that is quite what they apprehend—they and the writers and statesmen who speak for them. As I said before, what is feared in a case of industrial discontent is the army's preventive power. But I am myself uncertain what it is that these good souls dislike to have the army prevent. I shall take the customary means to learn."

Having occasion on the next day to enter the great audience hall of the palace I observed in gigantic letters running across the entire side opposite the entrance this surprising inscription:

IN A STRIKE, WHAT DO YOU FEAR THAT THE ARMY WILL PREVENT, WHICH OUGHT TO BE DONE?

Facing the entrance sat Grumsquutzy, in his robes of office and surrounded by an armed guard. At a little distance stood two great black slaves, each bearing a scourge of thongs. All about them the floor was slippery with blood. While I wondered at all this two policemen entered, having between them one whom I recognized as a professional Friend of the People, a great "orator," keenly concerned for the interests of Labor. Shown the inscription and unable or unwilling to answer, he was given over to the two blacks and, being stripped to the skin, was beaten with the whips until he bled copiously and his cries resounded through the palace. His ears were then shorn away and he was thrown into the street. By that time another Friend of the People was brought in, and treated in the same way; and the inquiry was continued, day after day, until all had been interrogated. But Grumsquutzy got no answer.

A most extraordinary and interesting custom of the Uggards is called the Naganag and has existed, I was told, for centuries. Immediately after every war, and before the returned army is put to death, the chieftains who have held high command and their official head, the Minister of National Displeasure, are conducted with much pomp to the public square of Nabootka, the capital. Here all are stripped naked, deprived of their sight with a hot iron and armed with a club each. They are then locked in the square, which has an inclosing wall thirty clowgebs high. A signal is given and they begin to fight. At the end of three days the place is entered and searched. If any of the dead bodies has an unbroken bone in it the survivors are boiled in wine; if not they are smothered in butter.

Upon the advantages of this custom—which surely has not its like in the whole world—I could get little light. One public official told me its purpose was "peace among the victorious"; another said it was "for gratification of the military instinct in high places," though if that is so one is disposed to ask "What was the war for?" The Prime Minister, profoundly learned in all things else, could not enlighten me and the commander-in-chief in the Wuggard war could only tell me, while on his way to the public square, that it was "to vindicate the truth of history."

In all the wars in which Ug has engaged in historic times that with Wug was the most destructive of life. Excepting among the comparatively few troops that had the hygienic and preservative advantage of personal collusion with the enemy, the mortality was appalling. Regiments exposed to the fatal conditions of camp life in their own country died like flies in a frost. So pathetic were the pleas of the sufferers to be led against the enemy and have a chance to live that none hearing them could forbear to weep. Finally a considerable number of them went to the seat of war, where they began an immediate attack upon a fortified city, for their health; but the enemy's resistance was too brief materially to reduce the death rate and the men were again in the hands of their officers. On their return to Ug they were so few that the public executioners charged with the duty of reducing the army to a peace footing were themselves made ill by inactivity.

As to the navy, the war with Wug having shown the Uggard sailors to be immortal, their Government knows not how to get rid of them, and remains a great sea power in spite of itself. I ventured to suggest mustering out, but neither the King nor any Minister of State was able to form a conception of any method of reduction and retrenchment but that of the public headsman.

THE WAR WITH WUG

It is said—I do not know with how much truth—that the defeat of Wug was made easy by a certain malicious prevision of the Wuggards themselves; something of the nature of heroic self-sacrifice, the surrender of a present advantage for a terrible revenge in the future. As an instance, the commander of the fortified city already mentioned is reported to have ordered his garrison to kill as few of their assailants as possible.

"It is true," he explained to his subordinates, who favored a defense to the death—"it is true this will lose us the place, but there are other places; you have not thought of that."

They had not thought of that.

"It is true, too, that we shall be taken prisoners, but"—and he smiled grimly—"we have fairly good appetites, and we must be fed. That will cost something, I take it. But that is not the best of it. Look at that vast host of our enemies—each one of them a future pensioner on a fool people. If there is among us one man who would willingly deprive the Uggard treasury of a single dependent—who would spare the Uggard pigs one gukwam of expense, let the traitor stand forth."

No traitor stood forth, and in the ensuing battles the garrison, it is said, fired only blank cartridges, and such of the assailants as were killed incurred that mischance by falling over their own feet.

It is estimated by Wuggard statisticians that in ten years from the close of the war the annual appropriation for pensions in Ug will amount to no less than one hundred and sixty gumdums to every pig in the kingdom.

E (11 Sept. 1898): 20. Incorporated into "The Land Beyond the Blow" in the chapter "Marooned on Ug."

NOTE

In this war, the strategy of Ug is completely and inhumanly economic. The narrow logic of the Uggard position is based on the assumption that army veterans entail a ruinous cost to the state in pensions. If and when Ug is victorious in battle, therefore, it prevents this future financial burden by executing its own soldiers. In this case, by allowing Wug to conquer Ug without casualties, the Uggards subversively saddle the victors—now the rulers of Ug—with the enormous expense of pensioning their huge army. Thus the Uggards avenge themselves on Wug and defeat it in the long run. The story can be read as an obvious allegory of the Spanish–American War, with Ug representing the United States, Wug representing Spain, and Scumadumclitchclitch representing Cuba.

MOXON'S MASTER

"Are you serious?—do you really believe that a machine thinks?"

I got no immediate reply; Moxon was apparently intent upon the coals in the grate, touching them deftly here and there with the fire-poker till they signified a sense of his attention by a brighter glow. For several weeks I had been observing in him a growing habit of delay in answering even the most trivial of commonplace questions. His air, however, was that of preoccupation rather than deliberation: one might have said that he had "something on his mind."

Presently he said:

"What is a 'machine'? The word has been variously defined. Here is one definition from a popular dictionary: 'Any instrument or organization by which power is applied and made effective, or a desired effect produced.' Well, then, is not a man a machine? And you will admit that he thinks—or thinks he thinks."[1]

"If you do not wish to answer my question," I said, rather testily, "why not say so?—all that you say is mere evasion. You know well enough that when I say 'machine' I do not mean a man, but something that man has made and controls."

"When it does not control him," he said, rising abruptly and looking out of a window, whence nothing was visible in the blackness of a stormy night. A moment later he turned about and with a smile said: "I beg your pardon; I had no thought of evasion. I considered the dictionary man's unconscious testimony suggestive and worth something in the discussion. I can give your question a direct answer easily enough: I do believe that a machine thinks about the work that it is doing."

That was direct enough, certainly. It was not altogether pleasing, for it tended to confirm a sad suspicion that Moxon's devotion to study and work in his machine-shop had not been good for him. I knew, for one thing, that he suffered from insomnia, and that is no light affliction. Had it affected his mind? His reply to my question seemed to me then evidence that it had; perhaps I should think differently about it now. I was younger then, and among the blessings that are not denied to youth is ignorance. Incited by that great stimulant to controversy, I said:

"And what, pray, does it think with—in the absence of a brain?"

The reply, coming with less than his customary delay, took his favorite form of counter-interrogation:

"With what does a plant think—in the absence of a brain?"

"Ah, plants also belong to the philosopher class! I should be pleased to know some of their conclusions; you may omit the premises."

"Perhaps," he replied, apparently unaffected by my foolish irony, "you may be able to infer their convictions from their acts. I will spare you the familiar examples of the sensitive mimosa, the several insectivorous flowers and those whose stamens bend down and shake their pollen upon the entering bee in order that he may fertilize their distant mates. But observe this. In an open spot in my garden I planted a climbing vine. When it was barely above the surface I set a stake into the soil a yard away. The vine at once made for it, but as it was about to reach it after several days I removed it a few feet. The vine at once altered its course, making an acute angle, and again made for the stake. This manœuvre was repeated several times, but finally, as if discouraged, the vine abandoned the pursuit and ignoring further attempts to divert it traveled to a small tree, farther away, which it climbed."

"Roots of the eucalyptus will prolong themselves incredibly in search of moisture. A well-known horticulturist relates that one entered an old drain pipe and followed it until it came to a break, where a section of the pipe had been removed to make way for a stone wall that had been built across its course. The root left the drain and followed the wall until it found an opening where a stone had fallen out. It crept through and following the other side of the wall back to the drain, entered the unexplored part and resumed its journey."

"And all this?"

"Can you miss the significance of it? It shows the consciousness of plants. It proves that they think."

"Even if it did—what then? We were speaking, not of plants, but of machines. They may be composed partly of wood—wood that has no longer vitality—or wholly of metal. Is thought an attribute also of the mineral kingdom?"

"How else do you explain the phenomena, for example, of crystallization?"

"I do not explain them."

"Because you cannot without affirming what you wish to deny, namely, intelligent co-operation among the constituent elements of the crystals. When soldiers form lines, or hollow squares, you call it reason. When wild geese in flight take the form of a letter V you say instinct. When the homogeneous atoms of a mineral, moving freely in solution, arrange themselves into shapes mathematically perfect, or particles of frozen moisture into the symmetrical and beautiful forms of snowflakes, you have nothing to say. You have not even invented a name to conceal your heroic unreason."

MOXON'S MASTER

Moxon was speaking with unusual animation and earnestness. As he paused I heard in an adjoining room known to me as his "machine-shop," which no one but himself was permitted to enter, a singular thumping sound, as of some one pounding upon a table with an open hand. Moxon heard it at the same moment and, visibly agitated, rose and hurriedly passed into the room whence it came. I thought it odd that any one else should be in there, and my interest in my friend—with doubtless a touch of unwarrantable curiosity—led me to listen intently, though, I am happy to say, not at the keyhole. There were confused sounds, as of a struggle or scuffle; the floor shook. I distinctly heard hard breathing and a hoarse whisper which said "Damn you!" Then all was silent, and presently Moxon reappeared and said, with a rather sorry smile:

"Pardon me for leaving you so abruptly. I have a machine in there that lost its temper and cut up rough."

Fixing my eyes steadily upon his left cheek, which was traversed by four parallel excoriations showing blood, I said:

"How would it do to trim its nails?"

I could have spared myself the jest; he gave it no attention, but seated himself in the chair that he had left and resumed the interrupted monologue as if nothing had occurred:

"Doubtless you do not hold with those (I need not name them to a man of your reading) who have taught that all matter is sentient, that every atom is a living, feeling, conscious being. *I* do. There is no such thing as dead, inert matter: it is all alive; all instinct with force, actual and potential; all sensitive to the same forces in its environment and susceptible to the contagion of higher and subtler ones residing in such superior organisms as it may be brought into relation with, as those of man when he is fashioning it into an instrument of his will. It absorbs something of his intelligence and purpose—more of them in proportion to the complexity of the resulting machine and that of its work.

"Do you happen to recall Herbert Spencer's definition of 'Life'? I read it thirty years ago. He may have altered it afterward, for anything I know, but in all that time I have been unable to think of a single word that could profitably be changed or added or removed. It seems to me not only the best definition, but the only possible one.

"'Life,' he says, 'is a definite combination of heterogeneous changes, both simultaneous and successive, in correspondence with external coexistences and sequences.'"[2]

"That defines the phenomenon," I said, "but gives no hint of its cause."

"That," he replied, "is all that any definition can do. As Mill points out, we know nothing of cause except as an antecedent—nothing of effect except as a consequent.[3] Of certain phenomena, one never occurs without another, which is dissimilar: the first in point of time we call cause, the second, effect. One who had many times seen a rabbit pursued by a dog, and had never seen rabbits and dogs otherwise, would think the rabbit the cause of the dog.[4]

"But I fear," he added, laughing naturally enough, "that my rabbit is leading me a long way from the track of my legitimate quarry: I'm indulging in the pleasure of the chase for its own sake. What I want you to observe is that in Herbert Spencer's definition of 'life' the activity of a machine is included—there is nothing in the definition that is not applicable to it. According to this sharpest of observers and deepest of thinkers, if a man during his period of activity is alive, so is a machine when in operation. As an inventor and constructor of machines I know that to be true."

Moxon was silent for a long time, gazing absently into the fire. It was growing late and I thought it time to be going, but somehow I did not like the notion of leaving him in that isolated house, all alone except for the presence of some person of whose nature my conjectures could go no further than that it was unfriendly, perhaps malign. Leaning toward him and looking earnestly into his eyes while making a motion with my hand through the door of his workshop, I said:

"Moxon, whom have you in there?"

Somewhat to my surprise he laughed lightly and answered without hesitation:

"Nobody; the incident that you have in mind was caused by my folly in leaving a machine in action with nothing to act upon, while I undertook the interminable task of enlightening your understanding. Do you happen to know that Consciousness is the creature of Rhythm?"

"O bother them both!" I replied, rising and laying hold of my overcoat. "I'm going to wish you good night; and I'll add the hope that the machine which you inadvertently left in action will have her gloves on the next time you think it needful to stop her."

Without waiting to observe the effect of my shot I left the house.

Rain was falling, and the darkness was intense. In the sky beyond the crest of a hill toward which I groped my way along precarious plank sidewalks and across miry, unpaved streets I could see the faint glow of the city's lights, but behind me nothing was visible but a single window of Moxon's house. It glowed with what seemed to me a mysterious and fateful meaning. I knew it was an uncurtained aperture in my friend's "machine-shop," and I had little doubt that he had resumed the studies interrupted by his duties as my instructor in mechanical consciousness and the fatherhood of Rhythm. Odd, and in some degree humorous, as his convictions seemed to me at that time, I could not wholly divest myself of the feeling that they had some tragic relation to his life and character—perhaps to his destiny—although I no longer entertained the notion that they were the vagaries of a disordered mind. Whatever might be thought of his views, his exposition of them was too logical for that. Over and over, his last words came back to me: "Consciousness is the creature of Rhythm." Bald and terse as the statement was, I now found it infinitely alluring. At each recurrence it broadened in meaning and deepened in suggestion. Why, here, (I thought) is something upon which to found a philosophy. If consciousness is the product of rhythm all things *are* conscious, for all have motion, and all motion is rhythmic. I wondered if Moxon knew the significance and breadth of his thought—the scope of this momentous generalization; or had he arrived at his philosophic faith by the tortuous and uncertain road of observation?

That faith was then new to me, and all Moxon's expounding had failed to make me a convert; but now it seemed as if a great light shone about me, like that which fell upon Saul of Tarsus;[5] and out there in the storm and darkness and solitude I experienced what Lewes calls "The endless variety and excitement of philosophic thought."[6] I exulted in a new sense of knowledge, a new pride of reason. My feet seemed hardly to touch the earth; it was as if I were uplifted and borne through the air by invisible wings.

Yielding to an impulse to seek further light from him whom I now recognized as my master and guide, I had unconsciously turned about, and almost before I was aware of having done so found myself again at Moxon's door. I was drenched with rain, but felt no discomfort. Unable in my excitement to find the doorbell I instinctively tried the knob. It turned and, entering, I mounted the stairs to the room that I had so recently left. All was dark and silent; Moxon, as I had supposed, was in the adjoining room—the "machine-shop." Groping along the wall until I found the communicating door I knocked loudly several times, but got no response, which I attributed to the uproar outside, for the wind was blowing a gale and dashing the rain against the thin walls in sheets. The drumming upon the shingle roof spanning the unceiled room was loud and incessant.

I had never been invited into the machine-shop—had, indeed, been denied admittance, as had all others, with one exception, a skilled metal worker, of whom no one knew anything except that his name was Haley and his habit silence. But in my spiritual exaltation, discretion and civility were alike forgotten and I opened the door. What I saw took all philosophical speculation out of me in short order.

Moxon sat facing me at the farther side of a small table upon which a single candle made all the light that was in the room. Opposite him, his back toward me, sat another person. On the table between the two was a chess-board; the men were playing. I knew little of chess, but as only a few pieces were on the board it was obvious that the game was near its close. Moxon was intensely interested—not so much, it seemed to me, in the game as in his antagonist, upon whom he had fixed so intent a look that, standing though I did directly in the line of his vision, I was altogether unobserved. His face was ghastly white, and his eyes glittered like diamonds. Of his antagonist I had only a back view, but that was sufficient; I should not have cared to see his face.

He was apparently not more than five feet in height, with proportions suggesting those of a gorilla—a tremendous breadth of shoulders, thick, short neck and broad, squat head, which had a tangled growth of black hair and was topped with a crimson fez. A tunic of the same color, belted tightly to the waist, reached the seat—apparently a box—upon which he sat; his legs and feet were not seen. His left forearm appeared to rest in his lap; he moved his pieces with his right hand, which seemed disproportionately long.

I had shrunk back and now stood a little to one side of the doorway and in shadow. If Moxon had looked farther than the face of his opponent he could have observed nothing now, except that the door was open. Something forbade me either to enter or to retire, a feeling—I know not how it came—that I was in the presence of an imminent tragedy and might serve my friend by remaining. With a scarcely conscious rebellion against the indelicacy of the act I remained.

The play was rapid. Moxon hardly glanced at the board before making his moves, and to my unskilled eye seemed to move the piece most convenient to his hand, his motions in doing so being quick, nervous and lacking in precision. The response of his antagonist, while equally prompt in the inception, was made with a slow, uniform, mechanical and, I thought, somewhat theatrical movement of the arm, that was a sore trial to my patience. There was something unearthly about it all, and I caught myself shuddering. But I was wet and cold.

Two or three times after moving a piece the stranger slightly inclined his head, and each time I observed that Moxon shifted his king. All at once the thought came to me that the man was dumb. And then that he was a machine—an automaton chess-player! Then I remembered that Moxon had once spoken to me of having invented such a piece of mechanism, though I did not understand that it had actually been constructed. Was all his talk about the consciousness and intelligence of machines merely a prelude to eventual exhibition of this device—only a trick to intensify the effect of its mechanical action upon me in my ignorance of its secret?

A fine end, this, of all my intellectual transports—my "endless variety and excitement of philosophic thought!" I was about to retire in disgust when something occurred to hold my curiosity. I observed a shrug of the thing's great shoulders, as if it were irritated; and so natural was this—so entirely human—that in my new view of the matter it startled me. Nor was that all, for a moment later it struck the table sharply with its clenched hand. At that gesture Moxon seemed even more startled than I: he pushed his chair a little backward, as in alarm.

Presently Moxon, whose play it was, raised his hand high above the board, pounced upon one of his pieces like a sparrow-hawk and with the exclamation "checkmate!" rose quickly to his feet and stepped behind his chair. The automaton sat motionless.

The wind had now gone down, but I heard, at lessening intervals and progressively louder, the rumble and roll of thunder. In the pauses between I now became conscious of a low humming or buzzing which, like the thunder, grew momentarily louder and more distinct. It seemed to come from the body of the automaton, and was unmistakably a whirring of wheels. It gave me the impression of a disordered mechanism which had escaped the repressive and regulating action of some controlling part—an effect such as might be expected if a pawl should be jostled from the teeth of a ratchet-wheel. But before I had time for much conjecture as to its nature my attention was taken by the strange motions of the automaton itself. A slight but continuous convulsion appeared to have possession of it. In body and head it shook like a

MOXON'S MASTER

man with palsy or an ague chill, and the motion augmented every moment until the entire figure was in violent agitation. Suddenly it sprang to its feet and with a movement almost too quick for the eye to follow shot forward across table and chair, with both arms thrust forth to their full length—the posture and lunge of a diver. Moxon tried to throw himself backward out of reach, but he was too late: I saw the horrible thing's hands close upon his throat, his own clutch its wrists. Then the table was overturned, the candle thrown to the floor and extinguished, and all was black dark. But the noise of the struggle was dreadfully distinct, and most terrible of all were the raucous, squawking sounds made by the strangled man's efforts to breathe. Guided by the infernal hubbub, I sprang to the rescue of my friend, but had hardly taken a stride in the darkness when the whole room blazed with a blinding white light that burned into my brain and heart and memory a vivid picture of the combatants on the floor, Moxon underneath, his throat still in the clutch of those iron hands, his head forced backward, his eyes protruding, his mouth wide open and his tongue thrust out; and— horrible contrast!—upon the painted face of his assassin an expression of tranquil and profound thought, as in the solution of a problem in chess! This I observed, then all was blackness and silence.

Three days later I recovered consciousness in a hospital. As the memory of that tragic night slowly evolved in my ailing brain I recognized in my attendant Moxon's confidential workman, Haley. Responding to a look he approached, smiling.

"Tell me about it," I managed to say, faintly—"all about it."

"Certainly," he said; "you were carried unconscious from a burning house— Moxon's. Nobody knows how you came to be there. You may have to do a little explaining. The origin of the fire is a bit mysterious, too. My own notion is that the house was struck by lightning."

"And Moxon?"

"Buried yesterday—what was left of him."

Apparently this reticent person could unfold himself on occasion. When imparting shocking intelligence to the sick he was affable enough. After some moments of the keenest mental suffering I ventured to ask another question:

"Who rescued me?"

"Well, if that interests you—I did."

"Thank you, Mr. Haley, and may God bless you for it. Did you rescue, also, that charming product of your skill, the automaton chess-player that murdered its inventor?"

The man was silent a long time, looking away from me. Presently he turned and gravely said:

"Do you know that?"

"I do," I replied; "I saw it done."

That was many years ago. If asked to-day I should answer less confidently.

E (16 Apr. 1899): 22 (as "A Night at Moxon's"); *CW* 3.88–105.

NOTES

In the classical tradition of the hoax, this tale begins with the absurd proposition that man is a machine and then proceeds speciously but ingeniously to make it seem plausible through the use of logical fallacies, subtly defective reasoning, and missing details that entice readers to make credulous inferences. Some strained interpretations have been written about this story, all more or less filling in blanks in the narrative with far-fetched explanations. For a discussion of this story as a hoax, see *PA* 153–55.

1. Cf. *DD*: "Cartesian, *adj.* Relating to Descartes, a famous philosopher, author of the celebrated dictum, *Cogito ergo sum*—whereby he was pleased to suppose he demonstrated the reality of human existence. The dictum might be improved, however, thus: *Cogito cogito ergo cogito sum*—'I think that I think, therefore I think that I am'; as close an approach to certainty as any pholosopher has yet made."

2. Herbert Spencer (1820–1903), British philosopher. The passage quoted was first propounded in rudimentary form in *The Principles of Psychology* (1855), in definitive form in *The Principles of Biology* (1864–67), part 1, chaps. 4–5. AB first cited it in "The Fables of Zambri, the Parsee," First Series, no. 12 (*F* 16 [27 July 1872]: 37; *CF,* no. 7), and again in "Prattle," *Ar* 1, no. 39 (15 Dec. 1877): 5, both times in contexts that ridiculed it for its obscurity.

3. See John Stuart Mill (1806–73), *A System of Logic, Ratiocinative and Inductive* (1843), especially book 2, chapter 5, "Of the Law of Universal Causation." In this treatise Mill presents a radical empiricist theory of knowledge, denying that even the truths of mathematics can be known deductively and asserting that all knowledge is acquired inductively through observation of particulars.

4. Cf. *DD*: "Effect, *n.* The second of two phenomena which always occur together in the same order. The first, called a Cause, is said to generate the other—which is no more sensible than it would be for one who has never seen a dog except in the pursuit of a rabbit to declare the rabbit the cause of the dog." AB also used the analogy in "Concerning Terrestrial Lunarians," *NYA* (18 May 1903): 14; *E* (30 May 1903): 14.

5. AB refers to Saint Paul, called Saul before his conversion to Christianity. "And as he journeyed, he came near Damascus: and suddenly there shined round about him a light from heaven: And he fell to the earth, and heard a voice saying unto him, Saul, Saul, why persecutest thou me?" (Acts 9:3–4).

6. George Henry Lewes (1817–78), historian, critic, and husband of George Eliot. The quotation is from his *The History of Philosophy from Thales to Comte* (London: Longmans, Green, 1867), 1:51. AB cites the remark in "The Model Philosopher" (*ND* 73). It is also found in "The Grizzly Papers: No. II," *OM* 6, no. 2 (February 1871): 181. Cf. *DD*: "Noumenon, *n.* That which exists, as distinguished from that which merely seems to exist, the latter being a phenomenon. The noumenon is a bit difficult to locate; it can be apprehended only by a process of reasoning—which is a phenomenon. Nevertheless, the discovery and exposition of noumena offer a rich field for what Lewes calls 'the endless variety and excitement of philosophic thought.' Hurrah (therefore) for the noumenon!" AB was scornful of abstract concepts which could not be verified and which bore no useful application to the practical world or life.

THE ALTERNATIVE PROPOSAL

A TRUE HISTORY OF THE GENESIS AND DEVELOPMENT OF AMERICA'S ULTIMATUM

Calumpit was lost—Calumpit on the Bag Bag—and Aguinaldo's hopes were broken.[1] All that Filipino valor could accomplish had been done, and it remained only to wring from the victor such terms as magnanimity might concede to helplessness running a bluff.

In the palace at Manila Gen. Otis and Admiral Dewey were in session in full uniform.[2] Behind them were their respective staffs (or staves) in full uniform too, a glittering array; on either hand were secretaries and stenographers, with pencils poised in air, expectant. Clad all in black and so masked that only his glowing eyes could be seen, a portentous figure, to whom the medieval ax and block would have been appropriate appurtenances, sat at the General's fateful typewriter, ready to strike the keys whose sound would be heard around the world,[3] attesting the hecatombs[4] of Filipino slain in the next battle—for still the remnants of Aguinaldo's forces were afield. Three newspaper correspondents, heavily muzzled, were tethered to iron rings in the wall. It was a notable gathering and the Muse of History held her breath.

"Have the Filipino Peace Commissioners arrived?" said Gen. Otis to a staff officer that stood glittering near by.

"Sir, they await," answered the Head of the Department of Negotiations with the Enemy.

"Have they been apprised of the sole condition on which we will accept the surrender of Aguinaldo and his army?"

"They have, sir, and have replied that they do not like it. I am to say to you that they will consider an alternative proposal."

"Good; we will retire and invent one. The Government of the United States is firm, but not stubborn."

With that General Otis and Admiral Dewey rose and withdrew to an inner apartment, and darkness fell upon the land and the sea. Within an hour they returned to the throne room. They walked slowly, as if infirm; their heads were bowed and their shoulders had a pronounced stoop as if beneath a great load of responsibility. Their faces were lined and seamed with thought. They were visibly grayer. Without a word they seated themselves as before. Then General Otis said:

"Let Señores Arguelles and Bergal[5] approach—show them in."

The Peace Commissioners of the Aguinalderos entered and stood in the Two Presences. They bowed ceremoniously. The General and the Admiral bowed ceremoniously. The staff officers glittered in silence, and a dashing young Lieutenant of sea cavalry ceased to dash. A slight tremor of the earth attested Nature's interest in the momentous event that was approaching its culmination. The phenomenon was impressive; it was the first earthquake that Manila had known for two hours.

"Señores," said the General, "I venture to presume that it is hardly needful to remind you that your hope of successful resistance is extinguished by our capture of your great stronghold on the Bag Bag."

The Filipino Commissioners bowed in silence. The General continued:

"Notwithstanding, we are told that you do not like our proposal for an unconditional surrender and that you invite us to make an alternative proposal."

The Commissioners bowed again. It was then observed that one-half the audience chamber was growing rapidly dark, and in a few seconds the gathering gloom had extinguished everything to the right of the median line of the vast room. One half of that distinguished company was invisible to the other half. A moment later the darkness began to lift and soon all was light as before. The incident was exhausted—Admiral Dewey had finished a wink of his starboard eye.

The General resumed, but this time he addressed one of his staff, the Chief Preparer of the Hostile Mind:

"Have the honorable Commissioners been instructed in the American pronunciation of their beautiful language?"

The staff officer saluted and replied:

"General (and Admiral) they have: they understand her as she is spoke here."[6]

"'Tis well," said the General,—then to the Commissioners: "The fateful moment arrives—the conference ends. Return to Señor Aguinaldo and say to him, with reference to our former proposal, that if he does not like it he may Calumpit!"

The Commissioners retired with tears in each other's eyes.

E (14 May 1899): 12 (under the heading "Two Stories by Bierce").

THE ALTERNATIVE PROPOSAL

NOTES

Following the Spanish-American War of 1898, the United States found itself fighting the Filipinos, who had been grateful for American help in achieving independence from Spain but now turned on their former ally because they did not want Spanish rule to be replaced by American. Just as Bierce had criticized the inept way the American military had prosecuted the war he now satirized the pomposity of the same military men, who were negotiating with the Filipinos. This entire piece, dripping with sarcasm, is written in the mock-heroic style.

Either AB or one of his editors printed this work as one of "Two Stories by Bierce." The other item, "John Smith's Ancestors," is only a mathematical conundrum, and by no stretch of definition a tale. It has been excluded from this edition. It can be found in *CW* 9.53–57.

1. AB refers to Emilio Aguinaldo (1869–1964), Filipino revolutionary who declared himself president of a revolutionary government on 22 March 1897. Later driven into exile, Aguinaldo returned when the U.S. captured the Philippines from Spain in the course of the Spanish-American War of 1898; in defiance of U.S. wishes, declared himself president again on 23 January 1899, setting up a capital at Calumpit or Kalumpit, on the Bagbag River 8 miles northwest of Malolos on the island of Luzon. U.S. troops fought Aguinaldo's forces, ultimately defeating them; he was captured on 23 March 1901. Calumpit was captured by U.S. forces led by Gen. Arthur McArthur in late April 1899.

2. Gen. Elwell S. Otis (1838–1909) was leader of all U.S. combat forces in the Philippines during the Spanish-American War and was appointed military governor on 29 August 1898. He directed the American forces in suppressing the Filipino insurgents until he was relieved of his duties on 5 May 1900 by Gen. Arthur McArthur. Adm. George Dewey (1837–1917) commanded the Asiatic Squadron of the U.S. Navy in the Spanish-American War and was chiefly responsible for defeating Spain in the Philippines.

3. Cf. Ralph Waldo Emerson (1803–82), "Concord Hymn" (1836), about the Battle of Lexington and Concord: "Here once the embattled farmers stood, / And fired the shot heard round the world" (ll. 3–4).

4. A term from classical Greek for a large slaughter or sacrifice.

5. Manuel Arguelles was one of three Filipinos nominated by Aguinaldo to meet American counterparts in January 1899 to defuse tensions and prevent the outbreak of war. But the conference (9–29 January) accomplished little, in large part because the United States deliberately strung out the negotiations so that naval reinforcements could arrive. Bergal is unidentified.

6. *English as She Is Spoke; or, A Jest in Sober Earnest* (1883) by José da Fonseca was a translation of a book of unintentionally grotesque instances of conversational English designed for Portuguese speakers. It was the object of derision throughout the English-speaking world.

THE ALTERNATIVE PROPOSAL

TRUSTLAND: A TALE OF A TRAVELER

Arriving at the capital of the country after many incredible adventures, I was promptly arrested by the police and taken before the Jumjum. He was an exceedingly grave and dignified person about three hundred years old, as I afterward learned, and held office by appointment, "for life or fitness," as their laws express it. With one necessary exception all offices are appointive and the tenure of all except that is the same. The Panjandrum, or, as we should call him, King, is elected for a term of one hundred and fifty years, at the expiration of which he is shot. It is held that any man who has been so long in high authority will have committed enough sins and blunders to deserve death, even if none can be specifically proved.

Brought into the presence of the Jumjum, who graciously saluted me by taking his right foot in his left hand and carrying it to his lips, I was seated on a beautiful rug and told in broken English by an interpreter brought from Kansas that I was at liberty to ask any questions that I chose.

"Your Highness," I said, addressing the Jumjum through the interpreting Populist, "I fear that I do not understand; I expected, not to ask questions, but to have to answer them. I am ready to give such an account of myself as will satisfy you that I am an honest man—neither a criminal nor a spy."

"The gentleman seems to regard himself with a considerable interest," said the Jumjum, aside to an officer of his suite—a remark which the interpreter, with characteristic intelligence, duly repeated to me. Then addressing me the Jumjum said:

"Doubtless your personal character is an alluring topic, but it is relevant to nothing in any proceedings that can be taken here. When a foreigner arrives in our capital he is brought before me to be instructed in whatever he may think it expedient for him to know of the manners, customs, laws and so forth, of the country that he honors with his presence. It matters nothing to us what he is, but much to him what we are. You are at liberty to inquire."

I was for a moment overcome with emotion by so noble an example of official civility and thoughtfulness, then, after a little reflection, I said: "May it please your Highness, I should greatly like to be informed of the origin of the name of your esteemed country."

"Our country," said the Jumjum, acknowledging the compliment by a movement of his ears, "is called Trustland because all its industries, trades and professions are conducted by great aggregations of capital known as 'trusts.' They do the entire business of the country."

"Good God!" I exclaimed; "what a terrible state of affairs that is! Why do your people not rise and throw off the yoke?"

"You are pleased to be unintelligible, honorable stranger," said the great man, with a smile. "Would you mind explaining what you mean by 'the yoke'?"

"I mean," said I, surprised by his ignorance of metaphor, but reflecting that possibly the figures of rhetoric were not used in that country—"I mean the oppression, the slavery under which your people groan, their bondage to the tyrannical trusts, entailing poverty, unrequited toil and loss of self-respect."

"Why, as to that," he replied, "our people are prosperous and happy. There is very little poverty and what there is is obviously the result of vice or improvidence. Our labor is light and all the necessaries of life, many of the comforts and some of the luxuries are abundant and cheap. I hardly know what you mean by the tyranny of the trusts; they do not seem to care to be tyrannous, for each, having the entire market for what it produces, its prosperity is assured and there is none of the strife and competition which, as I can imagine, might breed hardness and cruelty. Moreover, we should not let them be tyrannous. Why should we?"

"But, your Highness, suppose, for example, the trust that manufactures safety pins should decide to double the price of its product. What is to prevent great injury to the consumer?"

"The courts. Having but one man—the responsible manager—to deal with, protective legislation and its enforcement would be a very simple matter. If there were a thousand manufacturers of safety pins, scattered all over the country in as many jurisdictions, there would be no controlling them at all. They would cheat, not only one another but the consumers, with virtual immunity. But there is no disposition among our trusts to do any such thing. Each has the whole market, as I said, and each has learned by experience what the manager of a large business soon must learn, and what the manager of a small one probably would not learn and could not afford to apply if he knew it—namely, that low prices bring disproportionately large sales and therefore profits. Prices in this country are never put up except when some kind of scarcity increases the cost of production. Besides, nearly all the consumers are a part of the trusts, the stock of which is about the best kind of property for investment."

"What!" I cried,—"do not the managers so manipulate the stock by 'watering' it and otherwise as to fool and cheat the small investors?"

TRUSTLAND: A TALE OF A TRAVELER

"We should not permit them. That would be dishonest."

"So it is in my country," I replied, rather tartly, for I believed his apparent *naiveté* assumed for my confusion, "but we are unable to prevent it."

He looked at me somewhat compassionately, I thought. "Perhaps," he said, "not enough of you really wish to prevent it. Perhaps your people are—well, different from mine—not worse, you understand—just different."

I felt the blood go into my cheeks and hot words were upon my tongue's end, but I restrained them; the conditions for a quarrel were not favorable to my side of it. When I had mastered my chagrin and resentment I said:

"In my country when trusts are formed a great number of people suffer, whether the general consumer does or not—many small dealers, middle men, drummers and general employees. The small dealer is driven out of the business by underselling. The middle man is frequently ignored, the trust dealing directly, or nearly so, with the consumer. The drummer is discharged because, competition having disappeared, custom must come without solicitation. Consolidation lets out swarms of employees of the individual concerns consolidated, for it is nearly as easy to conduct one large concern as a dozen smaller ones. These people get great sympathy from the public and the newspapers and their case is obviously pitiable. Was it not so in this country during the transition stage, and did not these poor gentlemen have to"—the right words would not come; I hardly knew how to finish. "Were they not compelled to go to work?" I finally asked, rather humbly.

The great official crossed his legs over his neck, in the manner of his countrymen when reflecting, and was silent for several minutes. Then he resumed his former posture and spoke:

"I am not sure that I understand you about our transition state. So far as our history goes matters with us have always been as they are to-day. To suppose them to have been otherwise would be to impugn the common sense of our ancestors. Nor do I quite know what you mean by 'small dealers,' 'middle men,' 'drummers' and so forth."

He paused, fell into thought and was again in the act of absently crossing his legs over his neck when suddenly his face was suffused with the light of a happy thought. It so elated him that he sprang to his feet and with his staff of office broke the heads of his Chief Admonisher of the Inimical and his Second Assistant Audible Sycophant. Then he said:

"I think I comprehend. Some eighty-five years ago, soon after my induction into office, there came to the court of His Effulgency the Panjandrum a man who had been cast upon the island of Chicago (which I believe belongs to the American archipelago) and had passed many years there in business with the natives. Having learned all their customs and business methods he escaped to his own country and laid before the Panjandrum a comprehensive scheme of commercial reform. He and his scheme were referred to me, the Panjandrum being graciously pleased to be unable to make

TRUSTLAND: A TALE OF A TRAVELER

head or tail of it. I may best explain it in its application to a single industry—the manufacture and sale of gootles."

"What is a gootle? "I asked.

"A metal weight for attachment to the tail of a donkey to keep him from braying," was the answer. "It is known in this country that a donkey cannot utter a note unless he can lift his tail. Then, as now, gootles were made by a single concern having a great capital invested and an immense plant, and employing an army of workmen. It dealt, as it does to-day, directly with consumers. Afflicted with a sonant donkey a man would write to the trust and receive his gootle by return mail, or go personally to the factory and carry his purchase home on his shoulder—according to where he lived. The reformer said this was primitive, crude and injurious to the interests of the public and especially the poor. He proposed that the members of the gootle trust divide their capital and each member go into the business of making gootles for himself—I do not mean for his personal use—in different parts of the country. But none of them was to sell to consumers, but to other men, who would sell in quantity to still other men, who would sell single gootles for domestic use. Each manufacturer would of course require a full complement of officers, clerks and so forth, as would the other men—everybody but the consumer—and each would have to support them and make a profit himself. Competition would be so sharp that solicitors would have to be employed to make sales; and they too must have a living out of the business. Honored stranger, am I right in my inference that the proposed system has anything in common with the one which obtains in your own happy and enlightened country, and which you approve?"

I did not care to reply. "Of course," the Jumjum continued, "all this would greatly have enhanced the cost of gootles, thereby lessening the sales, thereby reducing the output, thereby throwing a number of workmen out of employment. You see this, do you not, O guest of my country?"

"Pray tell me," I said, "what became of the reformer who proposed all this change?"

"All this change? Why, sir, the one-thousandth part is not told: he proposed that his system should be general: not only in the gootle trust, but every trust in the country was to be broken up in the same way! When I had him before me, and had stated my objections to the plan, I asked him what were its advantages.

"'Sir,' he replied, 'I represent two-and-a-half millions of gentlemen in uncongenial employments, mostly manual and fatiguing. This would give them the kind of activity that they would like—such as their class enjoys in other countries where my system is in full flower, and where it is deemed so sacred that any proposal for its abolition or simplification by trusts is regarded with horror, especially by the working class.'

"Having reported to the Panjandrum (whose vermiform appendix may good angels have in charge) and received his orders, I called the reformer before me and addressed him thus:

"'Illustrious man, and friend of my sovereign, I have the honor to inform you that in the royal judgment your proposal is the most absurd, impudent and audacious ever made; that the system which you propose to set up is revolutionary and mischievous beyond the dreams of treason; that only in a nation of rogues and idiots could it have a moment's toleration.'

"He was about to reply, but cutting his throat to intimate that the hearing was at an end I withdrew from the Hall of Audience, as under similar circumstances I am about to do now."

I withdrew first, by way of a window.

E (19 Nov. 1899): 15. Incorporated into "The Land Beyond the Blow" under the title "The Jumjum of Gokeetle-Guk."

NOTE

This piece reflects the proliferation, in the United States at this time, of holding corporations which had been designed to evade the restrictions of the Sherman antitrust act of 1890. This proliferation continued until 1902, when President Theodore Roosevelt began initiating anti-monopoly suits. The Hearst newspapers, which employed AB, were vehemently critical of trusts, so this piece is in direct conflict with Hearst policy. Normally, a difference of opinion like this would mean the end of the writer's job, but AB had such respect and so strong a following that Hearst permitted him to dissent. AB's reasoning is fairly straightforward: the practice of encouraging competition is wasteful and results in duplication and the employment of redundant levels of management, wholesalers, and retailers, all of which adds costs that trusts eliminate through economies of scale. While AB's position in this matter was unpopular and seems merely contrarian, he does state that when trusts injure consumers through unfair practices, the courts might intervene and legislation might be enacted to rectify the situation. Interestingly enough, despite a more combative tone directed toward monopolies Roosevelt in effect took a similar position, objecting not to size per se but to illegalities. AB expresses many of the same opinions on trusts in the essay "Concerning Trusts" (*San Francisco Evening Post Magazine*, 3 June 1899; *FR* 173–77).

THE MAID OF PODUNK

Of the girlhood of Mrs. Nation (wrote the Historian of the Future) little that is authentic is known. She is commonly believed to have been born at Podunk, where as lately as the year 2730 a monument stood inscribed with her name, her virtues and her deeds.[1] In that year it was destroyed by the great earthquake that overthrew that famous city, which was then the national capital.

It is known that she was of humble origin and was brought up (her mother having died in giving birth to her) "on the bottle."[2] The meaning of that phrase, much in use among her contemporaries, is not now accurately understood, for it is obvious that unless the ardent spirits of that day were materially different from those of our time they would not have served as the sole diet of infants. To the deleterious effects of "the bottle" on the child's health we perhaps can trace that passionate antagonism to strong drink which was the keynote to her character and career.

When little Carrie was eleven years old, say about 1830, her father removed to Whitchita, or Whickity, a frontier town in Kansas, or Mormont—authorities disagree.[3] It was here that she began to hear the mysterious "voices" that moved her to take up arms against the "joints."[4] These, it appears, were places in which strong drinks were made by daring criminals and forced down the throats of persons who had been seized on the highways and carried into them.

The evolution of the word "joint," as given by the learned and ingenious Potwin Dumbleshaw,[5] in his great work on the philology of the ancients, is interesting. A man who had been carried into one of these terrible places and made to swallow the noxious liquid there produced was singularly affected by it: he was so limber as to be unable either to stand or sit—it was as if he had joints all over him. Hence he was known as a "jointer." Now, in the ancient Americanese tongue a "horser" was one who rode the now extinct animal called a "horse," a "schooner" was one who sailed in a ship called a "schoon," and so forth, the termination "er" implying always a certain relation to a place or thing.[6] So, by an odd forward-and-back analogy, the word "joint," meaning originally a point of flection in a limb, came to mean also, through its own derivative, a place where the "jointer" was jointed. "I know not," says Prof. Dumbleshaw, "a more curious instance of the perversion and shifting of words from thing to thing."

It is only fair to explain that Dr. Nubler, Professor of Extinct Languages at the Seacaucus University,[7] holds a different view, to the effect that Prof. Dumbleshaw is an ass.

For many centuries there has been much controversy regarding the "voices" said to have been heard by the young Carrie Slupsky[8] (that was her maiden name), and many duels are said to have resulted from the conflicting opinions.

The chief protagonists of Miss Slupsky—the men most solemnly convinced of her veracity and good faith in affirming her guidance by the "voices"—are Bastien Lapage, a famous author of the nineteenth century, and Mark Twain (or Duane), a painter of great renown.[9] Both these worthies, each in his way, have put upon record their profound persuasion of the maiden's actual inspiration by audible voices in the air, and both were her contemporaries and compatriots. Not much of the work of either has come down to us—a few leaves from the book of Lapage, a fragment of a painting by Twain—or Duane.

An odd circumstance is that in one of the former, Mrs. Nation's birthplace and home of her girlhood is mentioned as "Domremy."[10] The name occurs in several fragments of European literature of an even earlier date, and these facts have given rise to much discussion, evolving more heat than light.

Prof. Clambuck, writing in the year 2641, explains this apparent discrepancy somewhat as follows: In the Pottawottomy dialect,[11] which in the nineteenth century prevailed over the greater part of America among the illiterate, "po" and "dom" meant the same thing—a cow. Now, "dunk" meant a place of refreshment, or entertainment, and "remy" is an old Algonquin word for salt. Having these meanings in mind, it is easy, says the learned professor, to see that the names "Podunk" and "Domremy" are virtually the same: they signify a place of refreshment for cows, a place where those animals go for salt—a "cow-lick."

It is not, generally speaking, within the province of the historian to utter dogmatic judgment in such matters, but this seems to be a pretty flagrant instance of ingenuity. I mention it only to show to what lengths the learned will sometimes go in explaining what is obviously a grammatical error (like the "ablative absolute" in Latin)[12] or a mere slip of the pen, as when it was said that Edwin Markham was born in Bethlehem.[13]

There can be no reasonable doubt that Mrs. Nation was born in Podunk, nor that the writer who first used the name Domremy did so in a moment of abstraction. As to the cows coming to Podunk to lick salt, the acute reader will not fail to observe the similarity in sound between "lick" and "liquor," the ancient Americanese word for strong drink—a significant circumstance, though it is not the business of history to inquire what it signifies.

THE MAID OF PODUNK

At about thirteen years of age, Miss Slupsky said that the "voices" directed her to go to a certain place where she would find a hatchet—a small ax, sometimes called a "sword"—suitable for smashing joints. She did so, and, finding the implement, tried its edge on a cherry tree. Asked by her father if she knew who had felled the tree she replied: "I cannot tell a lie, father, you know I cannot tell a lie; I don't know a thing about it."[14]

The reception accorded to that statement is believed by Geezer ("The Ministry of Pain," iv., 327) to have had a stupendous effect upon the course of history. It gave the beautiful Maid of Podunk a distaste for a sedentary occupation and urged her forth to the tented field. From that day the demon Drink trembled in his frail glass armor, and when, in 1904, the lady was caught and burned as a witch there was not in all Topeka (says the Future Historian, in conclusion) enough wine to christen a canal boat.

NYJ (10 Mar. 1901): 26; *E* **(19 Mar. 1901): 14** (as "Ambrose Bierce's History of the Maid of Podunk").

NOTES

A satire of Carry Nation, the temperance activist famous for invading saloons with a hatchet and wrecking them. The humor is somewhat thin and forced, as the persona of a future historian lacks adequate information and so reconstructs the details of her life in a ridiculously erroneous biography.

In his later career, AB further developed this persona to project the idea that the civilization of AB's time would eventually be so thoroughly destroyed, as had happened to many once mighty ancient cultures, and leave so few records that it would be necessary for future historians to supplement the pitifully few and broken relics with wild guesses in order to form even some distorted notion of that civilization.

Title: A parody of "the maid of Orleans," the customary designation of Joan of Arc. AB may have been following the example of Voltaire's mock-epic poem *La Pucelle d'Orleans* (1755, 1762), a risqué burlesque in which Joan of Arc is depicted as a hapless maiden whose virginity is frequently in danger of being violated. The work was frequently translated as *The Maid of Orleans*. AB may also have had Mark Twain's *Personal Recollections of Joan of Arc* (1896) in mind, although that work is a respectful historical account of Joan. Note that Twain is mentioned in the sketch. Podunk is American slang for a small and backward town. See H. L. Mencken, "The Podunk Mystery," *New Yorker* 24, no. 31 (25 Sept. 1948): 75–81.

1. Carry (frequently but erroneously spelled Carrie) Nation was born Carry Amelia Moore on 25 November 1846 in Girard County, Kentucky. She was hardly a "maid"; she was six feet tall and weighed one hundred seventy-five pounds, and at the time the story was published she was sixty-four years old. She died 9 June 1911.

2. Cf. TC, *NL* 21, no. 9 (1 Apr. 1871): 9; reprinted in *FD* 102–3 under "Current Journalings": "Some raging iconoclast, after having overthrown religion by history, upset history by science, and then toppled over science, has now laid his impious hands upon babies' nursing bottles. 'The tubes of these infernal machines,' says this beast, 'are composed of India-rubber dissolved in bisulphide of carbon, and thickened with lead, resin, and sometimes oxysulphuret of antimony, from which, when it comes in contact with the milk, sulphuretted hydrogen is evolved, and lactate of lead formed in the stomach.' This logic is irresistible. Granting only that the tubes are made in that simple and intelligible manner (and anybody

can see for himself that they are), the sulpheretted hydrogen and the lactate of lead follow (down the œsophagus) as a logical sequence. But the scientific idiot seems to be profoundly unaware that these substances are not only harmless to the child but actually nutritious and essential to its growth. Not only so, but nature has implanted in its breast an instinctive craving for these very viands. Often have we seen some wee thing turn disgusted from the breast and lift up its voice: 'Not for Joseph; give me the bottle with the oxysulphuret of antimony tube. I take sulphuretted hydrogen and lactate of lead in mine every time!' And we have said: 'Nature is working in that darling. What God hath joined together let no man put asunder!' And we have thought of the wicked iconoclast."

3. Nation divorced her first husband, Dr. Charles Gloyd (an alcoholic), shortly after their marriage in 1867. In 1877 she married David Nation and by the 1890s had settled in Medicine Lodge, Kansas. She began entering saloons in various Kansas towns and destroying their liquor supplies. In January 1901 she elicited great notoriety when she destroyed one such saloon in Wichita with a hatchet, which henceforth became her defining symbol. AB's deliberate error "Mormont" is meant to refer to the Mormons, who are teetotalers.

4. Nation in fact admitted to hearing voices and having other mystical experiences. See her autobiography, *The Use and Need of the Life of Carry A. Nation* (1904).

5. Dumbleshaw is first mentioned in "John Smith: An Editorial Article from a Journal of May 3rd, A.D. 3873" (*F*, 10 May 1873). AB removed the reference to him in the revised version of the tale (see "John Smith, Liberator"). Dumbleshaw is cited again in "The Extinction of the Smugwumps," "Industrial Discontent in Ancient America," "A Screed of the Future Historian," "The Dispersal," and "Ashes of the Beacon."

6. AB railed tirelessly against such constructions. See "Prattle," *E* (19 Feb. 1888): 4: "*Roomer*, for *lodger.* This is one of the most abominable words in the language of illiteracy. How it came I cannot imagine. I have myself, by way of experiment, and perhaps revenge, tried to give it company, having 'invented and gone round advising' the words *bedder* and *mealer*, constructed on the same lines, but they lack some mysterious vital quality and will not 'stick.'"

7. In the summer of 1896 AB spent several months in Englewood, New Jersey, six miles northeast of Secaucus. AB's misspelling of the name here is presumably deliberate.

8. Cf. Worgum Slupsky, the "author" of some verses in the *DD* entry "Portable."

9. Jules Bastien-Lepage (1848–84), French painter. AB has misspelled the name, whether deliberately or not. For Twain see "The Great Strike of 1895," p. 904 note 19.

10. Domrémy-la-Pucelle, a small village in eastern France, is the birthplace of Joan of Arc.

11. The Potawatomi are a Native American tribe originally based in southern Michigan; they later expanded into Wisconsin, Illinois, and Indiana. In 1846 the U.S. government moved them to a reservation in Kansas; some later moved to Oklahoma.

12. See *DD*: "ABLATIVE, *adj.* A certain case of Latin nouns. The ablative absolute is an ancient form of grammatical error much admired by modern scholars."

13. Edwin Markham (1852–1940) was a California poet and once a friend of AB; but the latter severed relations with him shortly after publication of his celebrated poem "The Man with the Hoe" (1899), in which AB felt Markham had subordinated his artistic feeling to propaganda. Markham was actually born in Oregon City, Oregon.

14. A parody of the story of George Washington's chopping down the cherry tree, fabricated by Mason Locke (Parson) Weems (1759–1825), American clergyman and itinerant book agent. The fiction was inserted into the fifth edition (1806) of his book *The Life and Memorable Actions of George Washington* (1800).

THE MAID OF PODUNK

THE EXTINCTION OF
THE SMUGWUMPS

Although (wrote the Future Historian) the American climate, since the continent's discovery by the Swedish Admiral, Galumphus,[1] had never been what we Saharans of
to-day would call supportable, yet for several centuries a considerable population did
manage to withstand its horrors, and even multiplied. Indeed, so great was the fecun-
dity of the mongrel races inhabiting that continent that at one time the people of the
United States alone are believed to have numbered nearly twenty millions.

This estimate is based on an extant report of the United States Pension Bureau for
the year 1915, from which it appears that the whole number of pensioners on the rolls
was then 17,534,196. It is known that, as the learned Jupileter points out, "the entire
body of the people drew pensions, the only persons debarred from that civic privilege
being those who had served honorably in the wars and been sufficiently rewarded by
the gratitude and respect of their countrymen."

Professor Smiitthh, of the University of Timbuctoo, presents some reasons for his
belief that the astonishing multiplication of the ancient Americans was assisted by a
process called "immigration," the nature of which is not now understood. The word
is perhaps a medical term.

In their long battle with Nature the Americans were of course defeated.[2] With their
crude and fragmentary knowledge of natural laws and their inaptitude in the arts and
sciences they were unable to protect themselves against the increasing rigors of their
murderous climate, and paid with their lives the penalty of ignorance. In all that vast
territory lying east of the Mountain of Rocks the winters grew successively colder, the
summers successively warmer. Every year, in nearly all places in that region, the temperature was officially reported both lower in the one season and higher in the other
than it had ever been before and with a correspondingly unprecedented death rate.

During the Presidency of Samuel Gompers,[3] in 1908, no fewer than 16,042 persons perished in one summer's heat in New York City alone; and although in the

annual report of the Bureau of Vital Statistics this total is reduced to 7,993 by deduct-
ing the number that had perished of cold in the preceding winter, the figures were
sufficiently alarming to cause a general exodus from the place.

Other places, however, were no better off; the only persons who improved their
condition were the comparatively few who could reach the Pacific Coast or cross to
the Old World before all ships had been withdrawn from the transatlantic trade.

After the year 1908 no records of the mortality appear to have been made; none, at
least, have come down to us. It was not, however, until nearly a generation later that in
the mad struggle against these malign and terrible conditions all Government ceased,
and with it every form of human activity except for the immediate preservation of individual life. Out of that vast welter of death and the peril of death nothing could have
come but cries and lamentations, and these the perished arts did not record.

Not climate only—another dread, implacable agency of doom was concerned in
this unexampled tragedy! As early as 1870, in the Presidency of General Linkon, scientists had observed that the eastern littoral of North America was slowly sinking
into the sea, while the western was rising at the same rate. Year by year, while the
Bay San Francisco, now an inland village, but then a flourishing seaport, grew shallow the Atlantic made greater and greater inroads upon the land. The continent, as
Dumbleshaw has graphically expressed it, "was turning over like a man in bed."

The Eastern pleasure resorts, with their "bathing-beaches," were first to be en-
gulfed by the winter storms; then the rising tides invaded the great commercial cities
of New York, Pittsburg,[4] Podunk and many others, whose names are lost in the mists
of antiquity. By the end of the Twentieth century, as the ancients for some unknown
reason reckoned time, the entire vast region east of the Mountain of Rocks had disappeared. Yet not a living thing was drowned, for none had survived the terrible vicissitudes of that insupportable climate!

To the modern understanding it seems hardly credible that in order to reach the
ruins of Honolulu the ancient archaeologist had to traverse three hundred and ten
surindas of sea that rolled between them and the Califuranian coast! The journey is
now made, through the populous kingdom of Citrusia,[5] in two days.

NYJ (19 July 1901): 14; *E* (12 Aug. 1901): 12.

NOTES

Another Future Historian fantasy, this one also prophesies doom. The Smugwumps were
first cited in "For the Ahkoond" as a humorous variant of Mugwump. Originally a term
used for renegade Republicans in the election of 1884, it had come to be used for political
independents. AB was probably attracted to the term for its sound rather than its meaning.
1. The verb *galumph* means to move with a clumsy, heavy tread.
2. See "Nature as a Reformer," *Co* 45, no. 1 (June 1908): [1]: "As a habitation for man as he is,
this world—the material spheroid upon which he lives as long as he can—is a singularly

inhospitable dwelling-place. Upon only about one-eighth part of its surface can he live at all, and for only a little time, in an unequal struggle with the malign forces of nature."

3. Samuel Gompers (1850–1924), labor leader who founded the American Federation of Labor in 1886.

4. See "Retribution," note 1.

5. First cited in "For the Ahkoond," note 1.

THE EXTINCTION OF THE SMUGWUMPS

INDUSTRIAL DISCONTENT
IN ANCIENT AMERICA

Lighting a fresh cigar of tea leaves and putting on an electro-magnetic thinking-cap the Future Historian wrote as follows:

The capital weakness of the "Labor Movement" in ancient America—a fundamental disability which nothing could cure—was its reliance on moral qualities which are not universal; with which, indeed, human nature is but sparingly endowed.

Man then, as now, was a selfish animal, fond of high and noble sentiments when without occasion for their exercise, but in all practical affairs guided by short and narrow views of self-interest and incapable of general actions in furtherance of the general welfare.

Then, as now, it was easy to kindle a bright flame of enthusiasm for some great "cause" requiring concerted action and heroic devotion, but impossible to enlist in its service those who could see a personal advantage in standing aloof.

For "organized labor" to succeed, it was necessary that all laborers belong to the organizations; yet this was obviously impossible to bring about. Nor were matters much mended by a close approach to it.

The fewer that remained outside, with freedom of individual action, the greater was the demand for their labor during "strikes," and the higher were the wages that they could command; the result, as might have been foreseen, being greater defections from the unions. So the conditions that the unions strove to create were the very conditions most fatal to their success.

"Unionism" bore in its bosom the seeds of its own dissolution. At every step toward attainment of its end, it offered an added premium to desertion; its success was father to failure.

So paralyzing, so incurable and at last so universally obvious was this inherent disability that, as early as 1912, during the Presidency of General Gompers,[1] the Administration tried to force through Congress an amendment to the Constitution making labor unions unlawful and strikes felonious.

The measure failed, because, as Senator Debs[2] explained, it was needless: the common sense of the country was a "sufficient protection against the scheming of ambitious demagogues and the mischievous incitements of self-seeking agitators."

In Dumbleshaw's "History of Human Delusions," that ingenious investigator relates that, owing to the prevalence of "unionism," non-union workingmen so prospered through high wages and steady employment that they became one of the overcrowded professions, and they finally formed a league, the National Federation of Scabs, the chief purposes of which were to limit its own membership and secure by strikes and other appropriate means a monopoly of employment.

The immediate provocation to this action on their part is found in the fact that, yielding to the suasion of avarice, one J. P. Morgan,[3] a man unskilled in the use of his hands, threw up a very good position in a steel trust and went to work in a non-union coal mine.

"That," says a quaint chronicler of the period, rather obscurely, "was the limit and called for the kibosh." (The meaning of "kibosh" is not now understood. The word has a suggestive resemblance to "Bigosh," the name of a popular deity of the time, frequently invoked, particularly in agricultural affairs. "Kibosh" may have been the title of an officer of the constabulary.)[4]

As a practical working organization the National Federation of Scabs appears to have had but a brief existence and a rather stormy one. Of all labor leagues it was by far the most tyrannical and intolerant.

In 1907, during its famous strike against the employment of union men as nurse maids in the Podunk Asylum for Female Foundlings, it committed so many offenses against life and property that the entire military force of the State of Buffalo was called out for its suppression, but was defeated with great slaughter.

It was then attacked by the Grand Army of the Republic[5] and the Army of Government Pensioners, but, as neither of these forces had ever been accustomed to the use of arms, they shared the fate of their more experienced allies.

Finally the Federation was subdued by the Quakers, a powerful tribe in Pennsylvania, led by Matthew Quay;[6] its chiefs were banished to Nebraska and a general boycott declared against all its surviving members.

It went out of existence in the year 1915, during the Presidency of John Smith, known in his time as "the Dark Horse."[7]

After 1918 there were no more "labor troubles" in America. In that year, at a great Congress of all the industries, it was almost unanimously resolved that the wage system was a failure, Government ownership a delusion, co-operation impossible and combination disgusting.

The congress urged a return to the ancient and beneficent system of slavery. The advice was eagerly taken by all, and thenceforth until the submersion of the continent the term "industrial discontent" was heard no more in the speech of a happy, happy people.

NYJ (14 Aug. 1901): 14.

NOTES

AB criticized unions, as he earlier criticized big business, for using violence or the threat of it to promote their causes.

1. See "The Extinction of the Smugwumps," p. 951 note 3.
2. Eugene V. Debs (1855–1926), Socialist leader. While president of the American Railway Union he led a bitter strike against the Great Northern Railroad and the Pullman Company in 1895. AB remarked on the strike with considerable heat, so much so that William Randolph Hearst urged him to take a "vacation" until the strike was over.
3. John Pierpont Morgan (1837–1913), railroad magnate, founder of the U.S. Steel Corporation (1901), and accumulator of an immense personal fortune.
4. In his Little Johnny sketches, AB used Kibosh as the name of an Indian native and also as the name of a fictitious country. The word is used in slang, with a negative connotation. To "put the kibosh on" means "to put an end to."
5. See "Ashes of the Beacon," p. 1088 note 42.
6. Matthew Quay (1833–1904), U.S. representative (1865–67) and U.S. senator (1887–89, 1901–4) from Pennsylvania. See "The Passing Show," NYJ (20 Jan. 1901): 26; E (20 Jan. 1901): 25: "An esteemed, though Pennsylvanian, contemporary explains with reasonless levity that if Mr. Quay is elected to the Senate his supporters 'will be tickled half to death.' It is to be hoped that his actual instatement to office will tickle them the other half."
7. The original "dark horse" was James Knox Polk (1795–1849), who unexpectedly beat out Martin Van Buren as Democratic presidential candidate in 1844 and went on to become the eleventh president of the U.S. (1845–49). The term was coined by Andrew Jackson.

AT OLD MAN ECKERT'S

Philip Eckert lived for many years in an old, weather-stained wooden house about three miles from the little town of Marion, in Vermont.[1] There must be quite a number of persons living who remember him, not unkindly, I trust, and know something of the story that I am about to tell.

"Old Man Eckert," as he was always called, was not of a sociable disposition and lived alone. As he was never known to speak of his own affairs nobody thereabout knew anything of his past, nor of his relatives if he had any. Without being particularly ungracious or repellent in manner or speech, he managed somehow to be immune to impertinent curiosity, yet exempt from the evil repute with which it commonly revenges itself when baffled; so far as I know, Mr. Eckert's renown as a reformed assassin or a retired pirate of the Spanish Main had not reached any ear in Marion. He got his living cultivating a small and not very fertile farm.

One day he disappeared and a prolonged search by his neighbors failed to turn him up or throw any light upon his whereabouts or whyabouts. Nothing indicated preparation to leave: all was as he might have left it to go to the spring for a bucket of water. For a few weeks little else was talked of in that region; then "old man Eckert" became a village tale for the ear of the stranger. I do not know what was done regarding his property—the correct legal thing, doubtless. The house was standing, still vacant and conspicuously unfit, when I last heard of it, some twenty years afterward.

Of course it came to be considered "haunted," and the customary tales were told of moving lights, dolorous sounds and startling apparitions. At one time, about five years after the disappearance, these stories of the supernatural became so rife, or through some attesting circumstances seemed so important, that some of Marion's most serious citizens deemed it well to investigate, and to that end arranged for a night session on the premises. The parties to this undertaking were John Holcomb, an apothecary; Wilson Merle, a lawyer, and Andrus C. Palmer, the teacher of the public school, all men of consequence and repute. They were to meet at Holcomb's house at eight o'clock in the evening of the appointed day and go together to the scene of their vigil, where certain arrangements for their comfort, a provision of fuel and the like, for the season was winter, had been already made.

Palmer did not keep the engagement, and after waiting a half-hour for him the others went to the Eckert house without him. They established themselves in the principal room, before a glowing fire, and without other light than it gave, awaited events. It had been agreed to speak as little as possible: they did not even renew the exchange of views regarding the defection of Palmer, which had occupied their minds on the way.

Probably an hour had passed without incident when they heard (not without emotion, doubtless) the sound of an opening door in the rear of the house, followed by footfalls in the room adjoining that in which they sat. The watchers rose to their feet, but stood firm, prepared for whatever might ensue. A long silence followed—how long neither would afterward undertake to say. Then the door between the two rooms opened and a man entered.

It was Palmer. He was pale, as if from excitement—as pale as the others felt themselves to be. His manner, too, was singularly distrait: he neither responded to their salutations nor so much as looked at them, but walked slowly across the room in the light of the failing fire and opening the front door passed out into the darkness.

It seems to have been the first thought of both men that Palmer was suffering from fright—that something seen, heard or imagined in the back room had deprived him of his senses. Acting on the same friendly impulse both ran after him through the open door. But neither they nor any one ever again saw or heard of Andrus Palmer!

This much was ascertained the next morning. During the session of Messrs. Holcomb and Merle at the "haunted house" a new snow had fallen to a depth of several inches upon the old. In this snow Palmer's trail from his lodging in the village to the back door of the Eckert house was conspicuous. But there it ended: from the front door nothing led away but the tracks of the two men who swore that he preceded them. Palmer's disappearance was complete as that of "old man Eckert" himself—whom, indeed, the editor of the local paper somewhat graphically accused of having "reached out and pulled him in."

E (17 Nov. 1901): Editorial Section, p. 2 (as "At the Eckert House"); *CW* 3.389–92.

NOTES

A vignette of supernatural disappearance that resembles those narrated in "Whither?". The last line, however, may be a hint that the reader is being "pulled in."

1. The town is fictitious. In E, AB located the story in "Morton, in Missouri" (see "Selected Textual Variants").

A DIAGNOSIS OF DEATH

"I am not so superstitious as some of your physicians—men of science, as you are pleased to be called," said Hawver, replying to an accusation that had not been made. "Some of you—only a few, I confess—believe in the immortality of the soul, and in apparitions which you have not the honesty to call ghosts. I go no further than a conviction that the living are sometimes seen where they are not, but have been—where they have lived so long, perhaps so intensely, as to have left their impress on everything about them. I know, indeed, that one's environment may be so affected by one's personality as to yield, long afterward, an image of one's self to the eyes of another. Doubtless the impressing personality has to be the right kind of personality as the perceiving eyes have to be the right kind of eyes—mine, for example."

"Yes, the right kind of eyes, conveying sensations to the wrong kind of brain," said Dr. Frayley, smiling.

"Thank you; one likes to have an expectation gratified; that is about the reply that I supposed you would have the civility to make."

"Pardon me. But you say that you know. That is a good deal to say, don't you think? Perhaps you will not mind the trouble of saying how you learned."

"You will call it an hallucination," Hawver said, "but that does not matter." And he told the story.

"Last summer I went, as you know, to pass the hot weather term in the town of Meridian. The relative at whose house I had intended to stay was ill, so I sought other quarters. After some difficulty I succeeded in renting a vacant dwelling that had been occupied by an eccentric doctor of the name of Mannering, who had gone away years before, no one knew where, not even his agent. He had built the house himself and had lived in it with an old servant for about ten years. His practice, never very extensive, had after a few years been given up entirely. Not only so, but he had withdrawn himself almost altogether from social life and become a recluse. I was told by the village doctor, about the only person with whom he held any relations, that during his retirement he had devoted himself to a single line of study, the result of which he had expounded in a book that did not commend itself to the approval of his professional brethren, who, indeed, considered him not entirely sane. I have not seen the book and cannot now recall the title of it, but I am told that it expounded a rather startling theory. He held that it was possible in the case of many a person in good health to forecast his death with precision, several months in advance of the event. The limit, I think, was eighteen months. There were local tales of his having exerted his powers of prognosis, or perhaps you would say diagnosis; and it was said that in every instance the person whose friends he had warned had died suddenly at the appointed time, and from no assignable cause. All this, however, has nothing to do with what I have to tell; I thought it might amuse a physician.

"The house was furnished, just as he had lived in it. It was a rather gloomy dwelling for one who was neither a recluse nor a student, and I think it gave something of its character to me—perhaps some of its former occupant's character; for always I felt in it a certain melancholy that was not in my natural disposition, nor, I think, due to loneliness. I had no servants that slept in the house, but I have always been, as you know, rather fond of my own society, being much addicted to reading, though little to study. Whatever was the cause, the effect was dejection and a sense of impending evil; this was especially so in Dr. Mannering's study, although that room was the lightest and most airy in the house. The doctor's life-size portrait in oil hung in that room, and seemed completely to dominate it. There was nothing unusual in the picture; the man was evidently rather good looking, about fifty years old, with iron-gray hair, a smooth-shaven face and dark, serious eyes. Something in the picture always drew and held my attention. The man's appearance became familiar to me, and rather 'haunted' me.

"One evening I was passing through this room to my bedroom, with a lamp—there is no gas in Meridian. I stopped as usual before the portrait, which seemed in the lamplight to have a new expression, not easily named, but distinctly uncanny. It interested but did not disturb me. I moved the lamp from one side to the other and observed the effects of the altered light. While so engaged I felt an impulse to turn round. As I did so I saw a man moving across the room directly toward me! As soon as he came near enough for the lamplight to illuminate the face I saw that it was Dr. Mannering himself; it was as if the portrait were walking!

"'I beg your pardon,' I said, somewhat coldly, 'but if you knocked I did not hear.'

"He passed me, within an arm's length, lifted his right forefinger, as in warning, and without a word went on out of the room, though I observed his exit no more than I had observed his entrance.

"Of course, I need not tell you that this was what you will call an hallucination and I call an apparition. That room had only two doors, of which one was locked; the other led into a bedroom, from which there was no exit. My feeling on realizing this is not an important part of the incident.

"Doubtless this seems to you a very commonplace 'ghost story'—one constructed on the regular lines laid down by the old masters of the art. If that were so I should not have related it, even if it were true. The man was not dead; I met him to-day in Union Street. He passed me in a crowd."

Hawver had finished his story and both men were silent. Dr. Frayley absently drummed on the table with his fingers.

"Did he say anything to-day?" he asked—"anything from which you inferred that he was not dead?"

Hawver stared and did not reply.

"Perhaps," continued Frayley, "he made a sign, a gesture—lifted a finger, as in warning. It's a trick he had—a habit when saying something serious—announcing the result of a diagnosis, for example."

"Yes, he did—just as his apparition had done. But, good God! did you ever know him?"

Hawver was apparently growing nervous.

"I knew him. I have read his book, as will every physician some day. It is one of the most striking and important of the century's contributions to medical science. Yes, I knew him; I attended him in an illness three years ago. He died."

Hawver sprang from his chair, manifestly disturbed. He strode forward and back across the room; then approached his friend, and in a voice not altogether steady, said: "Doctor, have you anything to say to me—as a physician?"

"No, Hawver; you are the healthiest man I ever knew. As a friend I advise you to go to your room. You play the violin like an angel. Play it; play something light and lively. Get this cursed bad business off your mind."

The next day Hawver was found dead in his room, the violin at his neck, the bow upon the strings, his music open before him at Chopin's funeral march.[1]

NYJ (8 Dec. 1901): 41 (as "The Diagnosis of Death"); *CW* 3.81–87.

NOTES

The dramatic impact of the uncanny conclusion is possibly heightened by Hawver's initial denial of superstition and his insistence upon a rational, though empirically unprovable, explanation of apparition.

1. Hawver must have been playing a transcription for violin, for the "Funeral March" of Frédéric François Chopin (1810–49), originally composed as a piano solo in 1837, was incorporated as the third movement of his Piano Sonata No. 2 in B-flat minor, Opus 35 (1839).

A LETTER FROM A BTRUGUMIAN

TRANSLATED BY AMBROSE BIERCE

You ask me, my dear Tgnagogu, to relate my adventures among the Americans, as they call themselves. My adventures were very brief, lasting altogether not more than three gumkas, and most of the time was passed in taking measures for my own safety.

My skyship, which had been driven for three moons before an irresistible gale, passed over a great city just at daylight one morning, and rather than continue the voyage with a lost reckoning I demanded that I be permitted to disembark. My wish was respected, and my companions soared away without me. Before night I had escaped from the city, by what means you know, and with my remarkable experiences in returning to civilization all Btrugumia is familiar. The description of the strange city I have reserved for you, by whom only could I hope to be believed. Nyork, as its inhabitants call it, is a city of inconceivable extent—not less, I should judge, than seven square glepkeps! Of the number of its inhabitants I can only say that they are as the sands of the desert. They wear clothing—of a hideous kind, 'tis true—speak an apparently copious though harsh language, and seem to have a certain limited intelligence. They are puny in stature, the tallest of them being hardly higher than my breast.

Nevertheless, Nyork is a city of giants. The magnitude of all things artificial there is astounding! My dear Tgnagogu, words can give you no conception of it. Many of the buildings, I assure you, are as many as fifty sprugas in height, and shelter 5,000 persons each. And these stupendous structures are so crowded together that to the spectator in the narrow streets below they seem utterly devoid of design and symmetry—mere monstrous aggregations of brick, stone and metal—mountains of masonry, cliffs and crags of architecture hanging in the sky!

A city of giants inhabited by pigmies! For you must know, oh friend of my liver, that the rearing of these mighty structures could not be the work of the puny folk that swarm in ceaseless activity about their bases. These fierce little savages invaded the island in numbers so overwhelming that the giant builders had to fly before them. Some escaped across a great bridge which, with the help of their gods, they had suspended in the air from bank to bank of a wide river parting the island from the mainland, but many could do no better than mount the buildings that they had reared, and there, in these inaccessible altitudes, they dwell to-day, still piling stone upon stone. Whether they do this in obedience to their instinct as builders, or in hope to escape by way of the heavens, I had not the means to learn, being ignorant of the pigmy tongue and in continual fear of the crowds that followed me.

You can see the giants toiling away up there in the sky, laying in place the enormous blocks of stone which none but they could handle. They look no bigger than beetles, but you know that they are ten sprugas in stature, and you shudder to think what would ensue if one should lose his footing. Fancy that great bulk whirling down to earth from so dizzy an altitude! . . .

May birds ever sing above your grave.

JOQUOLK WAK MGAPY.

NYA (**30 Apr. 1903**): **16.** Incorporated into "The Land Beyond the Blow," in the chapter "An Execution in Batrugia."

NOTES

An unusual venture of AB into the relatively new genre of science fiction. When the tale was reprinted, AB changed the name of the place to Batrugia.

THE FUTURE HISTORIAN
AND HIS FATIGUE

"At last, in the year 1903, as, for some reason now unknown, time was then reckoned," wrote the Future Historian, "the Cup was won by Sir Thomas the Lifter, with the *Shamyacht III*. He had made twelve previous attempts, but had been foiled every time by some trick of construction or sailing. It was during these contests that the term 'Yan Kee trick' came into use, and we still have it. Yan Kee was the name of the Chinese mariner who always sailed the American boat, our knowledge of which fact we owe to that distinguished philologist, Dr. Joch Ooblebubber, who with Um Licomemsel, the archaeologist, discovered the ruins of Minnesota.

"Sir Thomas escaped the vengeance of the mob, but was drowned with all his crew on the voyage back to England, and the celebrated Cup was forever lost. His last words were 'Don't give up the ship!'[1]—one of the most memorable sayings of antiquity.

"Ten years later another cup was presented by the Irish Parliament, and the contests were renewed, continuing with varying fortunes for a quarter of a century, when they were forbidden by both governments under pressure of the Allied Powers.

"In reviewing the history of this extraordinary craze one cannot fail to be struck by its incredible unreason, in which it was unmatched even in those barbarous times. Compared with it the famous conflict between Science and Religion seems almost an intelligent contention, a manly sport.

"As a means of gambling these yacht races were distinctly inferior to flipping a coin, to running the 'horse,' whatever that animal may have been, or to the game (what we know of it) called draw-the-poker.

"It developed no useful qualities in either the men who built the boats or those who sailed them, for the boats were so absurdly unlike anything else afloat that both construction and handling were particular arts, without utility in the shipyard or on the sea. In fact, the vessels never were used for any purpose but racing, and in only the one race for which they were made did anybody take the faintest interest. The sole superiority of one over another consisted in a deeper draught—a lengthening downward and weighing of the 'fin keel' so as to make it possible to carry more sail without upsetting. The knowing ones talked and wrote very learnedly of a thousand other features of construction, but that was all moonshine; the yacht that could safely carry the greatest spread of sail always beat the other. With this controlling advantage any 'model' was good enough. True, it took these primitive reasoners many years to learn so simple a truth. Philosophers (who did not take the trouble to point it out) knew it as early as 1903, but the persons most interested did not perceive it until fifteen years later, when a remodeled old mudscow, with a fin keel fifty feet deep, met the cup winner of that year off the Irish coast and beat her out of sight.

"After this revelation there could be but one end of it all—keels grew deeper and deeper and more and more heavily weighted, masts taller, booms longer and sails bigger. Accidents and wrecks from trying to achieve both lightness and strength were even more frequent than they had been at the beginning of the century, and in the final race (before the interdiction) both yachts grounded in the middle of the Atlantic and were beaten to pieces in a half-hour, whereby both the King of New York and the Panjandrum of Great Britain and the Isle of Man, who were guests on board, had the bad luck to lose their lives.

"It is doubtful," concluded the Future Historian, smiling as the toes holding his pen flew rapidly across his sheet of prepared sky, "if the annals of folly contain anything so distressing to human pride as this yacht-racing episode in the history of the ancient inhabitants of Great Britain and her transatlantic dependency. In the words of our greatest and most original humorist, 'it makes me tired.'"

NYA (8 July 1903): 14; *E* **(5 Sept. 1903): 14**.

NOTES

The story concerns the yacht race between the United States and Great Britain whose winner would receive "America's Cup." Sir Thomas Lipton (1850–1931), the British merchant who in 1890 began vigorous marketing of the tea that bears his name, was an ardent yachtsman who tried on five occasions to win America's Cup (1899, 1901, 1903, 1920, and 1930), but lost every time. On each occasion his ship was called the *Shamrock*. In 1903, the race— in which the contestants were to sail ten to fifteen nautical miles from the Sandy Hook Lightship (stationed eight nautical miles southeast of Sandy Hook, New Jersey) and return—was to have been run in late August, but bad weather prevented it until September 3, when the U.S. yacht *Reliance* easily beat Lipton's *Shamrock*. AB's scorn for conspicuously expensive activities without practical utility is explicit in this transparent spoof.

1. In the War of 1812, Sir Oliver Hazard Perry (1785–1819) carried on his stricken flagship the *Lawrence* a blue flag emblazoned with the motto "Don't Give Up the Ship."

A CHRONICLE
OF THE TIME TO BE

The Future Historian sat paring his nails before his telepathic typewriter, which merrily clicked off his thoughts. "By the year 1907," it wrote, "the Japanese had so consolidated their power in Manchuria that Russia appears to have despaired of further success against them and to have relinquished all hopes of recovering the province. The Czar's death in the terrible battle of Harbin,[1] the destruction of the Baltic fleet in its desperate attempt to retake Port Arthur,[2] the frightful famine caused by the Chinese General Ma's possession of the Siberian railroad—all these untoward events had so subdued the spirit of the people of the Russian Empire that further war was impossible. 'The Colossus of the North' lay bleeding and helpless on the field of his ambition, while his hereditary enemy, Great Britain, restrained only by fear of Germany and France, rectified her Indian frontier almost as it pleased her.

"Germany, indeed, was almost a negligible quantity in the problem, her mountebank Emperor having troubles of his own. With the Socialist rebellion of 1906 he had barely been able to cope, and his hard-earned victory had left him with no stomach for fighting in the interest of his allies. France, still suffering from her brief but bloody contest with the United States of America over complications arising from the sale of the Panama Canal concession,[3] was equally averse to war, and had perfidiously repudiated her treaty obligations and turned a deaf ear to the demands of her ally. So it was that Russia as an Asiatic power was virtually effaced, while in Europe she had declined to the third rank among military nations.

"Matters stood in this unhappy plight when, as related in a former chapter of this history, the usurper Kuropatkin[4] seized the reins of power, overturning the Romanoff dynasty and either putting to death or banishing all its considerable adherents. This able, ambitious and unscrupulous man seemed for a time content with the glory of his achievement and the subjection of his own country to his will. He made an inglorious peace with Japan, satisfied Great Britain with shameful concessions and even consented to the permanent occupation of Trans-Baikal Siberia by China. But behind all these apparently cowardly surrenders the fierce, indomitable will of the ancient Huns burned with an inextinguishable flame. In the apathy of a hopeless people were still some vestiges of the same persistent spirit that had survived even the defeat at Chalons fifteen centuries before.[5] For two decades the new Czar devoted himself to a patient reorganization of the civil and military administration, to the promotion of the empire's industries and commerce, to creation of a powerful navy. So effectually, yet so secretly withal, was this gigantic task accomplished that in the year 1928 Russia was again a menace to the peace of Europe without having alarmed even the most suspicious of the Great Powers. Now and again, it is true, some voice in the wilderness of politics or journalism cried an unheeded warning, but these prophets of evil lacked the facts to verify their dismal predictions, for the Russian press was under a strict censorship, and the Imperial Government pursued a policy of silence. Statistics were among the secret archives of the Government, accessible to none but its own officials.

"Meantime, China was undergoing something of the same regeneration which for nearly a century had made Japan the paradox and marvel of the world. The entire form and texture of her civilization had begun to change, and—incredible fatuity!— the change was assisted and acclaimed by all the Caucasian nations of the world, which vied with one another to maintaining the one condition under which it was possible— 'the integrity of China.'[6] The imperial army had increased to vast though unknown numbers, and was trained by European mercenaries of all nationalities, without a protest from Russia, whom it seemed most to menace. Great arsenals manufactured and stored against a future need immense quantities of destructive modern weapons, and under the fostering care of European intelligence the Chinese navy grew to formidable proportions and efficiency. The new Emperor, Chon Lu, an enlightened but cunning and ambitious ruler, pursued during this period a policy of apparent hostility to Russia, resulting in frequent but trivial and fruitless disputes, in which neither side obtained an important advantage.

"Such was the situation when, on the ever-memorable fourth of September, 1928, the world was startled by an identical rescript from Pekin and St. Petersburg announcing an offensive alliance between the Russian and Chinese empires! Of the stupendous consequences that ensued, entailing nothing less than the effacement of the ancient European civilization, it is impossible to write even at this distant day without the profoundest emotion."

NYA (6 May 1904): 16.

NOTES

AB was an astute and sometimes prescient observer of the international scene, particularly from the military standpoint. Written on the very day of the Japanese attack on the Russian base of Port Arthur, it recognized the then new and underestimated military strength of Japan and predicted the transformation of then backward Russia and China into modern powers. AB often quoted the proverb: "in time of peace prepare for war." He did not believe that people or nations changed fundamentally in short periods of time; he was skeptical of the claims of those who had reason to oppose America or the West that they were now devoted to peace and amity; and he strongly opposed America's letting down its guard. The allusion to the few lonely voices which were not listened to included himself, for he increasingly thought of himself as a Cassandra.

1. Harbin is the second largest city of northeastern China and capital of Heilungkiang Province, on the Sungari River. A small fishing village before 1896, it thereafter became the construction center for the Chinese Eastern Railway, which by 1904 linked the Trans-Siberian Railroad with the Russian port of Vladivostok on the Sea of Japan. Harbin was a base for Russian military operations in Manchuria during the Russo-Japanese War.

2. Port Arthur was the name given by the British to a city in China, on the Yellow Sea at the top of Liaotung Peninsula in southern Manchuria. It was a strategically important naval base. The peninsula was leased to the Russians in 1898. Port Arthur was attacked by the Japanese on 5 May 1904, initiating the Russo-Japanese War; it fell the next year after a long siege.

3. France had sold its interest in the Panama Canal to the United States in February 1904. AB discusses the matter in another "future historian" passage included in the column "The Passing Show," *NYA* (7 Feb. 1904): 24; *E* (21 Feb. 1904): 44; see p. 1200.

4. Peter Alekseyevich Kropotkin (1842–1921), Russian scientist, revolutionary, and proponent of "anarchist communism," was imprisoned in 1874 but escaped two years later, spending the next thirty-one years in England before returning to Russia in 1917.

5. AB refers to the defeat in 451 of the ancient Huns, led by Attila, at the hands of the Romans, led by the general Aetius, at the battle of the Catalaunian Plains near the present-day town of Châlons-sur-Marne, France.

6. AB opposed the partition of China by Western nations, largely because of the impracticability of the task, not out of any respect for Chinese sovereignty. See "Ambrose Bierce Says: We Should Beware of Mixing in Partition of China," *NYJ* (10 July 1900): 8; *E* (11 July 1900): 6 (as "The 'Partition' of China").

THE DOG IN GANEGWAG

At about the end of the thirty-seventh month of our voyage due south into the Unknown Sea we sighted land, and although the coast appeared wild and inhospitable, the captain decided to send a boat ashore in search of fresh water and provisions, of which we were in sore need. I was of the boat's crew, and thought myself fortunate in being able to set foot again upon the earth. There were seven others in the landing party, including the mate, who commanded.

Selecting a sheltered cove, which appeared to be at the mouth of a small creek, we beached the boat, and, leaving two men to guard it, started inland toward a grove of trees. Before we reached it an animal came out of it and advanced confidently toward us, showing no signs of either fear or hostility. It was a hideous creature, not altogether like anything that we had ever seen, but on its close approach we recognized it as a dog, of an unimaginable breed. As we were nearly famished one of the sailors shot it for food. Instantly a great crowd of people, who had doubtless been watching us from among the trees, rushed upon us with fierce exclamations and surrounded us, making the most threatening gestures and brandishing unfamiliar weapons. Unable to resist such odds we were seized and bound with cords and dragged into the forest almost before we knew what had happened to us. Observing the nature of our reception the ship's crew hastily weighed anchor and sailed away, and we never again saw them.

Beyond the trees concealing it from the sea was a great city, and thither we were taken. It was Gumammam, the capital of Ganegwag, whose people are dog worshipers. The fate of my companions I never learned, for although I remained in the country, much of the time as a prisoner, for seven years, and learned to speak its language, no answer was ever given to my many inquiries about my unfortunate friends.

The Ganegwagians are an ancient race with a history covering a period of ten thousand supintroes. In stature they are large, in color blue, with crimson hair and yellow eyes. They live to a great age, sometimes as much as twenty supintroes, their climate being so wholesome that even the aged have to sail to a distant island in order to die. Whenever a sufficient number of them reach what they call "the age of going away" they embark on a government ship and in the midst of impressive public rites and ceremonies set sail for "the Isle of the Happy Change." Of their strange civilization, their laws, manners and customs, their copper clothing and liquid houses I have written—at perhaps too great length—in my famous book, "Ganegwag the Incredible." Here I shall confine myself to their religion, certainly the most amazing form of superstition in the world.

Nowhere, it is believed, but in Ganegwag has so vile a creature as the dog obtained general recognition as a deity. There this filthy beast is considered so divine that it is freely admitted to the domestic circle and cherished as an honored guest. Scarce a family that is able to support a dog is without one, and some have as many as a half-dozen. Indeed, the dog is the special deity of the poor, those families having most that are least able to maintain them, unless the domestic conditions forbid. In some sections of the country, particularly the southern and southwestern provinces, the number of dogs is estimated to be greater than that of the children, as is the cost of their maintenance. In families of the rich they are fewer in number, but more sacredly cherished, especially by the female members, who lavish upon them a wealth of affection not always granted to the husband and children and distinguish them with indescribable attentions and endearments.

Nowhere is the dog compelled to make any other return for all this honor and benefaction than a fawning and sycophantic demeanor toward those who bestow them and an insulting and injurious attitude toward strangers who have dogs of their own, and toward other dogs. In any considerable town of the realm not a day passes but the public newsman relates in the most matter-of-fact and unsympathetic way to his circle of listless auditors painful instances of human beings, mostly women and children, bitten and mangled by these ferocious animals without provocation.

In addition to these ravages of the dog in his normal state are a vastly greater number of outrages committed by the sacred animal in the fury of insanity, for he has an hereditary tendency to madness, and in that state his bite is incurable, the victim awaiting in the most horrible agony the sailing of the next ship to the Isle of the Happy Change, his suffering imperfectly medicined by expressions of public sympathy for the dog.

A cynical citizen of Gumammam said to the writer of this narrative: "My countrymen have invented three hundred kinds of dogs, and only one way to hang a thief." Yet all the dogs are alike in this, that none are respectable.

Withal, it must be said of this extraordinary people that their horrible religion is free from the hollow forms and meaningless ceremonies in which so many superstitions of the lower races find expression. It is a religion of love, practical, undemonstrative, knowing nothing of pageantry and spectacle. It is hidden in the lives and hearts of the people; a stranger would hardly know of its existence as a distinct faith. Indeed, other faiths and better ones (one of them having some resemblance to a debased form of Christianity) coexist with it, sometimes in the same mind. Caniolatry[1] is not intolerant so long as the dog is not denied an equal divinity with the deities of other faiths. Nevertheless, I cannot think of the inhabitants of Ganegwag without loathing and contempt.

NYA (12 May 1904): 14. Incorporated into "The Land Beyond the Blow."

NOTES

There is more to this sketch than an example of AB's well-known antipathy to dogs. In the last paragraph, he compliments for its warmth, sincerity, tolerance, and simplicity the caniolatry the rest of the piece attacks and contrasts it to the debased form of a better faith that is the popular religion. AB thus uses this piece to further his ongoing feud with what he considers a warped and superficial form of Christianity, which he implies should be loving, heartfelt, tolerant, and without pretensions.

1. See "Ashes of the Beacon," p. 1087 note 37.

PART 5

1905–1910

INTRODUCTION

In 1890, Bierce wrote his autobiographical memoir, "A Sole Survivor." He was only forty-eight years old at the time, yet although he acknowledged he had escaped death many times he was conscious of a certain loneliness as a consequence. In 1905, after a gap of another full year of not writing any fiction, he was sixty-three and had become old. He looked old and he *felt* old, and he knew that he would not be a sole survivor much longer. The self-education he pursued through his interest in philosophy, particularly the Stoics and Epicurus, and possibly Schopenhauer, still had not resulted in a settled comfort. On the contrary, the happiness that he believed was life's greatest good continued to elude him. Slowly and almost imperceptibly his hope for happiness dwindled to a search for means that might at least reduce if not end the frustrations, disappointments, and sorrows he kept encountering in life.

In his increasingly irregular and short journalistic contributions to Hearst publications, he now variously referred to himself as the Curmudgeon Philosopher, the Sentimental Bachelor, and the Bald Campaigner. These tags were certainly part of the self-depreciating humor he had begun many years ago when he called his column "Prattle," but now they also reflected self-knowledge, a recognition and acceptance of the aspects of his character revealed by the tags. He realized he was looked upon as a curmudgeon, but instead of being apologetic or defensive about it, he decided to make sure that his social criticisms would have at their core a steel frame of logic or philosophy. This was a continuation of his lifelong policy of seldom venting his opposition to a theory or practice without emplacing researched information or careful thought where they could stop counterattacks. He realized he had a streak of sentiment. For most of his life, he had labored to suppress or disguise it, but now he decided to live with it and let it be seen. He realized that his entire career had been a campaign to affirm certain values and oppose others. The habit of combat was too deeply ingrained in him to discard, so as a matter of honor he resolved to continue to fight as long as he wrote. A famous caricature depicts him, white-haired but defiant, dragging his pen from a scabbard. Vincent Starrett was exactly right when he called it "the undying portrait of the man." These accepted aspects of his character inspirit the fiction of his final period.

"The Jury in Ancient America," "The Conflagration in Ghargaroo," "Insurance in Ancient America," and "An Execution in Batrugia" all cover topics that angered Bierce. These and other previous stories that were thinly disguised social criticisms were collected in 1909 and amalgamated into the extended political satires "Ashes of the Beacon" and "The Land Beyond the Blow." As infuriating and perhaps painful as it may be to read his objections to cherished and even hallowed American institutions—republican government, the right of free speech, trial by jury, and our system of jurisprudence—it may be even more important today for those devoted to those institutions to read his criticisms than it was for his contemporaries. Even though his predictions may appear at first glance cantankerous and offensively reactionary today, the thoughtfulness and validity of many of his objections still remain in place.

As "The Ashes of the Beacon," especially, makes clear, Bierce realizes that at one extreme of the political spectrum is despotism, and at the other end is anarchy, and he is radically opposed to both. He does not attempt to propose and advocate any alternatives to what he criticizes; his main concern is that readers face the truth and stop deluding themselves with beliefs that are at odds with reality. He is more concerned with achieving the ends of justice and righteousness than with the means, and he is irate that revered means so often frustrate the ends that they are part of the problem. It is not only, for him, that the present system falls far short of its ideals. As one who saw that democracy and republican government resulted in the bloody horror that was the Civil War, and that the aftermath of that war was not any purification of the population but rather a rush to gain by hook or crook any advantages that were there for the taking, he refuses to extol or justify the political or legal culture capable of producing, permitting, and countenancing such moral enormities.

Not all of his objections to the culture he saw around him are well-founded. "Rise and Fall of the Aëroplane" is an exception to the rule about the thought that underpins even his curmudgeonly outbursts. His opposition to Theodore Roosevelt is evident in "An Ancient Hunter" and "A Leaf Blown In from Days to Be," which skillfully use humor to launch damaging attacks on the ex-president for self-serving egotism that crosses over into dishonesty. Bierce's attacks thus have both political and moral dimensions. Insofar as they are political, they reflect his partisan views and are mainly of interest for biographical purposes. Insofar as they are moral, they touch on a feature of Roosevelt that disturbed even supporters of Roosevelt as unseemly qualities in the president of the Republic. On the other hand, Bierce is somewhat self-indulgent in his criticism, for he cannot seriously expect only saints or exemplary philosophers to hold office.

"The Dispersal" is a chilling scenario of terrorism made possible by technological progress. The prediction expressed through an account of a Future Historian no longer, if ever, appears fanciful. Bierce had long since concluded that human nature does not change over time, and that its murderous proclivities will always discover new ways of turning scientific "advances" to evil purposes and using technology to multiply their effectiveness.

Easily written stories of the supernatural, such as "A Vine on a House," "Staley Fleming's Hallucination," and "Two Military Executions," probably served as a means of supplying a critical mass of fiction to Hearst's *Cosmopolitan* magazine, in which these and many of the other stories of the last years appeared, and of keeping his name before the public. They may have been written mainly for income, but Bierce was too exacting a thinker to be contented with writing only potboilers, and even the subject of the supernatural challenged his intellect. Some change in his attitude can be detected in "A Man with Two Lives," a tale perhaps inspired by one of those near misses which left him a sole survivor. Part of the story has its basis in history, but part is a fanciful meditation on a split personality, one part of which survived a massacre and one part which did not. This sort of reflection had played a part in the writing of a number of his Civil War stories, and it does again in "A Baffled Ambuscade" and "A Resumed Identity."

Once his mind turned to seriously speculating about inexplicable phenomena, "A Wireless Message" was not a far-out story, for the subject of telepathy was then, as it still is, occasionally attested to by testimonials. Similarly, the spectral jailer in "An Arrest" is no more improbable than the "dagger of the mind" was to Macbeth, a projection of a guilty conscience. From here, Bierce apparently began to address the possibility that spirits might possibly have an existence independent of bodies. For someone like himself, who had seen so much death and who was drawn to visiting battlefields and cemeteries, the desire to communicate with the spirits of the departed, this kind of speculation reflects the increased indulgence in sentiment of his last years. "The Moonlit Road" takes another step in that direction, not basing itself in the simple-minded superstition of "spooks" but seeking some rational justification for spirit surviving the death of the body. "The Other Lodgers" is, along the same line of thought, a tale in which a psychologically sensitive narrator registers lingering subliminal impressions, undetectable to others, of what a building had been used for. "The Stranger" moves even farther in its contemplation of spirits driven to telling their story to chance travelers, making them aware that the vicinity is, in a sense, hallowed ground.

As if he caught himself doing what he earlier ridiculed, "One Summer Night" is a reaction to the drift of his thought toward the supernatural, and a return to his familiar and unsentimental emphasis upon the foibles of the living. But "John Mortonson's Funeral" cuts both ways. On the one hand, it resembles the previous tale as a mocking of human credulity by shockingly affirming that the world operates by the laws of Nature, which have nothing to do with sentiment. On the other hand, the story is a memorial to his son, and betrays what even Bierce must have recognized was a natural but irrational wish for his son to be remembered.

Two more stories written at this time represent the culmination of a remarkable development in Bierce's style, a last new variation. Some of his Civil War stories reflected situations Bierce had either experienced, or had empathized with. These stories, however, although perhaps not as impressive as stand-alone tales as the war stories with great dramatic appeal, appear to have their origins in the self-examination made possible by his giving rein to sentiment. They do, of course, have intrinsic interest, but to anyone familiar with Bierce's biography they can be seen to be densely written, utilizing what must have been painful personal insights but subordinating them to literary purposes. "Beyond the Wall" is a story of a foolishly proud man who allows concern for his social station and family tradition to deny him his only chance for love. Although the story's details do not work as exact parallels to his biography, they are close enough to suggest an essential comparison. The happiness that Bierce sought for in vain during his lifetime also escaped the protagonist in the story, but not before a bond had been created that survived death and inspired hope. This is not only a unique story in Bierce's canon but also a powerful stand-alone tale especially impressive as an indication of how far he had traveled in his art and his life. "Three and One Are One," a story of a family tragically split by personality and political differences, also has biographical ramifications. It is similarly focused on the prospect of those who love each other finding reconciliation and reunion beyond the restrictions of life and human reason. Bierce could never bring himself to be a believer in God and Heaven, but the longing was in him and at the end he was honest enough not to deny it.

THE JURY IN
ANCIENT AMERICA

AN HISTORICAL SKETCH WRITTEN IN THE YEAR OF GRACE 3687

TRANSLATED BY AMBROSE BIERCE

Of all the nations of antiquity the one that has been most studied in our day by those desiring to profit by the lessons of experience and avoid the errors of an imperfect civilization is the great American republic known as the Connected States. In the study of some others we are aided by a greater and more varied literature (for the ancient Americans were not, even according to the standards of the time, a literary people), but of none are the writings that have come down to us so rich in warning significance.

The ancient Americans were a composite people; their blood was a blend of all the strains known in their time. Their government, while they had one, being merely a loose and mutable expression of the desires and caprices of the majority—that is to say, of the ignorant, restless and reckless—gave the freest rein and play to all the primal instincts and elemental passions of the race. In so far and for so long as it had any restraining force, it was only the restraint of the present over the power of the past— that of a new habit over an old and insistent tendency ever seeking expression in large liberties and indulgences impatient of control. In the history of that unhappy people, therefore, we see unveiled the workings of the human will in its most lawless state, without fear of authority or care of consequence. Nothing could be more instructive.

Of the American form of government, although itself the greatest of evils afflicting the victims of those that it entailed, but little needs to be said here; it has perished from the earth, a system discredited by an unbroken record of failure in all parts of the world, from the earliest historic times to its final extinction in its last stronghold, the Patagonian republic. Of living students of political history not one is known to have professed to see in it anything but a mischievous creation of theorists and visionaries—

persons whom our gracious sovereign has deigned to brand for the world's contempt as "dupes of hope purveying to sons of greed." The political philosopher of to-day is spared the trouble of pointing out the fallacies of republican government, as the mathematician is spared that of demonstrating the absurdity of the convergence of parallel lines; yet the ancient Americans not only clung to their error with a blind, unquestioning faith, even when groaning under its most insupportable burdens, but seem to have believed it of divine origin. It was thought by them to have been established by the god Woshington, whose worship, with that of such *dii minores* as Gufferson, Iaxon and Lancon (identical with the Hebru Abrem), runs like a shining thread through all the warp and woof of the stuff that garmented their moral nakedness. Some stones, very curiously inscribed in many tongues, of what is believed to have been a temple of this deity, were found by the explorer Droyhors in the wilderness bordering the river Bhitt (supposed by him to be the ancient Potumuc) as lately as the year 3157, as the Americans, for some reason not now known, reckoned time. If their tutelary deity really invented representative government, they were not the first by many to whom he imparted the malign secret of its inauguration and denied that of its maintenance.

One of the most "sacred" rights of the ancient American was the trial of an accused person by "a jury of his peers." This, in America, was a right secured to him by a written constitution. It was almost universally believed to have had its origin in Magna Carta, a famous document which certain rebellious English noblemen had compelled their sovereign to sign under a threat of death. That celebrated "bill of rights" has not come down to us, but researches of the learned have made it certain that it contained no mention of trial by jury, which, indeed, was unknown to its authors. The words *judicium parium* meant to them something entirely different—the judgment of the entire community of freemen. The words and the practice they represented antedated Magna Carta by many centuries and were common to the Franks and other Germanic nations, amongst whom a trial "jury" consisted of persons having a knowledge of the matter to be determined—persons who in later times were called "witnesses" and rigorously excluded from the seats of judgment.

It is difficult to conceive a more clumsy and ineffective machinery for ascertaining truth and doing justice than a jury of twelve men of the average intelligence, even among ourselves. What, then, must this device have been among the half-civilized tribes of the Connected States of America? Nay, the case is worse than that, for it was the practice to prevent men of even the average intelligence from serving as jurors. Jurors had to be residents of the locality of the crime charged, and every crime was made a matter of public notoriety by the "newspapers" long before the accused was brought to trial; yet, as a rule, he who had read or talked about the trial was held disqualified to serve. This in a country where, when a man who could read was not reading about local crimes, he was talking about them, or if doing neither was doing something worse.

THE JURY IN ANCIENT AMERICA

To the twelve men so chosen the opposing lawyers addressed their disingenuous pleas and for their consideration the witnesses presented their carefully rehearsed testimony, most of it false. So unintelligent were these juries that a great part of the time in every trial was consumed in keeping from them certain kinds of evidence with which they could not be trusted; yet the lawyers were permitted to submit to them any kind of misleading argument that they pleased and fortify it with innuendoes without relevancy and logic without sense. Appeals to their passions, their sympathies, their prejudices, were regarded as legitimate influences and tolerated by the judges on the theory that each side's offenses would about offset those of the other. In a criminal case it was expected that the prosecutor would declare repeatedly and in the most solemn manner his belief in the guilt of the person accused, and that the attorney for the defense would affirm with equal gravity his conviction of his client's innocence. How could they impress the jury with a belief which they did not themselves venture to affirm? It is not recorded that any lawyer ever rebelled against the iron authority of these conditions and stood for truth and conscience. They were, indeed, the conditions of his existence as a lawyer, a fact which they easily persuaded themselves mitigated the baseness of their obedience to them, or justified it altogether.

The judges, as a rule, were no better, for before they could become judges they must have been advocates. Most of them depended for their office upon the favor of the people, which was fatal to the independence, the dignity and the impartiality to which they laid so solemn claim. In their decisions they favored, so far as they dared to, every interest, class or person powerful enough to help or hurt them in an election. Holding their high office by so precarious a tenure, they were under strong temptation to enrich themselves from the serviceable purses of wealthy litigants, and in disregard of justice to cultivate the favor of the attorneys practicing before them, and before whom they might soon be compelled themselves to practice.

In the higher courts of the land, where juries were unknown and appointed judges held their seats for life, these awful conditions did not obtain, and there Justice might have been content to dwell, and there she actually did sometimes set her foot. Unfortunately, the great judges had the consciences of their education. They had crept to place through the slime of the lower courts and their robes of office bore the damnatory evidence. Unfortunately, too, the attorneys, the jury habit strong upon them, brought into the superior tribunals the moral characteristics and professional methods acquired in the lower. Instead of assisting the judges to ascertain the truth and the law, they cheated in argument and took liberties with fact, deceiving the court whenever they deemed it to the interest of their cause to do so, and as willingly won by a technicality or a trick as by the justice of their contention and their ability in supporting it. Altogether, the entire judicial system of the Connected States of America was inefficient, disreputable, corrupt.

The result might easily have been foreseen and doubtless was predicted by patriots whose admonitions have not come down to us. Denied protection of the law, neither property nor life was safe. Greed filled his coffers from the meager hoards of Thrift, private vengeance took the place of legal redress, mad multitudes rioted and slew with virtual immunity from punishment or blame, and all the land was red with crime. In the early years of the twentieth century the annual number of unpunished homicides was estimated by reputable statisticians at no fewer than ten thousand, in a population of less, it is now believed, than two hundred millions! If the chief and highest duty of government is protection of the citizen, these appalling figures are conclusive as to the kind of government this savage and reckless people preferred to have and the kind of machinery to which they entrusted the execution of their laws.

A singular phenomenon of the time was the immunity of criminal women. Among the ancient Americans woman held a place unique in the history of nations. If not actually worshiped as a deity, as some historians have affirmed, she was at least regarded with feelings of veneration which the modern mind has a difficulty in comprehending. Some degree of compassion for her mental inferiority, some degree of forbearance toward her infirmities of temper, some degree of immunity for the offenses which these peculiarities entail—these are common to all peoples above the grade of barbarians. In ancient America these chivalrous sentiments found open and lawful expression only in relieving woman of the burden of participation in political and military service; the laws gave her no express exemption from responsibility for crime. When she murdered, she was arrested; when arrested, brought to trial—though the origin and meaning of those observances are not now known. Gunkle, whose researches into the jurisprudence of antiquity enable him to speak with commanding authority of many things, gives us here nothing better than the conjecture that the trial of women for murder, in the nineteenth century and a part of the twentieth, was a survival of an earlier custom of actually convicting and punishing them, but it seems extremely improbable that a people that once put its female assassins to death would ever have relinquished the obvious advantages of the practice while retaining with purposeless tenacity some of its costly preliminary forms. Whatever may have been the reason, the custom was observed with all the gravity of a serious intention. Gunkle professes knowledge of one or two instances (he does not name his authorities) where matters went as far as conviction and sentence, and adds that the mischievous sentimentalists who had always lent themselves to the solemn jest by protestations of great *vraisemblance* against "the judicial killing of women," became really alarmed and filled the land with their lamentations. Among the phenomena of brazen effrontery he classes the fact that some of these loud protagonists of the right of women to assassinate unpunished were themselves women! Howbeit, the sentences, if ever pronounced, were never executed, and during the second quarter of the twentieth century the meaningless custom of bringing female assassins to trial was abandoned. What the effect was of their exemption from this considerable inconvenience we have not the data to conjecture, unless we understand as an allusion to it some otherwise obscure words of the famous Edward Bok, the only writer of the period whose work has survived. In his monumental essay on barbarous penology, entitled "Slapping the Wrist," he couples "woman's emancipation from the trammels of law" and "man's better prospect of death" in a way that some have construed as meaning that he regarded them as cause and effect. It must be said, however, that this interpretation finds no support in the general character of his writing, which is exceedingly humane, refined and womanly.

It has been said that the writings of this great man are the only surviving work of his period, but of that we are not altogether sure. There exists a fragment of an anonymous essay on woman's legal responsibility which many Americologists think belongs to the beginning of the twentieth century. Certainly it could not have been written later than the middle of it, for at that time woman had been definitively released from responsibility to any law but that of her own will. The essay is an argument against even such imperfect exemption as she had in its author's time.

"It has been urged," he says, "that women, being less rational and more emotional than men, should not be held accountable in the same degree. To this it may be answered that punishment for crime is not intended to be retaliatory, but admonitory and deterrent. It is, therefore, peculiarly necessary to those not easily reached by other forms of warning and dissuasion. Control of the wayward is not to be sought in reduction of restraints, but in their multiplication. One who cannot be curbed by reason may be curbed by fear, a familiar truth which lies at the foundation of all penological systems. The argument for exemption of women is equally cogent for exemption of habitual criminals, for they too are abnormally inaccessible to reason, abnormally disposed to obedience to the suasion of their unregulated impulses and passions. To free them from the restraints of the fear of punishment would be a bold innovation which has as yet found no proponent outside their own class.

"Very recently this dangerous enlargement of the meaning of the phrase 'emancipation of woman' has been fortified with a strange advocacy by the female 'champions of their sex.' Their argument runs this way: 'We are denied a voice in the making of the laws relating to infliction of the death penalty; it is unjust to hold us to an accountability to which we have not assented.' Of course this argument is as broad as the entire body of law; it amounts to nothing less than a demand for general immunity from all laws, for to none of them has woman's assent been asked or given. But let us consider this amazing claim with reference only to the proposal in the service and promotion of which it is now urged: exemption of women from the death penalty for murder. In the last analysis it is seen to be a simple demand for compensation. It says: 'You owe us a *solatium*. Since you deny us the right to vote, you should give us the right to assassinate. We do not appraise it at so high a valuation as the other franchise, but we do value it.'

"Apparently they do: without legal, but with virtual, immunity from punishment, the women of this country take an average of one thousand lives annually, nine in ten being the lives of men. Juries of men, incited and sustained by public opinion, have actually deprived every adult male American of the right to live. If the death of any man is desired by any woman for any reason, he is without protection. She has only to kill him and say that he wronged or insulted her. Certain almost incredible recent instances prove that no woman is too base to slay a man with impunity, no crime of that nature sufficiently rich in all the elements of depravity to compel a conviction of the assassin, or, if she is convicted and sentenced, her punishment by the public executioner."

In this interesting fragment, quoted by Bogul in his *History of an Extinct Civilization*, we learn something of the shame and peril of American citizenship under institutions which, not having run their foreordained course to the unhappy end, were still in some degree supportable. What these institutions became afterward is a familiar story. It is true that the law of trial by jury was repealed. It had broken down, but not until itself had broken down the whole nation's respect for all law, for all forms of authority, for order and private virtues. The people whose rude forefathers in another land it had served roughly to protect against their tyrants, it had lamentably failed to protect against themselves, and when in madness they swept it away, it was not as one renouncing an error, but as one impatient of the truth which the error is still believed to contain. They flung it away, not as an ineffectual restraint, but as a restraint; not because it was no longer an instrument of justice for the determination of truth, but because they feared that it might again become such. In brief, trial by jury was abolished only when it had produced anarchy.

In concluding this brief and imperfect historical sketch I cannot forbear to relate, after the learned and ingenious Bunkux, the only known instance of a public irony expressing itself in the sculptor's noble art. In the ancient and famous city of Hohokus once stood a bronze statue of colossal size and impressive dignity. It was erected by public subscription to the memory of a man whose only distinction consisted in a single term of service as a juror in a famous murder trial, the details of which have not come down to us. It occupied the court and held public attention for many weeks, being most bitterly contested by both prosecution and defense. When at last it was given to the jury by the judge in the most celebrated charge that had ever been delivered from the bench, a ballot was taken at once. The jury stood eleven for acquittal and one for conviction. And so it stood at every ballot of the more than fifty that were taken during the fortnight that the jury was locked up for deliberation. Moreover, the dissenting juror would not argue the matter; he would listen with patient attention while his eleven indignant opponents thundered their opinions into his ears, even when they supported them with threats of personal violence; but not a word would he say. At last a disagreement was formally entered, the jury discharged and the obstinate juror chased from the city by the maddened populace. Despairing of success in another trial and privately admitting his belief in the prisoner's innocence, the public prosecutor moved for his release, which the judge ordered with remarks plainly implying his own belief that the wrong man had been tried.

THE JURY IN ANCIENT AMERICA

Years afterward the accused person died confessing his guilt, and a little later one of the jurors who had been sworn to try the case admitted that he had attended the trial on the first day only, having been personated during the rest of the proceedings by a twin brother, the obstinate member, who was a deaf-mute.

The statue of this eminent public servant was overthrown and destroyed by an earthquake in the year 2742.

Co 39, no. 4 (Aug. 1905): 384–88. Incorporated into "Ashes of the Beacon."

NOTE

Among American authors of this time, only Mark Twain can vie with AB as an outspoken critic of the jury system. AB's scorn not just for juries but also for the entire legal system probably goes back at least to 1880, when he was for several months the superintendent of a gold-mining operation in the Black Hills, Dakota Territory. He became embroiled there in a number of lawsuits, some of which continued after he returned to San Francisco, that convinced him that justice and the legal system were too seldom on the same side. Subsequent observations of courtroom proceedings in California and Nevada only reinforced his disillusionment. His bias against juries was also augmented by his belief, especially strong in his last years, that democracy was turning into mobocracy, and that the country was pandering to the lowest common denominators of its diverse citizenry.

A VINE ON A HOUSE

About three miles from the little town of Norton, in Missouri, on the road leading to Maysville,[1] stands an old house that was last occupied by a family named Harding. Since 1886 no one has lived in it, nor is any one likely to live in it again. Time and the disfavor of persons dwelling thereabout are converting it into a rather picturesque ruin. An observer unacquainted with its history would hardly put it into the category of "haunted houses," yet in all the region round such is its evil reputation. Its windows are without glass, its doorways without doors; there are wide breaches in the shingle roof, and for lack of paint the weatherboarding is a dun gray. But these unfailing signs of the supernatural are partly concealed and greatly softened by the abundant foliage of a large vine overrunning the entire structure. This vine—of a species which no botanist has ever been able to name—has an important part in the story of the house.

The Harding family consisted of Robert Harding, his wife Matilda, Miss Julia Went, who was her sister, and two young children. Robert Harding was a silent, cold-mannered man who made no friends in the neighborhood and apparently cared to make none. He was about forty years old, frugal and industrious, and made a living from the little farm which is now overgrown with brush and brambles. He and his sister-in-law were rather tabooed by their neighbors, who seemed to think that they were seen too frequently together—not entirely their fault, for at these times they evidently did not challenge observation. The moral code of rural Missouri is stern and exacting.

Mrs. Harding was a gentle, sad-eyed woman, lacking a left foot.

At some time in 1884 it became known that she had gone to visit her mother in Iowa. That was what her husband said in reply to inquiries, and his manner of saying it did not encourage further questioning. She never came back, and two years later, without selling his farm or anything that was his, or appointing an agent to look after his interests, or removing his household goods, Harding, with the rest of the family, left the country. Nobody knew whither he went; nobody at that time cared. Naturally, whatever was movable about the place soon disappeared and the deserted house became "haunted" in the manner of its kind.

One summer evening, four or five years later, the Rev. J. Gruber, of Norton, and a Maysville attorney named Hyatt met on horseback in front of the Harding place. Having business matters to discuss, they hitched their animals and going to the house sat on the porch to talk. Some humorous reference to the somber reputation of the place was made and forgotten as soon as uttered, and they talked of their business affairs until it grew almost dark. The evening was oppressively warm, the air stagnant.

Presently both men started from their seats in surprise: a long vine that covered half the front of the house and dangled its branches from the edge of the porch above them was visibly and audibly agitated, shaking violently in every stem and leaf.

"We shall have a storm," Hyatt exclaimed.

Gruber said nothing, but silently directed the other's attention to the foliage of adjacent trees, which showed no movement; even the delicate tips of the boughs silhouetted against the clear sky were motionless. They hastily passed down the steps to what had been a lawn and looked upward at the vine, whose entire length was now visible. It continued in violent agitation, yet they could discern no disturbing cause.

"Let us leave," said the minister.

And leave they did. Forgetting that they had been traveling in opposite directions, they rode away together. They went to Norton, where they related their strange experience to several discreet friends. The next evening, at about the same hour, accompanied by two others whose names are not recalled, they were again on the porch of the Harding house, and again the mysterious phenomenon occurred: the vine was violently agitated while under the closest scrutiny from root to tip, nor did their combined strength applied to the trunk serve to still it. After an hour's observation they retreated, no less wise, it is thought, than when they had come.

No great time was required for these singular facts to rouse the curiosity of the entire neighborhood. By day and by night crowds of persons assembled at the Harding house "seeking a sign." It does not appear that any found it, yet so credible were the witnesses mentioned that none doubted the reality of the "manifestations" to which they testified.

By either a happy inspiration or some destructive design, it was one day proposed—nobody appeared to know from whom the suggestion came—to dig up the vine, and after a good deal of debate this was done. Nothing was found but the root, yet nothing could have been more strange!

For five or six feet from the trunk, which had at the surface of the ground a diameter of several inches, it ran downward, single and straight, into a loose, friable earth; then it divided and subdivided into rootlets, fibers and filaments, most curiously interwoven. When carefully freed from soil they showed a singular formation. In their

A VINE ON A HOUSE

ramifications and doublings back upon themselves they made a compact network, having in size and shape an amazing resemblance to the human figure.[2] Head, trunk and limbs were there; even the fingers and toes were distinctly defined; and many professed to see in the distribution and arrangement of the fibers in the globular mass representing the head a grotesque suggestion of a face. The figure was horizontal; the smaller roots had begun to unite at the breast.

In point of resemblance to the human form this image was imperfect. At about ten inches from one of the knees, the *cilia* forming that leg had abruptly doubled backward and inward upon their course of growth. The figure lacked the left foot.

There was but one inference—the obvious one; but in the ensuing excitement as many courses of action were proposed as there were incapable counselors. The matter was settled by the sheriff of the county, who as the lawful custodian of the abandoned estate ordered the root replaced and the excavation filled with the earth that had been removed.

Later inquiry brought out only one fact of relevancy and significance: Mrs. Harding had never visited her relatives in Iowa, nor did they know that she was supposed to have done so.

Of Robert Harding and the rest of his family nothing is known. The house retains its evil reputation, but the replanted vine is as orderly and well-behaved a vegetable as a nervous person could wish to sit under of a pleasant night, when the katydids grate out their immemorial revelation and the distant whippoorwill signifies his notion of what ought to be done about it.

Co 39, no. 6 (Oct. 1905): 617–18 (under the heading "Some Uncanny Tales"); *CW* 3.383–88.

NOTES

An invented story in the manner of "Two Haunted Houses" (p. 671).

1. Maysville is an actual town (the county seat of De Kalb County in northwestern Missouri), but Norton appears to be fictitious. (A small town named Norton is found in Saline County in central Missouri, but it is very far from Maysville.)

2. *A Fourteen Weeks' Course in Chemistry* (New York: A. S. Barnes, 1867) by Joel Dorman Steele (1836–66) contains an anecdote about the root of an apple tree that had enveloped the body of Roger Williams (pp. 259–60).

A VINE ON A HOUSE

A MAN WITH TWO LIVES

Here is the queer story of David William Duck, related by himself. Duck is an old man living in Aurora, Illinois, where he is universally respected. He is commonly known, however, as "Dead Duck."

"In the autumn of 1866 I was a private soldier of the Eighteenth Infantry. My company was one of those stationed at Fort Phil Kearney, commanded by Colonel Carrington. The country is more or less familiar with the history of that garrison, particularly with the slaughter by the Sioux of a detachment of eighty-one men and officers—not one escaping—through disobedience of orders by its commander, the brave but reckless Captain Fetterman. When that occurred, I was trying to make my way with important dispatches to Fort C. F. Smith, on the Big Horn.[1] As the country swarmed with hostile Indians, I traveled by night and concealed myself as best I could before daybreak. The better to do so, I went afoot, armed with a Henry rifle[2] and carrying three days' rations in my haversack.

"For my second place of concealment I chose what seemed in the darkness a narrow cañon leading through a range of rocky hills. It contained many large bowlders, detached from the slopes of the hills. Behind one of these, in a clump of sage-brush, I made my bed for the day, and soon fell asleep. It seemed as if I had hardly closed my eyes, though in fact it was near midday, when I was awakened by the report of a rifle, the bullet striking the bowlder just above my body. A band of Indians had trailed me and had me nearly surrounded; the shot had been fired with an execrable aim by a fellow who had caught sight of me from the hillside above. The smoke of his rifle betrayed him, and I was no sooner on my feet than he was off his and rolling down the declivity. Then I ran in a stooping posture, dodging among the clumps of sage-brush in a storm of bullets from invisible enemies. The rascals did not rise and pursue, which I thought rather queer, for they must have known by my trail that they had to deal with only one man. The reason for their inaction was soon made clear. I had not gone a hundred yards before I reached the limit of my run—the head of the gulch which I had mistaken for a cañon. It terminated in a concave breast of rock, nearly vertical and destitute of vegetation. In that cul-de-sac I was caught like a bear in a pen. Pursuit was needless; they had only to wait.

"They waited. For two days and nights, crouching behind a rock topped with a growth of mesquite, and with the cliff at my back, suffering agonies of thirst and absolutely hopeless of deliverance, I fought the fellows at long range, firing occasionally at the smoke of their rifles, as they did at that of mine. Of course, I did not dare to close my eyes at night, and lack of sleep was a keen torture.

"I remember the morning of the third day, which I knew was to be my last. I remember, rather indistinctly, that in my desperation and delirium I sprang out into the open and began firing my repeating rifle without seeing anybody to fire at. And I remember no more of that fight.

"The next thing that I recollect was my pulling myself out of a river just at nightfall. I had not a rag of clothing and knew nothing of my whereabouts, but all that night I traveled, cold and footsore, toward the north. At daybreak I found myself at Fort C. F. Smith, my destination, but without my dispatches. The first man that I met was a sergeant named William Briscoe, whom I knew very well. You can fancy his astonishment at seeing me in that condition, and my own at his asking who the devil I was.

"'Dave Duck,' I answered; 'who should I be?'

"He stared like an owl.

"'You do look it,' he said, and I observed that he drew a little away from me. 'What's up?' he added.

"I told him what had happened to me the day before. He heard me through, still staring; then he said:

"'My dear fellow, if you are Dave Duck I ought to inform you that I buried you two months ago. I was out with a small scouting party and found your body, full of bullet-holes and newly scalped—somewhat mutilated otherwise, too, I am sorry to say—right where you say you made your fight. Come to my tent and I'll show you your clothing and some letters that I took from your person; the commandant has your dispatches.'

"He performed that promise. He showed me the clothing, which I resolutely put on; the letters, which I put into my pocket. He made no objection, then took me to the commandant, who heard my story and coldly ordered Briscoe to take me to the guardhouse. On the way I said:

"'Bill Briscoe, did you really and truly bury the dead body that you found in these togs?'

"'Sure,' he answered—'just as I told you. It was Dave Duck, all right; most of us knew him. And now, you damned impostor, you'd better tell me who you are.'

"'I'd give something to know,' I said.

A MAN WITH TWO LIVES

"A week later, I escaped from the guardhouse and got out of the country as fast as I could. Twice I have been back, seeking for that fateful spot in the hills, but unable to find it."

Co 39, no. 6 (Oct. 1905): 618–20 (under the heading "Some Uncanny Tales"); *CW* 3.345–49.

NOTES

The historical background about the "brave but reckless" Captain Fetterman is basically accurate and is alluded to in AB's 1887 autobiographical memoir, "Across the Plains" (see *SS* 79). The account of David Duck, of course, is fanciful, in keeping with the story's designation in *Co* as an "uncanny" tale.

1. Fort Phil Kearny [*sic*] was located in north-central Wyoming, near the border of Montana. It was under the command of Col. (later Brig. Gen.) Henry Beebee Carrington (1824–1912). On 21 December 1866, Col. (not Capt.) William J. Fetterman of the 18th Infantry set out from the fort with a band of seventy-nine soldiers and two civilians to rescue a wagon train that was being attacked by Sioux Indians; Fetterman and his entire corps were killed in an ambush. Fort C. F. Smith was the first army post in Montana, just across the border from Wyoming. Founded in 1866, it was abandoned two years later, in part because of the Fetterman disaster.

2. The Henry rifle was the immediate forerunner of the Winchester rifle. About fourteen thousand Henrys were made between 1860 and 1866 by the New Haven Arms Company.

A WIRELESS MESSAGE

In the summer of 1896 Mr. William Holt, a wealthy manufacturer of Chicago, was living temporarily in a little town of central New York, the name of which the writer's memory has not retained. Mr. Holt had had "trouble with his wife," from whom he had parted a year before. Whether the trouble was anything more serious than "incompatibility of temper," he is probably the only living person that knows: he is not addicted to the vice of confidences. Yet he has related the incident herein set down to at least one person without exacting a pledge of secrecy. He is now living in Europe.

One evening he had left the house of a brother whom he was visiting, for a stroll in the country. It may be assumed—whatever the value of the assumption in connection with what is said to have occurred—that his mind was occupied with reflections on his domestic infelicities and the distressing changes that they had wrought in his life. Whatever may have been his thoughts, they so possessed him that he observed neither the lapse of time nor whither his feet were carrying him; he knew only that he had passed far beyond the town limits and was traversing a lonely region by a road that bore no resemblance to the one by which he had left the village. In brief, he was "lost."

Realizing his mischance, he smiled; central New York is not a region of perils, nor does one long remain lost in it. He turned about and went back the way that he had come. Before he had gone far he observed that the landscape was growing more distinct—was brightening. Everything was suffused with a soft, red glow in which he saw his shadow projected in the road before him. "The moon is rising," he said to himself. Then he remembered that it was about the time of the new moon, and if that tricksy orb was in one of its stages of visibility it had set long before. He stopped and faced about, seeking the source of the rapidly broadening light. As he did so, his shadow turned and lay along the road in front of him as before. The light still came from behind him. That was surprising; he could not understand. Again he turned, and again, facing successively to every point of the horizon. Always the shadow was before—always the light behind, "a still and awful red."[1]

Holt was astonished—"dumbfounded" is the word that he used in telling it—yet seems to have retained a certain intelligent curiosity. To test the intensity of the light whose nature and cause he could not determine, he took out his watch to see if he could make out the figures on the dial. They were plainly visible, and the hands indicated the hour of eleven o'clock and twenty-five minutes. At that moment the mysterious illumination suddenly flared to an intense, an almost blinding splendor, flushing the entire sky, extinguishing the stars and throwing the monstrous shadow of himself athwart the landscape. In that unearthly illumination he saw near him, but apparently in the air at a considerable elevation, the figure of his wife, clad in her night-clothing and holding to her breast the figure of his child. Her eyes were fixed upon his with an expression which he afterward professed himself unable to name or describe, further than that it was "not of this life."

The flare was momentary, followed by black darkness, in which, however, the apparition still showed white and motionless; then by insensible degrees it faded and vanished, like a bright image on the retina after the closing of the eyes. A peculiarity of the apparition, hardly noted at the time, but afterward recalled, was that it showed only the upper half of the woman's figure: nothing was seen below the waist.

The sudden darkness was comparative, not absolute, for gradually all objects of his environment became again visible.

In the dawn of the morning Holt found himself entering the village at a point opposite to that at which he had left it. He soon arrived at the house of his brother, who hardly knew him. He was wild-eyed, haggard and gray as a rat. Almost incoherently, he related his night's experience.

"Go to bed, my poor fellow," said his brother, "and—wait. We shall hear more of this."

An hour later came the predestined telegram. Holt's dwelling in one of the suburbs of Chicago had been destroyed by fire. Her escape cut off by the flames, his wife had appeared at an upper window, her child in her arms. There she had stood, motionless, apparently dazed. Just as the firemen had arrived with a ladder, the floor had given way, and she was seen no more.

The moment of this culminating horror was eleven o'clock and twenty-five minutes, standard time.

Co 39, no. 6 (Oct. 1905): 620–22 (under the heading "Some Uncanny Tales"); *CW* 3.340–42.

NOTES

Another uncanny tale, with an intimation of the possibility of telepathic communication. This notion was current at this time and enjoyed some degree of respectability. For instance, in an article on 6 January 1889 Dan De Quille recalled such an incident involving himself and Mark Twain, and in his 1891 essay "Mental Telegraph," Twain mentions the same incident and discussed further instances of the phenomenon.

1. Coleridge, *The Rime of the Ancient Mariner* (1798), l. 271.

AN ARREST

Having murdered his brother-in-law, Orrin Brower of Kentucky was a fugitive from justice. From the county jail where he had been confined to await his trial he had escaped by knocking down his jailer with an iron bar, robbing him of his keys and, opening the outer door, walking out into the night. The jailer being unarmed, Brower got no weapon with which to defend his recovered liberty. As soon as he was out of the town he had the folly to enter a forest; this was many years ago, when that region was wilder than it is now.

The night was pretty dark, with neither moon nor stars visible, and as Brower had never dwelt thereabout, and knew nothing of the lay of the land, he was, naturally, not long in losing himself. He could not have said if he were getting farther away from the town or going back to it—a most important matter to Orrin Brower. He knew that in either case a posse of citizens with a pack of bloodhounds would soon be on his track and his chance of escape was very slender; but he did not wish to assist in his own pursuit. Even an added hour of freedom was worth having.

Suddenly he emerged from the forest into an old road, and there before him saw, indistinctly, the figure of a man, motionless in the gloom. It was too late to retreat: the fugitive felt that at the first movement back toward the wood he would be, as he afterward explained, "filled with buckshot." So the two stood there like trees, Brower nearly suffocated by the activity of his own heart; the other—the emotions of the other are not recorded.

A moment later—it may have been an hour—the moon sailed into a patch of unclouded sky and the hunted man saw that visible embodiment of Law lift an arm and point significantly toward and beyond him. He understood. Turning his back to his captor, he walked submissively away in the direction indicated, looking to neither the right nor the left; hardly daring to breathe, his head and back actually aching with a prophecy of buckshot.

Brower was as courageous a criminal as ever lived to be hanged; that was shown by the conditions of awful personal peril in which he had coolly killed his brother-in-law. It is needless to relate them here; they came out at his trial, and the revelation of his calmness in confronting them came near to saving his neck. But what would you have?—when a brave man is beaten, he submits.

So they pursued their journey jailward along the old road through the woods. Only once did Brower venture a turn of the head: just once, when he was in deep shadow and he knew that the other was in moonlight, he looked backward. His captor was Burton Duff, the jailer, as white as death and bearing upon his brow the livid mark of the iron bar. Orrin Brower had no further curiosity.

Eventually they entered the town, which was all alight, but deserted; only the women and children remained, and they were off the streets. Straight toward the jail the criminal held his way. Straight up to the main entrance he walked, laid his hand upon the knob of the heavy iron door, pushed it open without command, entered and found himself in the presence of a half-dozen armed men. Then he turned. Nobody else entered.

On a table in the corridor lay the dead body of Burton Duff.

Co 39, no. 6 (Oct. 1905): 622 (under the heading "Some Uncanny Tales"); *CW* 3.340–42.

NOTE

Under the guise of another uncanny tale, AB appears to have composed a semi-psychological allegory of conscience.

THE CONFLAGRATION
IN GHARGAROO

While in Ghargaroo (said the Returned Traveler) I heard much of the great statesman and philosopher, Juptka-Getch, who was accounted the wisest person in the realm and was held in so high honor and esteem that none dared speak to him without permission of the sovereign. Having obtained this through the happy accident of having a wart on the left side of my nose, as had a cousin of the prime minister, I went humbly to the great man's dwelling, which to my astonishment I found to be an unfurnished cave in the side of a mountain. Inexpressibly surprised to observe that a favorite of the sovereign and the people was so meanly housed, I ventured, after my salutation, to ask how this could be so. Regarding me with an indulgent smile, the venerable man, who was about two hundred and fifty years old and entirely bald, explained.

"In one of our Sacred Books, of which we have three thousand," said he, "it is written, *'Golooloo ek wakwah betenka,'* and in another, *'Jebeb uq seedroy im aboltraqu ocrux ti smelkit.'*"

Translated, these mean, respectively, "The poor are blessed," and, "Heaven is not easily entered by those who are rich."

I asked Juptka-Getch if his countrymen really gave to these texts a practical application in the affairs of life.

"Why, surely," he replied, "you cannot think us such fools as to disregard the teachings of our gods! That would be madness. I cannot imagine a people so mentally and morally depraved as that! Can you?"

Observing me blushing and stammering, he inquired the cause of my embarrassment. "The thought of so incredible a thing confuses me," I managed to reply. "But tell me if in your piety and wisdom you really stripped yourself of all your property in order to obey the gods and get the benefit of indigence."

"I did not have to do so," he replied with a smile; "my king attended to that. When he wishes to distinguish one of his subjects by a mark of his favor, he impoverishes him to such a degree as will attest the exact measure of the royal approbation. I am proud to say that he took from me all that I had."

"But, pardon me," I said; "how does it occur that among a people which regards poverty as the greatest earthly good all are not poor? I observe here as much wealth and 'prosperity' as in my own country."

Juptka-Getch folded his legs across the back of his neck (an attitude which in Ghargaroo signifies profound reflection) and after a few moments answered: "The only person in this country that owns anything is the king; in the service of his people he afflicts himself with that burden. All property, of whatsoever kind, is his, to do with as he will. He divides it among his subjects in the ratio of their demerit, as determined by the waguks—local officers—whose duty it is to know personally every one in their jurisdiction. To the most desperate and irreclaimable criminals is allotted the greatest wealth, which is taken from them, little by little, as they show signs of reformation."

"But what," said I, "is to prevent the wicked from becoming poor at any time? How can the king and his officers keep the unworthy, suffering the punishment and peril of wealth, from giving it away?"

"To whom, for example?" replied the illustrious man, taking the great toe of his right foot in his mouth, as is the fashion in Ghargaroo when awaiting an important communication. The respectful formality of the posture imperfectly concealed the irony of the question, but I was not to be silenced.

"One might convert one's property into money," I persisted, "and throw the money into the sea."

Juptka-Getch released the toe and gravely answered: "Every person in Ghargaroo is compelled by law to keep minute accounts of his income and expenditures, and must swear to them. There is an annual appraisement by the waguk, and any needless decrease in the value of an estate is punished by skinning the offender's legs. Expenditures for luxuries and high living are, of course, approved, for it is universally known among us, and attested by many popular proverbs, that the pleasures of the rich are vain and disappointing. So they are considered a part of the punishment, and not only allowed but required. A man sentenced to wealth who lives frugally, indulging in only rational and inexpensive delights, has his ears cut off for the first offense, and for the second is compelled to pass six months at court, participating in all the gaieties of the capital."

"Most illustrious of mortals," I said, turning a somersault—the Ghargarese manner of interrupting a discourse—"I am as the dust upon your beard, but in my own country I am esteemed no fool, and right humbly do I perceive that you are *ecxroptug nemk puttog peleemy.*"

This expression translates, literally, "giving me a fill," a phrase without meaning in our tongue, but in Ghargarese appearing to imply incredulity.

"The gaieties of the king's court," I continued, "must be expensive. The courtiers of the sovereign's entourage, the great officers of the realm—surely they are not condemned to wealth, like common criminals!"

THE CONFLAGRATION IN GHARGAROO

"My son," said Juptka-Getch, tearing out a handful of his beard to signify his tranquility under accusation, "your doubt of my veracity is noted with satisfaction, but it is not permitted to you to impeach my sovereign's infallible knowledge of character. His courtiers, the great officers of the realm, as you truly name them, are the richest men in the country because he knows them to be the greatest rascals. After each annual reapportionment of the national wealth he settles all the unallotted surplus upon them."

Prostrating myself before the eminent philosopher, I craved his pardon for my doubt of his sovereign's wisdom and consistency, and begged him to cut off my head.

"Nay," he said, "you have committed the unpardonable sin and I cannot consent to bestow upon you the advantages of death. You shall continue to live the thing that you are."

"What!" I cried, "is it thought in Ghargaroo that death is an advantage, a blessing?"

"Our Sacred Books," he said, "are full of texts affirming the vanity of life."

My astonishment was for some moments too great for words. When I had recovered the power of speech, I said, "Then I infer that the death penalty is unknown to your laws!"

"We have the life penalty instead. Convicted criminals are not only enriched, as already explained, but by medical attendance kept alive as long as possible. On the other hand, the very righteous, who have been rewarded with poverty, are permitted to die whenever it pleases them."

Juptka-Getch again crossed his feet upon the back of his neck in meditation, and presently said, "Do not the Sacred Books of your country teach the vanity of life, the blessedness of poverty and the wickedness of wealth?"

"They do, O Most Illustrious, they do."

"And your countrymen believe?"

"Surely—none but the foolish and depraved entertain a doubt."

"Then I waste my breath in expounding laws and customs already known to you. You have, of course, the same."

At this I averted my face and blushed so furiously that the walls of the cave were illuminated with a wavering crimson like the light of a great conflagration! Thinking that the capital city was ablaze, Juptka-Getch ran from the cave's mouth, crying, "Fire, fire!" and I saw him no more.

Co 40, no. 4 (Feb. 1906): 457–58. Incorporated into "The Land Beyond the Blow."

NOTE

This sketch contrasts the literal teachings of Christianity with the practical interpretation of them that reverses their meaning. AB seems to be implying that either Christians do not truly believe their Scripture or that, especially as regards its views on the value of life, the religion's teachings are impractical.

THE CONFLAGRATION IN GHARGAROO

ONE SUMMER NIGHT

The fact that Henry Armstrong was buried did not seem to him to prove that he was dead: he had always been a hard man to convince. That he really was buried, the testimony of his senses compelled him to admit. His posture—flat upon his back, with his hands crossed upon his stomach and tied with something that he easily broke without profitably altering the situation—the strict confinement of his entire person, the black darkness and profound silence, made a body of evidence impossible to controvert and he accepted it without cavil.

But dead—no; he was only very, very ill. He had, withal, the invalid's apathy and did not greatly concern himself about the uncommon fate that had been allotted to him. No philosopher was he—just a plain, commonplace person gifted, for the time being, with a pathological indifference: the organ that he feared consequences with was torpid. So, with no particular apprehension for his immediate future, he fell asleep and all was peace with Henry Armstrong.

But something was going on overhead. It was a dark summer night, shot through with infrequent shimmers of lightning silently firing a cloud lying low in the west and portending a storm. These brief, stammering illuminations brought out with ghastly distinctness the monuments and headstones of the cemetery and seemed to set them dancing. It was not a night in which any credible witness was likely to be straying about a cemetery, so the three men who were there, digging into the grave of Henry Armstrong, felt reasonably secure.

Two of them were young students from a medical college a few miles away; the third was a gigantic negro known as Jess. For many years Jess had been employed about the cemetery as a man-of-all-work and it was his favorite pleasantry that he knew "every soul in the place." From the nature of what he was now doing it was inferable that the place was not so populous as its register may have shown it to be.

Outside the wall, at the part of the grounds farthest from the public road, were a horse and a light wagon, waiting.

The work of excavation was not difficult: the earth with which the grave had been loosely filled a few hours before offered little resistance and was soon thrown out. Removal of the casket from its box was less easy, but it was taken out, for it was a perquisite of Jess, who carefully unscrewed the cover and laid it aside, exposing the body in black trousers and white shirt. At that instant the air sprang to flame, a cracking shock of thunder shook the stunned world and Henry Armstrong tranquilly sat up. With inarticulate cries the men fled in terror, each in a different direction. For nothing on earth could two of them have been persuaded to return. But Jess was of another breed.

In the gray of the morning the two students, pallid and haggard from anxiety and with the terror of their adventure still beating tumultuously in their blood, met at the medical college.

"You saw it?" cried one.

"God! yes—what are we to do?"

They went around to the rear of the building, where they saw a horse, attached to a light wagon, hitched to a gatepost near the door of the dissecting-room. Mechanically they entered the room. On a bench in the obscurity sat the negro Jess. He rose, grinning, all eyes and teeth.

"I'm waiting for my pay," he said.

Stretched naked on a long table lay the body of Henry Armstrong, the head defiled with blood and clay from a blow with a spade.

Co 40, no. 5 (Mar. 1906): 543–44 (under the heading "Some Uncanny Tales"); *CW* 3.58–61.

NOTE

Despite its designation as an "uncanny" tale, this powerful sketch is a satire on human venality. The nineteenth century had a horrified fascination of burial alive and grave robbery, famously exploited, respectively, by Poe's "The Premature Burial" (1844) and chapter 9 of Twain's *The Adventures of Tom Sawyer* (1876). AB here combines these sensational topics first to raise sympathy for the victim of premature burial and then to induce shock at the willingness of medical students to rationalize in the pursuit of science their immoral and illegal desecration of a grave, and the readiness of a cemetery employee to do for money whatever it took to supply them with a fresh corpse. Rationalization and greed are thus shown to trump humanitarian sentiments as motivation.

JOHN MORTONSON'S FUNERAL*

John Mortonson was dead: his lines in "the tragedy 'Man'"[1] had all been spoken and he had left the stage.

The body rested in a fine mahogany coffin fitted with a plate of glass. All arrangements for the funeral had been so well attended to that had the deceased known he would doubtless have approved. The face, as it showed under the glass, was not disagreeable to look upon: it bore a faint smile, and as the death had been painless, had not been distorted beyond the repairing power of the undertaker. At two o'clock of the afternoon the friends were to assemble to pay their last tribute of respect to one who had no further need of friends and respect. The surviving members of the family came severally every few minutes to the casket and wept above the placid features beneath the glass. This did them no good; it did no good to John Mortonson; but in the presence of death reason and philosophy are silent.

As the hour of two approached the friends began to arrive and after offering such consolation to the stricken relatives as the proprieties of the occasion required, solemnly seated themselves about the room with an augmented consciousness of their importance in the scheme funeral. Then the minister came, and in that overshadowing presence the lesser lights went into eclipse. His entrance was followed by that of the widow, whose lamentations filled the room. She approached the casket and after leaning her face against the cold glass for a moment was gently led to a seat near her daughter. Mournfully and low the man of God began his eulogy of the dead, and his doleful voice, mingled with the sobbing which it was its purpose to stimulate and sustain, rose and fell, seemed to come and go, like the sound of a sullen sea. The gloomy day grew darker as

---

* Rough notes of this tale were found among the papers of the late Leigh Bierce. It is printed here with such revision only as the author might himself have made in transcription.

he spoke; a curtain of cloud underspread the sky and a few drops of rain fell audibly. It seemed as if all Nature were weeping for John Mortonson.

When the minister had finished his eulogy with prayer a hymn was sung and the pall-bearers took their places beside the bier. As the last notes of the hymn died away the widow ran to the coffin, cast herself upon it and sobbed hysterically. Gradually, however, she yielded to dissuasion, becoming more composed; and as the minister was in the act of leading her away her eyes sought the face of the dead beneath the glass. She threw up her arms and with a shriek fell backward insensible.

The mourners sprang forward to the coffin, the friends followed, and as the clock on the mantel solemnly struck three all were staring down upon the face of John Mortonson, deceased.

They turned away, sick and faint. One man, trying in his terror to escape the awful sight, stumbled against the coffin so heavily as to knock away one of its frail supports. The coffin fell to the floor, the glass was shattered to bits by the concussion.

From the opening crawled John Mortonson's cat, which lazily leapt to the floor, sat up, tranquilly wiped its crimson muzzle with a forepaw, then walked with dignity from the room.

Co 40, no. 5 (Mar. 1906): 544–45 (under the heading "Some Uncanny Tales"); *CW* 3.252–54.

NOTES

It is probably no accident that this tale and the previous one were written at the same time and thus appeared in the same issue of *Co*. For most of his career, AB had repeatedly reminded readers that animals, including pets, are prone to ultimately regard humans from an unsentimental and utilitarian perspective as a potential food source, just as humans regard them. In this tale the cat has no sympathetic attachment to its former owner; in "One Summer Night" humans are seen as being basically animalistic by nature, regarding each other as only means to their own benefit or survival.

AB's letter to George Sterling (12 March 1906) clarifies the issue of the story's authorship: "Yes, the 'Cosmopolitan' cat-story is Leigh's and is to be credited to him if ever published in covers. I fathered it as the only way to get it published at all. Of course I had to rewrite it; it was very crude and too horrible. A story may be terrible, but must not be horrible—there is a difference. I found the manuscript among his papers" (*MMM* 147–48). In short, it appears that Leigh had attempted to imitate his father's style without fully understanding it, and the grieving father rewrote the story to make the most of it, and as a memorial to his son.

1. "The play is the tragedy, 'Man,' / And its hero the Conqueror Worm." Edgar Allan Poe, "The Conqueror Worm" (1843), ll. 39–40.

STALEY FLEMING'S HALLUCINATION

Of two men who were talking one was a physician.

"I sent for you, Doctor," said the other, "but I don't think you can do me any good. May be you can recommend a specialist in psychopathy. I fancy I'm a bit loony."

"You look all right," the physician said.

"You shall judge—I have hallucinations. I wake every night and see in my room, intently watching me, a big black Newfoundland dog with a white forefoot."

"You say you wake; are you sure about that? 'Hallucinations' are sometimes only dreams."

"Oh, I wake, all right. Sometimes I lie still a long time, looking at the dog as earnestly as the dog looks at me—I always leave the light going. When I can't endure it any longer I sit up in bed—and nothing is there!"

"'M, 'm—what is the beast's expression?"

"It seems to me sinister. Of course I know that, except in art, an animal's face in repose has always the same expression. But this is not a real animal. Newfoundland dogs are pretty mild looking, you know; what's the matter with this one?"

"Really, my diagnosis would have no value: I am not going to treat the dog."

The physician laughed at his own pleasantry, but narrowly watched his patient from the corner of his eye. Presently he said: "Fleming, your description of the beast fits the dog of the late Atwell Barton."

Fleming half rose from his chair, sat again and made a visible attempt at indifference. "I remember Barton," he said; "I believe he was—it was reported that—wasn't there something suspicious in his death?"

Looking squarely now into the eyes of his patient, the physician said: "Three years ago the body of your old enemy, Atwell Barton, was found in the woods near his house and yours. He had been stabbed to death. There have been no arrests; there was no clew. Some of us had 'theories.' I had one. Have you?"

"I? Why, bless your soul, what could I know about it? You remember that I left for Europe almost immediately afterward—a considerable time afterward. In the few weeks since my return you could not expect me to construct a 'theory.' In fact, I have not given the matter a thought. What about his dog?"

"It was first to find the body. It died of starvation on his grave."

We do not know the inexorable law underlying coincidences. Staley Fleming did not, or he would perhaps not have sprung to his feet as the night wind brought in through the open window the long wailing howl of a distant dog. He strode several times across the room in the steadfast gaze of the physician; then, abruptly confronting him, almost shouted: "What has all this to do with my trouble, Dr. Halderman? You forget why you were sent for."

Rising, the physician laid his hand upon his patient's arm and said, gently: "Pardon me. I cannot diagnose your disorder offhand—to-morrow, perhaps. Please go to bed, leaving your door unlocked; I will pass the night here with your books. Can you call me without rising?"

"Yes, there is an electric bell."

"Good. If anything disturbs you push the button without sitting up. Good night."

Comfortably installed in an armchair the man of medicine stared into the glowing coals and thought deeply and long, but apparently to little purpose, for he frequently rose and opening a door leading to the staircase, listened intently; then resumed his seat. Presently, however, he fell asleep, and when he woke it was past midnight. He stirred the failing fire, lifted a book from the table at his side and looked at the title. It was Denneker's "Meditations."[1] He opened it at random and began to read:

"Forasmuch as it is ordained of God that all flesh hath spirit and thereby taketh on spiritual powers, so, also, the spirit hath powers of the flesh, even when it is gone out of the flesh and liveth as a thing apart, as many a violence performed by wraith and lemure sheweth. And there be who say that man is not single in this, but the beasts have the like evil inducement, and—"

The reading was interrupted by a shaking of the house, as by the fall of a heavy object. The reader flung down the book, rushed from the room and mounted the stairs to Fleming's bed-chamber. He tried the door, but contrary to his instructions it was locked. He set his shoulder against it with such force that it gave way. On the floor near the disordered bed, in his night clothes, lay Fleming gasping away his life.

The physician raised the dying man's head from the floor and observed a wound in the throat. "I should have thought of this," he said, believing it suicide.

When the man was dead an examination disclosed the unmistakable marks of an animal's fangs deeply sunken into the jugular vein.

But there was no animal.

Co 40, no. 5 (Mar. 1906): 545–47 (under the heading "Some Uncanny Tales"); *CW* 3.169–73.

STALEY FLEMING'S HALLUCINATION

Essentially a potboiler story of an incredible supernatural incident, made more solemn by the unexplained assertion of "the inexorable law underlying coincidences" and a fabricated quotation from a fabricated mystic.

1. First cited in "A Psychological Shipwreck" (p. 386).

INSURANCE IN
ANCIENT AMERICA

TRANSLATED FROM THE WORK OF THE FUTURE HISTORIAN

BY AMBROSE BIERCE

Among the principal causes of that popular discontent which brought about the stupendous events resulting in the downfall of the great American republic, historians and archaeologists are now agreed in reckoning insurance. Of the exact nature of this factor in the problem of national life in that distant day, the fragmentary literature of the period leaves us imperfectly informed; many of its details have perished from human record, yet its outlines loom large through the mist of the ages and can be traced with precision. In the monumental work of Professor Golunk-Dorstro ("Some Account of the Insurance Delusion in Ancient America") we have its most considerable modern exposition; and Gakler's well-known volume, "The Follies of Antiquity," contains much interesting matter relating to it. From these and other sources the student of human unreason can reconstruct that astounding fallacy of insurance as, from three joints of its tail, the great naturalist Bogramus restored the ancient elephant, from hoof to horn.

The game of insurance, as practiced by the ancient Americans (and, as Gakler conjectures, by some of the tribesmen of Europe), was gambling, pure and simple, despite the sentimental character that its proponents sought to impress upon some forms of it for the greater prosperity of their dealings with its dupes. Essentially, it was a bet between the insurer and the insured. The number of ways in which the wager was made—all devised by the insurer—was almost infinite, but in none of them was there a departure from the intrinsic nature of the transaction as seen in its simplest, frankest form, which we shall here expound.

To those unlearned in the economical institutions of antiquity it is necessary to explain that in ancient America, long prior to the Japanese conquest, individual ownership of property prevailed; every person was permitted to get as much as he was able, and to hold it as his own without regard to his needs, or whether he made any good use of it or not. By some plan of distribution not now understood even the habitable surface of the earth, with the minerals beneath, was parceled out among the favored few, and there was really no place except at sea where children of the others could lawfully be born. Upon a part of the dry land that he had been able to acquire, or had leased from another for the purpose, a man would build a house worth, say, ten thousand drusoes. (The ancient unit of value was the "dollar," but nothing is now known as to its actual worth.) Long before the building was complete the owner was beset by "touts" and "cappers" of the insurance game, who poured into his ears the most ingenious expositions of the advantages of betting that it would burn down—for with incredible fatuity the people of that time continued, generation after generation, to build inflammable habitations. The persons whom the capper represented—they called themselves an "insurance company"—stood ready to accept the bet, a fact which seems to have generated no suspicion in the mind of the house-owner. Theoretically, of course, if the house did burn, payment of the wager would partly or wholly recoup the winner of the bet for the loss of his house, but in fact the result of the transaction was commonly very different. For the privilege of betting that his property would be destroyed by fire, the owner had to pay to the gentleman betting that it would not be, a certain percentage of its value every year, called a "premium." The amount of this was determined by the company, which employed statisticians and actuaries to fix it at such a sum that, according to the law of probabilities, long before the house was "due to burn," the company would have received more than the value of it in premiums. In other words, the owner of the house would himself supply the money to pay his bet, and a good deal more.

But how, it may be asked, could the company's actuary know that the man's house would last until he had paid in more than its insured value in premiums—more, that is to say, than the company would have to pay back? He could not, but from his statistics he could know how many houses in ten thousand of that kind burned in their first year, how many in their second, their third, and so on. That was all that he needed to know, the house-owners knowing nothing about it. He fixed his rates according to the facts, and the occasional loss of a bet in an individual instance did not affect the certainty of a general winning. Like other professional gamblers, the company expected to lose sometimes, yet knew that in the long run it *must* win; which meant that in any special case it would *probably* win. With a thousand gambling games open to him in which the chances were equal, the infatuated dupe chose to "sit into" one where they were against him! Deceived by the cappers' fairy tales, dazed by the complex and incomprehensible "calculations" put forth for his undoing, and having ever in the ear of his imagination the crackle and roar of the impoverishing flames, he grasped at the hope of beating—in an unwelcome way, it is true—"the man that kept the table." He must have known for a certainty that if the company could afford to insure him, he

INSURANCE IN ANCIENT AMERICA

could not afford to let it. He must have known that the whole body of the insured paid to the insurers more than the insurers paid to them; otherwise the business could not have been conducted. This they cheerfully admitted; indeed, they proudly affirmed it. In fact, insurance companies were the only professional gamblers that had the incredible hardihood to parade their enormous winnings as an inducement to play against their game. These winnings ("assets," they called them) proved their ability, they said, to pay when they lost; and that was indubitably true. What they did not prove, unfortunately, was the *will* to pay, which, from the imperfect court records of the period that have come down to us, appears frequently to have been lacking. Gakler relates that in the instance of the city of San Farisco (somewhat doubtfully identified by Macronus as the modern fishing-village of Gharoo) the disinclination of the insurance companies to pay their bets had the most momentous consequences.

In the year 1906, as the ancients reckoned time, San Farisco was totally destroyed by fire. The conflagration was caused by the friction of a pig scratching itself against an angle of a wooden building. More than one hundred thousand persons perished, and the loss of property is estimated by Kobo-Dogarque at one and a half million drusoes. On more than two-thirds of this enormous sum the insurance companies had laid bets, and the greater part of it they refused to pay. In justification they pointed out that the deed performed by the pig was "an act of God," who in the analogous instance of the express companies had been specifically forbidden to take any action affecting the interests of parties to a contract, or the result of an agreed undertaking.

In the ensuing litigation their attorneys cited two notable precedents. Several years before the San Farisco disaster, another American city had experienced a similar one through the upsetting of a lamp by the kick of a cow. In that case, also, the insurance companies had successfully denied their liability on the ground that the cow, manifestly incited by some supernatural power, had unlawfully influenced the result of a wager to which she was a not a party. The companies defendant had contended that the recourse of the property-owners was against, not them, but the owner of the cow. In his decision sustaining that view and dismissing the case, a learned judge (afterward president of one of the defendant companies) had in the legal phraseology of the period pronounced the action of the cow an obvious and flagrant instance of "butting in." Kobo-Dogarque believes that this decision was afterward reversed by an appellate court of opposite political complexion and the companies were compelled to compromise, but of this there is no record. It is certain that in the San Farisco case the precedent was triumphantly urged.

Another precedent which the companies cited with a particular emphasis related to an unfortunate occurrence at a famous millionaires' club in London, the capital of the renowned king, Jon Bul. A gentleman passing in the street fell in a fit and was carried into the club in convulsions. Two members promptly made a bet upon his life. A physician who chanced to be present set to work upon the patient, when one of the members who had laid the wager came forward and restrained him, saying: "Sir, I beg that you will attend to your own business. I have my money on that fit."

Doubtless these two notable precedents did not constitute the entire case of the defendants in the San Farisco insurance litigation, but the additional arguments are lost to us. It is known only that after many years of bitter litigation public patience was exhausted and a comparatively trivial occurrence fired the combustible elements of popular indignation to a white heat in which the entire insurance business of the country was burned out of existence, together with all the gamblers who had invented and conducted it. The president of one of the defaulting companies was walking one morning in a street of the new San Farisco, when he had the bad luck to step on the tail of a dog and was bitten in retaliation. Frenzied by the pain of the wound he gave the creature a savage kick and it ran howling toward a group of idlers in front of a grocery store. In ancient America the dog was a sacred animal, worshiped by all sorts and conditions of tribesmen. The idlers at once raised a great cry and setting upon the offender beat him so that he died. Their act was infectious: men, women, and children trooped out of their dwellings by thousands to join them, brandishing whatever weapons they could snatch, and uttering wild cries of vengeance. This formidable mob overpowered the police, and marching from one insurance office to another, successively demolished them all, slew such officers as they could lay hands on, and chased the fugitive survivors into the sea, "where," says a quaint chronicle of the time, "they were eaten by their kindred, the sharks." The carnival of violence continued all the day, and at set of sun not one person connected with any form of insurance remained alive.

Ferocious and bloody as was the massacre, it was only the beginning. As the news of it went blazing and coruscating along the wires by which intelligence was then conveyed across the country, city after city caught the contagion. Everywhere, even in the small hamlets and the agricultural districts, the dupes rose against their dupers. The smouldering resentment of years burst into flame, and within a week all that was left of insurance in America was the record of a monstrous and cruel delusion written in the blood of its promoters.

Students of the history of those troublous times need not be told what other and bloodier events logically followed that awful reprisal, until the whole stupendous edifice of popular government, temple and citadel of all fallacies and abuses, crashed to ruin, and among its fallen columns and scattered stones gave shelter to a diminishing population of skulking anarchists, who finally vanished from history into a darkness impenetrable to conjecture.

It remains only to say in justice that of the many forms of gambling known of old as insurance, the kind called life insurance appears to have been most nearly a "square game." In essence it was the same as fire insurance, marine insurance, accident insurance, and so forth, with an added offensiveness in that it was a betting on human lives—commonly by the policy-holder on lives that should have been most sacred to him and all the more immune from any taint of traffic. But it seems to have a just claim to the second place in the scale of crime indicated in an epigram of the period: "The next worse thing to an insurance business dishonestly conducted is an insurance business conducted honestly." So far as we of to-day have knowledge of the matter, life insurance was conducted as honest gambling, as to both payment of bets and distribution of winnings. If accusations to the contrary were made they have not come down to us; the ink in which they were written has faded from the scroll of history. The only writer of antiquity who is known to have mentioned them at any considerable length is Tomlawson,[1] nicknamed, for some unknown reason, "the Bostonian," an author of great repute in that age, according to Ginkler. From certain fragments of the Bostonian's work that were extant in Ginkler's day, that acute historian inferred that life insurance was free from the base practices characterizing kindred forms of gambling, and that the care and investment of its profits were a trust honorably administered by those having them in custody—whom the elder author names. It is no small distinction to have been chosen by one's country's gods to instate in the seats of honor the philanthropists and benefactors worthy to sit in what the greatest and most original of our contemporary poets has called,

"The fierce light that beats upon a throne."[2]

Co 41, no. 5 (Sept. 1906): 555–57. Incorporated into "Ashes of the Beacon."

NOTES

AB obviously regarded property insurance not only as a form of gambling but also as a scam loaded unconscionably to the benefit of the company, and exacerbated by the fact that insurance companies often balked at paying the full amount of damages. The case of the destruction of much of San Francisco by fire after the devastating earthquake of 18 April 1906 was a particularly notorious instance of insurance companies resorting to litigation which few victims could afford. In this piece that AB links insurance to some of his other pet peeves: the legal system, popular government, and anarchists.

1. AB refers to Thomas W. Lawson (1857–1925), a banker and broker who attacked the banking and insurance industries in a series of papers published in *Everybody's Magazine* beginning in July 1904, entitled "Frenzied Finance" and signed "Thomas W. Lawson, of Boston." The papers were later gathered in the book *Frenzied Finance* (1905). See "The Views of One," *NYA* (22 Aug. 1905): 14; *E* (29 Aug. 1905): 16: "The effort to abolish frenzied finance by sending 'infernal machines' [bombs] to frenzied financiers is natural but futile. The victims of the method prefer it to Tom Lawson, but the disinterested public is a proponent of Things as They Are—and the greatest of these is Mr. Lawson."
2. Tennyson, *Idylls of the King* (1869–85), Dedication, l. 234 ("which" for "that" in Tennyson).

A BAFFLED AMBUSCADE

Connecting Readyville and Woodbury was a good, hard turnpike nine or ten miles long. Readyville was an outpost of the Federal army at Murfreesboro; Woodbury had the same relation to the Confederate army at Tullahoma.[1] For months after the big battle at Stone River these outposts were in constant quarrel, most of the trouble occurring, naturally, on the turnpike mentioned, between detachments of cavalry. Sometimes the infantry and artillery took a hand in the game by way of showing their good-will.

One night a squadron of Federal horse commanded by Major Siedel, a gallant and skillful officer, moved out from Readyville on an uncommonly hazardous enterprise requiring secrecy, caution and silence.

Passing the infantry pickets, the detachment soon afterward approached two cavalry videttes[2] staring hard into the darkness ahead. There should have been three.

"Where is your other man?" said the major. "I ordered Dunning to be here to-night."

"He rode forward, sir," the man replied. "There was a little firing afterward, but it was a long way to the front."

"It was against orders and against sense for Dunning to do that," said the officer, obviously vexed. "Why did he ride forward?"

"Don't know, sir; he seemed mighty restless. Guess he was skeered."

When this remarkable reasoner and his companion had been absorbed into the expeditionary force, it resumed its advance. Conversation was forbidden; arms and accouterments were denied the right to rattle. The horses' tramping was all that could be heard and the movement was slow in order to have as little as possible of that. It was after midnight and pretty dark, although there was a bit of moon somewhere behind the masses of cloud.

Two or three miles along, the head of the column approached a dense forest of cedars bordering the road on both sides. The major commanded a halt by merely halting, and, evidently himself a bit "skeered," rode on alone to reconnoiter. He was followed, however, by his adjutant and three troopers, who remained a little distance behind and, unseen by him, saw all that occurred.

After riding about a hundred yards toward the forest, the major suddenly and sharply reined in his horse and sat motionless in the saddle. Near the side of the road, in a little open space and hardly ten paces away, stood the figure of a man, dimly visible and as motionless as he. The major's first feeling was that of satisfaction in having left his cavalcade behind; if this were an enemy and should escape he would have little to report. The expedition was as yet undetected.

Some dark object was dimly discernible at the man's feet; the officer could not make it out. With the instinct of the true cavalryman and a particular indisposition to the discharge of firearms, he drew his saber. The man on foot made no movement in answer to the challenge. The situation was tense and a bit dramatic. Suddenly the moon burst through a rift in the clouds and, himself in the shadow of a group of great oaks, the horseman saw the footman clearly, in a patch of white light. It was Trooper Dunning, unarmed and bareheaded. The object at his feet resolved itself into a dead horse, and at a right angle across the animal's neck lay a dead man, face upward in the moonlight.

"Dunning has had the fight of his life," thought the major, and was about to ride forward. Dunning raised his hand, motioning him back with a gesture of warning; then, lowering the arm, he pointed to the place where the road lost itself in the blackness of the cedar forest.

The major understood, and turning his horse rode back to the little group that had followed him and was already moving to the rear in fear of his displeasure, and so returned to the head of his command.

"Dunning is just ahead there," he said to the captain of his leading company. "He has killed his man and will have something to report."

Right patiently they waited, sabers drawn, but Dunning did not come. In an hour the day broke and the whole force moved cautiously forward, its commander not altogether satisfied with his faith in Private Dunning. The expedition had failed, but something remained to be done.

In the little open space off the road they found the fallen horse. At a right angle across the animal's neck face upward, a bullet in the brain, lay the body of Trooper Dunning, stiff as a statue, hours dead.

Examination disclosed abundant evidence that within a half-hour the cedar forest had been occupied by a strong force of Confederate infantry—an ambuscade.

Co 42, no. 1 (Nov. 1906): 37–38 (under the heading "Soldiers and Ghosts"); *CW* 3.356–60.

A BAFFLED AMBUSCADE

NOTES

The Civil War never ceased to haunt AB, and his mind constantly reverted to it, reimagining scenes and scenarios with which he was familiar. The fierce battle of Stone (or Stone's or Stones) River had seared itself into his memory.

1. Murfreesboro, in Rutherford County in central Tennessee, was the site of the battle of Stone's River (31 December 1862–2 January 1863), in which AB took part (see *SS* 26–28). It resulted in a Federal victory, although at heavy cost in casualties. Readyville is a village about ten miles east of Murfreesboro, on the Woodbury Road; Woodbury is a town four miles east of Readyville. Tullahoma is a city in Coffee County, thirty miles south of Murfreesboro.

2. A vidette (or vedette) was a mounted sentinel posted on the periphery of a military position.

TWO MILITARY EXECUTIONS

In the spring of the year 1862 General Buell's big army lay in camp, licking itself into shape for the campaign which resulted in the victory at Shiloh.[1] It was a raw, untrained army, although some of its fractions had seen hard enough service, with a good deal of fighting, in the mountains of Western Virginia, and in Kentucky. The war was young and soldiering a new industry, imperfectly understood by the young American of the period, who found some features of it not altogether to his liking. Chief among these was that essential part of discipline, subordination. To one imbued from infancy with the fascinating fallacy that all men are born equal,[2] unquestioning submission to authority is not easily mastered, and the American volunteer soldier in his "green and salad days"[3] is among the worst known. That is how it happened that one of Buell's men, Private Bennett Story Greene, committed the indiscretion of striking his officer. Later in the war he would not have done that; like Sir Andrew Aguecheek, he would have "seen him damned" first.[4] But time for reformation of his military manners was denied him: he was promptly arrested on complaint of the officer, tried by court-martial and sentenced to be shot.

"You might have thrashed me and let it go at that," said the condemned man to the complaining witness; "that is what you used to do at school, when you were plain Will Dudley and I was as good as you. Nobody saw me strike you; discipline would not have suffered much."

"Ben Greene, I guess you are right about that," said the lieutenant. "Will you forgive me? That is what I came to see you about."

There was no reply, and an officer putting his head in at the door of the guard-tent where the conversation had occurred, explained that the time allowed for the interview had expired. The next morning, when in the presence of the whole brigade Private

Greene was shot to death by a squad of his comrades, Lieutenant Dudley turned his back upon the sorry performance and muttered a prayer for mercy, in which himself was included.

A few weeks afterward, as Buell's leading division was being ferried over the Tennessee River to assist in succoring Grant's beaten army, night was coming on, black and stormy. Through the wreck of battle the division moved, inch by inch, in the direction of the enemy, who had withdrawn a little to reform his lines. But for the lightning the darkness was absolute. Never for a moment did it cease, and ever when the thunder did not crack and roar were heard the moans of the wounded among whom the men felt their way with their feet, and upon whom they stumbled in the gloom. The dead were there, too—there were dead a-plenty.

In the first faint gray of the morning, when the swarming advance had paused to resume something of definition as a line-of-battle, and skirmishers had been thrown forward, word was passed along to call the roll. The first sergeant of Lieutenant Dudley's company stepped to the front and began to name the men in alphabetical order. He had no written roll, but a good memory. The men answered to their names as he ran down the alphabet to G.

"Gorham."

"Here!"

"Grayrock."[5]

"Here!"

The sergeant's good memory was affected by habit:

"Greene."

"Here!"

The response was clear, distinct, unmistakable!

A sudden movement, an agitation of the entire company front, as from an electric shock, attested the startling character of the incident. The sergeant paled and paused. The captain strode quickly to his side and said sharply:

"Call that name again."

Apparently the Society for Psychical Research[6] is not first in the field of curiosity concerning the Unknown.

"Bennett Greene."

"Here!"

All faces turned in the direction of the familiar voice; the two men between whom in the order of stature Greene had commonly stood in line turned and squarely confronted each other.

"Once more," commanded the inexorable investigator, and once more came—a trifle tremulously—the name of the dead man:

"Bennett Story Greene."

TWO MILITARY EXECUTIONS

"Here!"

At that instant a single rifle-shot was heard, away to the front, beyond the skirmish-line, followed, almost attended, by the savage hiss of an approaching bullet which, passing through the line, struck audibly, punctuating as with a full stop the captain's exclamation, "What the devil does it mean?"

Lieutenant Dudley pushed through the ranks from his place in the rear.

"It means this," he said, throwing open his coat and displaying a visibly broadening stain of crimson on his breast. His knees gave way; he fell awkwardly and lay dead.

A little later the regiment was ordered out of line to relieve the congested front, and through some misplay in the game of battle was not again under fire. Nor did Bennett Greene, expert in military executions, ever again signify his presence at one.

Co 42, no. 1 (Nov. 1906): 37–40 (under the heading "Soldiers and Ghosts"); *CW* 3.361–65.

NOTES

A sensational story, appropriate to its general heading of "Soldiers and Ghosts."

1. A variation of *Antony and Cleopatra*, 1.5.72–73: "My salad days, / When I was green in judgment."
2. Cf. "The Ashes of the Beacon": "They felt that words and phrases had some talismanic power, and charmed themselves asleep by repeating 'liberty,' 'all men equal before the law,' 'dictates of conscience,' 'free speech' and all manner of such incantation to exorcise the spirits of the night" (p. 1063).
3. See "One of the Missing," p. 534 note 4.
4. Sir Andrew Aguecheek, a character in Shakespeare's *Twelfth Night*, is known for his desire to please but frustrated by his intellectual limitations. The phrase "see him damn'd" occurs at 3.4.285.
5. A Private Grayrock is the protagonist of "The Mocking-Bird" (p. 790).
6. For the Society for Psychical Research, see "Behind the Veil," p. 605 note 2. Also "Ambrose Bierce Says: Not All Men Desire Immortality," *NYJ* (25 Apr. 1901): 14; *E* (26 June 1901): 14: "So, then, we are to have statistics showing the proportion of living persons who wish to continue living after the little formality of death. That, I take it, is the meaning of the action taken by the Society for Psychical Research in sending out 'circular letters' asking all manner of persons to signify their wish in the matter of immortality."

THE MOONLIT ROAD

I

STATEMENT OF JOEL HETMAN, JR.

I am the most unfortunate of men. Rich, respected, fairly well educated and of sound health—with many other advantages usually valued by those having them and coveted by those who have them not—I sometimes think that I should be less unhappy if they had been denied me, for then the contrast between my outer and my inner life would not be continually demanding a painful attention. In the stress of privation and the need of effort I might sometimes forget the somber secret ever baffling the conjecture that it compels.

I am the only child of Joel and Julia Hetman. The one was a well-to-do country gentleman, the other a beautiful and accomplished woman to whom he was passionately attached with what I now know to have been a jealous and exacting devotion. The family home was a few miles from Nashville, Tennessee, a large, irregularly built dwelling of no particular order of architecture, a little way off the road, in a park of trees and shrubbery.

At the time of which I write I was nineteen years old, a student at Yale. One day I received a telegram from my father of such urgency that in compliance with its unexplained demand I left at once for home. At the railway station in Nashville a distant relative awaited me to apprise me of the reason for my recall: my mother had been barbarously murdered—why and by whom none could conjecture, but the circumstances were these:

My father had gone to Nashville, intending to return the next afternoon. Something prevented his accomplishing the business in hand, so he returned on the same night, arriving just before the dawn. In his testimony before the coroner he explained that having no latchkey and not caring to disturb the sleeping servants, he had, with no clearly defined intention, gone round to the rear of the house. As he turned an angle of the building, he heard a sound as of a door gently closed, and saw in the darkness, indistinctly, the figure of a man, which instantly disappeared among the trees of the lawn. A hasty pursuit and brief search of the grounds in the belief that the trespasser was some one secretly visiting a servant proving fruitless, he entered at the unlocked door and mounted the stairs to my mother's chamber. Its door was open, and stepping into black darkness he fell headlong over some heavy object on the floor. I may spare myself the details; it was my poor mother, dead of strangulation by human hands!

Nothing had been taken from the house, the servants had heard no sound, and excepting those terrible finger-marks upon the dead woman's throat—dear God! that I might forget them!—no trace of the assassin was ever found.

I gave up my studies and remained with my father, who, naturally, was greatly changed. Always of a sedate, taciturn disposition, he now fell into so deep a dejection that nothing could hold his attention, yet anything—a footfall, the sudden closing of a door—aroused in him a fitful interest; one might have called it an apprehension. At any small surprise of the senses he would start visibly and sometimes turn pale, then relapse into a melancholy apathy deeper than before. I suppose he was what is called a "nervous wreck." As to me, I was younger then than now—there is much in that. Youth is Gilead, in which is balm for every wound.[1] Ah, that I might again dwell in that enchanted land! Unacquainted with grief,[2] I knew not how to appraise my bereavement; I could not rightly estimate the strength of the stroke.

One night, a few months after the dreadful event, my father and I walked home from the city. The full moon was about three hours above the eastern horizon; the entire countryside had the solemn stillness of a summer night; our footfalls and the ceaseless song of the katydids were the only sounds aloof. Black shadows of bordering trees lay athwart the road, which, in the short reaches between, gleamed a ghostly white. As we approached the gate to our dwelling, whose front was in shadow, and in which no light shone, my father suddenly stopped and clutched my arm, saying, hardly above his breath:

"God! God! what is that?"

"I hear nothing," I replied.

"But see—see!" he said, pointing along the road, directly ahead.

I said: "Nothing is there. Come, father, let us go in—you are ill."

He had released my arm and was standing rigid and motionless in the center of the illuminated roadway, staring like one bereft of sense. His face in the moonlight showed a pallor and fixity inexpressibly distressing. I pulled gently at his sleeve, but he had forgotten my existence. Presently he began to retire backward, step by step, never for an instant removing his eyes from what he saw, or thought he saw. I turned half round to follow, but stood irresolute. I do not recall any feeling of fear, unless a sudden chill was its physical manifestation. It seemed as if an icy wind had touched my face and enfolded my body from head to foot; I could feel the stir of it in my hair.

THE MOONLIT ROAD

At that moment my attention was drawn to a light that suddenly streamed from an upper window of the house: one of the servants, awakened by what mysterious premonition of evil who can say, and in obedience to an impulse that she was never able to name, had lit a lamp. When I turned to look for my father he was gone, and in all the years that have passed no whisper of his fate has come across the borderland of conjecture from the realm of the unknown.[3]

II
STATEMENT OF CASPAR GRATTAN

To-day I am said to live; to-morrow, here in this room, will lie a senseless shape of clay that all too long was I. If any one lift the cloth from the face of that unpleasant thing it will be in gratification of a mere morbid curiosity. Some, doubtless, will go further and inquire, "Who was he?" In this writing I supply the only answer that I am able to make—Caspar Grattan. Surely, that should be enough. The name has served my small need for more than twenty years of a life of unknown length. True, I gave it to myself, but lacking another I had the right. In this world one must have a name; it prevents confusion, even when it does not establish identity. Some, though, are known by numbers, which also seem inadequate distinctions.

One day, for illustration, I was passing along a street of a city, far from here, when I met two men in uniform, one of whom, half pausing and looking curiously into my face, said to his companion, "That man looks like 767." Something in the number seemed familiar and horrible. Moved by an uncontrollable impulse, I sprang into a side street and ran until I fell exhausted in a country lane.

I have never forgotten that number, and always it comes to memory attended by gibbering obscenity, peals of joyless laughter, the clang of iron doors. So I say a name, even if self-bestowed, is better than a number. In the register of the potter's field I shall soon have both. What wealth!

Of him who shall find this paper I must beg a little consideration. It is not the history of my life; the knowledge to write that is denied me. This is only a record of broken and apparently unrelated memories, some of them as distinct and sequent as brilliant beads upon a thread, others remote and strange, having the character of crimson dreams with interspaces blank and black—witch-fires glowing still and red in a great desolation.

Standing upon the shore of eternity, I turn for a last look landward over the course by which I came. There are twenty years of footprints fairly distinct, the impressions of bleeding feet. They lead through poverty and pain, devious and unsure, as of one staggering beneath a burden—

Remote, unfriended, melancholy, slow.[4]

Ah, the poet's prophecy of Me—how admirable, how dreadfully admirable!

Backward beyond the beginning of this *via dolorosa*[5]—this epic of suffering with episodes of sin—I see nothing clearly; it comes out of a cloud. I know that it spans only twenty years, yet I am an old man.

One does not remember one's birth—one has to be told. But with me it was different; life came to me full-handed and dowered me with all my faculties and powers. Of a previous existence I know no more than others, for all have stammering intimations that may be memories and may be dreams. I know only that my first consciousness was of maturity in body and mind—a consciousness accepted without surprise or conjecture. I merely found myself walking in a forest, half-clad, footsore, unutterably weary and hungry. Seeing a farm-house, I approached and asked for food, which was given me by one who inquired my name. I did not know, yet knew that all had names. Greatly embarrassed, I retreated, and night coming on, lay down in the forest and slept.

The next day I entered a large town which I shall not name. Nor shall I recount further incidents of the life that is now to end—a life of wandering, always and everywhere haunted by an overmastering sense of crime in punishment of wrong and of terror in punishment of crime. Let me see if I can reduce it to narrative.

I seem once to have lived near a great city, a prosperous planter, married to a woman whom I loved and distrusted. We had, it sometimes seems, one child, a youth of brilliant parts and promise. He is at all times a vague figure, never clearly drawn, frequently altogether out of the picture.

One luckless evening it occurred to me to test my wife's fidelity in a vulgar, commonplace way familiar to every one who has acquaintance with the literature of fact and fiction. I went to the city, telling my wife that I should be absent until the following afternoon. But I returned before daybreak and went to the rear of the house, purposing to enter by a door with which I had secretly so tampered that it would seem to lock, yet not actually fasten. As I approached it, I heard it gently open and close, and saw a man steal away into the darkness. With murder in my heart, I sprang after him, but he had vanished without even the bad luck of identification. Sometimes now I cannot even persuade myself that it was a human being.

Crazed with jealousy and rage, blind and bestial with all the elemental passions of insulted manhood, I entered the house and sprang up the stairs to the door of my wife's chamber. It was closed, but having tampered with its lock also, I easily entered and despite the black darkness soon stood by the side of her bed. My groping hands told me that although disarranged it was unoccupied.

"She is below," I thought, "and terrified by my entrance has evaded me in the darkness of the hall."

With the purpose of seeking her I turned to leave the room, but took a wrong direction—the right one! My foot struck her, cowering in a corner of the room. Instantly my hands were at her throat, stifling a shriek, my knees were upon her struggling body; and there in the darkness, without a word of accusation or reproach, I strangled her till she died!

There ends the dream. I have related it in the past tense, but the present would be the fitter form, for again and again the somber tragedy reenacts itself in my consciousness—over and over I lay the plan, I suffer the confirmation, I redress the wrong. Then all is blank; and afterward the rains beat against the grimy window-panes, or the snows fall upon my scant attire, the wheels rattle in the squalid streets where my life lies in poverty and mean employment. If there is ever sunshine I do not recall it; if there are birds they do not sing.

There is another dream, another vision of the night. I stand among the shadows in a moonlit road. I am aware of another presence, but whose I cannot rightly determine. In the shadow of a great dwelling I catch the gleam of white garments; then the figure of a woman confronts me in the road—my murdered wife! There is death in the face; there are marks upon the throat. The eyes are fixed on mine with an infinite gravity which is not reproach, nor hate, nor menace, nor anything less terrible than recognition. Before this awful apparition I retreat in terror—a terror that is upon me as I write. I can no longer rightly shape the words. See! they—

Now I am calm, but truly there is no more to tell: the incident ends where it began—in darkness and in doubt.

Yes, I am again in control of myself: "the captain of my soul."[6] But that is not respite; it is another stage and phase of expiation. My penance, constant in degree, is mutable in kind: one of its variants is tranquility. After all, it is only a life-sentence. "To Hell for life"—that is a foolish penalty: the culprit chooses the duration of his punishment. To-day my term expires.

To each and all, the peace that was not mine.

III
STATEMENT OF THE LATE JULIA HETMAN, THROUGH THE MEDIUM BAYROLLES[7]

I had retired early and fallen almost immediately into a peaceful sleep, from which I awoke with that indefinable sense of peril which is, I think, a common experience in that other, earlier life. Of its unmeaning character, too, I was entirely persuaded, yet that did not banish it. My husband, Joel Hetman, was away from home; the servants slept in another part of the house. But these were familiar conditions; they had never before distressed me. Nevertheless, the strange terror grew so insupportable that conquering my reluctance to move I sat up and lit the lamp at my bedside. Contrary to my expectation this gave me no relief; the light seemed rather an added danger, for I reflected that it would shine out under the door, disclosing my presence to whatever evil thing might lurk outside. You that are still in the flesh, subject to horrors of the imagination, think what a monstrous fear that must be which seeks in darkness security from malevolent existences of the night. That is to spring to close quarters with an unseen enemy—the strategy of despair!

Extinguishing the lamp I pulled the bedclothing about my head and lay trembling and silent, unable to shriek, forgetful to pray. In this pitiable state I must have lain for what you call hours—with us there are no hours, there is no time.

At last it came—a soft, irregular sound of footfalls on the stairs! They were slow, hesitant, uncertain, as of something that did not see its way; to my disordered reason all the more terrifying for that, as the approach of some blind and mindless malevolence to which is no appeal. I even thought that I must have left the hall lamp burning and the groping of this creature proved it a monster of the night. This was foolish and inconsistent with my previous dread of the light, but what would you have? Fear has no brains; it is an idiot. The dismal witness that it bears and the cowardly counsel that it whispers are unrelated. We know this well, we who have passed into the Realm of Terror, who skulk in eternal dusk among the scenes of our former lives, invisible even to ourselves and one another, yet hiding forlorn in lonely places; yearning for speech with our loved ones, yet dumb, and as fearful of them as they of us. Sometimes the disability is removed, the law suspended: by the deathless power of love or hate we break the spell—we are seen by those whom we would warn, console or punish. What form we seem to them to bear we know not; we know only that we terrify even those whom we most wish to comfort, and from whom we most crave tenderness and sympathy.

Forgive, I pray you, this inconsequent digression by what was once a woman. You who consult us in this imperfect way—you do not understand. You ask foolish questions about things unknown and things forbidden. Much that we know and could impart in our speech is meaningless in yours. We must communicate with you through a stammering intelligence in that small fraction of our language that you yourselves can speak. You think that we are of another world. No, we have knowledge of no world but yours, though for us it holds no sunlight, no warmth, no music, no laughter, no song of birds, nor any companionship. O God! what a thing it is to be a ghost, cowering and shivering in an altered world, a prey to apprehension and despair!

No, I did not die of fright: the Thing turned and went away. I heard it go down the stairs, hurriedly, I thought, as if itself in sudden fear. Then I rose to call for help. Hardly had my shaking hand found the door-knob when—merciful Heaven!—I heard it returning. Its footfalls as it remounted the stairs were rapid, heavy and loud; they shook the house. I fled to an angle of the wall and crouched upon the floor. I tried to pray. I tried to call the name of my dear husband. Then I heard the door thrown open. There was an interval of unconsciousness, and when I revived I felt a strangling clutch upon my throat—felt my arms feebly beating against something that bore me backward—felt my tongue thrusting itself from between my teeth! And then I passed into this life.

THE MOONLIT ROAD

No, I have no knowledge of what it was. The sum of what we knew at death is the measure of what we know afterward of all that went before. Of this existence we know many things, but no new light falls upon any page of that; in memory is written all of it that we can read. Here are no heights of truth overlooking the confused landscape of that dubitable domain. We still dwell in the Valley of the Shadow,[8] lurk in its desolate places, peering from brambles and thickets at its mad, malign inhabitants. How should we have new knowledge of that fading past?

What I am about to relate happened on a night. We know when it is night, for then you retire to your houses and we can venture from our places of concealment to move unafraid about our old homes, to look in at the windows, even to enter and gaze upon your faces as you sleep. I had lingered long near the dwelling where I had been so cruelly changed to what I am, as we do while any that we love or hate remain. Vainly I had sought some method of manifestation, some way to make my continued existence and my great love and poignant pity understood by my husband and son. Always if they slept they would wake, or if in my desperation I dared approach them when they were awake, would turn toward me the terrible eyes of the living, frightening me by the glances that I sought from the purpose that I held.

On this night I had searched for them without success, fearing to find them; they were nowhere in the house, nor about the moonlit dawn. For, although the sun is lost to us forever, the moon, full-orbed or slender, remains to us. Sometimes it shines by night, sometimes by day, but always it rises and sets, as in that other life.

I left the lawn and moved in the white light and silence along the road, aimless and sorrowing. Suddenly I heard the voice of my poor husband in exclamations of astonishment, with that of my son in reassurance and dissuasion; and there by the shadow of a group of trees they stood—near, so near! Their faces were toward me, the eyes of the elder man fixed upon mine. He saw me—at last, at last, he saw me! In the consciousness of that, my terror fled as a cruel dream. The death-spell was broken: Love had conquered Law! Mad with exultation I shouted—I *must* have shouted, "He sees, he sees: he will understand!" Then, controlling myself, I moved forward, smiling and consciously beautiful, to offer myself to his arms, to comfort him with endearments, and, with my son's hand in mine, to speak words that should restore the broken bonds between the living and the dead.

Alas! alas! his face went white with fear, his eyes were as those of a hunted animal. He backed away from me, as I advanced, and at last turned and fled into the wood—whither, it is not given to me to know.

To my poor boy, left doubly desolate, I have never been able to impart a sense of my presence. Soon he, too, must pass to this Life Invisible and be lost to me forever.

Co 42, no. 3 (Jan. 1907): 334–39; *CW* 3.62–80.

THE MOONLIT ROAD

Unlike most of AB's supernatural stories, this one goes beyond inexplicable happenings and uncanny coincidences to a thoughtful contemplation of the existence of spirits. As such, it shows AB in the last decade of his life giving serious attention to a subject he had only indulged himself with earlier.

1. Cf. Jer. 8:22: "Is there no balm in Gilead . . . ?"
2. Cf. Isa. 53.3: "He is despised and rejected of men; a man of sorrows, and acquainted with grief."
3. Cf. "The Mocking-Bird": "beyond which lay the Realm of Conjecture" (p. 793).
4. Oliver Goldsmith (1728–74), *The Traveller* (1764), l. 1.
5. The Path of Sorrow (literally, "sad road"), the street along which Jesus is said to have carried his cross.
6. William Ernest Henley (1849–1903), "Invictus" (1875), l. 16.
7. First mentioned in "An Inhabitant of Carcosa" (p. 457).
8. From Ps. 23:4.

THE MOONLIT ROAD

AN EXECUTION IN BATRUGIA

In the year 1892 (said the Returned Traveler), while on a voyage to Polati, I had the misfortune to disagree with the crew as to the expediency of killing the captain and his officers, taking possession of the ship and setting up as pirates. As a result of this inharmony I was marooned on the island of Batrugia, whose capital, Ogamwee,[1] is the most ancient city in the world. With my remarkable adventures in reaching it my countrymen are already familiar; it suffices here to say that the king received me with gracious hospitality, quartered me in the palace of his prime minister, gave me for wives the three daughters of his lord chamberlain and provided me with an ample income from the public revenues. Within a year I had made a fair acquaintance with the Batrugian language, and was appointed royal interpreter, with a princely salary, although no one speaking any other tongue, myself excepted, had ever been seen in the kingdom.

One day I heard a great tumult in the street, and going to a window saw, in a public square opposite, a crowd of persons surrounding some high officials who were engaged in cutting off a man's head. Just before the executioner delivered the fatal stroke, the victim was asked if he had anything to say. He explained with earnestness that the deed for which he was about to suffer had been inspired and commanded by a brass-headed cow and four bushels of nightingales' eggs.

"Hold! hold!" I shouted in Batrugian, leaping from the window and forcing a way through the throng; "the man is obviously insane!"

"Friend of my sovereign," said an aged man in a long blue robe, gently restraining me, "it is not proper for you to interrupt these high proceedings with irrelevant remarks. The luckless gentleman who, in accordance with my will as lord chief justice, has just had the unhappiness to part with his head was so inconsiderate as to take the life of a fellow-subject."

"But he was insane," I persisted, "clearly and indisputably *ptig nupy uggydug!*"—a phrase imperfectly translatable, meaning, as near as may be, having flittermice in his campanile.

Seating himself on the ground and carrying the great toe of his right foot to his ear (the Batrugian posture of interrogation), the great jurist said, "Am I to infer that in your own honorable country a person accused of murder is permitted to plead insanity as a reason why he should not be put to death?"

"Yes, illustrious one," I replied, respectfully spitting, "we regard that as a good defense."

"Well," said he slowly, but with extreme emphasis, "I'll be *Gook swottled!*"

(*"Gook,"* I may explain, is the name of the Batrugian chief deity; but for the verb "to swottle" the English tongue has no equivalent. It seems to signify the deepest disapproval, and by a promise to be *"swottled"* a Batrugian denotes acute astonishment.)

"Surely," I said, "so wise and learned person as you cannot think it just to punish with death one who does not know right from wrong. The gentleman who has just now renounced his future believed himself to have been commanded to do what he did by a brass-headed cow and four bushels of nightingales' eggs—powers to which he acknowledged a spiritual allegiance. To have disobeyed would have been, from his point of view, an infraction of a law higher than that of man."

"Honorable but erring stranger," replied the famous jurist, shaking his fist beneath my nose with deferential civility, "if we permitted the prisoner in a murder trial to urge such a consideration as that—if our laws recognized any other justification than that he believed himself in peril of immediate death or great bodily injury—nearly all assassins would make some such defense. They would plead insanity of some kind and degree, and it would be almost impossible to establish their guilt. Murder trials would be expensive and almost interminable, defiled with perjury and sentiment. Juries would be deluded and confused, justice baffled and red-handed mankillers turned loose to repeat their crimes and laugh at the law. Even as the law is, in a population of only one hundred million we have had no fewer than three homicides in less than twenty years. With such statutes and customs as yours we should have had at least twice as many. Believe me, I know my people; they have not the American respect for human life."

As blushing is deemed in Batrugia a sign of pride, I turned my back upon the speaker—an act which, fortunately, signifies a desire to hear more.

"The law," he continued, "is for the good of the greatest number. The execution of an actual lunatic now and then is not an evil to the community, nor, when rightly considered, to the lunatic himself. He is better off when dead, and society is profited by his removal. We are spared the cost of exposing imposture, the humiliation of acquitting the guilty, the peril of their freedom, the contagion of their evil example."

"In my country," I said, "we have a saying to the effect that it is better that ninety-nine guilty escape than that one innocent be punished."

AN EXECUTION IN BATRUGIA

"It is better," said he, "for the ninety-nine guilty, but distinctly worse for the community. Sir," he concluded with chilling austerity, "I infer from their proverb that your countrymen are the most offensive blockheads in existence."

By way of refutation I mentioned the English, and indignantly withdrew from the island.

Co 43, no. 1 (May 1907): 96–97 (under the heading "Small Contributions"). Later incorporated into "The Land Beyond the Blow."

NOTES

The use of the insanity plea as a defense in cases of murder gained in popularity in American law during the latter part of the nineteenth century. Mark Twain, as well as AB, openly ridiculed its increased employment. The rate of three homicides in twenty years is, of course, incredibly low, but is meant to embarrass American society, whose equivalent rate astronomically exceeded the supposed Batrugian one.

1. Probably a modification of Otamwee (see "The Kingdom of Tortirra," p. 576 note 4). See also Otumwee in "Oil of Dog" (p. 756).

THE OTHER LODGERS

"In order to take that train," said Colonel Levering, sitting in the Waldorf-Astoria hotel,[1] "you will have to remain nearly all night in Atlanta. That is a fine city, but I advise you not to put up at the Breathitt House, one of the principal hotels. It is an old wooden building in urgent need of repairs. There are breaches in the walls that you could throw a cat through. The bedrooms have no locks on the doors, no furniture but a single chair in each, and a bedstead without bedding—just a mattress. Even these meager accommodations you cannot be sure that you will have in monopoly; you must take your chance of being stowed in with a lot of others. Sir, it is a most abominable hotel.

"The night that I passed in it was an uncomfortable night. I got in late and was shown to my room on the ground floor by an apologetic night-clerk with a tallow candle, which he considerately left with me. I was worn out by two days and a night of hard railway travel and had not entirely recovered from a gunshot wound in the head, received in an altercation. Rather than look for better quarters I lay down on the mattress without removing my clothing and fell asleep.

"Along toward morning I awoke. The moon had risen and was shining in at the uncurtained window, illuminating the room with a soft, bluish light which seemed, somehow, a bit spooky, though I dare say it had no uncommon quality; all moonlight is that way if you will observe it. Imagine my surprise and indignation when I saw the floor occupied by at least a dozen other lodgers! I sat up, earnestly damning the management of that unthinkable hotel, and was about to spring from the bed to go and make trouble for the night-clerk—him of the apologetic manner and the tallow candle—when something in the situation affected me with a strange indisposition to move. I suppose I was what a story-writer might call 'frozen with terror.' For those men were obviously all dead!

"They lay on their backs, disposed orderly along three sides of the room, their feet to the walls—against the other wall, farthest from the door, stood my bed and the chair.

All the faces were covered, but under their white cloths the features of the two bodies that lay in the square patch of moonlight near the window showed in sharp profile as to nose and chin.

"I thought this a bad dream and tried to cry out, as one does in a nightmare, but could make no sound. At last, with a desperate effort I threw my feet to the floor and passing between the two rows of clouted faces and the two bodies that lay nearest the door, I escaped from the infernal place and ran to the office. The night-clerk was there, behind the desk, sitting in the dim light of another tallow candle—just sitting and staring. He did not rise: my abrupt entrance produced no effect upon him, though I must have looked a veritable corpse myself. It occurred to me then that I had not before really observed the fellow. He was a little chap, with a colorless face and the whitest, blankest eyes I ever saw. He had no more expression than the back of my hand. His clothing was a dirty gray.

"'Damn you!' I said; 'what do you mean?'

"Just the same, I was shaking like a leaf in the wind and did not recognize my own voice.

"The night-clerk rose, bowed (apologetically) and—well, he was no longer there, and at that moment I felt a hand laid upon my shoulder from behind. Just fancy that if you can! Unspeakably frightened, I turned and saw a portly, kind-faced gentleman, who asked:

"'What is the matter, my friend?'

"I was not long in telling him, but before I made an end of it he went pale himself. 'See here,' he said, 'are you telling the truth?'

"I had now got myself in hand and terror had given place to indignation. 'If you dare to doubt it,' I said, 'I'll hammer the life out of you!'

"'No,' he replied, 'don't do that; just sit down till I tell you. This is not a hotel. It used to be; afterward it was a hospital. Now it is unoccupied, awaiting a tenant. The room that you mention was the dead-room—there were always plenty of dead. The fellow that you call the night-clerk used to be that, but later he booked the patients as they were brought in. I don't understand his being here. He has been dead a few weeks.'

"'And who are you?' I blurted out.

"'Oh, I look after the premises. I happened to be passing just now, and seeing a light in here came in to investigate. Let us have a look into that room,' he added, lifting the sputtering candle from the desk.

"'I'll see you at the devil first!' said I, bolting out of the door into the street.

"Sir, that Breathitt House, in Atlanta, is a beastly place! Don't you stop there."

"God forbid! Your account of it certainly does not suggest comfort. By the way, Colonel, when did all that occur?"

"In September, 1864—shortly after the siege."[2]

Co 43, no. 4 (Aug. 1907): 445–46; *CW* 3.400–404.

THE OTHER LODGERS

NOTES

Another memory of the Civil War, a psychological impression masked as a ghost story.

1. The Waldorf-Astoria Hotel in New York City originally consisted of two separate hotels built in 1893 and 1897 at Fifth Avenue between Thirty-third and Thirty-fourth streets. The complex was demolished in 1929 to make way for the Empire State Building. A new Waldorf-Astoria Hotel was built in 1931 between Park and Lexington Avenues between Forty-ninth and Fiftieth Streets.

2. The Atlanta Campaign, led by Gen. William T. Sherman, began on 1 May 1864 and ended on 2 September, when the Confederate Army of Tennessee filed out of the city and the Federals marched in.

BEYOND THE WALL

Many years ago, on my way from Hongkong to New York, I passed a week in San Francisco. A long time had gone by since I had been in that city, during which my ventures in the Orient had prospered beyond my hope; I was rich and could afford to revisit my own country to renew my friendship with such of the companions of my youth as still lived and remembered me with the old affection. Chief of these, I hoped, was Mohun Dampier, an old schoolmate with whom I had held a desultory correspondence which had long ceased, as is the way of correspondence between men. You may have observed that the indisposition to write a merely social letter is in the ratio of the square of the distance between you and your correspondent. It is a law.[1]

I remembered Dampier as a handsome, strong young fellow of scholarly tastes, with an aversion to work and a marked indifference to many of the things that the world cares for, including wealth, of which, however, he had inherited enough to put him beyond the reach of want. In his family, one of the oldest and most aristocratic in the country, it was, I think, a matter of pride that no member of it had ever been in trade nor politics, nor suffered any kind of distinction. Mohun was a trifle sentimental, and had in him a singular element of superstition, which led him to the study of all manner of occult subjects, although his sane mental health safeguarded him against fantastic and perilous faiths. He made daring incursions into the realm of the unreal without renouncing his residence in the partly surveyed and charted region of what we are pleased to call certitude.

The night of my visit to him was stormy. The Californian winter was on, and the incessant rain plashed in the deserted streets, or, lifted by irregular gusts of wind, was hurled against the houses with incredible fury. With no small difficulty my cabman found the right place, away out toward the ocean beach, in a sparsely populated suburb. The dwelling, a rather ugly one, apparently, stood in the center of its grounds, which as nearly as I could make out in the gloom were destitute of either flowers or grass. Three or four trees, writhing and moaning in the torment of the tempest, appeared to be trying to escape from their dismal environment and take the chance of finding a better one out at sea. The house was a two-story brick structure with a tower, a story higher, at one corner. In a window of that was the only visible light. Something in the appearance of the place made me shudder, a performance that may have been assisted by a rill of rain-water down my back as I scuttled to cover in the doorway.

In answer to my note apprising him of my wish to call, Dampier had written, "Don't ring—open the door and come up." I did so. The staircase was dimly lighted by a single gas-jet at the top of the second flight. I managed to reach the landing without disaster and entered by an open door into the lighted square room of the tower. Dampier came forward in gown and slippers to receive me, giving me the greeting that I wished, and if I had held a thought that it might more fitly have been accorded me at the front door the first look at him dispelled any sense of his inhospitality.

He was not the same. Hardly past middle age, he had gone gray and had acquired a pronounced stoop. His figure was thin and angular, his face deeply lined, his complexion dead-white, without a touch of color. His eyes, unnaturally large, glowed with a fire that was almost uncanny.

He seated me, proffered a cigar, and with grave and obvious sincerity assured me of the pleasure that it gave him to meet me. Some unimportant conversation followed, but all the while I was dominated by a melancholy sense of the great change in him. This he must have perceived, for he suddenly said with a bright enough smile, "You are disappointed in me—*non sum qualis eram.*"[2]

I hardly knew what to reply, but managed to say: "Why, really, I don't know: your Latin is about the same."

He brightened again. "No," he said, "being a dead language, it grows in appropriateness. But please have the patience to wait: where I am going there is perhaps a better tongue. Will you care to have a message in it?"

The smile faded as he spoke, and as he concluded he was looking into my eyes with a gravity that distressed me. Yet I would not surrender myself to his mood, nor permit him to see how deeply his prescience of death affected me.

"I fancy that it will be long," I said, "before human speech will cease to serve our need; and then the need, with its possibilities of service, will have passed."

He made no reply, and I too was silent, for the talk had taken a dispiriting turn, yet I knew not how to give it a more agreeable character. Suddenly, in a pause of the storm, when the dead silence was almost startling by contrast with the previous uproar, I heard a gentle tapping, which appeared to come from the wall behind my chair. The sound was such as might have been made by a human hand, not as upon a door by one asking admittance, but rather, I thought, as an agreed signal, an assurance of some one's presence in an adjoining room; most of us, I fancy, have had more experience of such communications than we should care to relate. I glanced at Dampier. If possibly there was something of amusement in the look he did not observe it. He appeared to have forgotten my presence, and was staring at the wall behind me with an expression in his eyes that I am unable to name, although my memory of it is as vivid to-day as was my sense of it then. The situation was embarrassing; I rose to take my leave. At this he seemed to recover himself.

"Please be seated," he said; "it is nothing—no one is there."

But the tapping was repeated, and with the same gentle, slow insistence as before.

"Pardon me," I said, "it is late. May I call to-morrow?"

He smiled—a little mechanically, I thought. "It is very delicate of you," said he, "but quite needless. Really, this is the only room in the tower, and no one is there. At least—" He left the sentence incomplete, rose, and threw up a window, the only opening in the wall from which the sound seemed to come. "See."

Not clearly knowing what else to do I followed him to the window and looked out. A street-lamp some little distance away gave enough light through the murk of the rain that was again falling in torrents to make it entirely plain that "no one was there." In truth there was nothing but the sheer blank wall of the tower.

Dampier closed the window and signing me to my seat resumed his own.

The incident was not in itself particularly mysterious; any one of a dozen explanations was possible (though none has occurred to me), yet it impressed me strangely, the more, perhaps, from my friend's effort to reassure me, which seemed to dignify it with a certain significance and importance. He had proved that no one was there, but in that fact lay all the interest; and he proffered no explanation. His silence was irritating and made me resentful.

"My good friend," I said, somewhat ironically, I fear, "I am not disposed to question your right to harbor as many spooks as you find agreeable to your taste and consistent with your notions of companionship; that is no business of mine. But being just a plain man of affairs, mostly of this world, I find spooks needless to my peace and comfort. I am going to my hotel, where my fellow-guests are still in the flesh."

It was not a very civil speech, but he manifested no feeling about it. "Kindly remain," he said. "I am grateful for your presence here. What you have heard to-night I believe myself to have heard twice before. Now I *know* it was no illusion. That is much to me—more than you know. Have a fresh cigar and a good stock of patience while I tell you the story."

The rain was now falling more steadily, with a low, monotonous susurration, interrupted at long intervals by the sudden slashing of the boughs of the trees as the wind rose and failed. The night was well advanced, but both sympathy and curiosity held me a willing listener to my friend's monologue, which I did not interrupt by a single word from beginning to end.

"Ten years ago," he said, "I occupied a ground-floor apartment in one of a row of houses, all alike, away at the other end of the town, on what we call Rincon Hill.[3] This had been the best quarter of San Francisco, but had fallen into neglect and decay, partly because the primitive character of its domestic architecture no longer suited the

BEYOND THE WALL

maturing tastes of our wealthy citizens, partly because certain public improvements had made a wreck of it. The row of dwellings in one of which I lived stood a little way back from the street, each having a miniature garden, separated from its neighbors by low iron fences and bisected with mathematical precision by a box-bordered gravel walk from gate to door.

"One morning as I was leaving my lodging I observed a young girl entering the adjoining garden on the left. It was a warm day in June, and she was lightly gowned in white. From her shoulders hung a broad straw hat profusely decorated with flowers and wonderfully beribboned in the fashion of the time. My attention was not long held by the exquisite simplicity of her costume, for no one could look at her face and think of anything earthly. Do not fear; I shall not profane it by description; it was beautiful exceedingly. All that I had ever seen or dreamed of loveliness was in that matchless living picture by the hand of the Divine Artist. So deeply did it move me that, without a thought of the impropriety of the act, I unconsciously bared my head, as a devout Catholic or well-bred Protestant uncovers before an image of the Blessed Virgin. The maiden showed no displeasure; she merely turned her glorious dark eyes upon me with a look that made me catch my breath, and without other recognition of my act passed into the house. For a moment I stood motionless, hat in hand, painfully conscious of my rudeness, yet so dominated by the emotion inspired by that vision of incomparable beauty that my penitence was less poignant than it should have been. Then I went my way, leaving my heart behind. In the natural course of things I should probably have remained away until nightfall, but by the middle of the afternoon I was back in the little garden, affecting an interest in the few foolish flowers that I had never before observed. My hope was vain; she did not appear.

"To a night of unrest succeeded a day of expectation and disappointment,[4] but on the day after, as I wandered aimlessly about the neighborhood, I met her. Of course I did not repeat my folly of uncovering, nor venture by even so much as too long a look to manifest an interest in her; yet my heart was beating audibly. I trembled and consciously colored as she turned her big black eyes upon me with a look of obvious recognition entirely devoid of boldness or coquetry.

"I will not weary you with particulars; many times afterward I met the maiden, yet never either addressed her or sought to fix her attention. Nor did I take any action toward making her acquaintance. Perhaps my forbearance, requiring so supreme an effort of self-denial, will not be entirely clear to you. That I was heels over head in love is true, but who can overcome his habit of thought, or reconstruct his character?

"I was what some foolish persons are pleased to call, and others, more foolish, are pleased to be called—an aristocrat; and despite her beauty, her charms and graces, the girl was not of my class. I had learned her name—which it is needless to speak—and something of her family. She was an orphan, a dependent niece of the impossible elderly fat woman in whose lodging-house she lived. My income was small and I lacked the talent for marrying; it is perhaps a gift. An alliance with that family would condemn me to its manner of life, part me from my books and studies, and in a social sense reduce me to the ranks. It is easy to deprecate such considerations as these and I have not retained myself for the defense. Let judgment be entered against me, but in strict justice all my ancestors for generations should be made co-defendants and I be permitted to plead in mitigation of punishment the imperious mandate of heredity. To a mésalliance of that kind every globule of my ancestral blood spoke in opposition. In brief, my tastes, habits, instinct, with whatever of reason my love had left me—all fought against it. Moreover, I was an irreclaimable sentimentalist, and found a subtle charm in an impersonal and spiritual relation which acquaintance might vulgarize and marriage would certainly dispel. No woman, I argued, is what this lovely creature seems. Love is a delicious dream; why should I bring about my own awakening?

"The course dictated by all this sense and sentiment was obvious. Honor, pride, prudence, preservation of my ideals—all commanded me to go away, but for that I was too weak. The utmost that I could do by a mighty effort of will was to cease meeting the girl, and that I did. I even avoided the chance encounters of the garden, leaving my lodging only when I knew that she had gone to her music lessons, and returning after nightfall. Yet all the while I was as one in a trance, indulging the most fascinating fancies and ordering my entire intellectual life in accordance with my dream. Ah, my friend, as one whose actions have a traceable relation to reason, you cannot know the fool's paradise in which I lived.

"One evening the devil put it into my head to be an unspeakable idiot. By apparently careless and purposeless questioning I learned from my gossipy landlady that the young woman's bedroom adjoined my own, a party-wall[5] between. Yielding to a sudden and coarse impulse I gently rapped on the wall. There was no response, naturally, but I was in no mood to accept a rebuke. A madness was upon me and I repeated the folly, the offense, but again ineffectually, and I had the decency to desist.

"An hour later, while absorbed in some of my infernal studies, I heard, or thought I heard, my signal answered. Flinging down my books I sprang to the wall and as steadily as my beating heart would permit gave three slow taps upon it. This time the response was distinct, unmistakable: one, two, three—an exact repetition of my signal. That was all I could elicit, but it was enough—too much.

"The next evening, and for many evenings afterward, that folly went on, I always having 'the last word.' During the whole period I was deliriously happy, but with the perversity of my nature I persevered in my resolution not to see her. Then, as I should have expected, I got no further answers. 'She is disgusted,' I said to myself, 'with what she thinks my timidity in making no more definite advances'; and I resolved to seek her and make her acquaintance and—what? I did not know, nor do I now know, what might have come of it. I know only that I passed days and days trying to meet her, and all in vain; she was invisible as well as inaudible. I haunted the streets where we had met, but she did not come. From my window I watched the garden in front of her house, but she passed neither in nor out. I fell into the deepest dejection, believing that she had gone away, yet took no steps to resolve my doubt by inquiry of my landlady, to whom, indeed, I had taken an unconquerable aversion from her having once spoken of the girl with less of reverence than I thought befitting.

"There came a fateful night. Worn out with emotion, irresolution and despondency, I had retired early and fallen into such sleep as was still possible to me. In the middle of the night something—some malign power bent upon the wrecking of my peace forever—caused me to open my eyes and sit up, wide awake and listening intently for I knew not what. Then I thought I heard a faint tapping on the wall—the mere ghost of the familiar signal. In a few moments it was repeated: one, two, three—no louder than before, but addressing a sense alert and strained to receive it. I was about to reply when the Adversary of Peace again intervened in my affairs with a rascally suggestion of retaliation. She had long and cruelly ignored me; now I would ignore her. Incredible fatuity—may God forgive it! All the rest of the night I lay awake, fortifying my obstinacy with shameless justifications and—listening.

"Late the next morning, as I was leaving the house, I met my landlady, entering.

"'Good morning, Mr. Dampier,' she said. 'Have you heard the news?'

"I replied in words that I had heard no news; in manner, that I did not care to hear any. The manner escaped her observation.

"'About the sick young lady next door,' she babbled on. 'What! you did not know? Why, she has been ill for weeks. And now—'

"I almost sprang upon her. 'And now,' I cried, 'now what?'

"'She is dead.'

"That is not the whole story. In the middle of the night, as I learned later, the patient, awakening from a long stupor after a week of delirium, had asked—it was her last utterance—that her bed be moved to the opposite side of the room. Those in attendance had thought the request a vagary of her delirium, but had complied. And there the poor passing soul had exerted its failing will to restore a broken connection—a golden thread of sentiment between its innocence and a monstrous baseness owning a blind, brutal allegiance to the Law of Self.

"What reparation could I make? Are there masses that can be said for the repose of souls that are abroad such nights as this—spirits 'blown about by the viewless winds'[6]—coming in the storm and darkness with signs and portents, hints of memory and presages of doom?

"This is the third visitation. On the first occasion I was too skeptical to do more than verify by natural methods the character of the incident; on the second, I responded to the signal after it had been several times repeated, but without result. To-night's recurrence completes the 'fatal triad' expounded by Parapelius Necromantius. There is no more to tell."

BEYOND THE WALL

When Dampier had finished his story I could think of nothing relevant that I cared to say, and to question him would have been a hideous impertinence. I rose and bade him good night in a way to convey to him a sense of my sympathy, which he silently acknowledged by a pressure of the hand. That night, alone with his sorrow and remorse, he passed into the Unknown.

Co 44, no. 2 (Dec. 1907): 185–89; *CW* **3.210–26**.

NOTES

One of the very few tales in AB's canon that qualifies as a love story. Although somewhat melodramatic, it is rich in its hints of autobiographical insights, some of which might have been painful for AB to admit. Morris is probably right when he connects the story to AB's relationship with his former wife (*Ambrose Bierce: Alone in Bad Company*, 239). AB separated from Mollie in the late 1880s in a tragic misunderstanding and fit of pride. Like the young woman in the story, she was beautiful and black-eyed and attached to an "impossible, elderly fat" relative—her mother in real life. Mollie remained devoted to AB but filed for divorce in 1904 under the mistaken impression that he secretly wanted one, was granted it in 1905, and died several months later. Carey McWilliams reports that both the divorce and the death were a great shock to AB. Written in 1907, the story's protagonist Dampier is self-condemned for being too obsessed with his social class, family tradition, and pride to respond to love. In other respects, the tale is a recurrence to AB's characteristic themes of happiness as life's greatest good, and reason as an ambivalent virtue, but its conclusion hints at a transcendent spiritual dimension beyond earthly life and affirms that love is stronger than death.

1. "One's reluctance to write a letter increases in the ratio of the square of the distance it has to go. I don't know why that is so, but it is—at least in my case." AB to George Sterling (6 Dec. 1904, MS, NP).
2. "Non sum qualis eram bonae / sub regno Cinarae" (I am not the sort of person I used to be under the rule of the lovely Cinara). Horace, *Odes,* 4.1. See also Ernest Dowson (1867–1900), "Non Sum Qualis Eram Bonae Sub Regno Cynarae" (1896).
3. See "Killed at Resaca," p. 512 note 4.
4. Cf. "One Kind of Officer": "a night of discomfort succeeded a day of apprehension" (p. 834).
5. A "party-wall" is "a wall upon the line between the premises of adjoining owners, which each has the right to use as a support for his structure, and usually also to some extent for chimneys, water-pipes, etc." (*C*).
6. A misquotation of Shakespeare, *Measure for Measure,* 3.1.124–26: "To be imprisoned in the viewless winds / And blown with restless violence round about / The pendent world."

A RESUMED IDENTITY

THE REVIEW AS A FORM OF WELCOME

One summer night a man stood on a low hill overlooking a wide expanse of forest and field. By the full moon hanging low in the west he knew what he might not have known otherwise: that it was near the hour of dawn. A light mist lay along the earth, partly veiling the lower features of the landscape, but above it the taller trees showed in well-defined masses against a clear sky. Two or three farmhouses were visible through the haze, but in none of them, naturally, was a light. Nowhere, indeed, was any sign or suggestion of life except the barking of a distant dog, which, repeated with mechanical iteration, served rather to accentuate than dispel the loneliness of the scene.

The man looked curiously about him on all sides, as one who among familiar sur-roundings is unable to determine his exact place and part in the scheme of things. It is so, perhaps, that we shall act when, risen from the dead, we await the call to judgment.

A hundred yards away was a straight road, showing white in the moonlight. Endeavoring to orient himself, as a surveyor or navigator might say, the man moved his eyes slowly along its visible length and at a distance of a quarter-mile to the south of his station saw, dim and gray in the haze, a group of horsemen riding to the north. Behind them were men afoot, marching in column, with dimly gleaming rifles aslant above their shoulders. They moved slowly and in silence. Another group of horse-men, another regiment of infantry, another and another—all in unceasing motion toward the man's point of view, past it, and beyond. A battery of artillery followed, the cannoneers riding with folded arms on limber and caisson. And still the inter-minable procession came out of the obscurity to south and passed into the obscurity to north, with never a sound of voice, nor hoof, nor wheel.

The man could not rightly understand: he thought himself deaf; said so, and heard his own voice, although it had an unfamiliar quality that almost alarmed him;

it disappointed his ear's expectancy in the matter of *timbre* and resonance. But he was not deaf, and that for the moment sufficed.

Then he remembered that there are natural phenomena to which some one has given the name "acoustic shadows."[1] If you stand in an acoustic shadow there is one direction from which you will hear nothing. At the battle of Gaines's Mill,[2] one of the fiercest conflicts of the Civil War, with a hundred guns in play, spectators a mile and a half away on the opposite side of the Chickahominy valley heard nothing of what they clearly saw. The bombardment of Port Royal, heard and felt at St. Augustine, a hundred and fifty miles to the south, was inaudible two miles to the north in a still atmosphere.[3] A few days before the surrender at Appomattox a thunderous engagement between the commands of Sheridan and Pickett was unknown to the latter commander, a mile in the rear of his own line.[4]

These instances were not known to the man of whom we write, but less striking ones of the same character had not escaped his observation. He was profoundly disquieted, but for another reason than the uncanny silence of that moonlight march.

"Good Lord!" he said to himself—and again it was as if another had spoken his thought—"if those people are what I take them to be we have lost the battle and they are moving on Nashville!"

Then came a thought of self—an apprehension—a strong sense of personal peril, such as in another we call fear. He stepped quickly into the shadow of a tree. And still the silent battalions moved slowly forward in the haze.

The chill of a sudden breeze upon the back of his neck drew his attention to the quarter whence it came, and turning to the east he saw a faint gray light along the horizon—the first sign of returning day. This increased his apprehension.

"I must get away from here," he thought, "or I shall be discovered and taken."

He moved out of the shadow, walking rapidly toward the graying east. From the safer seclusion of a clump of cedars he looked back. The entire column had passed out of sight: the straight white road lay bare and desolate in the moonlight!

Puzzled before, he was now inexpressibly astonished. So swift a passing of so slow an army!—he could not comprehend it. Minute after minute passed unnoted; he had lost his sense of time. He sought with a terrible earnestness a solution of the mystery, but sought in vain. When at last he roused himself from his abstraction the sun's rim was visible above the hills, but in the new conditions he found no other light than that of day; his understanding was involved as darkly in doubt as before.

On every side lay cultivated fields showing no sign of war and war's ravages. From the chimneys of the farmhouses thin ascensions of blue smoke signaled preparations for a day's peaceful toil. Having stilled its immemorial allocution to the moon, the watch-dog was assisting a negro who, prefixing a team of mules to the plow, was flatting and sharping contentedly at his task. The hero of this tale stared stupidly at the pastoral picture as if he had never seen such a thing in all his life; then he put his hand to his head, passed it through his hair and, withdrawing it, attentively considered the palm—a singular thing to do. Apparently reassured by the act, he walked confidently toward the road.

II
WHEN YOU HAVE LOST YOUR LIFE CONSULT A PHYSICIAN

Dr. Stilling Malson, of Murfreesboro, having visited a patient six or seven miles away, on the Nashville road, had remained with him all night. At daybreak he set out for home on horseback, as was the custom of doctors of the time and region. He had passed into the neighborhood of Stone's River battlefield when a man approached him from the roadside and saluted in the military fashion, with a movement of the right hand to the hat-brim. But the hat was not a military hat, the man was not in uniform and had not a martial bearing. The doctor nodded civilly, half thinking that the stranger's uncommon greeting was perhaps in deference to the historic surroundings. As the stranger evidently desired speech with him he courteously reined in his horse and waited.

"Sir," said the stranger, "although a civilian, you are perhaps an enemy."

"I am a physician," was the non-committal reply.

"Thank you," said the other. "I am a lieutenant, of the staff of General Hazen."[5] He paused a moment and looked sharply at the person whom he was addressing, then added, "Of the Federal army."

The physician merely nodded.

"Kindly tell me," continued the other, "what has happened here. Where are the armies? Which has won the battle?"

The physician regarded his questioner curiously with half-shut eyes. After a professional scrutiny, prolonged to the limit of politeness, "Pardon me," he said; "one asking information should be willing to impart it. Are you wounded?" he added, smiling.

"Not seriously—it seems."

The man removed the unmilitary hat, put his hand to his head, passed it through his hair and, withdrawing it, attentively considered the palm.

"I was struck by a bullet and have been unconscious. It must have been a light, glancing blow: I find no blood and feel no pain. I will not trouble you for treatment, but will you kindly direct me to my command—to any part of the Federal army—if you know?"

Again the doctor did not immediately reply: he was recalling much that is recorded in the books of his profession—something about lost identity and the effect of familiar scenes in restoring it. At length he looked the man in the face, smiled and said:

"Lieutenant, you are not wearing the uniform of your rank and service."

At this the man glanced down at his civilian attire, lifted his eyes and said with hesitation:

"That is true. I—I don't quite understand."

Still regarding him sharply but not unsympathetically the man of science bluntly inquired:

"How old are you?"

"Twenty-three—if that has anything to do with it."

"You don't look it; I should hardly have guessed you to be just that."

The man was growing impatient. "We need not discuss that," he said: "I want to know about the army. Not two hours ago I saw a column of troops moving northward on this road. You must have met them. Be good enough to tell me the color of their clothing, which I was unable to make out, and I'll trouble you no more."

"You are quite sure that you saw them?"

"Sure? My God, sir, I could have counted them!"

"Why, really," said the physician, with an amusing consciousness of his own resemblance to the loquacious barber of the Arabian Nights,[6] "this is very interesting. I met no troops."

The man looked at him coldly, as if he had himself observed the likeness to the barber. "It is plain," he said, "that you do not care to assist me. Sir, you may go to the devil!"

He turned and strode away, very much at random, across the dewy fields, his half-penitent tormentor quietly watching him from his point of vantage in the saddle till he disappeared beyond an array of trees.

<h1 style="text-align:center">III
THE DANGER OF LOOKING
INTO A POOL OF WATER</h1>

After leaving the road the man slackened his pace, and now went forward, rather deviously, with a distinct feeling of fatigue. He could not account for this, though truly the interminable loquacity of that country doctor offered itself in explanation. Seating himself upon a rock, he laid one hand upon his knee, back upward, and casually looked at it. It was lean and withered. He lifted both hands to his face. It was seamed and furrowed; he could trace the lines with the tips of his fingers. How strange!—a mere bullet-stroke and a brief unconsciousness should not make one a physical wreck.

"I must have been a long time in hospital," he said aloud. "Why, what a fool I am! The battle was in December, and it is now summer!" He laughed. "No wonder that fellow thought me an escaped lunatic. He was wrong: I am only an escaped patient."

At a little distance a small plot of ground enclosed by a stone wall caught his attention. With no very definite intent he rose and went to it. In the center was a square, solid monument of hewn stone. It was brown with age, weather-worn at the angles, spotted with moss and lichen. Between the massive blocks were strips of grass the leverage of whose roots had pushed them apart. In answer to the challenge of this ambitious structure Time had laid his destroying hand upon it, and it would soon be "one with Nineveh and Tyre."[7] In an inscription on one side his eye caught a familiar name. Shaking with excitement, he craned his body across the wall and read:

HAZEN'S BRIGADE

to

The Memory of Its Soldiers
who fell at
Stone River, Dec. 31, 1862.[8]

The man fell back from the wall, faint and sick. Almost within an arm's length was a little depression in the earth; it had been filled by a recent rain—a pool of clear water. He crept to it to revive himself, lifted the upper part of his body on his trembling arms, thrust forward his head and saw the reflection of his face, as in a mirror. He uttered a terrible cry. His arms gave way; he fell, face downward, into the pool and yielded up the life that had spanned another life.

Co 45, no. 4 (Sept. 1908): 405–7 (as "The Man"); ***CW* 3.174–84.**

NOTES

AB had made sentimental visits in 1903 and 1907 to old battlefields, and they refreshed his feelings of unreality, of his life after the Civil War as an anticlimax, even somewhat of a dream. It is likely that during his 1907 trip he visited the Stone River site, where the monument described in the story had been erected by General Hazen. Stone River (see "Killed at Resaca," p. 512 note 2) had been an especially bloody battle, and it is not hard to see this story reflecting AB's spiritual and psychological reflections as to what part of him might have been left there.

1. The term describes an event in which a person who would ordinarily hear a sound does not, or that one who should not hear a sound does. Battles of the Civil War noted for this phenomenon include Gettysburg, Seven Pines, Iuka, Fort Donelson, Five Forks, Perryville, and Chancellorsville.

2. The battle of Gaines' Mill, won by the Confederates, took place on 27 June 1862; it is also known as the battle of Chickahominy or Cold Harbor (not to be confused with the 1864 battle of Cold Harbor), because of its nearness to the Chickahominy River in east-central Virginia.

3. The battle of Port Royal took place on 7 November 1861 when Federal ships sought control of Port Royal Sound, south of Charleston, by bombarding two nearby forts, Walker and Beauregard. After several hours the Confederates abandoned the forts.

4. AB refers to Gen. (USV) Philip Henry Sheridan (1831–88) and Gen. (CSA) George Edward Pickett (1825–75), who fought in the battle of Sayler's Creek, Virginia (6 April 1865), resulting in a devastating defeat for the Confederates and making surrender inevitable. Robert E. Lee surrendered to Grant at Appomattox Court House on 9 April 1865.

5. For Hazen, see "Mr. Jim Beckwourth's Adventure," p. 264 note 2.

6. AB refers to the tale of the tailor (nights 29–30 of the *Arabian Nights*) who speaks of a barber who relentlessly pesters him with questions when all he wants is a haircut.

7. Rudyard Kipling (1865–1936), "Recessional: June 22, 1897," l. 16.

8. General Hazen had caused this memorial to be erected at his own expense while the war was still in progress.

A RESUMED IDENTITY

THREE AND ONE ARE ONE

In the year 1861 Barr Lassiter, a young man of twenty-two, lived with his parents and an elder sister near Carthage, Tennessee.[1] The family were in somewhat humble circumstances, subsisting by cultivation of a small and not very fertile plantation. Owning no slaves, they were not rated among "the best people" of their neighborhood; but they were honest persons of good education, fairly well mannered and as respectable as any family could be if uncredentialed by personal dominion over the sons and daughters of Ham.[2] The elder Lassiter had that severity of manner that so frequently affirms an uncompromising devotion to duty, and conceals a warm and affectionate disposition. He was of the iron of which martyrs are made, but in the heart of the matrix had lurked a nobler metal, fusible at a milder heat, yet never coloring nor softening the hard exterior. By both heredity and environment something of the man's inflexible character had touched the other members of the family; the Lassiter home, though not devoid of domestic affection, was a veritable citadel of duty, and duty—ah, duty is as cruel as death!

When the war came on it found in the family, as in so many others in that State, a divided sentiment; the young man was loyal to the Union, the others savagely hostile. This unhappy division begot an insupportable domestic bitterness, and when the offending son and brother left home with the avowed purpose of joining the Federal army not a hand was laid in his, not a word of farewell was spoken, not a good wish followed him out into the world whither he went to meet with such spirit as he might whatever fate awaited him.

Making his way to Nashville, already occupied by the Army of General Buell,[3] he enlisted in the first organization that he found, a Kentucky regiment of cavalry, and in due time passed through all the stages of military evolution from raw recruit to experienced trooper. A right good trooper he was, too, although in his oral narrative from which this tale is made there was no mention of that; the fact was learned from his surviving comrades. For Barr Lassiter has answered "Here" to the sergeant whose name is Death.

Two years after he had joined it his regiment passed through the region whence he had come. The country thereabout had suffered severely from the ravages of war, having been occupied alternately (and simultaneously) by the belligerent forces, and a sanguinary struggle had occurred in the immediate vicinity of the Lassiter homestead. But of this the young trooper was not aware.

Finding himself in camp near his home, he felt a natural longing to see his parents and sister, hoping that in them, as in him, the unnatural animosities of the period had been softened by time and separation. Obtaining a leave of absence, he set out[4] in the late summer afternoon, and soon after the rising of the full moon was walking up the gravel path leading to the dwelling in which he had been born.

Soldiers in war age rapidly, and in youth two years are a long time. Barr Lassiter felt himself an old man, and had almost expected to find the place a ruin and a desolation. Nothing, apparently, was changed. At the sight of each dear and familiar object he was profoundly affected. His heart beat audibly, his emotion nearly suffocated him; an ache was in his throat. Unconsciously he quickened his pace until he almost ran, his long shadow making grotesque efforts to keep its place beside him.

The house was unlighted, the door open. As he approached and paused to recover control of himself his father came out and stood bare-headed in the moonlight.

"Father!" cried the young man, springing forward with outstretched hand— "Father!"

The elder man looked him sternly in the face, stood a moment motionless and without a word withdrew into the house. Bitterly disappointed, humiliated, inexpressibly hurt and altogether unnerved, the soldier dropped upon a rustic seat in deep dejection, supporting his head upon his trembling hand. But he would not have it so: he was too good a soldier to accept repulse as defeat. He rose and entered the house, passing directly to the "sitting-room."

It was dimly lighted by an uncurtained east window. On a low stool by the hearthside, the only article of furniture in the place, sat his mother, staring into a fireplace strewn with blackened embers and cold ashes. He spoke to her—tenderly, interrogatively and with hesitation, but she neither answered, nor moved, nor seemed in any way surprised. True, there had been time for her husband to apprise her of their guilty son's return. He moved nearer and was about to lay his hand upon her arm, when his sister entered from an adjoining room, looked him full in the face, passed him without a sign of recognition and left the room by a door that was partly behind him. He had turned his head to watch her, but when she was gone his eyes again sought his mother. She too had left the place.

Barr Lassiter strode to the door by which he had entered. The moonlight on the lawn was tremulous, as if the sward were a rippling sea. The trees and their black shadows shook as in a breeze. Blended with its borders, the gravel walk seemed

THREE AND THREE ARE ONE

unsteady and insecure to step on. This young soldier knew the optical illusions produced by tears. He felt them on his cheek, and saw them sparkle on the breast of his trooper's jacket. He left the house and made his way back to camp.

The next day, with no very definite intention, with no dominant feeling that he could rightly have named, he again sought the spot. Within a half-mile of it he met Bushrod Albro, a former playfellow and schoolmate, who greeted him warmly.

"I am going to visit my home," said the soldier.

The other looked at him rather sharply, but said nothing.

"I know," continued Lassiter, "that my folks have not changed, but———"

"There have been changes," Albro interrupted—"everything changes. I'll go with you if you don't mind. We can talk as we go."

But Albro did not talk.

Instead of a house they found only fire-blackened foundations of stone, enclosing an area of compact ashes pitted by rains.

Lassiter's astonishment was extreme.

"I could not find the right way to tell you," said Albro. "In the fight a year ago your house was burned by a Federal shell."

"And my family—where are they?"

"In Heaven, I hope. All were killed by the shell."

Co 45, no. 5 (Oct. 1908): 550–52; *CW* **3.350–55**.

NOTES

Although short, this fine story is written in richly dense prose. Compressed beneath its details is mature deliberation and deep emotion. The story sparely recalls elements of plot and theme previously developed in major stories: the issue of slavery in "An Occurrence at Owl Creek Bridge," a family divided in loyalties in "A Horseman in the Sky," and the destruction of the family by the war in "The Affair at Coulter's Notch." Despite their brevity, the characterizations of father and son are eloquent and that of the stiff father especially bears some resemblance to Bierce himself. As with other *Co* stories, its supernatural element has more of a spiritual than a merely uncanny quality.

1. Carthage is the county seat of Smith County in north-central Tennessee. It was the site of a skirmish between Federals and Confederates on 23 January 1863. There were Federal expeditions from Murfreesboro to Carthage on 1–8 April 1863 and from Gallatin to Carthage on 10 October 1863.
2. Ham was one of three sons of Noah. Because Ham saw the nakedness of Noah, Noah cursed him with the obligation to serve his brothers. It was generally believed that blacks were the descendants of Ham and the bearers of his curse; therefore, it was appropriate that they be slaves. See Gen. 9:20–27.
3. For the Federals' occupation of Nashville, see "George Thurston," p. 423 note 3. For Buell, see "An Affair of Outposts," p. 920 note 3.
4. In a letter to Walter Neale (28 November 1911, MS, HL), AB noted that *CW* is in error at this point in reading "set foot" and indicated that the text should read "set out."

RISE AND FALL OF
THE AËROPLANE

The craze for flying appears to have culminated in the year 369 Before Smith.[1] In that year the aëroplane (a word of unknown derivation) was almost the sole means of travel. These flying-machines were so simple and cheap that one who had not a spare half-hour in which to make one could afford to purchase. The price for a one-man machine was about two dollars—one-tenth of a gooble. Double-seated ones were of course a little more costly. No other kinds were allowed by law, for, as was quaintly explained by a chronicle of the period, "a man has a right to break his own neck, and that of his wife, but not those of his children and friends." It had been learned by experiment that for transportation of goods and for use in war the aëroplane was without utility. (Of balloons, dirigible and indirigible, we hear nothing after 348 B. S.; the price of gas, controlled by a single corporation, made them impossible.)

From extant fragments of Jobblecopper's "History of Invention" it appears that in America alone there were at one time no fewer then ten million aëroplanes in use. In and about the great cities the air was so crowded with them and collisions resulting in falls were so frequent that prudent persons neither ventured to use them nor dared to go out of cover. As a poet of the time expressed it:

> With falling fools so thick the sky is filled
> That wise men walk abroad but to be killed.
> Small comfort that the fool, too, dies in falling,
> For he'd have starved betimes in any calling.
> The earth is spattered red with their remains:
> Blood, flesh, bone, gristle—everything but brains.[2]

The reaction from this disagreeable state of affairs seems to have been brought about by a combination of causes.

First, the fierce animosities engendered by the perils to pedestrians and "motorists"—a word of disputed meaning. So savage did this hostility become that firing at aëroplanes in flight, with the newly invented silent rifle, grew to the character of a national custom. Dimshouck has found authority for the statement that in a single day thirty-one aëronauts fell from the heavens into the streets of Nebraska, the capital of Chocago, victims of popular disfavor; and a writer of that time relates, not altogether lucidly, the finding in a park in Ohio of the bodies of "the Wright brothers, each pierced with bullets from hip to shoulder, the ears cut off, and without other marks of identification."[3]

Second in importance of these adverse conditions was the natural disposition of the ancients to tire of whatever had engaged their enthusiasm—the fickleness that had led to abandonment of the bicycle, of republican government, of baseball and of respect for women. In the instance of the aëroplane this reaction was probably somewhat hastened by the rifle practice mentioned.

Third, invention of the electric leg.[4] As a means of going from place to place the ancients had from the earliest ages of history relied largely on the wheel. Just how they applied it, not in stationary machinery, as we do ourselves, but as an aid to locomotion, we cannot now hope to know, for all the literature of the subject has perished; but it was evidently a crude and clumsy device, giving a speed of less than two hundred miles (four and a half sikliks)[5] an hour, even on roadways specially provided with rails for its rapid revolution. We know, too, that wheels produced an intolerable jolting of the body, whereby many died of a disease known as "therapeutics." Indeed, a certain class of persons who probably traveled faster than others came to be called "rough riders,"[6] and for their sufferings were compensated by appointment to the most lucrative offices in the gift of the sovereign. Small wonder that the men of that day hailed the aëroplane with intemperate enthusiasm and used it with insupportable immoderation!

But when the younger Eddy invented that supreme space-conquering device, the electric leg, and within six months perfected it to virtually what it is to-day, the necessity for flight no longer existed. The aëroplane, ending its brief and bloody reign a discredited and discarded toy, was "sent to the scrap-heap," as one of our brightest and most original modern wits has expressed it.[7] The wheel followed it into oblivion, whither the horse had preceded it, and Civilization lifted her virgin fires as a dawn in Eden, and like Cytherea[8] leading her moonrise troop of nymphs and graces, literally legged it o'er the land!

Co 45, no. 5 (Oct. 1908): 565–66 (as "The Rise and Fall of the Aeroplane"; under the heading "Small Contributions"); *CW* 12.346–49 (as part of "The Future Historian").

NOTES

In keeping with other pieces by the Future Historian, this sketch deliberately gives the impression of having been cobbled together from misunderstood scraps of surviving sources. AB obviously misjudged the airplane as a passing fad, but he was not alone. It was a popular target for comic songs and humor in the early twentieth century, and AB taps into this vein with his not very subtle puns about the "rise and fall" of the airplane and its use with "insupportable" immoderation.

1. "Before Smith" seems to have been linked in AB's mind with his 1873 sketch "John Smith, Liberator" (p. 163).

2. The poem is by AB himself. The last line derives from an editorial in *W,* no. 525 (21 Aug. 1886): 5.

3. Wilbur (1867–1912) and Orville Wright (1871–1948) had been interested in aviation since the 1890s. They made the world's first successful flight in a heavier-than-air flying machine on 17 December 1903 at Kitty Hawk, North Carolina. Thereafter they returned to their hometown of Dayton, Ohio, where they continued their experiments. AB's mention of them here was probably triggered by their extensive flying demonstrations in Europe and the United States in the summer and fall of 1908.

4. AB disdained the therapeutic fads of his day. Cf. "The Dawn of a New Era," *W,* no. 270 (30 Sept. 1881): 211 (unsigned): "Never has the curative effects of electricity received so striking an illustration. All the electric belts, electric hair-brushes, electric garters, electric bustles and electric suspenders known to modern therapeutics are seen to be mere idle toys compared with the stupendous latent energy of the domestic cat."

5. Deriving from the word "cyclic," meaning of, relating to, or being a cycle.

6. See "An Ancient Hunter," p. 1057 note 3.

7. AB later gave the title "The Scrap-Heap" to a selection of minor verse in his book *Shapes of Clay* (rev. ed. 1910, in *CW* 4).

8. "Cytherea" is an attribute or nickname of Aphrodite, deriving from the island of Cythera, in the Aegean Sea, where she was worshipped.

THE STRANGER

A man stepped out of the darkness into the little illuminated circle about our failing camp-fire and seated himself upon a rock.

"You are not the first to explore this region," he said, gravely.

Nobody controverted his statement; he was himself proof of its truth, for he was not of our party and must have been somewhere near when we camped. Moreover, he must have companions not far away; it was not a place where one would be living or traveling alone. For more than a week we had seen, besides ourselves and our animals, only such living things as rattlesnakes and horned toads. In an Arizona desert one does not long coexist with only such creatures as these: one must have pack animals, supplies, arms—"an outfit." And all these imply comrades. It was perhaps a doubt as to what manner of men this unceremonious stranger's comrades might be, together with something in his words interpretable as a challenge, that caused every man of our half-dozen "gentlemen adventurers" to rise to a sitting posture and lay his hand upon a weapon—an act signifying, in that time and place, a policy of expectation. The stranger gave the matter no attention and began again to speak in the same deliberate, uninflected monotone in which he had delivered his first sentence:

"Thirty years ago Ramon Gallegos, William Shaw, George W. Kent and Berry Davis, all of Tucson, crossed the Santa Catalina mountains and traveled due west, as nearly as the configuration of the country permitted. We were prospecting and it was our intention, if we found nothing, to push through to the Gila river at some point near Big Bend, where we understood there was a settlement.[1] We had a good outfit but no guide—just Ramon Gallegos, William Shaw, George W. Kent and Berry Davis."

The man repeated the names slowly and distinctly, as if to fix them in the memories of his audience, every member of which was now attentively observing him, but with a slackened apprehension regarding his possible companions somewhere in the darkness that seemed to enclose us like a black wall; in the manner of this volunteer historian was no suggestion of an unfriendly purpose. His act was rather that of a harmless lunatic than an enemy. We were not so new to the country as not to know that the solitary life of many a plainsman had a tendency to develop eccentricities of conduct and character not always easily distinguishable from mental aberration. A man is like a tree: in a forest of his fellows he will grow as straight as his generic and individual nature permits; alone in the open, he yields to the deforming stresses and tortions that environ him. Some such thoughts were in my mind as I watched the man from the shadow of my hat, pulled low to shut out the firelight. A witless fellow, no doubt, but what could he be doing there in the heart of a desert?

Having undertaken to tell this story, I wish that I could describe the man's appearance; that would be a natural thing to do. Unfortunately, and somewhat strangely, I find myself unable to do so with any degree of confidence, for afterward no two of us agreed as to what he wore and how he looked; and when I try to set down my own impressions they elude me. Anyone can tell some kind of story; narration is one of the elemental powers of the race. But the talent for description is a gift.

Nobody having broken silence the visitor went on to say:

"This country was not then what it is now. There was not a ranch between the Gila and the Gulf. There was a little game here and there in the mountains, and near the infrequent water-holes grass enough to keep our animals from starvation. If we should be so fortunate as to encounter no Indians we might get through. But within a week the purpose of the expedition had altered from discovery of wealth to preservation of life. We had gone too far to go back, for what was ahead could be no worse than what was behind; so we pushed on, riding by night to avoid Indians and the intolerable heat, and concealing ourselves by day as best we could. Sometimes, having exhausted our supply of wild meat and emptied our casks, we were days without food or drink; then a water-hole or a shallow pool in the bottom of an *arroyo* so restored our strength and sanity that we were able to shoot some of the wild animals that sought it also. Sometimes it was a bear, sometimes an antelope, a coyote, a cougar—that was as God pleased; all were food.

"One morning as we skirted a mountain range, seeking a practicable pass, we were attacked by a band of Apaches who had followed our trail up a gulch—it is not far from here. Knowing that they outnumbered us ten to one, they took none of their usual cowardly precautions, but dashed upon us at a gallop, firing and yelling. Fighting was out of the question: we urged our feeble animals up the gulch as far as there was footing for a hoof, then threw ourselves out of our saddles and took to the *chaparral* on one of the slopes, abandoning our entire outfit to the enemy. But we retained our rifles, every man—Ramon Gallegos, William Shaw, George W. Kent and Berry Davis."

"Same old crowd," said the humorist of our party. He was an Eastern man, unfamiliar with the decent observances of social intercourse. A gesture of disapproval from our leader silenced him and the stranger proceeded with his tale:

THE STRANGER

"The savages dismounted also, and some of them ran up the gulch beyond the point at which we had left it, cutting off further retreat in that direction and forcing us on up the side. Unfortunately the *chaparral* extended only a short distance up the slope, and as we came into the open ground above we took the fire of a dozen rifles; but Apaches shoot badly when in a hurry, and God so willed it that none of us fell. Twenty yards up the slope, beyond the edge of the brush, were vertical cliffs, in which, directly in front of us, was a narrow opening. Into that we ran, finding ourselves in a cavern about as large as an ordinary room in a house. Here for a time we were safe: a single man with a repeating rifle could defend the entrance against all the Apaches in the land. But against hunger and thirst we had no defense. Courage we still had, but hope was a memory.

"Not one of those Indians did we afterward see, but by the smoke and glare of their fires in the gulch we knew that by day and by night they watched with ready rifles in the edge of the bush—knew that if we made a sortie not a man of us would live to take three steps into the open. For three days, watching in turn, we held out before our suffering became insupportable. Then—it was the morning of the fourth day—Ramon Gallegos said:

"'Señores, I know not well of the good God and what please him. I have live without religion, and I am not acquaint with that of you. Pardon, señores, if I shock you, but for me the time is come to beat the game of the Apache.'

"He knelt upon the rock floor of the cave and pressed his pistol against his temple. 'Madre de Dios,' he said, 'comes now the soul of Ramon Gallegos.'

"And so he left us—William Shaw, George W. Kent and Berry Davis.

"I was the leader: it was for me to speak.

"'He was a brave man,' I said—'he knew when to die, and how. It is foolish to go mad from thirst and fall by Apache bullets, or be skinned alive—it is in bad taste. Let us join Ramon Gallegos.'

"'That is right,' said William Shaw.

"'That is right,' said George W. Kent.

"I straightened the limbs of Ramon Gallegos and put a handkerchief over his face. Then William Shaw said: 'I should like to look like that—a little while.'

"And George W. Kent said that he felt that way, too.

"'It shall be so,' I said: 'the red devils will wait a week. William Shaw and George W. Kent, draw and kneel.'

"They did so and I stood before them.

"'Almighty God, our Father,' said I.

"'Almighty God, our Father,' said William Shaw.

"'Almighty God, our Father,' said George W. Kent.

"'Forgive us our sins,' said I.

"'Forgive us our sins,' said they.

THE STRANGER

"'And receive our souls.'

"'And receive our souls.'

"'Amen!'

"'Amen!'

"I laid them beside Ramon Gallegos and covered their faces."

There was a quick commotion on the opposite side of the camp-fire: one of our party had sprung to his feet, pistol in hand.

"And you!" he shouted—"*you* dared to escape?—you dare to be alive? You cowardly hound, I'll send you to join them if I hang for it!"

But with the leap of a panther the captain was upon him, grasping his wrist. "Hold it in, Sam Yountsey, hold it in!"

We were now all upon our feet—except the stranger, who sat motionless and apparently inattentive. Some one seized Yountsey's other arm.

"Captain," I said, "there is something wrong here. This fellow is either a lunatic or merely a liar—just a plain, every-day liar whom Yountsey has no call to kill. If this man was of that party it had five members, one of whom—probably himself—he has not named."

"Yes," said the captain, releasing the insurgent, who sat down, "there is something—unusual. Years ago four dead bodies of white men, scalped and shamefully mutilated, were found about the mouth of that cave. They are buried there; I have seen the graves—we shall all see them to-morrow."

The stranger rose, standing tall in the light of the expiring fire, which in our breathless attention to his story we had neglected to keep going.

"There were four," he said—"Ramon Gallegos, William Shaw, George W. Kent and Berry Davis."

With this reiterated roll-call of the dead he walked into the darkness and we saw him no more.

At that moment one of our party, who had been on guard, strode in among us, rifle in hand and somewhat excited.

"Captain," he said, "for the last half-hour three men have been standing out there on the *mesa*." He pointed in the direction taken by the stranger. "I could see them distinctly, for the moon is up, but as they had no guns and I had them covered with mine I thought it was their move. They have made none, but, damn it! they have got on to my nerves."

"Go back to your post, and stay till you see them again," said the captain. "The rest of you lie down again, or I'll kick you all into the fire."

The sentinel obediently withdrew, swearing, and did not return. As we were arranging our blankets the fiery Yountsey said: "I beg your pardon, Captain, but who the devil do you take them to be?"

"Ramon Gallegos, William Shaw and George W. Kent."

THE STRANGER

"But how about Berry Davis? I ought to have shot him."

"Quite needless; you couldn't have made him any deader. Go to sleep."

Co 46, no. 3 (Feb. 1909): 350–54 (as "A Stranger"); *CW* 3.315–24.

NOTES

One of AB's most memorable ghost stories, this tale is unusual in his canon in that its specificity of detail has so few points of contact with his biography that could help illuminate it: no known trips to Arizona, or contact with Apaches, or previously mentioned details from his mapping trip across the plains with General Hazen in 1866. Within its restriction as a short tale, a peculiarly moving account of a soul that could not rest but had to tell its story, it is almost a prose analogy to the Ancient Mariner.

1. Tucson lies in the southeast corner of Arizona. The Santa Catalina Mountains are located in what is now the Coronado National Forest, just north of Tucson. The Gila River runs from east to west through the southern part of Arizona, flowing near Phoenix and Yuma and emptying into the Gulf of California. "Big Bend" is an archaic term for the wide southward curve of the Gila River southwest of Phoenix, as it skirts the Gila Bend Mountains. A settlement named Gila Bend is located just south of this point; it had been settled by Native Americans from at least the late seventeenth century.

THE DISPERSAL

So somber a phenomenon as the effacement of an ancient and brilliant civilization within the lifetime of a single generation is, fortunately, known to have occurred only once in the history of the world. The catastrophe is not only unique in history, but all the more notable for having befallen, not a single state overrun by powerful barbarians, but half of the world; and for having been effected by a seemingly trivial agency that sprang from the civilization itself. Indeed, it was the work of one man.

Hiram Perry (or Percy) Maximus was born in the latter part of the nineteenth century of "the Christian Era," in Podunk, the capital of America.[1] Little is known of his ancestry, although Dumbleshaw[2] affirms on evidence not cited by him that he came of a family of pirates that infested the waters of Lake Erie (now the desert of Gobol) as early as "1813"—whenever that may have been.

The precise nature of Hiram Perry's invention, with its successive improvements, is not known—probably could not now be understood. It was called "the silent firearm"[3]—so much we learn from fragmentary chronicles of the period; also that it was of so small size that it could be put into the "pocket." (In his "Dictionary of Antiquities" the learned Pantin-Gwocx defines "pocket" as, first, "the main temple of the American deity;" second, a "a small receptacle worn on the person." The latter definition is the one, doubtless, that concerns us if the two things are not the same.) Regarding the work of "the silent firearm" we have light in abundance. Indeed, the entire history of the brief but bloody period between its invention and the extinction of the Christian civilization is an unbroken record of its fateful employment.

Of course the immense armies of the time were at once supplied with the new weapon, with results that none had foreseen. Soldiers were thenceforth as formidable to their officers as to their enemies. It was no longer possible to maintain discipline, for no officer dared offend, by punishment or reprimand, one who could fatally retaliate as secretly and securely, in the repose of camp as in the tumult of battle. In civic affairs the deadly device was malignly active. Statesmen in disfavor (and all were hateful to men of contrary politics) fell dead in the forum by means invisible and inaudible. Anarchy, discarding her noisy and imperfectly effective methods, gladly embraced the new and safe one.

In other walks of life matters were no better. Armed with the sinister power of life and death, any evil-minded person (and most of the ancient Caucasians appear to have been evil-minded) could gratify a private revenge or wanton malevolence by slaying whom he would, and nothing cried aloud the lamentable deed.

So horrible was the mortality, so futile all preventive legislation, that society was stricken with a universal panic. Cities were plundered and abandoned; villages without villagers fell to decay; homes were given up to bats and owls, and farms became jungles infested with wild beasts. The people fled to the mountains, the forests, the marshes, concealing themselves from one another in caves and thickets, and dying from privation and exposure and diseases more dreadful than the perils from which they had fled. When every human being distrusted and feared every other human being solitude was esteemed the only good; and solitude spells death. In one generation Americans and Europeans had slunk back into the night of barbarism.

Co 46, no. 4 (Mar. 1909): 472–73 (as "The Reversion to Barbarism," under the heading "Small Contributions"); *CW* 12.343–46 (as part of "The Future Historian").

NOTES

A sketch in the Future Historian mode, this piece is consonant with AB's gloomy prognostication that his culture was doomed. He was not, of course, alone in this activity. Various other authors of the time—for example, Jack London, H. G. Wells, Mark Twain, and Ignatius Donnelly—contemplated in their fiction the use of frighteningly deadly threats to established civilizations in their fiction, ranging from genocide to biological warfare to such "advanced" technological achievements as poison gas, electrified fences, and destructive rays. Compared to these, a silent pistol seems modest, but it is enough for AB to be successful in this short tale to capture the essence of terrorism and to show how little it might take for evil to extinguish the light of civilization.

1. Although Hiram Maximus is almost certainly fictitious, AB was probably alluding to Hudson Maxim (1853–1927), the inventor of improved gunpowder, explosives, and weaponry, including the Maxim silencer, which greatly reduces the sound of a gunshot. For Podunk, see "The Maid of Podunk."
2. For Dumbleshaw, see "The Maid of Podunk," p. 948 note 5.
3. See AB's article on "an absolutely noiseless and smokeless gunpowder," "Infumiferous Tacitite," *E* (11 Feb. 1894): 6 (unsigned); repr. *FR* 190–92.

AN ANCIENT HUNTER

In the nineteenth century of what, in honor of Christopher Columbum, a mythical hero, the ancients called the "Christian era," Africa was an unknown land of deserts, jungles, fierce wild beasts and degraded savages. It is believed that no white man had ever penetrated it to a distance of one league from the coast. All the literature of that time relating to African exploration, conquest and settlement is now known to be purely imaginative—what the ancients admired as "fiction" and we punish as felony.

Authentic African history begins in the early years of the twentieth century of the "era" mentioned, and its most stupendous events are the first recorded, the record being made, chiefly, by the hand that wrought the work—that of Tudor Rosenfelt, the most illustrious figure of antiquity. Of this astonishing man's parentage and early life nothing is certainly known: legend is loquacious, but history is silent. There are traditions affirming his connection with a disastrous explosion at Bronco, a city of the Chinese province of Wyo Ming,[1] his subjugation of the usurper Tammano[2] in the American city of N'yorx (now known to have had no existence outside the imagination of the poets) and his conquest of the island of Cubebs;[3] but from all this bushel of fable we get no grain of authenticated fact. The tales appear to be merely hero-myths, such as belong to the legendary age of every people of the ancient world except the Greeks and Romans. Further than that he was an American Indian nothing can be positively affirmed of Tudor Rosenfelt before the year "1909" of the "Christian [Columbian] era." In that year we glimpse him disembarking from two ships on the African coast near Bumbassa,[4] and, with one foot in the sea and the other on dry land, swearing through clenched teeth that other forms of life than Man shall be no more. He then strides, unarmed and unattended, into the jungle, and is lost to view for ten years!

Legend and myth now reassert their ancient reign. In that memorable decade, as we know from the ancient author of "Who's Whoest in Africa," the most incredible tales were told and believed by those who, knowing the man and his mission, suffered insupportable alternations of hope and despair. It was said that the Dark Continent into which he had vanished was frequently shaken from coast to coast as by the trampling and wrestling of titanic energies in combat and the fall of colossal bulks on the yielding crust of the earth; that mariners in adjacent waters heard recurrent growls and roars of rage and shouts of triumph—an enormous uproar that smote their ships like a gale from the land and swept them affrighted out to sea; that so loud were these terrible sounds as to be simultaneously audible in the Indian and Atlantic oceans, as was proved by comparing the logs of vessels arriving from both seas at the port of Berlin. As is quaintly related in one of these marine diaries, "The noise was so strenuous that our ears was nigh to busting with the wolume of the sound." Through all this monstrous opulence of the primitive rhetorical figure known as the Lie[5] we easily discern a nucleus of truth: something uncommon was going on in Africa.[6]

At the close of the memorable decade (*circa* "1919") authentic history again appears in the fragmentary work of Antrolius:[7] Rosenfelt walks out of the jungle at Mbongwa on the side of the continent opposite Bumbassa. He is now attended by a caravan of twenty thousand camels and ten thousand native porters, all bearing trophies of the chase. A complete list of these would require more pages than Homer Wheeler Wilcox's catalogue of ships,[8] but among them were heads of elephants with antlers attached; pelts of the checkered lion and the spiny hippopotentot, respectively the most ferocious and the most venomous of their species; a skeleton of the missing lynx (*Pithecanthropos erectus compilatus*);[9] entire bodies of pterodactyls and broncosauruses; a slithy tove[10] mounted on a fine specimen of the weeping wanderoo; the downy electrical whacknasty (*Ananias flabbergastor*);[11] the carnivorous mastodon; ten specimens of the skinless tiger (*Felis decorticata*);[12] a saber-toothed python, whose bite produced the weeping sickness; three ribnosed gazzadoodles; a pair of blood-sweating bandicoots; a night-blooming jeewhillikins;[13] three and a half varieties of the crested skynoceros; a purring crocodile, or buzz-saurian; two Stymphalian[14] linnets; a skeleton of the three footed swammigolsis—afterwards catalogued at the Podunk Museum of Defective Types as *Talpa unopede noninvento*;[15] a hydra from Lerna;[16] the ring-tail mollycoddle and the fawning polecat (*Civis nondesiderabilis*).[17]

These terrible monsters, which from the dawning of time had ravaged all Africa, baffling every attempt at exploration and settlement, the Exterminator, as he came to be called, had strangled or captured with his bare hands; and the few remaining were so cowed that they gave milk. Indeed, such was their terror of his red right arm that all forsook their evil ways, offered themselves as beasts of burden to the whites that came afterward, and in domestication and servitude sought the security that he denied to their ferocity and power. Within a single generation prosperous colonies of Caucasians sprang up all along the coasts, and the silk hat and pink shirt, immemorial pioneers and promoters of civilization, penetrated the remotest fastnesses, spreading peace and plenty o'er a smiling land!

The later history of this remarkable man is clouded in obscurity. Much of his own account of his exploits, curiously intertangled with those of an earlier hero named

AN ANCIENT HUNTER

Hercules, is extant, but it closes with his re-embarkation for America. Some hold that on returning to his native land he was assailed with opprobrium, loaded with chains and cast into Chicago; others contend that he was enriched by gifts from the sovereigns of the world, received with acclamation by his grateful countrymen, and even mentioned for the presidency to succeed Samuel Gompers[18]—an honor that he modestly declined on the ground of inexperience and unfitness. Whatever may be the truth of these matters, he doubtless did not long suffer affliction nor enjoy prosperity, for in the great catastrophe of the year 254 B. S. the entire continent of North America and the contiguous island of Omaha were swallowed up by the sea. Fortunately his narrative is preserved in the Royal Library of Timbuktu, in which capital of civilization stands his colossal statue of ivory and gold. In the shadow of that renowned memorial I write this imperfect tribute to his worth.

Co 46, no. 5 (Apr. 1909): 597–98 (as "The Advance Agent"; under the heading "Small Contributions"); CW 12.349–55 (as part of "The Future Historian").

NOTES

A send-up of the two-year hunting trip to Africa that Theodore Roosevelt undertook, beginning on 23 March 1909, following the end of his presidency. The disdain AB had for Roosevelt can be inferred from the way this sketch treats him as a myth, and downgrades to mere parts of that myth some of his more famous real exploits, but excludes any mention of him as the president of the United States. Readers of the time would have picked up the piece's vicious innuendoes of monarchy and Jewish background in the name Tudor Rosenfelt. Roosevelt's love of hunting, notorious even when big game hunting was a glamorous sport, is characterized as the main achievement for which he will be remembered. The humorist Finley Peter Dunne had his literary creation Mr. Dooley suggest that Roosevelt's egocentric account of the Spanish-American War might have been fittingly titled "Alone in Cubia," and AB correspondingly launches Roosevelt from two ships into Africa "unarmed and unattended." After ten years, during which sounds of awesome struggles are hyperbolically reported as emanating from the Dark Continent, the hero emerges at the head of an incredible retinue and an exuberantly Rabelaisian menagerie of legendary beasts, having single-handedly subdued Africa and made it safe for Caucasian settlement. Given the short length of this piece and its commitment to the mode of humor, it is difficult to imagine what more AB might have done to make it more defamatory. Roosevelt's defeat as a third-party candidate in the presidential election of 1912 led AB to remark: "The defeat of Teddy fills the soul of me with a great white peace" (letter to Helen [Bierce] Cowden, 6 Nov. [1912]; MMM 227).

1. AB makes this same joke ("Wyo Ming" regarded as a Chinese province) in the fable "The Massacre," E (6 Aug. 1893): 12 (CF no. 435).
2. The political organization known as Tammany Hall, associated with the Democratic Party, began in 1789 and largely controlled New York City politics up to the 1930s, when it was finally weakened by the joint efforts of Mayor Fiorello La Guardia (1934–45) and Franklin Delano Roosevelt. Theodore Roosevelt was in fact instrumental in limiting Tammany Hall's

control of New York City politics, working in 1884 as an assemblyman with Gov. Grover Cleveland on a variety of municipal reforms.

3. A reference to Theodore Roosevelt's leading the Rough Riders into battle on San Juan Hill in Cuba in July 1898, during the Spanish-American War.

4. For the imaginary realm of Bumbassa, see "The Wizard of Bumbassa" (p. 826).

5. Cf. "Prattle," *E* (30 Sept. 1894): 6: "Obviously the Chinese literary class is not ignorant of that engaging rhetorical figure known as the Lie, and can use it with a truly Western largess and liberality."

6. Cf. "The Passing Show," *NYJ* (2 Dec. 1900): 26; *E* (2 Dec. 1900): 30: "It looks as if human anger found its most acceptable expression, not in cruelty, but in the rhetorical figure known as the lie." In book 4 of *Gulliver's Travels*, the Houyhnhnms have no word for the lie and so call it "the thing that is not."

7. Antrolius was first cited in "The Fall of the Republic."

8. A parodic reference to Ella Wheeler Wilcox (see "John Smith, Liberator," p. 165 note 8) and to Homer's catalog of ships in book 2 of the *Iliad*.

9. AB's mock Latin means "hairy erect ape-man." Ernst Heinrich Haeckel (1834–1919), German philosopher and naturalist, coined the term "Pithecanthropos" to denote the putative link between apes and human beings.

10. From Lewis Carroll's "Jabberwocky," in *Through the Looking-Glass* (1871), ll. 1, 25 (plural in Caroll).

11. AB's mock Latin means "Ananias the flabbergaster." Ananias is the name given to three different individuals in the Bible. AB frequently alluded to the one cited in Acts 2:24–27 and 4:32–37, whom God punished for deceit.

12. AB's mock Latin means "skinned cat."

13. For "jeewhillikins" see "Little Johnny," *E* (15 Jan. 1888): 4, in which there is an "Ovis geewhillikins" ("Common Doe-headed Sheep of California"), and the Little Johnny sketch "The Snowty Geewhillikins and Other Animals," *NYA* (14 Oct. 1904): 16, in which the characteristics of the beast are not specified other than that it is "snowty" and a foe of the whale. As H. L. Mencken (*The American Language: Supplement I* [New York: Knopf, 1945], 664) notes, the word is a euphemism for the expletive "Jesus."

14. The adjective derives from Stymphalos, a city and mountain in Arcadia. AB alludes to one of the labors of Herakles, in which he subdued the Stymphalian Birds.

15. AB's mock Latin means "unlocated one-footed mole."

16. The Hydra of Lerna, near Argos, was destroyed by Herakles.

17. AB's mock Latin means "undesirable citizen."

18. For Gompers, see "The Extinction of the Smugwumps," p. 951 note 3.

AN ANCIENT HUNTER

ASHES OF THE BEACON

AN HISTORICAL MONOGRAPH WRITTEN IN 4930

Of the many causes that conspired to bring about the lamentable failure of "self-government" in ancient America the most general and comprehensive was, of course, the impracticable nature of the system itself. In the light of modern culture, and instructed by history, we readily discern the folly of those crude ideas upon which the ancient Americans based what they knew as "republican institutions," and maintained, as long as maintenance was possible, with something of a religious fervor, even when the results were visibly disastrous.

To us of to-day it is clear that the word "self-government" involves a contradiction,[1] for government means control by something other than the thing to be controlled. When the thing governed is the same as the thing governing there is no government, though for a time there may be, as in the case under consideration there was, a considerable degree of forbearance, giving a misleading appearance of public order. This, however, soon must, as in fact it soon did, pass away with the delusion that gave it birth. The habit of obedience to written law, inculcated by generations of respect for actual government able to enforce its authority, will persist for a long time, with an ever lessening power upon the imagination of the people; but there comes a time when the tradition is forgotten and the delusion exhausted. When men perceive that nothing is restraining them but their consent to be restrained, then at last there is nothing to obstruct the free play of that selfishness which is the dominant characteristic and fundamental motive of human nature and human action respectively. Politics, which may have had something of the character of a contest of principles, becomes a struggle of interests, and its methods are frankly serviceable to personal and class advantage. Patriotism and respect for law pass like a tale that is told. Anarchy, no longer disguised as "government by consent," reveals his hidden hand, and in the words of our greatest living poet,

lets the curtain fall,
And universal darkness buries all![2]

The ancient Americans were a composite people; their blood was a blend of all the strains known in their time.[3] Their government, while they had one, being merely a loose and mutable expression of the desires and caprices of the majority—that is to say, of the ignorant, restless and reckless—gave the freest rein and play to all the primal instincts and elemental passions of the race. In so far and for so long as it had any restraining force, it was only the restraint of the present over the power of the past—that of a new habit over an old and insistent tendency ever seeking expression in large liberties and indulgences impatient of control. In the history of that unhappy people, therefore, we see unveiled the workings of the human will in its most lawless state, without fear of authority or care of consequence. Nothing could be more instructive.

Of the American form of government, although itself the greatest of evils afflicting the victims of those that it entailed, but little needs to be said here; it has perished from the earth,[4] a system discredited by an unbroken record of failure in all parts of the world, from the earliest historic times to its final extinction. Of living students of political history not one professes to see in it anything but a mischievous creation of theorists and visionaries—persons whom our gracious sovereign has deigned to brand for the world's contempt as "dupes of hope purveying to sons of greed."[5] The political philosopher of to-day is spared the trouble of pointing out the fallacies of republican government, as the mathematician is spared that of demonstrating the absurdity of the convergence of parallel lines; yet the ancient Americans not only clung to their error with a blind, unquestioning faith, even when groaning under its most insupportable burdens, but seem to have believed it of divine origin. It was thought by them to have been established by the god Washington, whose worship, with that of such *dii minores* as Gufferson, Jaxon and Lincon (identical probably with the Hebru Abrem), runs like a shining thread through all the warp and woof of the stuff that garmented their moral nakedness. Some stones, very curiously inscribed in many tongues, were found by the explorer Droyhors in the wilderness bordering the river Bhitt (supposed by him to be the ancient Potomac) as lately as the reign of Barukam IV. These stones appear to be fragments of a monument or temple erected to the glory of Washington in his divine character of Founder and Preserver of republican institutions. If this tutelary deity of the ancient Americans really invented representative government they were not the first by many to whom he imparted the malign secret of its inauguration and denied that of its maintenance.

Although many of the causes which finally, in combination, brought about the downfall of the great American republic were in operation from the beginning—

being, as has been said, inherent in the system—it was not until the year 1995 (as the ancients for some reason not now known reckoned time) that the collapse of the vast, formless fabric was complete. In that year the defeat and massacre of the last army of law and order in the lava beds of California extinguished the final fires of enlightened patriotism and quenched in blood the monarchical revival. Thenceforth armed opposition to anarchy was confined to desultory and insignificant warfare waged by small gangs of mercenaries in the service of wealthy individuals and equally feeble bands of proscripts fighting for their lives. In that year, too, "the Three Presidents"[6] were driven from their capitals, Cincinnati, New Orleans and Duluth, their armies dissolving by desertion and themselves meeting death at the hands of the populace.

The turbulent period between 1920 and 1995, with its incalculable waste of blood and treasure, its dreadful conflicts of armies and more dreadful massacres by passionate mobs, its kaleidoscopic changes of government and incessant effacement and redrawing of boundaries of states, its interminable tale of political assassinations and proscriptions—all the horrors incident to intestinal wars of a naturally lawless race—had so exhausted and dispirited the surviving protagonists of legitimate government that they could make no further head against the inevitable, and were glad indeed and most fortunate to accept life on any terms that they could obtain.

But the purpose of this sketch is not bald narration of historic fact, but examination of antecedent germinal conditions; not to recount calamitous events familiar to students of that faulty civilization, but to trace, as well as the meager record will permit, the genesis and development of the causes that brought them about. Historians in our time have left little undone in the matter of narration of political and military phenomena. In Golpek's "Decline and Fall of the American Republics," in Soseby's "History of Political Fallacies," in Holobom's[7] "Monarchical Renascence," and notably in Gunkux's immortal work, "The Rise, Progress, Failure and Extinction of The Connected States of America" the fruits of research have been garnered, a considerable harvest. The events are set forth with such conscientiousness and particularity as to have exhausted the possibilities of narration. It remains only to expound causes and point the awful moral.

To a delinquent observation it may seem needless to point out the inherent defects of a system of government which the logic of events has swept like political rubbish from the face of the earth, but we must not forget that ages before the inception of the American republics and that of France and Ireland[8] this form of government had been discredited by emphatic failures among the most enlightened and powerful nations of antiquity: the Greeks, the Romans, and long before them (as we now know) the Egyptians and the Chinese. To the lesson of these failures the founders of the eighteenth and nineteenth century republics were blind and deaf. Have we then reason to believe that our posterity will be wiser because instructed by a greater number of examples? And is the number of examples which they will have in memory really greater? Already the instances of China, Egypt, Greece and Rome are almost lost in the mists of antiquity; they are known, except by infrequent report, to the archæologist only, and but dimly and uncertainly to him. The brief and imperfect record of yesterdays which we call History is like that traveling vine of India which, taking new root as it advances, decays at one end while it grows at the other, and so is constantly perishing and finally lost in all the spaces which it has over-passed.

From the few and precious writings that have descended to us from the early period of the American republic we get a clear if fragmentary view of the disorders and lawlessness affecting that strange and unhappy nation. Leaving the historically famous "labor troubles" for more extended consideration, we may summarize here a few of the results of hardly more than a century and a quarter of "self-government" as it existed on this continent just previously to the awful end. At the beginning of the "twentieth century" a careful study by trustworthy contemporary statisticians of the public records and those apparently private ones known as "newspapers" showed that in a population of about 80,000,000[9] the annual number of homicides was not less than 10,000; and this continued year after year to increase, not only absolutely, but proportionately, until, in the words of Dumbleshaw, who is thought to have written his famous "Memoirs of a Survivor"[10] in the year 1908 of their era, "it would seem that the practice of suicide is a needless custom, for if a man but have patience his neighbor is sure to put him out of his misery." Of the 10,000 assassins less than three per cent. were punished, further than by incidental imprisonment if unable to give bail while awaiting trial. If the chief end of government is the citizen's security of life and his protection from aggression, what kind of government do these appalling figures disclose? Yet so infatuated with their imaginary "liberty"[11] were these singular people that the contemplation of all this crime abated nothing of the volume and persistence of their patriotic ululations, and affected not their faith in the perfection of their system. They were like a man standing on a rock already submerged by the rising tide, and calling to his neighbors on adjacent cliffs to observe his superior security.

When three men engage in an undertaking in which they have an equal interest, and in the direction of which they have equal power, it necessarily results that any action approved by two of them, with or without the assent of the third, will be taken. This is called—or was called when it was an accepted principle in political and other affairs—"the rule of the majority."[12] Evidently, under the malign conditions supposed, it is the only practicable plan of getting anything done. A and B rule and overrule C, not because they ought, but because they can; not because they are wiser, but because they are stronger. In order to avoid a conflict in which he is sure to be worsted, C submits as soon as the vote is taken. C is as likely to be right as A and B; nay, that eminent ancient philosopher, Professor Richard A. Proctor[13] (or Proroctor, as the learned now spell the name), has clearly shown by the law of probabilities that any one of the three, all being of the same intelligence, is far likelier to be right than the other two.

It is thus that the "rule of the majority" as a political system is established. It is in essence nothing but the discredited and discreditable principle that "might makes right"; but early in the life of a republic this essential character of government by majority is not seen. The habit of submitting all questions of policy to the arbitrament of counting noses and assenting without question to the result invests the ordeal with a seeming sanctity, and what was at first obeyed as the command of power comes to be revered as the oracle of wisdom. The innumerable instances—such as the famous ones of Galileo and Keeley[14]—in which one man has been right and all the rest of the race wrong, are overlooked, or their significance missed, and "public opinion" is followed as a divine and infallible guide through every bog into which it blindly stumbles and over every precipice in its fortuitous path. Clearly, sooner or later will be encountered a bog that will smother or a precipice that will crush. Thoroughly to apprehend the absurdity of the ancient faith in the wisdom of majorities let the loyal reader try to fancy our gracious Sovereign by any possibility wrong, or his unanimous Ministry by any possibility right!

During the latter half of the "nineteenth century" there arose in the Connected States a political element opposed to all government, which frankly declared its object to be anarchy. This astonishing heresy was not of indigenous growth: its seeds were imported from Europe by the emigration or banishment thence of criminals congenitally incapable of understanding and valuing the blessings of monarchical institutions, and whose method of protest was murder. The governments against which they conspired in their native lands were too strong in authority and too enlightened in policy for them to overthrow. Hundreds of them were put to death, thousands imprisoned and sent into exile. But in America, whither those who escaped fled for safety, they found conditions entirely favorable to the prosecution of their designs.

A revered fetish of the Americans was "freedom of speech": it was believed that if bad men were permitted to proclaim their evil wishes they would go no further in the direction of executing them—that if they might say what they would like to do they would not care to do it. The close relation between speech and action was not understood. Because the Americans themselves had long been accustomed, in their own political debates and discussions, to the use of unmeaning declamations and threats which they had no intention of executing, they reasoned that others were like them, and attributed to the menaces of these desperate and earnest outcasts no greater importance than to their own. They thought also that the foreign anarchists, having exchanged the tyranny of kings for that of majorities, would be content with their new and better lot and become in time good and law-abiding citizens.

The anarchist of that far day (thanks to the firm hands of our gracious sovereigns the species is now extinct) was a very different person from what our infatuated ancestors imagined him. He struck at government, not because it was bad, but because it was government. He hated authority, not for its tyranny, but for its power. And in order to make this plain to observation he frequently chose his victim from amongst those whose rule was most conspicuously benign.

Of the seven early Presidents of the American republic who perished by assassination no fewer than four were slain by anarchists with no personal wrongs to impel them to the deed—nothing but an implacable hostility to law and authority. The fifth victim, indeed, was a notorious demagogue who had pardoned the assassin of the fourth.[15]

The field of the anarchist's greatest activity was always a republic, not only to emphasize his impartial hatred of all government, but because of the inherent feebleness of that form of government, its inability to protect itself against any kind of aggression by any considerable number of its people having a common malevolent purpose. In a republic the crust that confined the fires of violence and sedition was thinnest.

No improvement in the fortunes of the original anarchists through immigration to what was then called the New World would have made them good citizens. From centuries of secret war against particular forms of authority in their own countries they had inherited a bitter antagonism to all authority, even the most beneficent. In their new home they were worse than in their old. In the sunshine of opportunity the rank and sickly growth of their perverted natures became hardy, vigorous, bore fruit. They surrounded themselves with proselytes from the ranks of the idle, the vicious, the unsuccessful. They stimulated and organized discontent. Every one of them became a center of moral and political contagion. To those as yet unprepared to accept anarchy was offered the milder dogma of Socialism, and to those even weaker in the faith something vaguely called Reform. Each was initiated into that degree to which the induration of his conscience and the character of his discontent made him eligible, and in which he could be most serviceable, the body of the people still cheating themselves with the false sense of security begotten of the belief that they were somehow exempt from the operation of all agencies inimical to their national welfare and integrity. Human nature, they thought, was different in the West from what it was in the East: in the New World the old causes would not have the old effects: a republic had some inherent vitality of its own, entirely independent of any action intended to keep it alive. They felt that words and phrases had some talismanic power, and charmed themselves asleep by repeating "liberty," "all men equal before the law," "dictates of conscience," "free speech" and all manner of such incantation to exorcise the spirits of the night. And when they could no longer close their eyes to the dangers environing them; when they saw at last that what they had mistaken for the magic power of their form of government and its assured security was really its radical weakness and subjective peril— they found their laws inadequate to repression of the enemy, the enemy too strong to permit the enactment of adequate laws. The belief that a malcontent armed with freedom of speech, a newspaper, a vote and a rifle less dangerous than a malcontent with a still tongue in his head, empty hands and under police surveillance was abandoned, but all too late. From its fatuous dream the nation was awakened by the noise of arms, the shrieks of women and the red glare of burning cities.

Beginning with the slaughter at St. Louis on a night in the year 1920, when no fewer than twenty-two thousand citizens were slain in the streets and half the city destroyed, massacre followed massacre with frightful rapidity. New York fell in the month following, many thousands of its inhabitants escaping fire and sword only to be driven into the bay and drowned, "the roaring of the water in their ears," says Bardeal, "augmented by the hoarse clamor of their red-handed pursuers, whose blood-thirst was unsated by the sea." A week later Washington was destroyed, with all its public buildings and archives; the President and his Ministry were slain, Congress was dispersed, and an unknown number of officials and private citizens perished. Of all the principal cities only Chicago and San Francisco escaped. The people of the former were all anarchists and the latter was valorously and successfully defended by the Chinese.[16]

The urban anarchists were eventually subdued and some semblance of order was restored, but greater woes and sharper shames awaited this unhappy nation, as we shall see.

In turning from this branch of our subject to consider the causes of the failure and bloody disruption of the great American republic other than those inherent in the form of government, it may not be altogether unprofitable to glance briefly at what seems to a superficial view the inconsistent phenomenon of great material prosperity. It is not to be denied that this unfortunate people was at one time singularly prosperous, in so far as national wealth is a measure and proof of prosperity. Among nations it was the richest nation. But at how great a sacrifice of better things was its wealth obtained! By the neglect of all education except that crude, elementary sort which fits men for the coarse delights of business and affairs but confers no capacity of rational enjoyment; by exalting the worth of wealth and making it the test and touchstone of merit; by ignoring art, scorning literature and despising science, except as these might contribute to the glutting of the purse; by setting up and maintaining an artificial standard of morals which condoned all offenses against the property and peace of every one but the condoner; by pitilessly crushing out of their natures every sentiment and aspiration unconnected with accumulation of property, these civilized savages and commercial barbarians attained their sordid end. Before they had rounded the first half-century of their existence as a nation they had sunk so low in the scale of morality that it was considered nothing discreditable to take the hand and even visit the house of a man who had grown rich by means notoriously corrupt and dishonorable; and Harley declares that even the editors and writers of newspapers, after fiercely assailing such men in their journals, would be seen "hobnobbing" with them in public places.[17] (The nature of the social ceremony named the "hobnob" is not now understood, but it is known that it was a sign of amity and favor.) When men or nations devote all the powers of their minds and bodies to the heaping up of wealth, wealth is heaped up. But what avails it? It may not be amiss to quote here the words of one of the greatest of the ancients whose works—fragmentary, alas—have come down to us.

ASHES OF THE BEACON

"Wealth has accumulated itself into masses; and poverty, also in accumulation enough, lies impassably separated from it; opposed, uncommunicating, like forces in positive and negative poles. The gods of this lower world sit aloft on glittering thrones, less happy than Epicurus's gods, but as indolent, as impotent; while the boundless living chaos of ignorance and hunger welters, terrific in its dark fury, under their feet. How much among us might be likened to a whited sepulcher: outwardly all pomp and strength, but inwardly full of horror and despair and dead men's bones! Iron highways, with their wains fire-winged, are uniting all the ends of the land; quays and moles, with their innumerable stately fleets, tame the ocean into one pliant bearer of burdens; labor's thousand arms, of sinew and of metal, all-conquering everywhere, from the tops of the mount down to the depths of the mine and the caverns of the sea, ply unweariedly for the service of man; yet man remains unserved. He has subdued this planet, his habitation and inheritance, yet reaps no profit from the victory. Sad to look upon: in the highest stage of civilization nine-tenths of mankind have to struggle in the lowest battle of savage or even animal man—the battle against famine. Countries are rich, prosperous in all manner of increase, beyond example; but the men of these countries are poor, needier than ever of all sustenance, outward and inward; of belief, of knowledge, of money, of food."[18]

To this somber picture of American "prosperity" in the nineteenth century nothing of worth can be added by the most inspired artist. Let us simply inscribe upon the gloomy canvas the memorable words of an illustrious poet of the period:

> That country speeds to an untoward fate,
> Where men are trivial and gold is great.[19]

One of the most "sacred" rights of the ancient American was the trial of an accused person by "a jury of his peers."[20] This, in America, was a right secured to him by a written constitution. It was almost universally believed to have had its origin in Magna Carta, a famous document which certain rebellious noblemen of another country had compelled their sovereign to sign under a threat of death. That celebrated "bill of rights" has not all come down to us, but researches of the learned have made it certain that it contained no mention of trial by jury, which, indeed, was unknown to its authors. The words *judicium parium*[21] meant to them something entirely different—the judgment of the entire community of freemen. The words and the practice they represented antedated Magna Carta by many centuries and were common to the Franks and other Germanic nations, amongst whom a trial "jury" consisted of persons having a knowledge of the matter to be determined—persons who in later times were called "witnesses" and rigorously excluded from the seats of judgment.[22]

It is difficult to conceive a more clumsy and ineffective machinery for ascertaining truth and doing justice than a jury of twelve men of the average intelligence, even among ourselves. What, then, must this device have been among the half-civilized tribes of the Connected States of America! Nay, the case is worse than that, for it was the practice to prevent men of even the average intelligence from serving as jurors. Jurors had to be residents of the locality of the crime charged, and every crime was made a matter of public notoriety long before the accused was brought to trial; yet, as a rule, he who had read or talked about the trial was held disqualified to serve. This in a country where, when a man who could read was not reading about local crimes he was talking about them, or if doing neither was doing something worse!

To the twelve men so chosen the opposing lawyers addressed their disingenuous pleas and for their consideration the witnesses presented their carefully rehearsed testimony, most of it false. So unintelligent were these juries that a great part of the time in every trial was consumed in keeping from them certain kinds of evidence with which they could not be trusted; yet the lawyers were permitted to submit to them any kind of misleading argument that they pleased and fortify it with innuendoes without relevancy and logic without sense. Appeals to their passions, their sympathies, their prejudices, were regarded as legitimate influences and tolerated by the judges on the theory that each side's offenses would about offset those of the other. In a criminal case it was expected that the prosecutor would declare repeatedly and in the most solemn manner his belief in the guilt of the person accused, and that the attorney for the defense would affirm with equal gravity his conviction of his client's innocence. How could they impress the jury with a belief which they did not themselves venture to affirm? It is not recorded that any lawyer ever rebelled against the iron authority of these conditions and stood for truth and conscience. They were, indeed, the conditions of his existence as a lawyer, a fact which they easily persuaded themselves mitigated the baseness of their obedience to them, or justified it altogether.

The judges, as a rule, were no better, for before they could become judges they must have been advocates, with an advocate's fatal disabilities of judgment. Most of them depended for their office upon the favor of the people, which, also, was fatal to the independence, the dignity and the impartiality to which they laid so solemn claim. In their decisions they favored, so far as they dared, every interest, class or person powerful enough to help or hurt them in an election. Holding their high office by so precarious a tenure, they were under strong temptation to enrich themselves from the serviceable purses of wealthy litigants, and in disregard of justice to cultivate the favor of the attorneys practicing before them, and before whom they might soon be compelled themselves to practice.

In the higher courts of the land, where juries were unknown and appointed judges held their seats for life, these awful conditions did not obtain, and there Justice might have been content to dwell, and there she actually did sometimes set her foot. Unfortunately, the great judges had the consciences of their education. They had crept to place through the slime of the lower courts and their robes of office bore the damnatory evidence. Unfortunately, too, the attorneys, the jury habit strong upon them, brought into the superior tribunals the moral characteristics and professional methods acquired in the lower. Instead of assisting the judges to ascertain the truth and the law, they cheated in argument and took liberties with fact, deceiving the court whenever they deemed it to the interest of their cause to do so, and as willingly won by a technicality or a trick as by the justice of their contention and their ability in supporting it. Altogether, the entire judicial system of the Connected States of America was inefficient, disreputable, corrupt.

The result might easily have been foreseen and doubtless was predicted by patriots whose admonitions have not come down to us. Denied protection of the law, neither property nor life was safe. Greed filled his coffers from the meager hoards of Thrift, private vengeance took the place of legal redress, mad multitudes rioted and slew with virtual immunity from punishment or blame, and the land was red with crime.

A singular phenomenon of the time was the immunity of criminal women. Among the Americans woman held a place unique in the history of nations. If not actually worshiped as a deity, as some historians, among them the great Sagab-Joffoy, have affirmed, she was at least regarded with feelings of veneration which the modern mind has a difficulty in comprehending. Some degree of compassion for her mental inferiority, some degree of forbearance toward her infirmities of temper, some degree of immunity for the offenses which these peculiarities entail—these are common to all peoples above the grade of barbarians.[23] In ancient America these chivalrous sentiments found open and lawful expression only in relieving woman of the burden of participation in political and military service; the laws gave her no express exemption from responsibility for crime. When she murdered, she was arrested; when arrested, brought to trial—though the origin and meaning of those observances are not now known. Gunkux, whose researches into the jurisprudence of antiquity enable him to speak with commanding authority of many things, gives us here nothing better than the conjecture that the trial of women for murder, in the nineteenth century and a part of the twentieth, was the survival of an earlier custom of actually convicting and punishing them, but it seems extremely improbable that a people that once put its female assassins to death would ever have relinquished the obvious advantages of the practice while retaining with purposeless tenacity some of its costly preliminary forms. Whatever may have been the reason, the custom was observed with all the gravity of a serious intention. Gunkux professes knowledge of one or two instances (he does not name his authorities) where matters went so far as conviction and sentence, and adds that the mischievous sentimentalists who had always lent themselves to the solemn jest by protestations of great *vraisemblance* against "the judicial killing of women," became really alarmed and filled the land with their lamentations. Among the phenomena of brazen effrontery he classes the fact that some of these loud protagonists of the right of women to assassinate unpunished were themselves women! Howbeit, the sentences, if ever pronounced, were never executed, and during the first quarter of the twentieth century the meaningless custom of bringing female assassins to trial was abandoned.[24] What the effect was of their exemption from this considerable inconvenience we have not the data to conjecture, unless we understand as an allusion to it some otherwise obscure words of the famous Edward Bok,[25] the only writer of the period whose work has survived. In his monumental essay on barbarous penology, entitled "Slapping the Wrist," he couples "woman's emancipation from the trammels of law" and "man's better prospect of death" in a way that some have construed as meaning that he regarded them as cause and effect. It must be said, however, that this interpretation finds no support in the general character of his writing, which is exceedingly humane, refined and womanly.

It has been said that the writings of this great man are the only surviving work of his period, but of that we are not altogether sure. There exists a fragment of an anonymous essay on woman's legal responsibility which many Americologists think belongs to the beginning of the twentieth century. Certainly it could not have been written later than the middle of it, for at that time woman had been definitely released from any responsibility to any law but that of her own will. The essay is an argument against even such imperfect exemption as she had in its author's time.

"It has been urged," the writer says, "that women, being less rational and more emotional than men, should not be held accountable in the same degree. To this it may be answered that punishment for crime is not intended to be retaliatory, but admonitory and deterrent. It is, therefore, peculiarly necessary to those not easily reached by other forms of warning and dissuasion. Control of the wayward is not to be sought in reduction of restraints, but in their multiplication. One who cannot be curbed by reason may be curbed by fear, a familiar truth which lies at the foundation of all penological systems. The argument for exemption of women is equally cogent for exemption of habitual criminals, for they too are abnormally inaccessible to reason, abnormally disposed to obedience to the suasion of their unregulated impulses and passions. To free them from the restraints of the fear of punishment would be a bold innovation which has as yet found no respectable proponent outside their own class.

"Very recently this dangerous enlargement of the meaning of the phrase 'emancipation of woman' has been fortified with a strange advocacy by the female 'champions of their sex.' Their argument runs this way: 'We are denied a voice in the making of the laws relating to infliction of the death penalty; it is unjust to hold us to an accountability to which we have not assented.' Of course this argument is as broad as the entire body of law; it amounts to nothing less than a demand for general immunity from all laws, for to none of them has woman's assent been asked or given. But let us consider this amazing claim with reference only to the proposal in the service and promotion of which it is now urged: exemption of women from the death penalty for murder. In the last analysis it is seen to be a simple demand for compensation. It says: 'You owe us a *solatium*.[26] Since you deny us the right to vote, you should give us the right to assassinate. We do not appraise it at so high a valuation as the other franchise, but we do value it.'

"Apparently they do: without legal, but with virtual, immunity from punishment, the women of this country take an average of one thousand lives annually, nine in ten being the lives of men. Juries of men, incited and sustained by public opinion, have actually deprived every adult male American of the right to live. If the death of any man is desired by any woman for any reason he is without protection. She has only to kill him and say that he wronged or insulted her. Certain almost incredible recent instances prove that no woman is too base for immunity, no crime against life sufficiently rich in all the elements of depravity to compel a conviction of the assassin, or, if she is convicted and sentenced, her punishment by the public executioner."[27]

In this interesting fragment, quoted by Bogul in his "History of an Extinct Civilization," we learn something of the shame and peril of American citizenship under institutions which, not having run their foreordained course to the unhappy end, were still in some degree supportable. What these institutions became afterward is a familiar story. It is true that the law of trial by jury was repealed. It had broken down, but not until it had sapped the whole nation's respect for all law, for all forms of authority, for order and private virtues. The people whose rude forefathers in another land it had served roughly to protect against their tyrants, it had lamentably failed to protect against themselves, and when in madness they swept it away, it was not as one renouncing an error, but as one impatient of the truth which the error is still believed to contain. They flung it away, not as an ineffectual restraint, but as a restraint; not because it was no longer an instrument of justice for the determination of truth, but because they feared that it might again become such. In brief, trial by jury was abolished only when it had provoked anarchy.

Before turning to another phase of this ancient civilization I cannot forbear to relate, after the learned and ingenious Gunkux, the only known instance of a public irony expressing itself in the sculptor's noble art. In the ancient city of Hohokus[28] once stood a monument of colossal size and impressive dignity. It was erected by public subscription to the memory of a man whose only distinction consisted in a single term of service as a juror in a famous murder trial, the details of which have not come down to us. This occupied the court and held public attention for many weeks, being bitterly contested by both prosecution and defense. When at last it was given to the jury by the judge in the most celebrated charge that had ever been delivered from the bench, a ballot was taken at once. The jury stood eleven for acquittal to one for conviction. And so it stood at every ballot of the more than fifty that were taken during the fortnight that the jury was locked up for deliberation. Moreover, the dissenting juror would not argue the matter; he would listen with patient attention while his eleven indignant opponents thundered their opinions into his ears, even when they supported them with threats of personal violence; but not a word would he say. At last a disagreement was formally entered, the jury discharged and the obstinate juror chased from the city by the maddened populace. Despairing of success in another trial and privately admitting his belief in the prisoner's innocence, the public prosecutor moved for his release, which the judge ordered with remarks plainly implying his own belief that the wrong man had been tried.

Years afterward the accused person died confessing his guilt, and a little later one of the jurors who had been sworn to try the case admitted that he had attended the trial on the first day only, having been personated during the rest of the proceedings by a twin brother, the obstinate member, who was a deaf-mute.

The monument to this eminent public servant was overthrown and destroyed by an earthquake in the year 2342.

One of the causes of that popular discontent which brought about the stupendous events resulting in the disruption of the great republic, historians and archæologists are agreed in reckoning "insurance."[29] Of the exact nature of that factor in the problem of the national life of that distant day we are imperfectly informed; many of its details have perished from the record, yet its outlines loom large through the mist of ages and can be traced with greater precision than is possible in many more important matters.

In the monumental work of Professor Golunk-Dorstro ("Some Account of the Insurance Delusion in Ancient America") we have its most considerable modern exposition; and Gakler's well-known volume, "The Follies of Antiquity," contains much interesting matter relating to it. From these and other sources the student of human unreason can reconstruct that astounding fallacy of insurance as, from three joints of its tail, the great naturalist Bogramus restored the ancient elephant, from hoof to horn.

The game of insurance, as practiced by the ancient Americans (and, as Gakler conjectures, by some of the tribesmen of Europe), was gambling, pure and simple, despite the sentimental character that its proponents sought to impress upon some forms of it for the greater prosperity of their dealings with its dupes. Essentially, it was a bet between the insurer and the insured. The number of ways in which the wager was made—all devised by the insurer—was almost infinite, but in none of them was there a departure from the intrinsic nature of the transaction as seen in its simplest, frankest form, which we shall here expound.

To those unlearned in the economical institutions of antiquity it is necessary to explain that in ancient America, long prior to the disastrous Japanese war, individual ownership of property was unrestricted; every person was permitted to get as much as he was able, and to hold it as his own without regard to his needs, or whether he made any good use of it or not. By some plan of distribution not now understood even the habitable surface of the earth, with the minerals beneath, was parceled out among the favored few, and there was really no place except at sea where children of the others could lawfully be born. Upon a part of the dry land that he had been able to acquire, or had leased from another for the purpose, a man would build a house worth, say, ten thousand *drusoes*. (The ancient unit of value was the "dollar," but nothing is now known as to its actual worth.) Long before the building was complete the owner was beset by "touts" and "cappers"[30] of the insurance game, who poured into his ears the most ingenious expositions of the advantages of betting that it would burn down—for with incredible fatuity the people of that time continued, generation after generation, to build inflammable habitations. The persons whom the capper represented—they called themselves an "insurance company"—stood ready to accept the bet, a fact which seems to have generated no suspicion in the mind of the house-owner. Theoretically, of course, if the house did burn payment of the wager would partly or wholly recoup the winner of the bet for the loss of his house, but in fact the result of the transaction was commonly very different. For the privilege of betting that his property would be destroyed by fire the owner had to pay to the gentleman betting that it would not be, a certain percentage of its value every year, called a "premium." The amount of this was determined by the company, which employed statisticians and actuaries to fix it at such a sum that, according to the law of probabilities, long before the house was "due to burn," the company would have received more than the value of it in premiums. In other words, the owner of the house would himself supply the money to pay his bet, and a good deal more.

But how, it may be asked, could the company's actuary know that the man's house would last until he had paid in more than its insured value in premiums—more, that is to say, than the company would have to pay back? He could not, but from his statistics he could know how many houses in ten thousand of that kind burned in their first year, how many in their second, their third, and so on. That was all that he needed to know, the house-owners knowing nothing about it. He fixed his rates according to the facts, and the occasional loss of a bet in an individual instance did not affect the certainty of a general winning. Like other professional gamblers, the company expected to lose sometimes, yet knew that in the long run it *must* win; which meant that in any special case it would *probably* win. With a thousand gambling games open to him in which the chances were equal, the infatuated dupe chose to "sit into" one where they were against him! Deceived by the cappers' fairy tales, dazed by the complex and incomprehensible "calculations" put forth for his undoing, and having ever in the ear of his imagination the crackle and roar of the impoverishing flames, he grasped at the hope of beating—in an unwelcome way, it is true—"the man that kept the table."[31] He must have known for a certainty that if the company could afford to insure him he could not afford to let it. He must have known that the whole body of the insured paid to the insurers more than the insurers paid to them; otherwise the business could not have been conducted. This they cheerfully admitted; indeed, they proudly affirmed it. In fact, insurance companies were the only professional gamblers that had the incredible hardihood to parade their enormous winnings as an inducement to play against their game. These winnings ("assets," they called them) proved their ability, they said, to pay when they lost; and that was indubitably true. What they did not prove, unfortunately, was the *will* to pay, which from the imperfect court records of the period that have come down to us, appears frequently to have been lacking. Gakler relates that in the instance of the city of San Francisco (somewhat doubtfully identified by Macronus as the modern fishing-village of Gharoo) the disinclination of the insurance companies to pay their bets had the most momentous consequences.

In the year 1906 San Francisco was totally destroyed by fire. The conflagration was caused by the friction of a pig scratching itself against an angle of a wooden building. More than one hundred thousand persons perished, and the loss of property is estimated by Kobo-Dogarque at one and a half million *drusoes*.[32] On more than two-thirds of this enormous sum the insurance companies had laid bets, and the greater part of it they refused to pay. In justification they pointed out that the deed performed by the pig was "an act of God," who in the analogous instance of the express companies had been specifically forbidden to take any action affecting the interests of parties to a contract, or the result of an agreed undertaking.

In the ensuing litigation their attorneys cited two notable precedents. A few years before the San Francisco disaster, another American city had experienced a similar one through the upsetting of a lamp by the kick of a cow.[33] In that case, also, the insurance companies had successfully denied their liability on the ground that the cow, manifestly incited by some supernatural power, had unlawfully influenced the result of a wager to which she was not a party. The companies defendant had contended that the recourse of the property-owners was against, not them, but the owner of the cow. In his decision sustaining that view and dismissing the case, a learned judge (afterward president of one of the defendant companies) had in the legal phraseology of the period pronounced the action of the cow an obvious and flagrant instance of unwarrantable intervention.[34] Kobo-Dogarque believes that this decision was afterward reversed by an appellate court of contrary political complexion and the companies were compelled to compromise, but of this there is no record. It is certain that in the San Francisco case the precedent was urged.[35]

Another precedent which the companies cited with particular emphasis related to an unfortunate occurrence at a famous millionaires' club in London, the capital of the renowned king, John Bul. A gentleman passing in the street fell in a fit and was carried into the club in convulsions. Two members promptly made a bet upon his life. A physician who chanced to be present set to work upon the patient, when one of the members who had laid the wager came forward and restrained him, saying: "Sir, I beg that you will attend to your own business. I have my money on that fit."

Doubtless these two notable precedents did not constitute the entire case of the defendants in the San Francisco insurance litigation, but the additional pleas are lost to us.

Of the many forms of gambling known as insurance that called life insurance appears to have been the most vicious.[36] In essence it was the same as fire insurance, marine insurance, accident insurance and so forth, with an added offensiveness in that it was a betting on human lives—commonly by the policy-holder on lives that should have been held most sacred and altogether immune from the taint of traffic. In point of practical operation this ghastly business was characterized by a more fierce and flagrant dishonesty than any of its kindred pursuits. To such lengths of robbery did the managers go that at last the patience of the public was exhausted and a comparatively trivial occurrence fired the combustible elements of popular indignation to a white heat in which the entire insurance business of the country was burned out of existence, together with all the gamblers who had invented and conducted it. The president of one of the companies was walking one morning in a street of New York, when he had the bad luck to step on the tail of a dog and was bitten in retaliation. Frenzied by the pain of the wound, he gave the creature a savage kick and it ran howling toward a group of idlers in front of a grocery store. In ancient America the dog was a sacred animal, worshiped by all sorts and conditions of tribesmen. The idlers at once raised a great cry, and setting upon the offender beat him so that he died.

Their act was infectious: men, women and children trooped out of their dwellings by thousands to join them, brandishing whatever weapons they could snatch, and uttering wild cries of vengeance. This formidable mob overpowered the police, and marching from one insurance office to another, successively demolished them all, slew such officers as they could lay hands on and chased the fugitive survivors into the sea, "where," says a quaint chronicle of the time, "they were eaten by their kindred, the sharks." This carnival of violence continued all the day, and at set of sun not one person connected with any form of insurance remained alive.

Ferocious and bloody as was the massacre, it was only the beginning. As the news of it went blazing and coruscating along the wires by which intelligence was then conveyed across the country, city after city caught the contagion. Everywhere, even in the small hamlets and the agricultural districts, the dupes rose against their dupers. The smouldering resentment of years burst into flame, and within a week all that was left of insurance in America was the record of a monstrous and cruel delusion written in the blood of its promoters.

A remarkable feature of the crude and primitive civilization of the Americans was their religion. This was polytheistic, as is that of all backward peoples, and among their minor deities were their own women. This has been disputed by respectable authorities, among them Gunkux and the younger Kekler, but the weight of archæological testimony is against them, for, as Sagab-Joffoy ingeniously points out, none of less than divine rank would by even the lowest tribes be given unrestricted license to kill. Among the Americans woman, as already pointed out, indubitably had that freedom, and exercised it with terrible effect, a fact which makes the matter of their religion pertinent to the purpose of this monograph. If ever an American woman was punished by law for murder of a man no record of the fact is found; whereas, such American literature as we possess is full of the most enthusiastic adulation of the impossible virtues and imaginary graces of the human female. One writer even goes to the length of affirming that respect for the sex is the foundation of political stability, the cornerstone of civil and religious liberty! After the breakup of the republic and the savage intertribal wars that followed, Gyneolatry[37] was an exhausted cult and woman was relegated to her old state of benign subjection.

Unfortunately, we know little of the means of travel in ancient America, other than the names. It seems to have been done mainly by what were called "railroads," upon which wealthy associations of men transported their fellow-citizens in some kind of vehicle at a low speed, seldom exceeding fifty or sixty miles an hour, as distance and time were then reckoned—about equal to seven *kaltabs* a *grillog*. Notwithstanding this slow movement of the vehicles, the number and fatality of accidents were incredible. In the Zopetroq Museum of Archæology is preserved an official report (found in the excavations made by Droyhors on the supposed site of Washington) of a Government Commission of the Connected States. From that document we learn that in the year 1907 of their era the railroads of the country killed 5,000 persons and wounded 72,286—a mortality which is said by the commissioners to be twice that of the battle of Gettysburg, concerning which we know nothing but the name.[38] This was about the annual average of railroad casualties of the period, and if it provoked comment it at least led to no reform, for at a later period we find the mortality even greater. That it was preventable is shown by the fact that in the same year the railroads of Great Britain, where the speed was greater and the intervals between vehicles less, killed only one passenger. It was a difference of government: Great Britain had a government that governed; America had not. Happily for humanity, the kind of government that does not govern, self-government, "government of the people, by the people and for the people"[39] (to use a meaningless paradox of that time) has perished from the face of the earth.

An inherent weakness in republican government was that it assumed the honesty and intelligence of the majority, "the masses," who were neither honest nor intelligent. It would doubtless have been an excellent government for a people so good and wise as to need none. In a country having such a system the leaders, the politicians, must necessarily all be demagogues, for they can attain to place and power by no other method than flattery of the people and subserviency to the will of the majority. In all the ancient American political literature we look in vain for a single utterance of truth and reason regarding these matters. In none of it is a hint that the multitude was ignorant and vicious, as we know it to have been, and as it must necessarily be in any country, to whatever high average of intelligence and morality the people attain; for "intelligence" and "morality" are comparative terms, the standard of comparison being the intelligence and morality of the wisest and best, who must always be the few. Whatever general advance is made, those not at the head are behind—are ignorant and immoral according to the new standard, and unfit to control in the higher and broader policies demanded by the progress made. Where there is true and general progress the philosopher of yesterday would be the ignoramus of to-day, the honorable of one generation the vicious of another. The peasant of our time is incomparably superior to the statesman of ancient America, yet he is unfit to govern, for there are others more fit.

That a body of men can be wiser than its wisest member seems to the modern understanding so obvious and puerile an error that it is inconceivable that any people, even the most primitive, could ever have entertained it;[40] yet we know that in America it was a fixed and steadfast political faith. The people of that day did not, apparently, attempt to explain how the additional wisdom was acquired by merely assembling in council, as in their "legislatures"; they seem to have assumed that it was so, and to have based their entire governmental system upon that assumption, with never a suspicion of its fallacy. It is like assuming that a mountain range is higher than its highest peak. In the words of Golpek, "The early Americans believed that units of intelligence were addable quantities," or as Soseby more wittily puts it, "They thought that in a combination of idiocies they had the secret of sanity."

The Americans, as has been said, never learned that even among themselves majorities ruled, not because they ought, but because they could—not because they were wise, but because they were strong. The count of noses determined, not the better policy, but the more powerful party. The weaker submitted, as a rule, for it had to or risk a war in which it would be at a disadvantage. Yet in all the early years of the republic they seem honestly to have dignified their submission as "respect for the popular verdict." They even quoted from the Latin language the sentiment that "the voice of the people is the voice of God."[41] And this hideous blasphemy was as glib upon the lips of those who, without change of mind, were defeated at the polls year after year as upon those of the victors.

Of course, their government was powerless to restrain any aggression or encroachment upon the general welfare as soon as a considerable body of voters had banded together to undertake it. A notable instance has been recorded by Bamscot in his great work, "Some Evil Civilizations." After the first of America's great intestinal wars the surviving victors formed themselves into an organization which seems at first to have been purely social and benevolent, but afterward fell into the hands of rapacious politicians who in order to preserve their power corrupted their followers by distributing among them enormous sums of money exacted from the government by threats of overturning it. In less than a half-century after the war in which they had served, so great was the fear which they inspired in whatever party controlled the national treasury that the total sum of their exactions was no less annually than seventeen million *prastams!*[42] As Dumbleshaw naïvely puts it, "having saved their country, these gallant gentlemen naturally took it for themselves." The eventual massacre of the remnant of this hardy and impenitent organization by the labor unions more accustomed to the use of arms is beyond the province of this monograph to relate. The matter is mentioned at all only because it is a typical example of the open robbery that marked that period of the republic's brief and inglorious existence; the Grand Army, as it called itself, was no worse and no better than scores of other organizations having no purpose but plunder and no method but menace. A little later nearly all classes and callings became organized conspiracies, each seeking an unfair advantage through laws which the party in power had not the firmness to withhold, nor the party hoping for power the courage to oppose. The climax of absurdity in this direction was reached in 1918, when an association of barbers, known as Noblemen of the Razor, procured from the parliament of the country a law giving it a representative in the President's Cabinet, and making it a misdemeanor to wear a beard.

In Soseby's "History of Popular Government" he mentions "a monstrous political practice known as 'Protection to American Industries.'" Modern research has not ascertained precisely what it was; it is known rather from its effects than in its true character, but from what we can learn of it to-day I am disposed to number it among those malefic agencies concerned in the destruction of the American republics, particularly the Connected States, although it appears not to have been peculiar to "popular government." Some of the contemporary monarchies of Europe were afflicted with it, but by the divine favor which ever guards a throne its disastrous effects were averted. "Protection" consisted in a number of extraordinary expedients, the purposes of which and their relations to one another cannot with certainty be determined in the present state of our knowledge. Debrethin and others agree that one feature of it was the support, by general taxation, of a few favored citizens in public palaces, where they passed their time in song and dance and all kinds of revelry. They were not, however, altogether idle, being required, out of the sums bestowed upon them, to employ a certain number of men each in erecting great piles of stone and pulling them down again, digging holes in the ground and then filling them with earth, pouring water into casks and then drawing it off, and so forth. The unhappy laborers were subject to the most cruel oppressions, but the knowledge that their wages came from the pockets of those whom their work nowise benefited was so gratifying to them that nothing could induce them to leave the service of their heartless employers to engage in lighter and more useful labor.

Another characteristic of "Protection" was the maintenance at the principal seaports of "customs-houses," which were strong fortifications armed with heavy guns for the purpose of destroying or driving away the trading ships of foreign nations. It was this that caused the Connected States to be known abroad as the "Hermit Republic," a name of which its infatuated citizens were strangely proud, although they had themselves sent armed ships to open the ports of Japan and other Oriental countries to their own commerce. In their own case, if a foreign ship came empty and succeeded in evading the fire of the "customs-house," as sometimes occurred, she was permitted to take away a cargo.

It is obvious that such a system was distinctly evil, but it must be confessed our uncertainty regarding the whole matter of "Protection" does not justify us in assigning it a definite place among the causes of national decay. That in some way it produced an enormous revenue is certain, and that the method was dishonest is no less so; for this revenue—known as a "surplus"—was so abhorred while it lay in the treasury that all were agreed upon the expediency of getting rid of it, two great political parties existing for apparently no other purpose than the patriotic one of taking it out.

But how, it may be asked, could people so misgoverned get on, even as well as they did?

From the records that have come down to us it does not appear that they got on very well. They were preyed upon by all sorts of political adventurers, whose power in most instances was limited only by the contemporaneous power of other political adventurers equally unscrupulous. A full half of the taxes wrung from them was stolen. Their public lands, millions of square miles, were parceled out among banded conspirators. Their roads and the streets of their cities were nearly impassable. Their public buildings, conceived in abominable taste and representing enormous sums of money, which never were used in their construction, began to tumble about the ears of the workmen before they were completed. The most delicate and important functions of government were intrusted to men with neither knowledge, heart nor experience, who by their corruption imperiled the public interest and by their blundering disgraced the national name. In short, all the train of evils inseparable from government of any kind beset this unhappy people with tenfold power, together with hundreds of worse ones peculiar to their own faulty and unnatural system. It was thought that their institutions would give them peace, yet in the first three-quarters of a century of their existence they fought three important wars: one of revenge, one of aggression and one—the bloodiest and most wasteful known up to that time—among themselves.[43] And before a century and a half had passed they had the humiliation to see many of their seaport cities destroyed by the Emperor of Japan in a quarrel which they had themselves provoked by their greed of Oriental dominion.

By far the most important factor concerned in bringing about the dissolution of the republic and the incredible horrors that followed it was what was known as "the contest between capital and labor." This momentous struggle began in a rather singular way through an agitation set afoot by certain ambitious women who preached at first to inattentive and inhospitable ears, but with ever increasing acceptance, the doctrine of equality of the sexes, and demanded the "emancipation" of woman. True, woman was already an object of worship and had, as noted before, the right to kill. She was treated with profound and sincere deference, because of certain humble virtues, the product of her secluded life. Men of that time appear to have felt for women, in addition to religious reverence, a certain sentiment known as "love." The nature of this feeling is not clearly known to us, and has been for ages a matter of controversy evolving more heat than light. This much is plain: it was largely composed of good will, and had its root in woman's dependence. Perhaps it had something of the character of the benevolence with which we regard our slaves, our children and our domestic animals—everything, in fact, that is weak, helpless and inoffensive.

Woman was not satisfied; her superserviceable advocates taught her to demand the right to vote, to hold office, to own property, to enter into employment in competition with man. Whatever she demanded she eventually got. With the effect upon her we are not here concerned; the predicted gain to political purity did not ensue, nor did commercial integrity receive any stimulus from her participation in commercial pursuits. What indubitably did ensue was a more sharp and bitter competition in the industrial world through this increase of more than thirty per cent. in its wage-earning population. In no age nor country has there ever been sufficient employment for those requiring it. The effect of so enormously increasing the already disproportionate number of workers in a single generation could be no other than disastrous. Every woman employed displaced or excluded some man, who, compelled to seek a lower employment, displaced another, and so on, until the least capable or most unlucky of the series became a tramp—a nomadic mendicant criminal! The number of these dangerous vagrants in the beginning of the twentieth century of their era has been estimated by Holobom at no less than seven and a half *blukuks!* Of course, they were as tow to the fires of sedition, anarchy and insurrection. It does not very nearly relate to our present purpose, but it is impossible not to note in passing that this unhappy result, directly flowing from woman's invasion of the industrial field, was unaccompanied by any material advantage to herself. Individual women, here and there one, may themselves have earned the support that they would otherwise not have received, but the sex as a whole was not benefited. They provided for themselves no better than they had previously been provided for, and would still have been provided for, by the men whom they displaced. The whole somber incident is unrelieved by a single gleam of light.

Previously to this invasion of the industrial field by woman there had arisen conditions that were in themselves peculiarly menacing to the social fabric. Some of the philosophers of the period, rummaging amongst the dubious and misunderstood facts of commercial and industrial history, had discovered what they were pleased to term "the law of supply and demand"; and this they expounded with so ingenious a sophistry, and so copious a wealth of illustration and example that what is at best but a faulty and imperfectly applicable principle, limited and cut into by all manner of other considerations, came to be accepted as the sole explanation and basis of material prosperity and an infallible rule for the proper conduct of industrial affairs. In obedience to this "law"—for, interpreting it in its straitest sense they understood it to be mandatory—employers and employees alike regulated by its iron authority all their dealings with one another, throwing off the immemorial relations of mutual dependence and mutual esteem as tending to interfere with beneficent operation. The employer came to believe conscientiously that it was not only profitable and expedient, but under all circumstances his duty, to obtain his labor for as little money as possible, even as he sold its product for as much. Considerations of humanity were not banished from his heart, but most sternly excluded from his business. Many of these misguided men would give large sums to various charities; would found universities, hospitals, libraries; would even stop on their way to relieve beggars in the street; but for their own work-people they had no care. Straman relates in his "Memoirs" that a wealthy manufacturer once said to one of his mill-hands who had asked for an increase of his wages because unable to support his family on the pay that he was getting: "Your family is nothing to me. I cannot afford to mix benevolence with my business." Yet this man, the author adds, had just given a thousand *drusoes* to a "seaman's home." He could afford to care for other men's employees, but not for his own. He could not see that the act which he performed as truly, and to the same degree, cut down his margin of profit in his business as the act which he refused to perform would have done, and had not the advantage of securing him better service from a grateful workman.

On their part the laborers were no better. Their relations to their employers being "purely commercial," as it was called, they put no heart into their work, seeking ever to do as little as possible for their money, precisely as their employers sought to pay as little as possible for the work they got. The interests of the two classes being thus antagonized, they grew to distrust and hate each other, and each accession of ill feeling produced acts which tended to broaden the breach more and more. There was neither cheerful service on the one side nor ungrudging payment on the other.

The harder industrial conditions generated by woman's irruption into a new domain of activity produced among laboring men a feeling of blind discontent and concern. Like all men in apprehension, they drew together for mutual protection, they knew not clearly against what. They formed "labor unions," and believed them to be something new and effective in the betterment of their condition; whereas, from the earliest historical times, in Rome, in Greece, in Egypt, in Assyria, labor unions with their accepted methods of "striking" and rioting had been discredited by an almost unbroken record of failure. One of the oldest manuscripts then in existence, preserved in a museum at Turin, but now lost, related how the workmen employed in the necropolis at Thebes, dissatisfied with their allowance of corn and oil, had refused to work, broken out of their quarters and, after much rioting, been subdued by the arrows of the military. And such, despite the sympathies and assistance of brutal mobs of the populace, was sometimes the end of the American "strike."

Originally organized for self-protection, and for a time partly successful, these leagues became great tyrannies, so reasonless in their demands and so unscrupulous in their methods of enforcing them that the laws were unable to deal with them, and frequently the military forces of the several States were ordered out for the protection of life and property; but in most cases the soldiers fraternized with the leagues, ran away or were easily defeated. The cruel and mindless mobs had always the hypocritical sympathy and encouragement of the newspapers and the politicians, for both feared their power and courted their favor. The judges, dependent for their offices not only on "the labor vote," but, to obtain it, on the approval of the press and the politicians, boldly set aside the laws against conspiracy and strained to the utmost tension those relating to riot, arson and murder. To such a pass did all this come that in the year 1931 an innkeeper's denial of a half-holiday to an undercook resulted in the peremptory closing of half the factories in the country, the stoppage of all railroad travel and movement of freight by land and water and a general paralysis of the industries of the land. Many thousands of families, including those of the "strikers" and their friends, suffered from famine; armed conflicts occurred in every State; hundreds were slain and incalculable amounts of property wrecked and destroyed.

Failure, however, was inherent in the method, for success depended upon unanimity, and the greater the membership of the unions and the more serious their menace to the industries of the country, the higher was the premium for defection; and at last strike-breaking became a regular employment, organized, officered and equipped for the service required by the wealth and intelligence that directed it. From that moment the doom of labor unionism was decreed and inevitable. But labor unionism did not live long enough to die that way.

Naturally combinations of labor entailed combinations of capital. These were at first purely protective. They were brought into being by the necessity of resisting the aggressions of the others. But the trick of combination once learned, it was seen to have possibilities of profit in directions not dreamed of by its early promoters; its activities were not long confined to fighting the labor unions with their own weapons and with superior cunning and address. The shrewd and energetic men whose capacity and commercial experience had made them rich while the laborers remained poor were not slow to discern the advantages of coöperation over their own former method of competition among themselves. They continued to fight the labor unions, but ceased to fight one another. The result was that in the brief period of two generations almost the entire business of the country fell into the hands of a few gigantic corporations controlled by bold and unscrupulous men, who, by daring and ingenious methods, made the body of the people pay tribute to their greed.

In a country where money was all-powerful the power of money was used without stint and without scruple. Judges were bribed to do their duty, juries to convict, newspapers to support and legislators to betray their constituents and pass the most oppressive laws. By these corrupt means, and with the natural advantage of greater skill in affairs and larger experience in concerted action, the capitalists soon restored their ancient reign and the state of the laborer was worse than it had ever been before. Straman says that in his time two millions of unoffending workmen in the various industries were once discharged without warning and promptly arrested as vagrants and deprived of their ears because a sulking canal-boatman had kicked his captain's dog into the water. And the dog was a retriever.

Had the people been honest and intelligent, as the politicians affirmed them to be, the combination of capital could have worked no public injury—would, in truth, have been a great public benefit. It enormously reduced the expense of production and distribution, assured greater permanency of employment, opened better opportunities to general and special aptitude, gave an improved product and at first supplied it at a reduced price. Its crowning merit was that the industries of the country, being controlled by a few men from a central source, could themselves be easily controlled by law if law had been honestly administered. Under the old order of scattered jurisdictions, requiring a multitude of actions at law, little could be done, and little was done, to put a check on commercial greed; under the new, much was possible, and at times something was accomplished. But not for long; the essential dishonesty of the American character enabled these capable and conscienceless managers—"captains of industry" and "kings of finance"—to buy with money advantages and immunities superior to those that the labor unions could obtain by menaces and the promise of votes. The legislatures, the courts, the executive officers, all the sources of authority and springs of control, were defiled and impested until right and justice fled affrighted from the land, and the name of the country became a stench in the nostrils of the world.

Let us pause in our narrative to say here that much of the abuse of the so-called "trusts" by their victims took no account of the folly, stupidity and greed of the victims themselves. A favorite method by which the great corporations crushed out the competition of the smaller ones and of the "individual dealers" was by underselling them—a method made possible by nothing but the selfishness of the purchasing consumers who loudly complained of it. These could have stood by their neighbor, the "small dealer," if they had wanted to, and no underselling could have been done. When the trust lowered the price of its product they eagerly took the advantage offered, then cursed the trust for ruining the small dealer. When it raised the price they cursed it for ruining themselves. It is not easy to see what the trust could have done that would have been acceptable, nor is it surprising that it soon learned to ignore their clamor altogether and impenitently plunder those whom it could not hope to appease.

Another of the many sins justly charged against the "kings of finance" was this: They would buy properties worth, say, ten millions of "dollars" (the value of the dollar is now unknown) and issue stock upon it to the face value of, say, fifty millions. This their clamorous critics called "creating" for themselves forty millions of dollars. They created nothing; the stock had no dishonest value unless sold, and even at the most corrupt period of the government nobody was compelled by law to buy. In nine cases in ten the person who bought did so in the hope and expectation of getting much for little and something for nothing. The buyer was no better than the seller. He was a gambler. He "played against the game of the man who kept the table" (as the phrase went), and naturally he lost. Naturally, too, he cried out, but his lamentations, though echoed shrilly by the demagogues, seem to have been unavailing. Even the rudimentary intelligence of that primitive people discerned the impracticability of laws forbidding the seller to set his own price on the thing he would sell and declare it worth that price. Then, as now, nobody had to believe him. Of the few who bought these "watered" stocks in good faith as an investment in the honest hope of dividends it seems sufficient to say, in the words of an ancient Roman, "Against stupidity the gods themselves are powerless."[44] Laws that would adequately protect the foolish from the consequence of their folly would put an end to all commerce. The sin of "over-capitalization" differed in magnitude only, not in kind, from the daily practice of every salesman in every shop. Nevertheless, the popular fury that it aroused must be reckoned among the main causes contributory to the savage insurrections that accomplished the downfall of the republic.

With the formation of powerful and unscrupulous trusts of both labor and capital to subdue each other the possibilities of combination were not exhausted; there remained the daring plan of combining the two belligerents! And this was actually effected. The laborer's demand for an increased wage was always based upon an increased cost of living, which was itself chiefly due to increased cost of production from reluctant concessions of his former demands. But in the first years of the twentieth century observers noticed on the part of capital a lessening reluctance. More frequent and more extortionate and reasonless demands encountered a less bitter and stubborn resistance; capital was apparently weakening just at the time when, with its strong organizations of trained and willing strike-breakers, it was most secure. Not so; an ingenious malefactor, whose name has perished from history, had thought out a plan for bringing the belligerent forces together to plunder the rest of the population. In the accounts that have come down to us details are wanting, but we know that, little by little, this amazing project was accomplished. Wages rose to incredible rates. The cost of living rose with them, for employers—their new allies wielding in their service the weapons previously used against them, intimidation, the boycott and so forth—more than recouped themselves from the general public. Their employees got rebates on the prices of products, but for consumers who were neither laborers nor capitalists there was no mercy. Strikes were a thing of the past; strike-breakers threw themselves gratefully into the arms of the unions; "industrial discontent" vanished, in the words of a contemporary poet, "as by the stroke of an enchanter's wand."[45] All was peace, tranquility and order! Then the storm broke.

A man in St. Louis purchased a sheep's kidney for seven-and-a-half dollars. In his rage at the price he exclaimed: "As a public man I have given twenty of the best years of my life to bringing about a friendly understanding between capital and labor. I have succeeded, and may God have mercy on my meddlesome soul!"

The remark was resented, a riot ensued, and when the sun went down that evening his last beams fell upon a city reeking with the blood of a hundred millionaires and twenty thousand citizens and sons of toil!

Students of the history of those troublous times need not to be told what other and more awful events followed that bloody reprisal. Within forty-eight hours the country was ablaze with insurrection, followed by intestinal wars which lasted three hundred and seventy years and were marked by such hideous barbarities as the modern historian can hardly bring himself to relate. The entire stupendous edifice of popular government, temple and citadel of fallacies and abuses, had crashed to ruin. For centuries its fallen columns and scattered stones sheltered an ever diminishing number of skulking anarchists, succeeded by hordes of skin-clad savages subsisting on offal and raw flesh—the race-remnant of an extinct civilization. All finally vanished from history into a darkness impenetrable to conjecture.

In concluding this hasty and imperfect sketch I cannot forbear to relate an episode of the destructive and unnatural contest between labor and capital, which I find recorded in the almost forgotten work of Antrolius, who was an eye-witness to the incident.

At a time when the passions of both parties were most inflamed and scenes of violence most frequent it was somehow noised about that at a certain hour of a certain day some one—none could say who—would stand upon the steps of the Capitol and speak to the people, expounding a plan for reconciliation of all conflicting interests and pacification of the quarrel. At the appointed hour thousands had assembled to hear—glowering capitalists attended by hireling body-guards with firearms, sullen laborers with dynamite bombs concealed in their clothing. All eyes were directed to the specified spot, where suddenly appeared (none saw whence—it seemed as if he had been there all the time, such his tranquility) a tall, pale man clad in a long robe, bare-headed, his hair falling lightly upon his shoulders, his eyes full of compassion, and with such majesty of face and mien that all were awed to silence ere he spoke. Stepping slowly forward toward the throng and raising his right hand from the elbow, the index finger extended upward, he said, in a voice ineffably sweet and serious:

"Whatsoever ye would that men should do unto you, even so do ye also unto them."[46]

These strange words he repeated in the same solemn tones three times; then, as the expectant multitude waited breathless for his discourse, stepped quietly down into the midst of them, every one afterward declaring that he passed within a pace of where himself had stood. For a moment the crowd was speechless with surprise and disappointment, then broke into wild, fierce cries: "Lynch him, lynch him!" and some have testified that they heard the word "crucify." Struggling into looser order, the infuriated mob started in mad pursuit; but each man ran a different way and the stranger was seen again by none of them.

NYA (19 Feb. 1905): 22; E (26 Feb. 1905): 44 (with subtitle: "Written in 3940: An Historical Monograph"; an exhaustive revision of "The Fall of the Republic"); CW 1.17–86 (incorporating "The Jury in Ancient America" and "Insurance in Ancient America").

NOTES

The tendency to characterize AB's early career as merely contrarian and his later career as curmudgeonly is a victory for the impulse to pigeonhole but a defeat for careful analysis. Although AB took on a number of fights, he almost always went in prepared with background information and carefully thought out arguments. It is why although the arguments of many of his contemporaries are dated and today seem period pieces, his arguments still have vigor and point. He was more than merely outspoken and irritating; he had a real respect for truth, and hard truths have a place in his stands. His *DD* definition of a cynic as "A blackguard whose faulty vision sees things as they are, not as they ought to be" is a thinly disguised description of himself. The social satire "Ashes of the Beacon" is an outstanding example. Even when it seems most reactionary, biased, and outré, it has a clarity, depth, and persuasiveness that cannot be dismissed out of hand.

It is the logical conclusion of his lifelong assault on the willing surrender to belief, the full-time antithesis of Coleridge's "willing suspension of disbelief for the moment, which constitutes poetic faith." While AB did spend an inordinate amount of time and energy attacking fools and rogues, fads, and what—such as the entire enterprise of insurance—he believed were frauds or what—such as the suffrage movement—he believed were overstated follies, the main thrust of his journalism was employed in combating the spread and elevation to the status of absolute principles of two related notions of doubtful validity: the beliefs that human nature is basically good and that democracy is the supreme achievement of political development. "Ashes of the Beacon" is his most focused and extensive critique of those and related propositions.

For fuller treatments of AB's social philosophy, see Berkove's "Two Impossible Dreams: Ambrose Bierce on Utopia and America," and the introduction to *FR*.

1. See *DD*: "REPUBLIC, *n.* A nation in which, the thing governing and the thing governed being the same, there is only a permitted authority to enforce an optional obedience. In a republic the foundation of public order is the ever lessening habit of submission inherited from ancestors who, being truly governed, submitted because they had to. There are as many kinds of republics as there are gradations between the despotism whence they came and the anarchy whither they lead."
2. Alexander Pope, *The Dunciad* (rev. ed. 1742–43), 4.655–56.
3. This paragraph and the following were inserted from "The Jury in Ancient America."
4. AB mockingly alludes to the concluding words of Abraham Lincoln's Gettysburg Address. See also note 39 below.
5. In reference to an "Altrurian" colony near Santa Rosa, California (i.e., a colony inspired by W. D. Howells's *A Traveler in Altruria* [1894]), AB speaks scornfully of "the Ancient and Honorable Order of the Dupes of Hope" ("Prattle," *E* [13 Dec. 1896]: 6).
6. Perhaps meant to echo the "Year of the Four Emperors" in Roman history, when the emperors Pertinax, Didius Julianus, Pescennius Niger, and Septimius Severus all vied for supremacy in 193 C.E.
7. See "His Waterloo," p. 742 note 1.
8. Ireland did not officially become a republic until 1948, but it had been virtually independent since 1921, with the establishment of the Irish Free State. AB's prescient remark points to his belief that Home Rule for Ireland (involving the establishment of an independent parliament but still entailing recognition of the British Crown), widely discussed in the later nineteenth century, would lead eventually to actual independence.
9. The census of 1900 recorded the U.S. population at 75,994,575.
10. For Dumbleshaw, see "The Maid of Podunk," p. 948 note 5. AB himself wrote a brief memoir entitled "A Sole Survivor" (1890, *SS* 298–306).
11. In *DD*, AB defined liberty as "one of Imagination's most precious possessions."
12. See "Prattle," *E* (6 Aug. 1893): 6: "The essential principle in this rule of the majority . . . is the right of might. The majority governs, not for it ought, but for it can. Majorities are no

more likely to hold correct views than minorities, and there is only one valid reason why Tom's and Dick's views should prevail over Harry's, namely, that it is the only practical way to get on. In the last analysis a balloting is only a counting of noses to ascertain the relative military strength of the parties balloting. Commonly the weaker submits rather than risk a war for principles or interest not deemed vital to the national welfare. But when the principles at stake are embedded in the consciences and sentiments of the voters, and when those 'defeated at the polls' think themselves sufficiently strong in other ways to make up for their numerical weakness, they do not submit: they rebel and deliver such battle as they can. If beaten in the field the rising remains a rebellion; by success it becomes a revolution, and has, usually, the approval of the world and of posterity."

13. Richard Anthony Proctor (1837–88), British writer on mathematics, astronomy, and other scientific subjects. AB probably refers to his book, *Chance and Luck: A Discussion of the Laws of Luck, Coincidences, Wagers, Lotteries, and the Fallacies of Gambling* (1887).

14. AB apparently refers to a charlatan named John Ernst Worrell Keely (1827–98). In the 1870s Keely proposed to build a motor powered "from intermolecular vibrations of ether" and sold many shares of stock to fund the Keely Motor Company; but investigations after his death proved the venture to be a fraud. AB mentions Keely in some of his columns, spelling his name correctly there; the misspelling here is presumably deliberate.

15. The U.S. presidents up to 1909 who died in office were William Henry Harrison (1841), Abraham Lincoln (1865), James A. Garfield (1881), and William McKinley (1901). Harrison died of illness; the other three were assassinated. Only McKinley died at the hands of a professed anarchist.

16. From the earliest days of his writing career, AB had defended the Chinese against popular prejudices, especially virulent in the West. By now making this despised minority the saviors of San Francisco he was emphasizing again how wrong the majority could be.

17. In 1896, when AB was in Washington attacking the efforts of railroad magnate C. P. Huntington to persuade Congress to pass legislation granting him a long extension in repaying government debts, Huntington maintained that *E*'s opposition to him was a result of his cutting off payment of $12,000 a year to the paper. In a letter published as "Bierce to Huntington," AB stated: "if he makes his accusation good I will take him by the hand, which recently I have twice refused when he offered it—once in presence of three members of the press in the corridor of the Capitol, and again in the room of the Senate Committee on Pacific Railroads in the presence of the committee and many gentlemen attending one of its meetings. As to this latter promise I exact but one condition: Mr. Huntington is not to object to my glove." *E* (21 Mar. 1896): 14.

18. The quotation is from Thomas Carlyle's "Characteristics" (1831); reprinted in Carlyle's *Critical and Miscellaneous Essays* (New York: Scribner's, 1904), 3:20–21. AB quotes it in "Prattle," *E* (6 July 1890): 6.

19. AB himself is probably the author of these lines.

20. Beginning with this sentence, most of "The Jury in Ancient America" is inserted into the narrative, beginning with the fourth paragraph.

21. "A jury of [one's] peers."

22. Magna Carta was a charter of liberties that King John was pressured into proclaiming in 1215 following a rebellion of barons who objected to his exploitation of royal power. As AB suggests, at the time of the Magna Carta the term "peers" in *judicium parium* referred only to equally ranking noblemen.

23. The question of AB's position on women's equality is a complex one and cannot be adequately treated here. Although he supported woman suffrage in the early essay "Female Suffrage" (*Californian*, 7–28 Dec. 1867), he was opposed to it for most of his life. Part of the reason was that he was after all typical of his time in preferring to "relieve woman of the burden of participation in political and military service." Part of the reason was his restricted attitude toward suffrage in general. Part of the reason also was his coolness toward vociferous advocacy of any political agendas—including feminism. On the other hand, AB gave warm and generous support to a number of women writers, and among the individuals he sometimes praised in "Prattle" for outstanding acumen or courage were women. See, for example, his comments on women and war, particularly Jessie Schley, in *SD* 130–34. In short, a full and adequate treatment of the subject would have to deal in particulars (who was advocating what, and in what way) and would have to take the context of the times into account.

24. AB is probably thinking of two notorious cases in the early years of the twentieth century, the Nan Patterson case and the Mary Mabel Rogers case. Nan Patterson was a young actress in New York who was accused of killing a bookmaker, a married man named "Caesar" Young, while they were riding in a hansom cab on 4 May 1904. After two separate trials ended in hung juries, Patterson was freed in May 1905. Evidently AB regarded her as manifestly guilty; see "Views of One," *NYA* (14 June 1905): 14; *E* (21 June 1905): 16. Mary Mabel Rogers was convicted of killing her husband, Marcus Rogers, on 13 August 1902. She was hanged on 8 December 1905—the first woman in Vermont to be executed. Gov. Charles J. Bell refused to grant a reprieve, even though he had been vociferously lobbied by many groups and individuals to do so, including a petition by 30,000 women in Ohio. AB wrote about the case in "Some Thoughts on the Hanging," *NYA* (12 Dec. 1905): 16; *E* (19 Dec. 1905): 20 (as "The Views of One").

25. Edward William Bok (1863–1930), editor and essayist. In 1899 he took over editorship of the *Ladies' Home Journal*.

26. Compensation for injured feelings (as distinct from financial loss or physical suffering).

27. The source of this quotation appears to be AB himself.

28. Actually Ho-Ho-Kus, a town in northeastern New Jersey. AB apparently found the name humorous, for he uses it so from time to time in his writings.

29. Beginning with this paragraph, the bulk of the sketch "Insurance in Ancient America" is inserted into the narrative.

30. These two slang terms overlap in meaning. The function of a "tout" is to overpraise, and of a "capper" to decoy. As AB uses these terms, the "capper" appears to be a sales representative, and the "tout" a giver of testimonials.

31. See *DD*: "INSURANCE, *n*. An ingenious modern game of chance in which the player is permitted to enjoy the comfortable conviction that he is beating the man who keeps the table."

32. In the San Francisco earthquake and fire of 18 April 1906, 452 people were officially reported killed (although the actual number was probably higher, perhaps as high as two or three thousand), and damage was estimated at $350 million.

33. The Chicago fire of 8–11 October 1871 was reputed to have been started when a cow belonging to a Mrs. O'Leary kicked over a lantern. In fact, the fire was started in the barn of a laborer, Patrick O'Leary.

34. The Chicago fire resulted in damage estimated at $196 million, of which only $96.5 million was covered by insurance. Nevertheless, fifty-eight insurance companies across the country

went out of business as a result of claims. In fact, most insurance companies fulfilled their contractual obligations following the fire.

35. Most insurance companies in San Francisco insured against fire, but not earthquake. Some companies claimed that they were not liable for fires caused directly by the earthquake; however, most of the fire damage was determined not to be a direct result of the earthquake. In the ensuing months, twenty-seven insurance companies paid claims in full or close to full; nineteen paid ninety cents and up on the dollar; four companies settled for eighty cents and up; twenty-eight paid seventy-five cents and up; twenty-six paid less than seventy-five cents; and four European companies denied liability because of the earthquake and paid nothing. Many of the companies that eventually paid spent months or years in litigation to avoid meeting their commitments. AB commented on the matter in a letter written two months after the earthquake: "Yes, I've observed the . . . determination to 'beat' the insurance companies. Insurance is a hog game, and if they (the companies) can be beaten out of their dishonest gains by superior dishonesty I have no objection; but in my judgment they are neither legally nor morally liable for the half that is claimed of them. Those of them that took no earthquake risks don't owe a cent" (AB to George Sterling, 11 June 1911, MS, NP).

36. Between August 1905 and 1909, when AB revised this work, he reversed himself on the issue of life insurance. In "Insurance in Ancient America," he called it "most nearly a 'square game'" and said it "was conducted as honest gambling." The reason for the reversal is not presently known.

37. In the appearance of this story in *NYA* (19 Feb. 1905) and *E* (26 Feb. 1905), the text reads "Muliolatry." See AB to George Sterling (17 Apr. 1905, MS, NP): "The compound 'Mulolatry,' [*sic*] which I made in 'Ashes of the Beacon', would not, of course, be allowable in composition altogether serious. I used it because I could not at the moment think of the right word, 'gyneolatry', or 'gynecolatry', according as you make use of the nominative or the accusative. I once made 'caniolatry' [see "The Dog in Ganegwag" and "The Land Beyond the Blow" (p. 1131 note 36)] for a similar reason—just laziness. It's not nice to do things o' that kind, even in newspapers." AB refers to the erroneous creation of a compound word from both Latin (*mulier*, woman) and Greek (*latreia*, servitude) rather than from one language only (in this case, the Greek *gyne*, and *latreia*).

38. At the battle of Gettysburg (1–3 July 1863), the combined Federal and Confederate casualties are officially estimated as 7,053 killed, 33,264 wounded, and 10,790 missing. Other estimates yield substantially lower casualties for the Confederates and slightly lower ones for the Federals.

39. From Lincoln's Gettysburg Address (19 November 1863): "that government of the people, by the people, for the people, shall not perish from the earth."

40. Cf. *DD*: "MULTITUDE, *n.* A crowd; the source of political wisdom and virtue. In a republic, the object of the statesman's adoration. 'In a multitude of counsellors there is wisdom,' saith the proverb. If many men of equal individual wisdom are wiser than any one of them, it must be that they acquire the excess of wisdom by the mere act of getting together. Whence comes it? Obviously from nowhere—as well say that a range of mountains is higher than the single mountains composing it. A multitude is as wise as its wisest member if it obey him; if not, it is no wiser than its most foolish."

41. *Vox populi vox Dei.* The earliest recorded expression of the utterance occurs in Alcuin's letter to Charlemagne (ca. 800 C.E.). AB uses the Latin expression in the earlier appearance of this story as "The Fall of the Republic."

42. The Grand Army of the Republic was formed in 1866 by veterans of the Federal army. By the 1880s, with a membership of over 400,000, it was a formidable political force. In 1887 Congress passed legislation granting pensions to all veterans suffering from any type of disability; President Cleveland's veto of the bill was a significant factor in his defeat in the presidential election the next year. In 1890 Congress passed a similar bill, and it was signed by President Benjamin Harrison. By 1949 the pensions had totaled $8 billion.

43. The reference is to the American War of Independence (1775–83), the War of 1812 (1812–14), and the Civil War (1861–65).

44. The statement actually derives from a line by the German poet and dramatist Friedrich von Schiller (1759–1805), in his verse drama *Die Jungfrau von Orleans* (1801), act 3, scene 6: "Mit die Dummheit kämpfen Götter selbst vergebens" (Against stupidity the gods themselves battle in vain). In "Aphorisms of a Late Spring," *NYA* (24 Apr. 1904): 25, AB wrote: "Against stupidity the gods are said to be powerless; against intelligence they do not contend."

45. "I stood in Venice, on the Bridge of Sighs; / A palace and a prison on each hand: / I saw from out the waves her structures rise / As from the stroke of the enchanter's wand." Byron, *Childe Harold's Pilgrimage* (1812–18), canto 4, ll. 1–4. AB quotes the line also in "Mr. Masthead, Journalist" and "Prattle," *E* (18 Nov. 1894): 6.

46. Cf. Matt. 7:12: "Therefore all things whatsoever ye would that men should do to you, do ye even so to them: for this is the Law and the Prophets." Commonly known as the Golden Rule. AB frequently noted, as he does here, the discrepancies between the ideals of Jesus and the practices of professing and professional Christians.

THE LAND BEYOND THE BLOW

(After the method of Swift, who followed Lucian, and was himself followed by Voltaire and many others.)[1]

THITHER

A crowd of men were assisting at a dog-fight. The scene was one of indescribable confusion. In the center of the tumult the dogs, obscure in a cloud of dust, rolled over and over, howling, yarring, tearing each other with sickening ferocity. About them the hardly less ferocious men shouted, cursed and struck, encouraged the animals with sibilant utterances and threatened with awful forms of death and perdition all who tried to put an end to the combat. Caught in the thick of this pitiless mob I endeavored to make my way to a place of peace, when a burly blackguard, needlessly obstructing me, said derisively:

"I guess you are working pockets."

"You are a liar!" I retorted hotly.

That is all the provocation that I remember to have given.

SONS OF THE FAIR STAR

When consciousness returned the sun was high in the heavens, yet the light was dim, and had that indefinable ghastly quality that is observed during a partial eclipse. The sun itself appeared singularly small, as if it were at an immensely greater distance than usual. Rising with some difficulty to my feet, I looked about me. I was in an open space among some trees growing on the slope of a mountain range whose summit on the one hand was obscured by a mist of a strange pinkish hue, and on the other rose into peaks glittering with snow. Skirting the base at a distance of two or three miles flowed a wide river, and beyond it a nearly level plain stretched away to the horizon, dotted with villages and farmhouses and apparently in a high state of cultivation. All was unfamiliar in its every aspect. The trees were unlike any that I had ever seen or even imagined, the trunks being mostly square and the foliage consisting of slender filaments resembling hair, in many instances long enough to reach the earth. It was of many colors, and I could not perceive that there was any prevailing one, as green is in the vegetation to which I was accustomed. As far as I could see there were no grass, no weeds, no flowers; the earth was covered with a kind of lichen, uniformly blue. Instead of rocks, great masses of metals protruded here and there, and above me on the mountain were high cliffs of what seemed to be bronze veined with brass. No animals were visible, but a few birds as uncommon in appearance as their surroundings glided through the air or perched upon the rocks. I say glided, for their motion was not true flight, their wings being mere membranes extended parallel to their sides, and having no movement independent of the body. The bird was, so to say, suspended between them and moved forward by quick strokes of a pair of enormously large webbed feet, precisely as a duck propels itself in water. All these things excited in me no surprise, nor even curiosity; they were merely unfamiliar. That which most interested me was what appeared to be a bridge several miles away, up the river, and to this I directed my steps, crossing over from the barren and desolate hills to the populous plain.

For a full history of my life and adventures in Mogon-Zwair,[2] and a detailed description of the country, its people, their manners and customs, I must ask the reader to await the publication of a book, now in the press, entitled *A Blackened Eye;* in this brief account I can give only a few of such particulars as seem instructive by contrast with our own civilization.[3]

The inhabitants of Mogon-Zwair call themselves Golampis, a word signifying Sons of the Fair Star. Physically they closely resemble ourselves, being in all respects the equals of the highest Caucasian type. Their hair, however, has a broader scheme of color, hair of every hue known to us, and even of some imperceptible to my eyes but brilliant to theirs, being too common to excite remark. A Golampian assemblage with uncovered heads resembles, indeed, a garden of flowers, vivid and deep in color, no two alike. They wear no clothing of any kind, excepting for adornment and protection from the weather, resembling in this the ancient Greeks and the Japanese of yesterday;[4] nor was I ever able to make them comprehend that clothing could be worn for those reasons for which it is chiefly worn among ourselves. They are destitute of those feelings of delicacy and refinement which distinguish us from the lower animals, and which, in the opinion of our acutest and most pious thinkers, are evidences of our close relation to the Power that made us.

Among this people certain ideas which are current among ourselves as mere barren faiths expressed in disregarded platitudes receive a practical application to the affairs of life. For example, they hold, with the best, wisest and most experienced of our own race, and one other hereafter to be described, that wealth does not bring happiness and is a misfortune and an evil. None but the most ignorant and depraved, therefore, take the trouble to acquire or preserve it. A rich Golampi is naturally regarded with contempt and suspicion, is shunned by the good and respectable and subjected to police surveillance. Accustomed to a world where the rich man is profoundly and justly respected for his goodness and wisdom (manifested in part by his own deprecatory protests against the wealth of which, nevertheless, he is apparently unable to rid himself) I was at first greatly pained to observe the contumelious manner of the Golampis toward this class of men, carried in some instances to the length of personal violence; a popular amusement being the pelting them with coins. These the victims would carefully gather from the ground and carry away with them, thus increasing their hoard and making themselves all the more liable to popular indignities.

When the cultivated and intelligent Golampi finds himself growing too wealthy he proceeds to get rid of his surplus riches by some one of many easy expedients. One of these I have just described; another is to give his excess to those of his own class who have not sufficient to buy employment and so escape leisure, which is considered the greatest evil of all. "Idleness," says one of their famous authors, "is the child of poverty and the parent of discontent"; and another great writer says: "No one is without employment; the indolent man works for his enemies."

In conformity to these ideas the Golampis—all but the ignorant and vicious rich—look upon labor as the highest good, and the man who is so unfortunate as not to have enough money to purchase employment in some useful industry will rather engage in a useless one than not labor at all. It is not unusual to see hundreds of men carrying water from a river and pouring it into a natural ravine or artificial channel, through which it runs back into the stream. Frequently a man is seen conveying stones—or the masses of metal which there correspond to stones—from one pile to another. When all have been heaped in a single place he will convey them back again, or to a new place, and so proceed until darkness puts an end to the work. This kind of labor, however, does not confer the satisfaction derived from the consciousness of being useful, and is never performed by any person having the means to hire another to employ him in some beneficial industry. The wages usually paid to employers are from three to six *balukan* a day. This statement may seem incredible, but I solemnly assure the reader that I have known a bad workman or a feeble woman to pay as high as eight; and there have been instances of men whose incomes had outgrown their desires paying even more.

Labor being a luxury which only those in easy circumstances can afford, the poor are the more eager for it, not only because it is denied them, but because it is a sign of respectability. Many of them, therefore, indulge in it on credit and soon find themselves deprived of what little property they had to satisfy their hardfisted employers. A poor woman once complained to me that her husband spent every *rylat* that he could get in the purchase of the most expensive kinds of employment, while she and the children were compelled to content themselves with such cheap and coarse activity as dragging an old wagon round and round in a small field which a kind-hearted neighbor permitted them to use for the purpose. I afterward saw this improvident husband and

THE LAND BEYOND THE BLOW

unnatural father. He had just squandered all the money he had been able to beg or borrow in buying six tickets, which entitled the holder to that many days' employment in pitching hay into a barn. A week later I met him again. He was broken in health, his limbs trembled, his walk was an uncertain shuffle. Clearly he was suffering from overwork. As I paused by the wayside to speak to him a wagon loaded with hay was passing. He fixed his eyes upon it with a hungry, wolfish glare, clutched a pitchfork and leaned eagerly forward, watching the vanishing wagon with breathless attention and heedless of my salutation. That night he was arrested, streaming with perspiration, in the unlawful act of unloading that hay and putting it into its owner's barn. He was tried, convicted and sentenced to six months' detention in the House of Indolence.

The whole country is infested by a class of criminal vagrants known as *strambaltis*, or, as we should say, "tramps."[5] These persons prowl about among the farms and villages begging for work in the name of charity. Sometimes they travel in groups, as many as a dozen together, and then the farmer dares not refuse them; and before he can notify the constabulary they will have performed a great deal of the most useful labor that they can find to do and escaped without paying a *rylat*. One trustworthy agriculturist assured me that his losses in one year from these depredations amounted to no less a sum than seven hundred *balukan!* On nearly all the larger and more isolated farms a strong force of guards is maintained during the greater part of the year to prevent these outrages, but they are frequently overpowered, and sometimes prove unfaithful to their trust by themselves working secretly by night.

The Golampi priesthood has always denounced overwork as a deadly sin, and declared useless and apparently harmless work, such as carrying water from the river and letting it flow in again, a distinct violation of the divine law, in which, however, I could never find any reference to the matter; but there has recently risen a sect which holds that all labor being pleasurable, each kind in its degree is immoral and wicked. This sect, which embraces many of the most holy and learned men, is rapidly spreading and becoming a power in the state. It has, of course, no churches, for these cannot be built without labor, and its members commonly dwell in caves and live upon such roots and berries as can be easily gathered, of which the country produces a great abundance though all are exceedingly unpalatable. These *Gropoppsu* (as the members of this sect call themselves) pass most of their waking hours sitting in the sunshine with folded hands, contemplating their navels; by the practice of which austerity they hope to obtain as reward an eternity of hard labor after death.

The Golampis are an essentially pious and religious race. There are few, indeed, who do not profess at least one religion. They are nearly all, in a certain sense, polytheists: they worship a supreme and beneficent deity by one name or another, but all believe in the existence of a subordinate and malevolent one, whom also, while solemnly execrating him in public rites, they hold at heart in such reverence that needlessly to mention his name or that of his dwelling is considered sin of a rank hardly inferior to blasphemy.[6] I am persuaded that this singular tenderness toward a being whom their theology represents as an abominable monster, the origin of all evil and the foe to souls, is a survival of an ancient propitiatory adoration. Doubtless this wicked deity was once so feared that his conciliation was one of the serious concerns of life. He is probably as greatly feared now as at any former time, but is apparently less hated, and is by some honestly admired.

It is interesting to observe the important place held in Golampian affairs by religious persecution.[7] The Government is a pure theocracy, all the Ministers of State and the principal functionaries in every department of control belonging to the priesthood of the dominant church. It is popularly believed in Mogon-Zwair that persecution, even to the extent of taking life, is in the long run beneficial to the cause enduring it. This belief has, indeed, been crystallized into a popular proverb, not capable of accurate translation into our tongue, but to the effect that martyrs fertilize religion by pouring out their blood about its roots. Acting upon this belief with their characteristically logical and conscientious directness, the sacerdotal rulers of the country mercilessly afflict the sect to which themselves belong. They arrest its leading members on false charges, throw them into loathsome and unwholesome dungeons, subject them to the cruelest tortures and sometimes put them to death. The provinces in which the state religion is especially strong are occasionally raided and pillaged by government soldiery, recruited for the purpose by conscription among the dissenting sects, and are sometimes actually devastated with fire and sword. The result is not altogether confirmatory of the popular belief and does not fulfil the pious hope of the governing powers who are cruel to be kind. The vitalizing efficacy of persecution is not to be doubted, but the persecuted of too feeble faith frequently thwart its beneficent intent and happy operation by apostasy.

Having in mind the horrible torments which a Golampian general had inflicted upon the population of a certain town I once ventured to protest to him that so dreadful a sum of suffering, seeing that it did not accomplish its purpose, was needless and unwise.

"Needless and unwise it may be," said he, "and I am disposed to admit that the result which I expected from it has not followed; but why do you speak of the *sum* of suffering? I tortured those people in but a single, simple way—by skinning their legs."

"Ah, that is very true," said I, "but you skinned the legs of one thousand."

"And what of that?" he asked. "Can one thousand, or ten thousand, or any number of persons suffer more agony than one? A man may have his leg broken, then his nails pulled out, then be seared with a hot iron. Here is suffering added to suffering, and the effect is really cumulative. In the true mathematical sense it is a *sum* of suffering. A single person can experience it. But consider, my dear sir. How can you add one man's agony to another's? They are not addable quantities. Each is an individual pain, unaffected by the other. The limit of anguish which ingenuity can inflict is that utmost pang which one man has the vitality to endure."

I was convinced but not silenced.

THE LAND BEYOND THE BLOW

The Golampis all believe, singularly enough, that truth possesses some inherent vitality and power that give it an assured prevalence over falsehood; that a good name cannot be permanently defiled and irreparably ruined by detraction, but, like a star, shines all the brighter for the shadow through which it is seen; that justice cannot be stayed by injustice; that vice is powerless against virtue. I could quote from their great writers hundreds of utterances affirmative of these propositions. One of their poets, for example, has some striking and original lines, of which the following is a literal but unmetrical translation:

> A man who is in the right has three arms,[8]
> But he whose conscience is rotten with wrong
> Is stripped and confined in a metal cell.

Imbued with these beliefs, the Golampis think it hardly worth while to be truthful, to abstain from slander, to do justice and to avoid vicious actions. "The practice," they say, "of deceit, calumniation, oppression and immorality cannot have any sensible and lasting injurious effect, and it is most agreeable to the mind and heart. Why should there be personal self-denial without commensurate general advantage?"

In consequence of these false views, affirmed by those whom they regard as great and wise, the people of Mogon-Zwair are, as far as I have observed them, the most conscienceless liars, cheats, thieves, rakes and all-round, many-sided sinners that ever were created to be damned.[9] It was, therefore, with inexpressible joy that I received one day legal notification that I had been tried in the High Court of Conviction and sentenced to banishment to Lalugnan. My offense was that I had said that I regarded consistency as the most detestable of all vices.

AN INTERVIEW WITH GNARMAG-ZOTE

Mogon-Zwair and Lalugnan, having the misfortune to lie on opposite sides of a line, naturally hate each other; so each country sends its dangerous political criminals into the other, where they usually enjoy high honors and are sometimes elevated to important office under the crown. I was therefore received in Lalugnan with hospitality and given every encouragement in prosecuting my researches into the history and intellectual life of the people. They are so extraordinary a people, inhabiting so marvelous a country, that everything which the traveler sees, hears or experiences makes a lively and lasting impression upon his mind, and the labor of a lifetime would be required to relate the observation of a single year. I shall notice here only one or two points of national character—those which differ most conspicuously from ours, and in which, consequently, they are least worthy.

With a fatuity hardly more credible than creditable, the Lalugwumps, as they call themselves, deny the immortality of the soul. In all my stay in their country I found only one person who believed in a life "beyond the grave," as we should say, though as the Lalugwumps are cannibals they would say "beyond the stomach." In testimony to the consolatory value of the doctrine of another life, I may say that this one true believer had in this life a comparatively unsatisfactory lot, for in early youth he had been struck by a flying stone from a volcano and had lost a considerable part of his brain.

I cannot better set forth the nature and extent of the Lalugwumpian error regarding this matter than by relating a conversation that occurred between me and one of the high officers of the King's household—a man whose proficiency in all the vices of antiquity, together with his service to the realm in determining the normal radius of curvature in cats' claws, had elevated him to the highest plane of political preferment. His name was Gnarmag-Zote.

"You tell me," said he, "that the soul is immaterial. Now, matter is that of which we can have knowledge through one or more of our senses. Of what is immaterial—not matter—we can gain no knowledge in that way. How, then, can we know anything about it?"[10]

Perceiving that he did not rightly apprehend my position I abandoned it and shifted the argument to another ground. "Consider," I said, "the analogous case of a thought. You will hardly call thought material, yet we know there are thoughts."

"I beg your pardon, but we do not know that. Thought is not a thing, therefore cannot *be* in any such sense, for example, as the hand *is*. We use the word 'thought' to designate the result of an action of the brain, precisely as we use the word 'speed' to designate the result of an action of a horse's legs. But can it be said that speed *exists* in the same way as the legs which produce it exist, or in any way? Is it a thing?"

I was about to disdain to reply, when I saw an old man approaching, with bowed head, apparently in deep distress. As he drew near he saluted my distinguished interlocutor in the manner of the country, by putting out his tongue to its full extent and moving it slowly from side to side. Gnarmag-Zote acknowledged the civility by courteously spitting, and the old man, advancing, seated himself at the great officer's feet, saying: "Exalted Sir, I have just lost my wife by death, and am in a most melancholy frame of mind. He who has mastered all the vices of the ancients and wrested from nature the secret of the normal curvature of cats' claws can surely spare from his wisdom a few rays of philosophy to cheer an old man's gloom. Pray tell me what I shall do to assuage my grief."

The reader can, perhaps, faintly conceive my astonishment when Gnarmag-Zote gravely replied: "Kill yourself."

"Surely," I cried, "you would not have this honest fellow procure oblivion (since you think that death is nothing else) by so rash an act!"

"An act that Gnarmag-Zote advises," he said, coldly, "is not rash."

"But death," I said, "death, whatever else it may be, is an end of life. This old man is now in sorrow almost insupportable. But a few days and it will be supportable; a few months and it will have become no more than a tender melancholy. At last it will disappear, and in the society of his friends, in the skill of his cook, the profits of avarice, the study of how to be querulous and in the pursuit of loquacity, he will again experience the joys of age. Why for a present grief should he deprive himself of all future happiness?"

Gnarmag-Zote looked upon me with something like compassion. "My friend," said he, "guest of my sovereign and my country, know that in any circumstances, even those upon which true happiness is based and conditioned, death is preferable to life. The sum of miseries in any life (here in Lalugnan at least) exceeds the sum of pleasures; but suppose that it did not.[11] Imagine an existence in which happiness, of whatever intensity, is the rule, and discomfort, of whatever moderation, the exception. Still there is some discomfort. There is none in death, for (as it is given to us to know) that is oblivion, annihilation.[12] True, by dying one loses his happiness as well as his sorrows, but he is not conscious of the loss. Surely, a loss of which one will never know, and which, if it operate to make him less happy, at the same time takes from him the desire and capacity and need of happiness, cannot be an evil. That is so intelligently understood among us here in Lalugnan that suicide is common, and our word for sufferer is the same as that for fool. If this good man had not been an idiot he would have taken his life as soon as he was bereaved."

"If what you say of the blessing of death is true," I said, smilingly, for I greatly prided myself on the ingenuity of my thought, "it is unnecessary to commit suicide through grief for the dead; for the more you love the more glad you should be that the object of your affection has passed into so desirable a state as death."

"So we are—those of us who have cultivated philosophy, history and logic; but this poor fellow is still under the domination of feelings inherited from a million ignorant and superstitious ancestors—for Lalugnan was once as barbarous a country as your own. The most grotesque and frightful conceptions of death, and life after death, were current; and now many of even those whose understandings are emancipated wear upon their feelings the heavy chain of heredity."

"But," said I, "granting for the sake of the argument which I am about to build upon the concession" (I could not bring myself to use the idiotic and meaningless phrase, "for the sake of argument") "that death, especially the death of a Lalugwump, is desirable, yet the act of dying, the transition state between living and being dead, may be accompanied by the most painful physical, and most terrifying mental phenomena. The moment of dissolution may seem to the exalted sensibilities of the moribund a century of horrors."

The great man smiled again, with a more intolerable benignity than before. "There is no such thing as dying," he said; "the 'transition state' is a creation of your fancy and an evidence of imperfect reason. One is at any time either alive or dead. The one condition cannot shade off into the other. There is no gradation like that between waking and sleeping.[13] By the way, do you recognize a certain resemblance between death and a dreamless sleep?"

"Yes—death as you conceive it to be."

THE LAND BEYOND THE BLOW

"Well, does any one fear sleep? Do we not seek it, court it, wish that it may be sound—that is to say, dreamless? We desire occasional annihilation—wish to be dead for eight and ten hours at a time. True, we expect to awake, but that expectation, while it may account for our alacrity in embracing sleep, cannot alter the character of the state that we cheerfully go into. Suppose we did *not* wake in the morning, never did wake! Would our mental and spiritual condition be in any respect different through all eternity from what it was during the first few hours? After how many hours does oblivion begin to be an evil? The man who loves to sleep yet hates to die might justly be granted everlasting life with everlasting insomnia."

Gnarmag-Zote paused and appeared to be lost in the profundity of his thoughts, but I could easily enough see that he was only taking breath. The old man whose grief had given this turn to the conversation had fallen asleep and was roaring in the nose like a beast. The rush of a river near by, as it poured up a hill from the ocean, and the shrill singing of several kinds of brilliant quadrupeds were the only other sounds audible. I waited deferentially for the great antiquarian, scientist and courtier to resume, amusing myself meantime by turning over the leaves of an official report by the Minister of War on a new and improved process of making thunder from snail slime. Presently the oracle spoke.

"You have been born," he said, which was true. "There was, it follows, a time when you had not been born. As we reckon time, it was probably some millions of ages. Of this considerable period you are unable to remember one unhappy moment, and in point of fact there was none. To a Lalugwump that is entirely conclusive as to the relative values of consciousness and oblivion, existence and non-existence, life and death.[14] This old man lying here at my feet is now, if not dreaming, as if he had never been born. Would not it be cruel and inhuman to wake him back to grief? Is it, then, kind to permit him to wake by the natural action of his own physical energies? I have given him the advice for which he asked. Believing it good advice, and seeing him too irresolute to act, it seems my clear duty to assist him."

Before I could interfere, even had I dared take the liberty to do so, Gnarmag-Zote struck the old man a terrible blow upon the head with his mace of office. The victim turned upon his back, spread his fingers, shivered convulsively and was dead.

"You need not be shocked," said the distinguished assassin, coolly: "I have but performed a sacred duty and religious rite. The religion (established first in this realm by King Skanghutch, the sixty-second of that name) consists in the worship of Death. We have sacred books, some three thousand thick volumes, said to be written by inspiration of Death himself, whom no mortal has ever seen, but who is described by our priests as having the figure of a fat young man with a red face and wearing an affable smile. In art he is commonly represented in the costume of a husbandman sowing seeds.

"The priests and sacred books teach that death is the supreme and only good—that the chief duties of man are, therefore, assassination and suicide. Conviction of these cardinal truths is universal among us, but I am sorry to say that many do not honestly live up to the faith. Most of us are commendably zealous in assassination, but slack and lukewarm in suicide. Some justify themselves in this half-hearted observance of the Law and imperfect submission to the Spirit by arguing that if they destroy themselves their usefulness in destroying others will be greatly abridged. 'I find,' says one of our most illustrious writers, not without a certain force, it must be confessed, 'that I can slay many more of others than I can of myself.'

"There are still others, more distinguished for faith than works, who reason that if A kill B, B cannot kill C. So it happens that although many Lalugwumps die, mostly by the hands of others, though some by their own, the country is never wholly depopulated."

"In my own country," said I, "is a sect holding somewhat Lalugwumpian views of the evil of life; and among the members it is considered a sin to bestow it. The philosopher Schopenhauer taught the same doctrine,[15] and many of our rulers have shown strong sympathetic leanings toward it by procuring the destruction of many of their own people and those of other nations in what is called war."

"They are greatly to be commended," said Gnarmag-Zote, rising to intimate that the conversation was at an end. I respectfully protruded my tongue while he withdrew into his palace, spitting politely and with unusual copiousness in acknowledgment. A few minutes later, but before I had left the spot, two lackeys in livery emerged from the door by which he had entered, and while one shouldered the body of the old man and carried it into the palace kitchen the other informed me that his Highness was graciously pleased to desire my company at dinner that evening. With many expressions of regret I declined the invitation, unaware that to do so was treason. With the circumstances of my escape to the island of Tamtonia the newspapers have made the world already familiar.

THE TAMTONIANS

In all my intercourse with the Tamtonians I was treated with the most distinguished consideration and no obstacles to a perfect understanding of their social and political life were thrown in my way. My enforced residence on the island was, however, too brief to enable me to master the whole subject as I should have liked to do.

The government of Tamtonia is what is known in the language of the island as a *cilbuper.*[16] It differs radically from any form known in other parts of the world and is supposed to have been invented by an ancient chief of the race, named Natas,[17] who was for many centuries after his death worshiped as a god, and whose memory is still held in veneration. The government is of infinite complexity, its various functions distributed among as many officers as possible, multiplication of places being regarded as of the greatest importance, and not so much a means as an end. The Tamtonians seem to think that the highest good to which a human being can attain is the possession of an office; and in order that as many as possible may enjoy that advantage they have as many offices as the country will support, and make the tenure brief and in no way dependent on good conduct and intelligent administration of official duty. In truth, it occurs usually that a man is turned out of his office (in favor of an incompetent successor) before he has acquired sufficient experience to perform his duties with credit to himself or profit to the country. Owing to this incredible folly, the affairs of the island are badly mismanaged. Complaints are the rule, even from those who have had their way in the choice of officers. Of course there can be no such thing as a knowledge of the science of government among such a people, for it is to nobody's interest to acquire it by study of political history. There is, indeed, a prevalent belief that nothing worth knowing is to be learned from the history of other nations—not even from the history of their errors—such is this extraordinary people's national vanity! One of the most notable consequences of this universal and voluntary ignorance is that Tamtonia is the home of all the discreditable political and fiscal heresies from which many other nations, and especially our own, emancipated themselves centuries ago. They are there in vigorous growth and full flower, and believed to be of purely Tamtonian origin.

It needs hardly to be stated that in their personal affairs these people pursue an entirely different course, for if they did not there could be no profitable industries and professions among them, and no property to tax for the support of their government. In his private business a Tamtonian has as high appreciation of fitness and experience as anybody, and having secured a good man keeps him in service as long as possible.

The ruler of the nation, whom they call a *Tnediserp*, is chosen every five years but may be rechosen for five more. He is supposed to be selected by the people themselves, but in reality they have nothing to do with his selection. The method of choosing a man for *Tnediserp* is so strange that I doubt my ability to make it clear.

The adult male population of the island divides itself into two or more *seitrap*.* Commonly there are three or four, but only two ever have any considerable numerical strength, and none is ever strong morally or intellectually. All the members of each *ytrap* profess the same political opinions, which are provided for them by their leaders every five years and written down on pieces of paper so that they will not be forgotten. The moment that any Tamtonian has read his piece of paper, or *mroftalp*, he unhesitatingly adopts all the opinions that he finds written on it, sometimes as many as forty or fifty, although these may be altogether different from, or even antagonistic to, those with which he was supplied five years before and has been advocating ever since.[18] It will be seen from this that the Tamtonian mind is a thing whose processes

---

* The Tamtonian language forms its plurals most irregularly, but usually by an initial inflection. It has a certain crude and primitive grammar, but in point of orthoepy is extremely difficult. With our letters I can hardly hope to give an accurate conception of its pronunciation. As nearly as possible I write its words as they sounded to my ear when carefully spoken for my instruction by intelligent natives. It is a harsh tongue.

THE LAND BEYOND THE BLOW

no American can hope to respect, or even understand. It is instantaneously convinced without either fact or argument, and when these are afterward presented they only confirm it in its miraculous conviction; those which make against that conviction having an even stronger confirmatory power than the others. I have said any Tamtonian, but that is an overstatement. A few usually persist in thinking as they did before; or in altering their convictions in obedience to reason instead of authority, as our own people do; but they are at once assailed with the most opprobrious names, accused of treason and all manner of crimes, pelted with mud and stones and in some instances deprived of their noses and ears by the public executioner.[19] Yet in no country is independence of thought so vaunted as a virtue, and in none is freedom of speech considered so obvious a natural right or so necessary to good government.

At the same time that each *ytrap* is supplied with its political opinions for the next five years, its leaders—who, I am told, all pursue the vocation of sharpening axes— name a man whom they wish chosen for the office of *Tnediserp*. He is usually an idiot from birth, the Tamtonians having a great veneration for such, believing them to be divinely inspired. Although few members of the *ytrap* have ever heard of him before, they at once believe him to have been long the very greatest idiot in the country; and for the next few months they do little else than quote his words and point to his actions to prove that his idiocy is of entirely superior quality to that of his opponent— a view that he himself, instructed by his discoverers, does and says all that he can to confirm. His inarticulate mumblings are everywhere repeated as utterances of profound wisdom, and the slaver that drools from his chin is carefully collected and shown to the people, evoking the wildest enthusiasm of his supporters. His opponents all this time are trying to blacken his character by the foulest conceivable falsehoods, some even going so far as to assert that he is not an idiot at all! It is generally agreed among them that if he were chosen to office the most dreadful disasters would ensue, and that, *therefore,* he will not be chosen.

To this last mentioned conviction, namely that the opposing candidate *(rehtot lacsar)* cannot possibly be chosen, I wish to devote a few words here, for it seems to me one of the most extraordinary phenomena of the human mind. It implies, of course, a profound belief in the wisdom of majorities and the error of minorities. This belief can and does in some mysterious way co-exist, in the Tamtonian understanding, with the deepest disgust and most earnest disapproval of a decision which a majority has made.[20] It is of record, indeed, that one political *ytrap* sustained no fewer than six successive defeats without at all impairing its conviction that the right side must win.[21] In each recurring contest this *ytrap* was as sure that it would succeed as it had been in all the preceding ones—and sure *because* it believed itself in the right! It has been held by some native observers that this conviction is not actually entertained, but only professed for the purpose of influencing the action of others; but this is disproved by the fact that even after the contest is decided, though the result is unknown—when nobody's action can have effect—the leaders (ax-sharpeners) continue earnestly to "claim" this province and that, up to the very last moment of uncertainty, and the common people murder one another in the streets for the crime of doubting that the man is chosen whom the assassin was pleased to prefer. When the majority of a province has chosen one candidate and a majority of the nation another, the mental situation of the worthy Tamtonian is not over-easy of conception, but there can be no doubt that his faith in the wisdom of majorities remains unshaken.

One of the two antagonistic idiots having been chosen as ruler, it is customary to speak of him as "the choice of the people," whereas it is obvious that he is one of the few men, seldom exceeding two or three, whom it is certainly known that nearly one-half the people regard as unfit for the position.[22] He is less certainly "the people's choice" than any other man in the country excepting his unsuccessful opponents; for while it is known that a large body of his countrymen did not want him, it cannot be known how many of his supporters really preferred some other person, but had no opportunity to make their preference effective.

The Tamtonians are very proud of their form of government, which gives them so much power in selecting their rulers. This power consists in the privilege of choosing between two men whom but a few had a voice in selecting from among many millions, any one of whom the rest might have preferred to either. Yet every Tamtonian is as vain of possessing this incalculably small influence as if he were a Warwick in making kings and a Bismarck in using them.[23] He gives himself as many airs and graces as would be appropriate to the display of an honest pin-feather upon the pope's-nose[24] of a mooley peacock.

Each congenital idiot whom the ax-grinders name for the office of *Tnediserp* has upon the "ticket" with him a dead man, who stands or falls with his leader. There is no way of voting for the idiot without voting for the corpse also, and *vice versa*. When one of these precious couples has been chosen the idiot in due time enters upon the duties of his office and the corpse is put into an ice-chest and carefully preserved from decay. If the idiot should himself become a corpse he is buried at once and the other body is then haled out of its ice to take his place. It is propped up in the seat of authority and duly instated in power. This is the signal for a general attack upon it. It is subjected to every kind of sacrilegious indignity, vituperated as a usurper and an "accident," struck with rotten eggs and dead cats, and undergoes the meanest misrepresentation.[25] Its attitude in the chair, its fallen jaw, glazed eyes and degree of decomposition are caricatured and exaggerated out of all reason. Yet such as it is it must be endured for the unexpired term for which its predecessor was chosen. To guard against a possible interregnum, however, a law has recently been passed providing that if it should tumble out of the chair and be too rotten to set up again its clerks (*seiraterces*) are eligible to its place in a stated order of succession. Here we have the amazing anomaly of the rulers of a "free" people actually appointing their potential successors!—a thing inexpressibly repugnant to all our ideas of popular government, but apparently regarded in Tamtonia as a matter of course.

THE LAND BEYOND THE BLOW

During the few months intervening between the ax-men's selection of candidates and the people's choice between those selected (a period known as the *laitnediserp ngiapmac*) the Tamtonian character is seen at its worst. There is no infamy too great or too little for the partisans of the various candidates to commit and accuse their opponents of committing. While every one of them declares, and in his heart believes, that honest arguments have greater weight than dishonest; that falsehood reacts on the falsifier's cause; that appeals to passion and prejudice are as ineffectual as dishonorable, few have the strength and sense to deny themselves the luxury of all these methods and worse ones. The laws against bribery, made by themselves, are set at naught and those of civility and good breeding are forgotten. The best of friends quarrel and openly insult one another. The women, who know almost as little of the matters at issue as the men, take part in the abominable discussions; some even encouraging the general demoralization by showing themselves at the public meetings, sometimes actually putting themselves into uniform and marching in procession with banners, music and torchlights.[26]

I feel that this last statement will be hardly understood without explanation. Among the agencies employed by the Tamtonians to prove that one set of candidates is better than another, or to show that one political policy is more likely than another to promote the general prosperity, a high place is accorded to colored rags, flames of fire, noises made upon brass instruments, inarticulate shouts, explosions of gunpowder and lines of men walking and riding through the streets in cheap and tawdry costumes more or less alike. Vast sums of money are expended to procure these strange evidences of the personal worth of candidates and the political sanity of ideas. It is very much as if a man should paint his nose pea-green and stand on his head to convince his neighbors that his pigs are fed on acorns. Of course the money subscribed for these various controversial devices is not all wasted; the greater part of it is pocketed by the ax-grinders by whom it is solicited, and who have invented the system. That they have invented it for their own benefit seems not to have occurred to the dupes who pay for it. In the universal madness everybody believes whatever monstrous and obvious falsehood is told by the leaders of his own *ytrap,* and nobody listens for a moment to the exposures of their rascality. Reason has flown shrieking from the scene; Caution slumbers by the wayside with unbuttoned pocket. It is the opportunity of thieves!

With a view to abating somewhat the horrors of this recurring season of depravity, it has been proposed by several wise and decent Tamtonians to extend the term of office of the *Tnediserp* to six years instead of five, but the sharpeners of axes are too powerful to be overthrown. They have made the people believe that if the man whom the country chooses to rule it because it thinks him wise and good were permitted to rule it too long it would be impossible to displace him in punishment for his folly and wickedness. It is, indeed, far more likely that the term of office will be reduced to four years than extended to six. The effect can be no less than hideous!

In Tamtonia there is a current popular saying dating from many centuries back and running this way: *"Eht eciffo dluohs kees eht nam, ton eht nam eht eciffo"*—which may be translated thus: "No citizen ought to try to secure power for himself, but should be selected by others for his fitness to exercise it." The sentiment which this wise and decent phrase expresses has long ceased to have a place in the hearts of those who are everlastingly repeating it, but with regard to the office of *Tnediserp* it has still a remnant of the vitality of habit. This, however, is fast dying out, and a few years ago one of the congenital idiots who was a candidate for the highest dignity boldly broke the inhibition and made speeches to the people in advocacy of himself, all over the country. Even more recently another has uttered his preferences in much the same way, but with this difference: he did his speechmaking at his own home, the ax-grinders in his interest rounding up audiences for him and herding them before his door.[27] One of the two corpses, too, was galvanized into a kind of ghastly activity and became a talking automaton; but the other had been too long dead. In a few years more the decent tradition that a man should not blow his own horn will be obsolete in its application to the high office, as it is to all the others, but the popular saying will lose none of its currency for that.

To the American mind nothing can be more shocking than the Tamtonian practice of openly soliciting political preferment and even paying money to assist in securing it. With us such immodesty would be taken as proof of the offender's unfitness to exercise the power which he asks for, or bear the dignity which, in soliciting it, he belittles. Yet no Tamtonian ever refused to take the hand of a man guilty of such conduct, and there have been instances of fathers giving these greedy vulgarians the hands of their daughters in marriage and thereby assisting to perpetuate the species. The kind of government given by men who go about begging for the right to govern can be more easily imagined than endured. In short, I cannot help thinking that when, unable longer to bear with patience the evils entailed by the vices and follies of its inhabitants, I sailed away from the accursed island of Tamtonia, I left behind me the most pestilent race of rascals and ignoramuses to be found anywhere in the universe; and I never can sufficiently thank the divine Power who spared me the disadvantage and shame of being one of them, and cast my lot in this favored land of goodness and right reason, the blessed abode of public morality and private worth—of liberty, conscience and common sense.

I was not, however, to reach it without further detention in barbarous countries. After being at sea four days I was seized by my mutinous crew, set ashore upon an island, and having been made insensible by a blow upon the head was basely abandoned.

MAROONED ON UG

When I regained my senses I found myself lying on the strand a short remove from the margin of the sea. It was high noon and an insupportable itching pervaded my entire frame, that being the effect of sunshine in that country, as heat is in ours. Having observed that the discomfort was abated by the passing of a light cloud between me and the sun, I dragged myself with some difficulty to a clump of trees near by and found permanent relief in their shade. As soon as I was comfortable enough to examine my surroundings I saw that the trees were of metal, apparently copper, with leaves of what resembled pure silver, but may have contained alloy. Some of the trees bore burnished flowers shaped like bells, and in a breeze the tinkling as they clashed together was exceedingly sweet. The grass with which the open country was covered as far as I could see amongst the patches of forest was of a bright scarlet hue, excepting along the water-courses, where it was white. Lazily cropping it at some little distance away, or lying in it, indolently chewing the cud and attended by a man half-clad in skins and bearing a crook, was a flock of tigers.[28] My travels in New Jersey[29] having made me proof against surprise, I contemplated these several visible phenomena without emotion, and with a merely expectant interest in what might be revealed by further observation.

The tigerherd having perceived me, now came striding forward, brandishing his crook and shaking his fists with great vehemence, gestures which I soon learned were, in that country, signs of amity and good-will. But before knowing that fact I had risen to my feet and thrown myself into a posture of defense, and as he approached I led for his head with my left, following with a stiff right upon his solar plexus, which sent him rolling on the grass in great pain. After learning something of the social customs of the country I felt extreme mortification in recollecting this breach of etiquette, and even to this day I cannot think upon it without a blush.

Such was my first meeting with Jogogle-Zadester, Pastor-King of Ug, the wisest and best of men. Later in our acquaintance, when I had for a long time been an honored guest at his court, where a thousand fists were ceremoniously shaken under my nose daily, he explained that my lukewarm reception of his hospitable advances gave him, for the moment, an unfavorable impression of my breeding and culture.

The island of Ug, upon which I had been marooned, lies in the Southern Hemisphere, but has neither latitude nor longitude. It has an area of nearly seven hundred square *samtains* and is peculiar in shape, its width being considerably greater than its length. Politically it is a limited monarchy, the right of succession to the throne being vested in the sovereign's father, if he have one; if not in his grandfather, and so on upward in the line of ascent. (As a matter of fact there has not within historic times been a legitimate succession, even the great and good Jogogle-Zadester being a usurper chosen by popular vote.) To assist him in governing, the King is given a parliament, the Uggard word for which is *gabagab,* but its usefulness is greatly circumscribed by the *Blubosh,* or Constitution, which requires that every measure, in order to become a law, shall have an affirmative majority of the actual members, yet forbids any member to vote who has not a distinct pecuniary interest in the result. I was once greatly amused by a spirited contest over a matter of harbor improvement, each of two proposed harbors having its advocates. One of these gentlemen, a most eloquent patriot, held the floor for hours in advocacy of the port where he had an interest in a projected mill for making dead kittens into cauliflower pickles; while other members were being vigorously persuaded by one who at the other place had a clam ranch.[30] In a debate in the Uggard *gabagab* no one can have a "standing" except a party in interest; and as a consequence of this enlightened policy every bill that is passed is found to be most intelligently adapted to its purpose.

The original intent of this requirement was that members having no pecuniary interest in a proposed law at the time of its inception should not embarrass the proceedings and pervert the result; but the inhibition is now thought to be sufficiently observed by formal public acceptance of a nominal bribe to vote one way or the other. It is of course understood that behind the nominal bribe is commonly a more substantial one of which there is no record. To an American accustomed to the incorrupt methods of legislation in his own country the spectacle of every member of the Uggard *gabagab* qualifying himself to vote by marching up, each in his turn as his name is called, to the proponent of the bill, or to its leading antagonist, and solemnly receiving a *tonusi* (the smallest coin of the realm) is exceedingly novel. When I ventured to mention to the King my lack of faith in the principle upon which this custom is founded, he replied:

"Heart of my soul, if you and your compatriots distrust the honesty and intelligence of an interested motive why is it that in your own courts of law, as you describe them, no private citizen can institute a civil action to right the wrongs of anybody but himself?"

I had nothing to say and the King proceeded: "And why is it that your judges will listen to no argument from any one who has not acquired a selfish concern in the matter?"

"O, your Majesty," I answered with animation, "they listen to attorneys-general, district attorneys and salaried officers of the law generally, whose prosperity depends in no degree upon their success; who prosecute none but those whom they believe to be guilty; who are careful to present no false nor misleading testimony and argument; who are solicitous that even the humblest accused person shall be accorded every legal right and every advantage to which he is entitled; who, in brief, are animated by the most humane sentiments and actuated by the purest and most unselfish motives."

The King's discomfiture was pitiful: he retired at once from the capital and passed a whole year pasturing his flock of tigers in the solitudes beyond the River of Wine. Seeing that I would henceforth be *persona non grata* at the palace, I sought obscurity in the writing and publication of books. In this vocation I was greatly assisted by a few standard works that had been put ashore with me in my sea-chest.

The literature of Ug is copious and of high merit, but consists altogether of fiction— mainly history, biography, theology and novels. Authors of exceptional excellence receive from the state marks of signal esteem, being appointed to the positions of laborers in the Department of Highways and Cemeteries. Having been so fortunate as to win public favor and attract official attention by my locally famous works, "The Decline and Fall of the Roman Empire," "David Copperfield," "Pilgrim's Progress," and "Ben Hur,"[31] I was myself that way distinguished and my future assured. Unhappily, through

THE LAND BEYOND THE BLOW

ignorance of the duties and dignities of the position I had the mischance to accept a gratuity for sweeping a street crossing and was compelled to flee for my life.

Disguising myself as a sailor I took service on a ship that sailed due south into the Unknown Sea.

It is now many years since my marooning on Ug, but my recollection of the country, its inhabitants and their wonderful manners and customs is exceedingly vivid. Some small part of what most interested me I shall here set down.

The Uggards are, or fancy themselves, a warlike race: nowhere in those distant seas are there any islanders so vain of their military power, the consciousness of which they acquired chiefly by fighting one another. Many years ago, however, they had a war with the people of another island kingdom, called Wug. The Wuggards held dominion over a third island, Scamadumclitchclitch,[32] whose people had tried to throw off the yoke. In order to subdue them—at least to tears—it was decided to deprive them of garlic, the sole article of diet known to them and the Wuggards, and in that country dug out of the ground like coal. So the Wuggards in the rebellious island stopped up all the garlic mines, supplying their own needs by purchase from foreign trading proas. Having few cowrie shells, with which to purchase, the poor Scamadumclitch-clitchians suffered a great distress, which so touched the hearts of the compassionate Uggards—a most humane and conscientious people—that they declared war against the Wuggards and sent a fleet of proas to the relief of the sufferers. The fleet established a strict blockade of every port in Scamadumclitchclitch, and not a clove of garlic could enter the island. That compelled the Wuggard army of occupation to reopen the mines for its own subsistence.[33]

All this was told to me by the great and good and wise Jogogle-Zadester, King of Ug.

"But, your Majesty," I said, "what became of the poor Scamadumclitchclitchians?"

"They all died," he answered with royal simplicity.

"Then your Majesty's humane intervention," I said, "was not entirely—well, fattening?"

"The fortune of war," said the King, gravely, looking over my head to signify that the interview was at an end; and I retired from the Presence on hands and feet, as is the etiquette in that country.

As soon as I was out of hearing I threw a stone in the direction of the palace and said: "I never in my life heard of such a cold-blooded scoundrel!"

In conversation with the King's Prime Minister, the famous Grumsquutzy, I asked him how it was that Ug, being a great military power, was apparently without soldiers.

"Sir," he replied, courteously shaking his fist under my nose in sign of amity, "know that when Ug needs soldiers she enlists them. At the end of the war they are put to death."

"Visible embodiment of a great nation's wisdom," I said, "far be it from me to doubt the expediency of that military method; but merely as a matter of economy would it not be better to keep an army in time of peace than to be compelled to create one in time of war?"

"Ug is rich," he replied; "we do not have to consider matters of economy. There is among our people a strong and instinctive distrust of a standing army."

"What are they afraid of," I asked—"what do they fear that it will do?"

"It is not what the army may do," answered the great man, "but what it may prevent others from doing. You must know that we have in this land a thing known as Industrial Discontent."

"Ah, I see," I exclaimed, interrupting—"the industrial classes fear that the army may destroy, or at least subdue, their discontent."

The Prime Minister reflected profoundly, standing the while, in order that he might assist his faculties by scratching himself, even as we, when thinking, scratch our heads.

"No," he said presently; "I don't think that is quite what they apprehend—they and the writers and statesmen who speak for them. As I said before, what is feared in a case of industrial discontent is the army's preventive power. But I am myself uncertain what it is that these good souls dislike to have the army prevent. I shall take the customary means to learn."

Having occasion on the next day to enter the great audience hall of the palace I observed in gigantic letters running across the entire side opposite the entrance this surprising inscription:

"In a strike, what do you fear that the army will prevent which ought to be done?"

Facing the entrance sat Grumsquutzy, in his robes of office and surrounded by an armed guard. At a little distance stood two great black slaves, each bearing a scourge of thongs. All about them the floor was slippery with blood. While I wondered at all this two policemen entered, having between them one whom I recognized as a professional Friend of the People, a great orator, keenly concerned for the interests of Labor. Shown the inscription and unable or unwilling to answer, he was given over to the two blacks and, being stripped to the skin, was beaten with the whips until he bled copiously and his cries resounded through the palace. His ears were then shorn away and he was thrown into the street. Another Friend of the People was brought in, and treated in the same way; and the inquiry was continued, day after day, until all had been interrogated. But Grumsquutzy got no answer.

A most extraordinary and interesting custom of the Uggards is called the *Naganag* and has existed, I was told, for centuries. Immediately after every war, and before the returned army is put to death, the chieftains who have held high command and their official head, the Minister of National Displeasure, are conducted with much pomp to the public square of Nabootka, the capital. Here all are stripped naked, deprived of their sight with a hot iron and armed with a club each. They are then locked in the square, which has an enclosing wall thirty *clowgebs* high. A signal is given and they begin to fight. At the end of three days the place is entered and searched. If any of the dead bodies has an unbroken bone in it the survivors are boiled in wine; if not they are smothered in butter.

Upon the advantages of this custom—which surely has not its like in the whole world—I could get little light. One public official told me its purpose was "peace among the victorious"; another said it was "for gratification of the military instinct in high places," though if that is so one is disposed to ask "What was the war for?" The Prime Minister, profoundly learned in all things else, could not enlighten me, and the commander-in-chief in the Wuggard war could only tell me, while on his way to the public square, that it was "to vindicate the truth of history."

In all the wars in which Ug has engaged in historic times that with Wug was the most destructive of life. Excepting among the comparatively few troops that had the hygienic and preservative advantage of personal collusion with the enemy, the mortality was appalling. Regiments exposed to the fatal conditions of camp life in their own country died like flies in a frost.[34] So pathetic were the pleas of the sufferers to be led against the enemy and have a chance to live that none hearing them could forbear to weep. Finally a considerable number of them went to the seat of war, where they began an immediate attack upon a fortified city, for their health; but the enemy's resistance was too brief materially to reduce the death rate and the men were again in the hands of their officers. On their return to Ug they were so few that the public executioners charged with the duty of reducing the army to a peace footing were themselves made ill by inactivity.

As to the navy, the war with Wug having shown the Uggard sailors to be immortal, their government knows not how to get rid of them, and remains a great sea power in spite of itself. I ventured to suggest mustering out, but neither the King nor any Minister of State was able to form a conception of any method of reduction and retrenchment but that of the public headsman.

It is said—I do not know with how much truth—that the defeat of Wug was made easy by a certain malicious prevision of the Wuggards themselves: something of the nature of heroic self-sacrifice, the surrender of a present advantage for a terrible revenge in the future. As an instance, the commander of the fortified city already mentioned is reported to have ordered his garrison to kill as few of their assailants as possible.

"It is true," he explained to his subordinates, who favored a defense to the death— "it is true this will lose us the place, but there are other places; you have not thought of that."

They had not thought of that.

"It is true, too, that we shall be taken prisoners, but"—and he smiled grimly— "we have fairly good appetites, and we must be fed. That will cost something, I take it. But that is not the best of it. Look at that vast host of our enemies—each one of them a future pensioner on a fool people. If there is among us one man who would willingly deprive the Uggard treasury of a single dependent—who would spare the Uggard pigs one *gukwam* of expense, let the traitor stand forth."

No traitor stood forth, and in the ensuing battles the garrison, it is said, fired only blank cartridges, and such of the assailants as were killed incurred that mischance by falling over their own feet.

It is estimated by Wuggard statisticians that in twenty years from the close of the war the annual appropriation for pensions in Ug will amount to no less than one hundred and sixty *gumdums* to every enlisted man in the kingdom. But they know not the Uggard customs of exterminating the army.

THE DOG IN GANEGWAG

At about the end of the thirty-seventh month of our voyage due south from Ug we sighted land, and although the coast appeared wild and inhospitable, the captain decided to send a boat ashore in search of fresh water and provisions, of which we were in sore need. I was of the boat's crew and thought myself fortunate in being able to set foot again upon the earth. There were seven others in the landing party, including the mate, who commanded.

Selecting a sheltered cove, which appeared to be at the mouth of a small creek, we beached the boat, and leaving two men to guard it started inland toward a grove of trees. Before we reached it an animal came out of it and advanced confidently toward us, showing no signs of either fear or hostility. It was a hideous creature, not altogether like anything that we had ever seen, but on its close approach we recognized it as a dog, of an unimaginably loathsome breed. As we were nearly famished one of the sailors shot it for food. Instantly a great crowd of persons, who had doubtless been watching us from among the trees, rushed upon us with fierce exclamations and surrounded us, making the most threatening gestures and brandishing unfamiliar weapons. Unable to resist such odds we were seized, bound with cords and dragged into the forest almost before we knew what had happened to us. Observing the nature of our reception the ship's crew hastily weighed anchor and sailed away. We never again saw them.[35]

Beyond the trees concealing it from the sea was a great city, and thither we were taken. It was Gumammam, the capital of Ganegwag, whose people are dog-worshipers. The fate of my companions I never learned, for although I remained in the country for seven years, much of the time as a prisoner, and learned to speak its language, no answer was ever given to my many inquiries about my unfortunate friends.

The Ganegwagians are an ancient race with a history covering a period of ten thousand *supintroes*. In stature they are large, in color blue, with crimson hair and yellow eyes. They live to a great age, sometimes as much as twenty *supintroes,* their climate being so wholesome that even the aged have to sail to a distant island in order to die. Whenever a sufficient number of them reach what they call "the age of going away" they embark on a government ship and in the midst of impressive public rites and ceremonies set sail for "the Isle of the Happy Change." Of their strange civilization, their laws, manners and customs, their copper clothing and liquid houses I have written—at perhaps too great length—in my famous book, "Ganegwag the Incredible." Here I shall confine myself to their religion, certainly the most amazing form of superstition in the world.

Nowhere, it is believed, but in Ganegwag has so vile a creature as the dog obtained general recognition as a deity.[36] There this filthy beast is considered so divine that it is freely admitted to the domestic circle and cherished as an honored guest. Scarcely a family that is able to support a dog is without one, and some have as many as a half-dozen. Indeed, the dog is the special deity of the poor, those families having most that are least able to maintain them. In some sections of the country, particularly the southern and southwestern provinces, the number of dogs is estimated to be greater than that of the children, as is the cost of their maintenance. In families of the rich they are fewer in number, but more sacredly cherished, especially by the female members, who lavish upon them a wealth of affection not always granted to the husband and children, and distinguish them with indescribable attentions and endearments.

Nowhere is the dog compelled to make any other return for all this honor and benefaction than a fawning and sycophantic demeanor toward those who bestow them and an insulting and injurious attitude toward strangers who have dogs of their own, and toward other dogs. In any considerable town of the realm not a day passes but the public newsman relates in the most matter-of-fact and unsympathetic way to his circle of listless auditors painful instances of human beings, mostly women and children, bitten and mangled by these ferocious animals without provocation.

In addition to these ravages of the dog in his normal state are a vastly greater number of outrages committed by the sacred animal in the fury of insanity, for he has an hereditary tendency to madness, and in that state his bite is incurable, the victim awaiting in the most horrible agony the sailing of the next ship to the Isle of the Happy Change, his suffering imperfectly medicined by expressions of public sympathy for the dog.

A cynical citizen of Gumammam said to the writer of this narrative: "My countrymen have three hundred kinds of dogs, and only one way to hang a thief." Yet all the dogs are alike in this, that none is respectable.

Withal, it must be said of this extraordinary people that their horrible religion is free from the hollow forms and meaningless ceremonies in which so many superstitions of the lower races find expression. It is a religion of love, practical, undemonstrative, knowing nothing of pageantry and spectacle. It is hidden in the lives and hearts of the people; a stranger would hardly know of its existence as a distinct faith. Indeed, other faiths and better ones (one of them having some resemblance to a debased form of Christianity) co-exist with it, sometimes in the same mind. Cynolatry[37] is tolerant so long as the dog is not denied an equal divinity with the deities of other faiths. Nevertheless, I could not think of the people of Ganegwag without contempt and loathing; so it was with no small joy that I sailed for the contiguous island of Ghargaroo[38] to consult, according to my custom, the renowned statesman and philosopher, Juptka-Getch, who was accounted the wisest man in all the world, and held in so high esteem that no one dared speak to him without the sovereign's permission, countersigned by the Minister of Morals and Manners.

A CONFLAGRATION IN GHARGAROO

Through the happy accident of having a mole on the left side of my nose, as had also a cousin of the Prime Minister, I obtained a royal rescript permitting me to speak to the great Juptka-Getch, and went humbly to his dwelling, which, to my astonishment, I found to be an unfurnished cave in the side of a mountain. Inexpressibly surprised to observe that a favorite of the sovereign and the people was so meanly housed, I ventured, after my salutation, to ask how this could be so. Regarding me with an indulgent smile, the venerable man, who was about two hundred and fifty years old and entirely bald, explained.

"In one of our Sacred Books, of which we have three thousand," said he, "it is written, *'Golooloo ek wakwah betenka,'* and in another, *'Jebeb uq seedroy im aboltraqu ocrux ti smelkit.'"*[39]

Translated, these mean, respectively, "The poor are blessed," and, "Heaven is not easily entered by those who are rich."[40]

I asked Juptka-Getch if his countrymen really gave to these texts a practical application in the affairs of life.

"Why, surely," he replied, "you cannot think us such fools as to disregard the teachings of our gods! That would be madness. I cannot imagine a people so mentally and morally depraved as that! Can you?"

Observing me blushing and stammering, he inquired the cause of my embarrassment. "The thought of so incredible a thing confuses me," I managed to reply. "But tell me if in your piety and wisdom you really stripped yourself of all your property in order to obey the gods and get the benefit of indigence."

"I did not have to do so," he replied with a smile; "my King attended to that. When he wishes to distinguish one of his subjects by a mark of his favor, he impoverishes him to such a degree as will attest the exact measure of the royal approbation. I am proud to say that he took from me all that I had."

"But, pardon me," I said; "how does it occur that among a people which regards poverty as the greatest earthly good all are not poor? I observe here as much wealth and 'prosperity' as in my own country."

Juptka-Getch smiled and after a few moments answered: "The only person in this country that owns anything is the King; in the service of his people he afflicts himself with that burden. All property, of whatsoever kind, is his, to do with as he will. He divides it among his subjects in the ratio of their demerit, as determined by the *waguks*—local officers—whose duty it is to know personally every one in their jurisdiction. To the most desperate and irreclaimable criminals is allotted the greatest wealth, which is taken from them, little by little, as they show signs of reformation."

"But what," said I, "is to prevent the wicked from becoming poor at any time? How can the King and his officers keep the unworthy, suffering the punishment and peril of wealth, from giving it away?"

"To whom, for example?" replied the illustrious man, taking the forefinger of his right hand into his mouth, as is the fashion in Ghargaroo when awaiting an important communication. The respectful formality of the posture imperfectly concealed the irony of the question, but I was not of the kind to be easily silenced.

"One might convert one's property into money," I persisted, "and throw the money into the sea."

Juptka-Getch released the finger and gravely answered: "Every person in Ghargaroo is compelled by law to keep minute accounts of his income and expenditures, and must swear to them. There is an annual appraisement by the *waguk,* and any needless decrease in the value of an estate is punished by breaking the offender's legs. Expenditures for luxuries and high living are, of course, approved, for it is universally known among us, and attested by many popular proverbs, that the pleasures of the rich are vain and disappointing. So they are considered a part of the punishment, and not only allowed but required. A man sentenced to wealth who lives frugally, indulging in only rational and inexpensive delights, has his ears cut off for the first offense, and for the second is compelled to pass six months at court, participating in all the gaieties, extravagances and pleasures of the capital, and—"

"Most illustrious of mortals," I said, turning a somersault—the Ghargarese manner of interrupting a discourse without offense—"I am as the dust upon your beard, but in my own country I am esteemed no fool, and right humbly do I perceive that you are *ecxroptug nemk puttog peleemy."*

This expression translates, literally, "giving me a fill," a phrase without meaning in our tongue, but in Ghargarese it appears to imply incredulity.

"The gaieties of the King's court," I continued, "must be expensive. The courtiers of the sovereign's entourage, the great officers of the realm—surely they are not condemned to wealth, like common criminals!"

"My son," said Juptka-Getch, tearing out a handful of his beard to signify his tranquility under accusation, "your doubt of my veracity is noted with satisfaction, but it is not permitted to you to impeach my sovereign's infallible knowledge of character. His courtiers, the great officers of the realm, as you truly name them, are the richest men in the country because he knows them to be the greatest rascals. After each annual reapportionment of the national wealth he settles upon them the unallotted surplus."

THE LAND BEYOND THE BLOW

Prostrating myself before the eminent philosopher, I craved his pardon for my doubt of his sovereign's wisdom and consistency, and begged him to cut off my head.

"Nay," he said, "you have committed the unpardonable sin and I cannot consent to bestow upon you the advantages of death. You shall continue to live the thing that you are."

"What!" I cried, remembering the Lalugwumps and Gnarmag-Zote, "is it thought in Ghargaroo that death is an advantage, a blessing?"

"Our Sacred Books," he said, "are full of texts affirming the vanity of life."[41]

"Then," I said, "I infer that the death penalty is unknown to your laws!"

"We have the life penalty instead.[42] Convicted criminals are not only enriched, as already explained, but by medical attendance kept alive as long as possible. On the contrary, the very righteous, who have been rewarded with poverty, are permitted to die whenever it pleases them.

"Do not the Sacred Books of your country teach the vanity of life, the blessedness of poverty and the wickedness of wealth?"

"They do, O Most Illustrious, they do."

"And your countrymen believe?"

"Surely—none but the foolish and depraved entertain a doubt."

"Then I waste my breath in expounding laws and customs already known to you. You have, of course, the same."

At this I averted my face and blushed so furiously that the walls of the cave were illuminated with a wavering crimson like the light of a great conflagration! Thinking that the capital city was ablaze, Juptka-Getch ran from the cave's mouth, crying, "Fire, fire!" and I saw him no more.

AN EXECUTION IN BATRUGIA

My next voyage was not so prosperous. By violent storms lasting seven weeks, during which we saw neither the sun nor the stars, our ship was driven so far out of its course that the captain had no knowledge of where we were. At the end of that period we were blown ashore and wrecked on a coast so wild and desolate that I had never seen anything so terrifying. Through a manifest interposition of Divine Providence I was spared, though all my companions perished miserably in the waves that had crushed the ship among the rocks.

As soon as I was sufficiently recovered from my fatigue and bruises, and had rendered thanks to merciful Heaven for my deliverance, I set out for the interior of the country, taking with me a cutlass for protection against wild beasts and a bag of sea-biscuit for sustenance. I walked vigorously, for the weather was then cool and pleasant, and after I had gone a few miles from the inhospitable coast I found the country open and level. The earth was covered with a thick growth of crimson grass, and at wide intervals were groups of trees. These were very tall, their tops in many instances invisible in a kind of golden mist, or haze, which proved to be, not a transient phe-nomenon, but a permanent one, for never in that country has the sun been seen, nor is there any night. The haze seems to be self-luminous, giving a soft, yellow light, so diffused that shadows are unknown. The land is abundantly supplied with pools and rivulets, whose water is of a beautiful orange color and has a pleasing perfume some-what like attar of rose. I observed all this without surprise and with little apprehen-sion, and went forward, feeling that anything, however novel and mysterious, was better than the familiar terrors of the sea and the coast.

After traveling a long time, though how long I had not the means to determine, I arrived at the city of Momgamwo, the capital of the kingdom of Batrugia, on the main-land of the Hidden Continent, where it is always twelve o'clock.

The Batrugians are of gigantic stature, but mild and friendly disposition. They offered me no violence, seeming rather amused by my small stature. One of them, who appeared to be a person of note and consequence, took me to his house (their houses are but a single story in height and built of brass blocks), set food before me, and by signs manifested the utmost good will. A long time afterward, when I had learned the language of the country, he explained that he had recognized me as an American pigmy, a race of which he had some little knowledge through a letter from a brother, who had been in my country. He showed me the letter, of which the chief part is here presented in translation:

"You ask me, my dear Tgnagogu, to relate my adventures among the Americans, as they call themselves. My adventures were very brief, lasting altogether not more than three *gumkas,* and most of the time was passed in taking measures for my own safety.

"My skyship, which had been driven for six moons before an irresistible gale, passed over a great city just at daylight one morning, and rather than continue the voy-age with a lost reckoning I demanded that I be permitted to disembark. My wish was respected, and my companions soared away without me. Before night I had escaped from the city, by what means you know, and with my remarkable experiences in returning to civilization all Batrugia is familiar. The description of the strange city I have reserved for you, by whom only could I hope to be believed. Nyork, as its inhabi-tants call it, is a city of inconceivable extent—not less, I should judge, than seven square *glepkeps!* Of the number of its inhabitants I can only say that they are as the sands of the desert. They wear clothing—of a hideous kind, 'tis true—speak an apparently copious though harsh language, and seem to have a certain limited intelligence. They are puny in stature, the tallest of them being hardly higher than my breast.

"Nevertheless, Nyork is a city of giants. The magnitude of all things artificial there is astounding! My dear Tgnagogu, words can give you no conception of it. Many of the buildings, I assure you, are as many as fifty *sprugas* in height, and shelter five thousand persons each. And these stupendous structures are so crowded together that to the spectator in the narrow streets below they seem utterly devoid of design and symmetry—mere monstrous aggregations of brick, stone and metal—mountains of masonry, cliffs and crags of architecture hanging in the sky!

"A city of giants inhabited by pigmies! For you must know, oh friend of my liver, that the rearing of these mighty structures could not be the work of the puny folk that swarm in ceaseless activity about their bases. These fierce little savages invaded the island in numbers so overwhelming that the giant builders had to flee before them. Some escaped across great bridges which, with the help of their gods, they had suspended in the air from bank to bank of a wide river parting the island from the mainland, but many could do no better than mount some of the buildings that they had reared, and there, in these inaccessible altitudes, they dwell to-day, still piling stone upon stone. Whether they do this in obedience to their instinct as builders, or in hope to escape by way of the heavens, I had not the means to learn, being ignorant of the pigmy tongue and in continual fear of the crowds that followed me.[43]

"You can see the giants toiling away up there in the sky, laying in place the enormous beams and stones which none but they could handle. They look no bigger than beetles, but you know that they are many *sprugas* in stature, and you shudder to think what would ensue if one should lose his footing. Fancy that great bulk whirling down to earth from so dizzy an altitude! . . .

"May birds ever sing above your grave.

"JOQUOLK WAK MGAPY."

By my new friend, Tgnagogu, I was presented to the King, a most enlightened monarch, who not only reigned over, but ruled absolutely, the most highly civilized people in the world. He received me with gracious hospitality, quartered me in the palace of his Prime Minister, gave me for wives the three daughters of his Lord Chamberlain, and provided me with an ample income from the public revenues. Within a year I had made a fair acquaintance with the Batrugian language, and was appointed royal interpreter, with a princely salary, although no one speaking any other tongue, myself and two native professors of rhetoric excepted, had ever been seen in the kingdom.

One day I heard a great tumult in the street, and going to a window saw, in a public square opposite, a crowd of persons surrounding some high officials who were engaged in cutting off a man's head. Just before the executioner delivered the fatal stroke, the victim was asked if he had anything to say. He explained with earnestness that the deed for which he was about to suffer had been inspired and commanded by a brass-headed cow and four bushels of nightingales' eggs!

"Hold! hold!" I shouted in Batrugian, leaping from the window and forcing a way through the throng; "the man is obviously insane!"

"Friend," said a man in a long blue robe, gently restraining me, "it is not proper for you to interrupt these high proceedings with irrelevant remarks. The luckless gentleman who, in accordance with my will as Lord Chief Justice, has just had the happiness to part with his head was so inconsiderate as to take the life of a fellow-subject."

THE LAND BEYOND THE BLOW

"But he was insane," I persisted, "clearly and indisputably *ptig nupy uggydug!*"—a phrase imperfectly translatable, meaning, as near as may be, having flitter-mice in his campanile.[44]

"Am I to infer," said the Lord Chief Justice, "that in your own honorable country a person accused of murder is permitted to plead insanity as a reason why he should not be put to death?"

"Yes, illustrious one," I replied, respectfully, "we regard that as a good defense."

"Well," said he slowly, but with extreme emphasis, "I'll be *Gook swottled!*"

(*"Gook,"* I may explain, is the name of the Batrugian chief deity; but for the verb "to swottle" the English tongue has no equivalent. It seems to signify the deepest disapproval, and by a promise to be *"swottled"* a Batrugian denotes acute astonishment.)

"Surely," I said, "so wise and learned person as you cannot think it just to punish with death one who does not know right from wrong. The gentleman who has just now renounced his future believed himself to have been commanded to do what he did by a brass-headed cow and four bushels of nightingales' eggs—powers to which he acknowledged spiritual allegiance. To have disobeyed would have been, from his point of view, an infraction of a law higher than that of man."

"Honorable but erring stranger," replied the famous jurist, "if we permitted the prisoner in a murder trial to urge such a consideration as that—if our laws recognized any other justification than that he believed himself in peril of immediate death or great bodily injury—nearly all assassins would make some such defense. They would plead insanity of some kind and degree, and it would be almost impossible to establish their guilt. Murder trials would be expensive and almost interminable, defiled with perjury and sentiment. Juries would be deluded and confused, justice baffled, and red-handed man-killers turned loose to repeat their crimes and laugh at the law. Even as the law is, in a population of only one hundred million we have had no fewer than three homicides in less than twenty years! With such statutes and customs as yours we should have had at least twice as many. Believe me, I know my people; they have not the American respect for human life."

As blushing is deemed in Batrugia a sign of pride, I turned my back upon the speaker—an act which, fortunately, signifies a desire to hear more.

"Law," he continued, "is for the good of the greatest number. Execution of an actual lunatic now and then is not an evil to the community, nor, when rightly considered, to the lunatic himself. He is better off when dead, and society is profited by his removal. We are spared the cost of exposing imposture, the humiliation of acquitting the guilty, the peril of their freedom, the contagion of their evil example."

"In my country," I said, "we have a saying to the effect that it is better that ninety-nine guilty escape than that one innocent be punished."

"It is better," said he, "for the ninety-nine guilty, but distinctly worse for everybody else.[45] Sir," he concluded with chilling austerity, "I infer from their proverb that your countrymen are the most offensive blockheads in existence."

THE LAND BEYOND THE BLOW

By way of refutation I mentioned the English, indignantly withdrew from the country and set sail for Gokeetle-guk, or, as we should translate the name, Trustland.

THE JUMJUM OF GOKEETLE-GUK

Arriving at the capital of the country after many incredible adventures, I was promptly arrested by the police and taken before the Jumjum. He was an exceedingly affable person, and held office by appointment, "for life or fitness," as their laws express it. With one necessary exception all offices are appointive and the tenure of all except that is the same. The Panjandrum, or, as we should call him, King, is elected for a term of ten years, at the expiration of which he is shot. It is held that any man who has been so long in high authority will have committed enough sins and blunders to deserve death, even if none can be specifically proved.

Brought into the presence of the Jumjum, who graciously saluted me, I was seated on a beautiful rug and told in broken English by an interpreter who had escaped from Kansas that I was at liberty to ask any questions that I chose.

"Your Highness," I said, addressing the Jumjum through the interpreting Populist,[46] "I fear that I do not understand; I expected, not to ask questions, but to have to answer them. I am ready to give such an account of myself as will satisfy you that I am an honest man—neither a criminal nor a spy."

"The gentleman seems to regard himself with a considerable interest," said the Jumjum, aside to an officer of his suite—a remark which the interpreter, with characteristic intelligence, duly repeated to me. Then addressing me the Jumjum said:

"Doubtless your personal character is an alluring topic, but it is relevant to nothing in any proceedings that can be taken here. When a foreigner arrives in our capital he is brought before me to be instructed in whatever he may think it expedient for him to know of the manners, customs, laws, and so forth, of the country that he honors with his presence. It matters nothing to us what he is, but much to him what we are. You are at liberty to inquire."

I was for a moment overcome with emotion by so noble an example of official civility and thoughtfulness, then, after a little reflection, I said: "May it please your Highness, I should greatly like to be informed of the origin of the name of your esteemed country."

"Our country," said the Jumjum, acknowledging the compliment by a movement of his ears, "is called Trustland because all its industries, trades and professions are conducted by great aggregations of capital known as 'trusts.' They do the entire business of the country."

"Good God!" I exclaimed; "what a terrible state of affairs that is! I know about trusts. Why do your people not rise and throw off the yoke?"

"You are pleased to be unintelligible," said the great man, with a smile. "Would you mind explaining what you mean by 'the yoke'?"

"I mean," said I, surprised by his ignorance of metaphor, but reflecting that possibly the figures of rhetoric were not used in that country—"I mean the oppression,

THE LAND BEYOND THE BLOW

the slavery under which your people groan, their bondage to the tyrannical trusts, entailing poverty, unrequited toil and loss of self-respect."

"Why, as to that," he replied, "our people are prosperous and happy. There is very little poverty and what there is is obviously the result of vice or improvidence. Our labor is light and all the necessaries of life, many of the comforts and some of the luxuries are abundant and cheap. I hardly know what you mean by the tyranny of the trusts; they do not seem to care to be tyrannous, for each having the entire market for what it produces, its prosperity is assured and there is none of the strife and competition which, as I can imagine, might breed hardness and cruelty. Moreover, we should not let them be tyrannous. Why should we?"

"But, your Highness, suppose, for example, the trust that manufactures safety pins should decide to double the price of its product. What is to prevent great injury to the consumer?"

"The courts. Having but one man—the responsible manager—to deal with, protective legislation and its enforcement would be a very simple matter. If there were a thousand manufacturers of safety pins, scattered all over the country in as many jurisdictions, there would be no controlling them at all. They would cheat, not only one another but the consumers, with virtual immunity. But there is no disposition among our trusts to do any such thing. Each has the whole market, as I said, and each has learned by experience what the manager of a large business soon must learn, and what the manager of a small one probably would not learn and could not afford to apply if he knew it—namely, that low prices bring disproportionately large sales and therefore profits. Prices in this country are never put up except when some kind of scarcity increases the cost of production. Besides, nearly all the consumers are a part of the trusts, the stock of which is about the best kind of property for investment."

"What!" I cried,—"do not the managers so manipulate the stock by 'watering' it and otherwise as to fool and cheat the small investors?"

"We should not permit them. That would be dishonest."

"So it is in my country," I replied, rather tartly, for I believed his apparent *naïveté* assumed for my confusion, "but we are unable to prevent it."

He looked at me somewhat compassionately, I thought. "Perhaps," he said, "not enough of you really wish to prevent it. Perhaps your people are—well, different from mine—not worse, you understand—just different."

I felt the blood go into my cheeks and hot words were upon my tongue's end, but I restrained them; the conditions for a quarrel were not favorable to my side of it. When I had mastered my chagrin and resentment I said:

"In my country when trusts are formed a great number of persons suffer, whether the general consumer does or not—many small dealers, middle men, drummers[47] and general employees. The small dealer is driven out of the business by underselling. The middle man is frequently ignored, the trust dealing directly, or nearly so, with the consumer. The drummer is discharged because, competition having disappeared, custom must come without solicitation. Consolidation lets out swarms of employees of the individual concerns consolidated, for it is nearly as easy to conduct one large concern as a dozen smaller ones. These people get great sympathy from the public and the newspapers and their case is obviously pitiable. Was it not so in this country during the transition stage, and did not these poor gentlemen have to"—the right words would not come; I hardly knew how to finish. "Were they not compelled to go to work?" I finally asked, rather humbly.

The great official was silent for several minutes. Then he spoke.

"I am not sure that I understand you about our transition state. So far as our history goes matters with us have always been as they are to-day. To suppose them to have been otherwise would be to impugn the common sense of our ancestors. Nor do I quite know what you mean by 'small dealers,' 'middle men,' 'drummers,' and so forth."

He paused and fell into meditation, when suddenly his face was suffused with the light of a happy thought. It so elated him that he sprang to his feet and with his staff of office broke the heads of his Chief Admonisher of the Inimical and his Second Assistant Audible Sycophant. Then he said:

"I think I comprehend. Some eighty-five years ago, soon after my induction into office, there came to the court of the Panjandrum a man of this city who had been cast upon the island of Chicago (which I believe belongs to the American archipelago) and had passed many years there in business with the natives. Having learned all their customs and business methods he returned to his own country and laid before the Panjandrum a comprehensive scheme of commercial reform. He and his scheme were referred to me, the Panjandrum being graciously pleased to be unable to make head or tail of it. I may best explain it in its application to a single industry—the manufacture and sale of gootles."

"What is a gootle?" I asked.

"A metal weight for attachment to the tail of a donkey to keep him from braying," was the answer.[48] "It is known in this country that a donkey cannot utter a note unless he can lift his tail. Then, as now, gootles were made by a single concern having a great capital invested and an immense plant, and employing an army of workmen. It dealt, as it does today, directly with consumers. Afflicted with a sonant donkey a man would write to the trust and receive his gootle by return mail, or go personally to the factory and carry his purchase home on his shoulder—according to where he lived. The reformer said this was primitive, crude and injurious to the interests of the public and especially the poor. He proposed that the members of the gootle trust divide their capital and each member go into the business of making gootles for himself—I do not mean for his personal use—in different parts of the country. But none of them was to sell to consumers, but to other men, who would sell in quantity to still other men, who would sell single gootles for domestic use. Each manufacturer would of course require a full complement of officers, clerks and so forth, as would the other men—everybody but the consumer—and each would have to support them and make a profit himself.

THE LAND BEYOND THE BLOW

Competition would be so sharp that solicitors would have to be employed to make sales; and they too must have a living out of the business. Honored stranger, am I right in my inference that the proposed system has something in common with the one which obtains in your own happy, enlightened and prosperous country, and which you would approve?"

I did not care to reply.

"Of course," the Jumjum continued, "all this would greatly have enhanced the cost of gootles, thereby lessening the sales, thereby reducing the output, thereby throwing a number of workmen out of employment. You see this, do you not, O guest of my country?"

"Pray tell me," I said, "what became of the reformer who proposed all this change?"

"All this change? Why, sir, the one-thousandth part is not told: he proposed that his system should be general: not only in the gootle trust, but every trust in the country was to be broken up in the same way! When I had him before me, and had stated my objections to the plan, I asked him what were its advantages.

"'Sir,' he replied, 'I speak for millions of gentlemen in uncongenial employments, mostly manual and fatiguing. This would give them the kind of activity that they would like—such as their class enjoys in other countries where my system is in full flower, and where it is deemed so sacred that any proposal for its abolition or simplification by trusts is regarded with horror, especially by the working men.'

"Having reported to the Panjandrum (whose vermiform appendix may good angels have in charge) and received his orders, I called the reformer before me and addressed him thus:

"'Illustrious economist, I have the honor to inform you that in the royal judgment your proposal is the most absurd, impudent and audacious ever made; that the system which you propose to set up is revolutionary and mischievous beyond the dreams of treason;[49] that only in a nation of rogues and idiots could it have a moment's toleration.'

"He was about to reply, but cutting his throat to intimate that the hearing was at an end, I withdrew from the Hall of Audience, as under similar circumstances I am about to do now."

I withdrew first by way of a window, and after a terrible journey of six years in the Dolorous Mountains and on the Desert of Despair came to the western coast. Here I built a ship and after a long voyage landed on one of the islands constituting the Kingdom of Tortirra.

THE KINGDOM OF TORTIRRA

Of this unknown country and its inhabitants I have written a large volume which nothing but the obstinacy of publishers has kept from the world, and which I trust will yet see the light. Naturally, I do not wish to publish at this time anything that will sate public curiosity, and this brief sketch will consist of such parts only of the work as I think can best be presented in advance without abating interest in what is to follow when Heaven shall have put it into the hearts of publishers to square their conduct with their interests. I must, however, frankly confess that my choice has been partly determined by other considerations. I offer here those parts of my narrative which I conceive to be the least credible—those which deal with the most monstrous and astounding follies of a strange people. Their ceremony of marriage by decapitation; their custom of facing to the rear when riding on horseback; their practice of walking on their hands in all ceremonial processions; their selection of the blind for military command; their pig-worship—these and many other comparatively natural particulars of their religious, political, intellectual and social life I reserve for treatment in the great work for which I shall soon ask public favor and acceptance.

In Tortirran politics, as in Tamtonian, the population is always divided into two, and sometimes three or four "parties," each having a "policy" and each conscientiously believing the policy of the other, or others, erroneous and destructive. In so far as these various and varying policies can be seen to have any relation whatever to practical affairs they can be seen also to be the result of purely selfish considerations. The self-deluded people flatter themselves that their elections are contests of principles, whereas they are only struggles of interests. They are very fond of the word *slagthrit*, "principle"; and when they believe themselves acting from some high moral motive they are capable of almost any monstrous injustice or stupid folly. This insane devotion to principle is craftily fostered by their political leaders who invent captivating phrases intended to confirm them in it; and these deluding aphorisms are diligently repeated until all the people have them in memory, with no knowledge of the fallacies which they conceal. One of these phrases is "Principles, not men." In the last analysis this is seen to mean that it is better to be governed by scoundrels professing one set of principles than by good men holding another. That a scoundrel will govern badly, regardless of the principles which he is supposed somehow to "represent," is a truth which, however obvious to our own enlightened intelligence, has never penetrated the dark understandings of the Tortirrans. It is chiefly through the dominance of the heresy fostered by this popular phrase that the political leaders are able to put base men into office to serve their own nefarious ends.

I have called the political contests of Tortirra struggles of interests. In nothing is this more clear (to the looker-on at the game) than in the endless disputes concerning restrictions on commerce. It must be understood that lying many leagues to the southeast of Tortirra are other groups of islands, also wholly unknown to people of our race. They are known by the general name of *Gropilla-Stron* (a term signifying "the Land of the Day-dawn"), though it is impossible to ascertain why, and are inhabited by a powerful and hardy race, many of whom I have met in the capital of Tanga. The Stronagu, as they are called, are bold navigators and traders, their proas making long and hazardous voyages in all the adjacent seas to exchange commodities with other tribes. For many years they were welcomed in Tortirra with great hospitality and their goods eagerly purchased. They took back with them all manner of Tortirran

THE LAND BEYOND THE BLOW

products and nobody thought of questioning the mutual advantages of the exchange. But early in the present century a powerful Tortirran demagogue named Pragam began to persuade the people that commerce was piracy—that true prosperity consisted in consumption of domestic products and abstention from foreign.[50] This extraordinary heresy soon gathered such head that Pragam was appointed Regent and invested with almost dictatorial powers. He at once distributed nearly the whole army among the seaport cities, and whenever a Stronagu trading proa attempted to land, the soldiery, assisted by the populace, rushed down to the beach, and with a terrible din of gongs and an insupportable discharge of stink-pots—the only offensive weapon known to Tortirran warfare—drove the laden vessels to sea, or if they persisted in anchoring destroyed them and smothered their crews in mud. The Tortirrans themselves not being a sea-going people, all communication between them and the rest of their little world soon ceased. But with it ceased the prosperity of Tortirra. Deprived of a market for their surplus products and compelled to forego the comforts and luxuries which they had obtained from abroad, the people began to murmur at the effect of their own folly. A reaction set in, a powerful opposition to Pragam and his policy was organized, and he was driven from power.

But the noxious tree that Pragam had planted in the fair garden of his country's prosperity had struck root too deeply to be altogether eradicated. It threw up shoots everywhere, and no sooner was one cut down than from roots underrunning the whole domain of political thought others sprang up with a vigorous and baleful growth. While the dictum that trade is piracy no longer commands universal acceptance, a majority of the populace still hold a modified form of it, and that "importation is theft" is to-day a cardinal political "principle" of a vast body of Tortirra's people. The chief expounders and protagonists of this doctrine are all directly or indirectly engaged in making or growing such articles as were formerly got by exchange with the Stronagu traders. The articles are generally inferior in quality, but consumers, not having the benefit of foreign competition, are compelled to pay extortionate prices for them, thus maintaining the unscrupulous producers in needless industries and a pernicious existence. But these active and intelligent rogues are too powerful to be driven out. They persuade their followers, among whom are many ignorant consumers, that this vestigial remnant of the old Pragam policy is all that keeps the nation from being desolated by small-pox and an epidemic of broken legs.

It is impossible within these limits to give a full history of the strange delusion whose origin I have related. It has undergone many modifications and changes, as it is the nature of error to do, but the present situation is about this. The trading proas of the Stronagu are permitted to enter certain ports, but when one arrives she must anchor at a little distance from shore. Here she is boarded by an officer of the government, who ascertains the thickness of her keel, the number of souls on board and the amount and character of the merchandise she brings. From these data—the last being the main factor in the problem—the officer computes her unworthiness and adjudges a suitable penalty. The next day a scow manned by a certain number of soldiers pushes out and anchors within easy throw of her, and there is a frightful beating of gongs. When this has reached its lawful limit as to time it is hushed and the soldiers throw a stated number of stink-pots on board the offending craft. These, exploding as they strike, stifle the captain and crew with an intolerable odor. In the case of a large proa having a cargo of such commodities as the Tortirrans particularly need, this bombardment is continued for hours. At its conclusion the vessel is permitted to land and discharge her cargo without further molestation. Under these hard conditions importers find it impossible to do much business, the exorbitant wages demanded by seamen consuming most of the profit. No restrictions are now placed on the export trade, and vessels arriving empty are subjected to no penalties; but the Stronagu having other markets, in which they can sell as well as buy, cannot afford to go empty handed to Tortirra.

It will be obvious to the reader that in all this no question of "principle" is involved. A well-informed Tortirran's mental attitude with regard to the matter may be calculated with unfailing accuracy from a knowledge of his interests. If he produces anything which his countrymen want, and which in the absence of all restriction they could get more cheaply from the Stronagu than they can from him, he is in politics a *Gakphew,* or "Stinkpotter"; if not he is what that party derisively calls a *Shokerbom,* which signifies "Righteous Man"—for there is nothing which the Gakphews hold in so holy detestation as righteousness.

Nominally, Tortirra is an hereditary monarchy; virtually it is a democracy, for under a peculiar law of succession there is seldom an occupant of the throne, and all public affairs are conducted by a Supreme Council sitting at Felduchia, the capital of Tanga, to which body each island of the archipelago, twenty-nine in number, elects representatives in proportion to its population, the total membership being nineteen hundred and seventeen. Each island has a Subordinate Council for the management of local affairs and a Head Chief charged with execution of the laws. There is also a Great Court at Felduchia, whose function it is to interpret the general laws of the Kingdom, passed by the Supreme Council, and a Minor Great Court at the capital of each island, with corresponding duties and powers.[51] These powers are very loosely and vaguely defined, and are the subject of endless controversy everywhere, and nowhere more than in the courts themselves—such is the multiplicity of laws and so many are the contradictory decisions upon them, every decision constituting what is called a *lantrag,* or, as we might say, "precedent." The peculiarity of a *lantrag,* or previous decision, is that it is, or is not, binding, at the will of the honorable judge making a later one on a similar point. If he wishes to decide in the same way he quotes the previous decision with all the gravity that he would give to an exposition of the law itself; if not, he either ignores it altogether, shows that it is not applicable to the case under consideration (which, as the circumstances are never exactly the same, he can always do), or substitutes a contradictory *lantrag* and fortifies himself with that. There is a precedent for any decision that a judge may wish to make, but sometimes he is too indolent to search it out and cite it.

THE LAND BEYOND THE BLOW

Frequently, when the letter and intent of the law under which an action is brought are plainly hostile to the decision which it pleases him to render, the judge finds it easier to look up an older law, with which it is compatible, and which the later one, he says, does not repeal, and to base his decision on that; and there is a law for everything, just as there is a precedent. Failing to find, or not caring to look for, either precedent or statute to sustain him, he can readily show that any other decision than the one he has in will would be *tokoli impelly;* that is to say, contrary to public morals, and this, too, is considered a legitimate consideration, though on another occasion he may say, with public assent and approval, that it is his duty, not to make the law conform to justice, but to expound and enforce it as he finds it.[52] In short, such is the confusion of the law and the public conscience that the courts of Tortirra do whatever they please, subject only to overruling by higher courts in the exercise of *their* pleasure; for great as is the number of minor and major tribunals, a case originating in the lowest is never really settled until it has gone through all the intermediate ones and been passed upon by the highest, to which it might just as well have been submitted at first. The evils of this astonishing system could not be even baldly catalogued in a lifetime. They are infinite in number and prodigious in magnitude. To the trained intelligence of the American observer it is incomprehensible how any, even the most barbarous, nation can endure them.

An important function of the Great Court and the Minor Great Court is passing upon the validity of all laws enacted by the Supreme Council and the Subordinate Councils, respectively. The nation as a whole, as well as each separate island, has a fundamental law called the *Trogodal,* or, as we should say, the Constitution; and no law whatever that may be passed by the Council is final and determinate until the appropriate court has declared that it conforms to the Trogodal. Nevertheless every law is put in force the moment it is perfected and before it is submitted to the court. Indeed, not one in a thousand ever is submitted at all, that depending upon the possibility of some individual objecting to its action upon his personal interests, which few, indeed, can afford to do. It not infrequently occurs that some law which has for years been rigorously enforced, even by fines and imprisonment, and to which the whole commercial and social life of the nation has adjusted itself with all its vast property interests, is brought before the tribunal having final jurisdiction in the matter and coolly declared no law at all. The pernicious effect may be more easily imagined than related, but those who by loyal obedience to the statute all those years have been injured in property, those who are ruined by its erasure and those who may have suffered the severest penalties for its violation are alike without redress. It seems not to have occurred to the Tortirrans to require the court to inspect the law and determine its validity before it is put in force. It is, indeed, the traditional practice of these strange tribunals, when a case is forced upon them, to decide, not as many points of law as they can, but as few as they may; and this dishonest inaction is not only tolerated but commended as the highest wisdom. The consequence is that only those who make a profession of the law and live by it and find their account in having it as little understood by others as is possible can know which acts and parts of acts are in force and which are not. The higher courts, too, have arrogated to themselves the power of declaring unconstitutional even parts of the Constitution, frequently annulling most important provisions of the very instrument creating them!

A popular folly in Tortirra is the selection of representatives in the Councils from among that class of men who live by the law, whose sole income is derived from its uncertainties and perplexities. Obviously, it is to the interest of these men to make laws which shall be uncertain and perplexing—to confuse and darken legislation as much as they can. Yet in nearly all the Councils these men are the most influential and active element, and it is not uncommon to find them in a numerical majority. It is evident that the only check upon their ill-doing lies in the certainty of their disagreement as to the particular kind of confusion which they may think it expedient to create. Some will wish to accomplish their common object by one kind of verbal ambiguity, some by another; some by laws clearly enough (to them) unconstitutional, others by contradictory statutes, or statutes secretly repealing wholesome ones already existing. A clear, simple and just code would deprive them of their means of livelihood and compel them to seek some honest employment.

So great are the uncertainties of the law in Tortirra that an eminent judge once confessed to me that it was his conscientious belief that if all cases were decided by the impartial arbitrament of the *do-tusis* (a process similar to our "throw of the dice") substantial justice would be done far more frequently than under the present system; and there is reason to believe that in many instances cases at law are so decided—but only at the close of tedious and costly trials which have impoverished the litigants and correspondingly enriched the lawyers.[53]

Of the interminable train of shames and brutalities entailed by this pernicious system, I shall mention here only a single one—the sentencing and punishment of an accused person in the midst of the proceedings against him, and while his guilt is not finally and definitively established. It frequently occurs that a man convicted of crime in one of the lower courts is at once hurried off to prison while he has still the right of appeal to a higher tribunal, and while that appeal is pending. After months and sometimes years of punishment his case is reached in the appellate court, his appeal found valid and a new trial granted, resulting in his acquittal. He has been imprisoned for a crime of which he is eventually declared not to have been properly convicted. But he has no redress; he is simply set free to bear through all his after life the stain of dishonor and nourish an ineffectual resentment. Imagine the storm of popular indignation that would be evoked in America by an instance of so foul injustice![54]

In the great public square of Itsami, the capital of Tortirra, stands a golden statue of Estari-Kumpro, a famous judge of the Civil Court.* This great man was celebrated

* Klikat um Delu Ovwi.

throughout the kingdom for the wisdom and justice of his decisions and the virtues of his private life. So profound were the veneration in which he was held and the awe that his presence inspired, that none of the advocates in his court ever ventured to address him except in formal pleas: all motions, objections, and so forth, were addressed to the clerk and by him disposed of without dissent: the silence of the judge, who never was heard to utter a word, was understood as sanctioning the acts of his subordinate. For thirty years, promptly at sunrise, the great hall of justice was thrown open, disclosing the judge seated on a lofty dais beneath a black canopy, partly in shadow, and quite inaccessible. At sunset all proceedings for the day terminated, everyone left the hall and the portal closed. The decisions of this august and learned jurist were always read aloud by the clerk, and a copy supplied to the counsel on each side. They were brief, clear and remarkable, not only for their unimpeachable justice, but for their conformity to the fundamental principles of law. Not one of them was ever set aside, and during the last fifteen years of the great judge's service no litigant ever took an appeal, although none ever ventured before that infallible tribunal unless conscientiously persuaded that his cause was just.

One day it happened during the progress of an important trial that a sharp shock of earthquake occurred, throwing the whole assembly into confusion. When order had been restored a cry of horror and dismay burst from the multitude—the judge's head lay flattened upon the floor, a dozen feet below the bench, and from the neck of the rapidly collapsing body, which had pitched forward upon his desk, poured a thick stream of sawdust! For thirty years that great and good man had been represented by a stuffed manikin. For thirty years he had not entered his own court, nor heard a word of evidence or argument. At the moment of the accident to his simulacrum he was in his library at his home, writing his decision of the case on trial, and was killed by a falling chandelier. It was afterward learned that his clerk, twenty-five years dead, had all the time been personated by a twin brother, who was an idiot from birth and knew no law.

HITHER

Listening to the history of the golden statue in the great square, as related by a Tortirran storyteller, I fell asleep. On waking I found myself lying in a cot-bed amidst unfamiliar surroundings. A bandage was fastened obliquely about my head, covering my left eye, in which was a dull throbbing pain. Seeing an attendant near by I beckoned him to my bedside and asked: "Where am I?"

"Hospital," he replied, tersely but not unkindly. He added: "You have a bad eye."

"Yes," I said, "I always had; but I could name more than one Tortirran who has a bad heart."

"What is a Tortirran?" he asked.

CW 1.87–196: "Thither" (original); "Sons of the Fair Star" (*E*, 10 June 1888); "An Interview with Gnarmag-Zote" (*E*, 24 Nov. 1889 [as "The Golampians"]); "The Tamtonians" (*E*, 11 Nov. 1888); "Marooned on Ug" (*E*, 20 Feb. 1898 and 11 Sept. 1898 [as "The War with Wug"]); "The Dog in Ganegwag" (*NYA*, 12 May 1904); "A Conflagration in Ghargaroo" (*Co*, Feb. 1906); "An Execution in Batrugia" (*NYA*, 30 Apr. 1903 [as "A Letter from a Btrugumian"] and *Co*, May 1907); "The Jumjum of Gokeetle-Guk" (*E*, 19 Nov. 1899 [as "Trustland"]); "The Kingdom of Tortirra" (*E*, 22 Apr. 1888); "Hither" (partly from "Sons of the Fair Star," *E*, 10 June 1888).

NOTES

Compiled from individual sketches originally published between 1888 and 1907 (and collected in volumes 2 and 3 of this edition), this extended satire was rearranged and polished by AB in 1909 for *CW* 1. As was the case with *Gulliver's Travels*, on which it is largely modeled, the work heavily criticizes the narrator's native country, in this case America. Maneuvering his readers into viewing American practices from the fresh perspective of a traveler to strange lands, AB makes it inescapable to see that some of America's most cherished assumptions are inefficient if not ludicrous, and that its principles and practices are often in conflict with each other.

The appearance of Schopenhauerian and classical Epicurean elements of thought directed toward pessimistic conclusions is an indication of a late stage of Biercian development. Led by his reading, his mind continued to grow, but whereas he had been tentative and ambivalent before, now he was increasingly definite and negative. Although he undoubtedly read Stoic and Epicurean philosophy, it is not presently clear how well grounded he was in Schopenhauer. He might have been led to him through the writings of Edgar Saltus (1855–1921), an American popularizer of Schopenhauer whose columns appeared weekly in the same section of the Sunday Hearst papers that carried AB's columns. AB referred to Saltus infrequently, but with respect.

For a more extended background to "The Land Beyond the Blow," see the introduction to *FR*.

1. AB refers to Swift's *Gulliver's Travels* (1726), Lucian's *Alethōn diegēmatōn* (*True Story*) (second century C.E.), Voltaire's *Micromégas* (1752), and perhaps to other, more recent works such as W. D. Howells's *A Traveler from Altruria* (1894) and *Through the Eye of the Needle* (1907).

2. AB's original coinage here was Doosno-Zwair, but he amended it probably because he had used the name Doosnoswair in several fables in *Fantastic Fables* (1899), including "The Reform School Board" (*CF*, no. 166).

3. AB may be imitating *Gulliver* here: "But I shall not anticipate the reader with farther descriptions of this kind, because I reserve them for a greater work, which is now almost ready for the press, containing a general description of this empire . . . : their plants and animals, their peculiar manners and customs, with other matters very curious and useful." Jonathan Swift, *Gulliver's Travels* (1726), in *Gulliver's Travels, A Tale of a Tub, The Battle of the Books, etc.*, ed. William Alfred Eddy (New York: Oxford Univ. Press, 1933), 51; hereafter abbreviated *GT*.

4. See "Prattle," *E* (14 July 1895): 6:

In nations that cover the body for another purpose than decoration and protection from the weather, disputes as to how much of it, and under what circumstances, should be covered are inevitable and uncompassable. Alike in nature and in art, the question of the nude will be always demanding adjustment and be never adjusted. This eternal wrangle we have always with us as a penalty for the prudery of conceal-ment, creating and suggesting the prurience of exposure.

> Offended Nature hides her lash
> In the purple-black of a dyed mustache,

and the lash lurks in every fold of the clothing wherewith Man has insulted her. In ancient Greece the disgraceful squabble was unknown: it did not occur to the great-hearted, broad-brained and wholesome people of that blessed land that any of the handiwork of the gods was ignoble. Nor are the modern Japanese vexed with 'the question of the nude'; save where their admirable civilization has suffered the pollut-ing touch of ours they have not learned the infamy of sex. Among the blessings in store for them are their conversion to decorous lubricity and instruction in the nice conduct of a clouded mind.

[The last phrase plays off Pope's sarcastic description of Sir Plume in *The Rape of the Lock*, 4.123–24.]

5. See "The Death of Halpin Frayser," p. 817 note 18.
6. Satan. See "A Jug of Sirup," p. 856 note 1.
7. See "Prattle," *E* (4 Aug. 1895): 6: "nothing is so practical and logical as religious persecution. If carried to the point of extermination—and despite the hoary platitudes about the blood of the martyrs being the seed of the church, and so forth, it is easily capable of that exten-sion—it is from the view point of religion the most wisest and most rational of religious methods. That it is acceptable to God—to his God—every religionist is bound to believe, and in his heart does believe. If I can exterminate a heresy that is peopling Hell I am a ras-cal not to do so—an unfaithful servant of the Lord. If by putting to the sword one genera-tion of the irreclaimable and already damned I can save many generations from damnation, that, clearly, is mercy—that, clearly, is duty. Women being both religious and practical will favor the remarriage of Church and State—will set up a Theocracy and the Devil will do the rest."
8. AB is possibly suggesting how the literal meanings of some familiar cultural sentiments, such as "Thrice armed is he who is in the right," might appear to readers from another culture.
9. Cf., in *GT*, the King of Brobdingnag's comment after Gulliver has recounted the political, legal, and social customs of the English: "by what I have gathered from your own relation, and the answers I have with much pains wringed and extorted from you, I cannot but con-clude the bulk of your natives to be the most pernicious race of little odious vermin that nature ever suffered to crawl upon the surface of the earth" (*GT* 154).
10. "Now it is impossible to conceive the incorporeal as a separate existence, except the void: and the void can neither act nor be acted upon, but only provides opportunity of motion through itself to bodies. So that those who say that the soul is incorporeal are talking idly." Epicurus, *Letter to Herodotus,* in Cyril Bailey, *Epicurus: The Extant Fragments* (Oxford: Clarendon Press, 1926), 41, 43.
11. Cf. Arthur Schopenhauer (1788–1860): "The pleasure in this world, it has been said, out-weighs the pain; or, at any rate, there is an even balance between the two. If the reader wishes to see shortly whether this statement is true, let him compare the respective feelings

of two animals, one of which is engaged in eating the other." *Studies in Pessimism,* trans. T. Bailey Saunders (London: George Allen & Co., 1890), 12.

12. "Death is nothing to us. For all good and evil consists in sensation, but death is deprivation of sensation." Epicurus, *Letter to Menoeceus,* in Bailey, *Epicurus,* 85.

13. "So death, the most terrifying of ills, is nothing to us, since so long as we exist, death is not with us; but when death comes, then we do not exist." Epicurus, *Letter to Menoeceus;* in Bailey, *Epicurus,* 85.

14. Cf. Schopenhauer, *Studies in Pessimism*: "A man finds himself, to his great astonishment, suddenly existing, after thousands and thousands of years of non-existence: he lives for a little while; and then, again, comes an equally long period when he must exist no more" (33–34).

15. This view of Schopenhauer is inaccurate. Schopenhauer maintained that the will to live has as its purpose only the continuation of the species, not the production of individuals. The urge to procreate, therefore, may be regarded pessimistically by individuals as they are reduced to mere agents in the scheme of things. AB may have been referring to such provocative passages as the following from *Studies in Pessimism*: "If children were brought into the world by an act of pure reason alone, would the human race continue to exist? Would not a man rather have so much sympathy with the coming generation as to spare it the burden of existence? . . . Human life must be some kind of mistake" (15, 37).

16. The meaning of these terms is revealed by spelling them backward. Thus, a "cilbuper" is a republic; "ytrap," a party; "seirtrap," parties; etc.

17. "Natas" spelled backward is "Satan."

18. See "The Passing Show," *E* (22 Apr. 1900): 26; *NYA* (22 Apr. 1900): 26: "If I rightly understand [the slogan 'Principles, not men'] it means that so long as the party platform is all right, the characters of the party candidates are of little or no importance. If it does mean that, or anything like that, it is a reasonless and pernicious thing which one should be ashamed to say. There is no political principle or set of political principles of which the profession and possession by men in power can give us good government. That can be assured only by personal character. . . . 'Principles, not men,' when not the motto of a dupe is the motto of a duper. It is a pickpocket's claim to inattention." AB also treats of this matter in the fable "Party Manager and Gentleman" (*CF,* no. 243). AB is probably alluding to the Democratic Party's renunciation of its long-standing support for bimetallism in the presidential campaign of 1904, when the Democratic candidate, Alton B. Parker, came out emphatically in favor of the gold standard.

19. The reference is to the Mugwumps, who refused to support the Republican presidential candidate James G. Blaine in the election of 1884. See "For the Ahkoond," p. 542 note 9.

20. Cf. AB's comment to his readers during the presidential campaign of 1888: "Every man Jack of the lot of you honestly and calmly believes that the election is going his way. He is incapable of the conception of so worthy a man as he in a minority; he could as soon think of an archangel caught in a quail trap; and when the ugly fact is borne in upon the consciousness of him he feels as if he had fallen out of a clear sky and struck astride of his own neck." "Prattle," *E* (8 July 1888): 4.

21. An allusion to the six consecutive defeats suffered by the Democrats in the presidential elections of 1860 (J. C. Breckinridge lost to Abraham Lincoln), 1864 (George B. McClellan lost to Lincoln), 1868 (Horatio Seymour lost to U. S. Grant), 1872 (Horace Greeley lost to Grant), 1876 (Samuel J. Tilden lost to Rutherford B. Hayes), and 1880 (Winfield S. Hancock lost to James A. Garfield).

THE LAND BEYOND THE BLOW

22. Cf. AB's pungent comment, addressed to the wife of President Benjamin Harrison, who declared, "I do not wish my husband to be President again": "Wishes, madam, do not appear to count for much in this matter. With a single exception, your husband is the only man in the United States of whom it is certainly known that several millions of his fellow citizens did not wish him to be President this time." "Prattle," *E* (3 Nov. 1889): 6. Cf. *DD*: "PRESIDENT, *n*. The leading figure in a small group of men of whom—and of whom only—it is positively known that immense numbers of their countrymen did not want any of them for President."

23. Richard Neville, Earl of Warwick (1428–71) was called the "Kingmaker" because he was largely responsible for establishing Edward IV as king of England in 1461; Warwick actually ruled England for the next three years. In 1470 he helped to place Henry VI on the throne. Otto von Bismarck (1815–98) helped to free Prussia from Austrian control, unified the German states, and then became chancellor of Germany (1871–90). Throughout his term he was a stronger political and military force than the German emperors of the period.

24. "Pope's-nose" (or "pastor's nose") is a vulgar term for the tail of a dressed bird.

25. AB presumably witnessed such actions when Andrew Johnson succeeded Lincoln in 1865 and Chester Alan Arthur succeeded Garfield in 1881.

26. Cf. AB's comment following the presidential campaign of 1884, then regarded as one of the most vicious in American history: "Thank Heaven, it is over, and may we never have any more of it! . . . If ever, O good Satan, this faithful people celebrated thy praise, served thine altars and walked with humility along the line of thy desires; if ever it dedicated to thy service its hearts and brains and blood and bones; if ever it lied and cheated with incessant iteration and the heat of a noble zeal; if ever, in short, it was wholly overgiven to the love and lust of a folly that is barbarous, an ignorance that is brutal and a wickedness that is savage, mean and unspeakable, may it please thee now to reward the service and waive its repetition." "Prattle," *W,* no. 432 (8 Nov. 1884): 5.

27. In the presidential election of 1884, candidate James G. Blaine violated Republican precedent by going on the stump himself, while Democratic candidate Grover Cleveland delivered two speeches and attended a large celebration in his hometown, Buffalo.

28. AB bristled at the use of the word "flock" for other than a group of birds; cf. *DD*: "FOLD, *n*. In the miserable nomenclature of those outlying dark corners of the universe beyond the boundaries of the Pacific Slope, a sheep corral. The wretched barbarians infesting those remote dependencies have also the bad taste to call a band of sheep a 'flock' and a sheepherder a 'shepherd,' besides being linguistically disgusting in a reasonless multitude of other ways."

29. AB spent most of the summer of 1896 (one and a half years before writing this segment) in Englewood, New Jersey, recovering from the grueling four months (February–May) spent in Washington writing more than sixty articles against C. P. Huntington (see "Ashes of the Beacon," p. 1085 note 17).

30. Probably an allusion to C. P. Huntington's scheme to convince Congress to appropriate funds for a harbor at Santa Monica (near property owned by him), which would have resulted in a virtual private harbor, as opposed to a harbor at San Pedro, which several Congressional investigations had deemed a superior harbor for the Los Angeles area. The specific target of AB's attack may have been Stephen Benton Elkins (1841–1911), who as secretary of war in the Harrison administration (1891–93) had opposed the Santa Monica harbor but as U.S. senator from West Virginia (1895–1911) favored it. In "Another Thieves' Scheme on the Pacific Coast," *NYJ* (4 May 1896): 4, AB casts doubt on the sincerity of Elkins's about-face.

31. For *Ben-Hur*, see "The Great Strike of 1895," note 21.

32. The name Scamadumclitchclitch (Scumadumclitchclitch in "The War with Wug") resembles the name of Gulliver's "little nurse" in Brobdingnag, Glumdalclitch.

33. A parodic description of the Spanish-American War. The Spaniards (Wuggards) refused to countenance the independence of their colony, Cuba (Scamadumclitchclitch). Two months after the explosion of the U.S. battleship *Maine* in Havana harbor on 15 February 1898, the United States (Uggards) declared war on Spain, and on 22 April, President McKinley ordered the blockading of all Cuban ports, chiefly to prevent the export of sugar. The war was over by August.

34. In the Spanish-American War, only 379 U.S. soldiers died in combat, but more than 5,000 died of disease.

35. This scene appears to be an imitation of the opening chapter of book 4 ("A Voyage to the Houyhnhnms") of *GT*, when Gulliver, encountering a hideous monster (who later turns out to be a Yahoo), attacks him: "I drew my hanger [sword], and gave him a good blow with the flat side of it, for I durst not strike him with the edge, fearing the inhabitants might be provoked against me, if they should come to know that I had killed or maimed any of their cattle. When the beast felt the smart, he drew back, and roared so loud that a herd of at least forty came flocking about me from the next field, howling and making odious faces" (*GT* 266–67). Gulliver is finally saved by a Houyhnhnm (analagous to a horse).

36. In fact, the Egyptians worshipped a god, Anubis, who was conceived as having the head of a dog or jackal.

37. See "Ashes of the Beacon," p. 1087 note 37.

38. For the name Ghargaroo see "The Wizard of Bumbassa," p. 828 note 3.

39. Perhaps an imitation of the bizarre language of Luggnagg in *GT*: "I pronounced the following words, as they had been taught me the night before, *Ickpling gloffthrobb squutserumm blhiop mlashnalt zwin tnodbalkguffh slhiophad gurdlubh asht*. This is the compliment established by the laws of the land for all persons admitted to the King's presence. It may be rendered into English thus: *May your Celestial Majesty outlive the sun, eleven moons and a half*" (*GT* 244).

40. AB refers to such utterances by Jesus as "Blessed are the poor in spirit: for theirs is the kingdom of heaven" (Matt. 5:3) and "Verily I say unto you, that a rich man shall hardly enter into the kingdom of heaven. And again I say unto you, It is easier for a camel to go through the eye of a needle, than for a rich man to enter into the kingdom of God" (Matt. 19:23–24).

41. Cf. Eccles. 1:2–4: "Vanity of vanities, saith the Preacher, all is vanity. What profit hath a man of all his labour which he taketh under the sun? One generation passeth away, and another generation cometh: but the earth abideth for ever."

42. Cf. *DD*: "PARDON, *v*. To remit a penalty and restore to a life of crime. To add to the lure of crime the temptation of ingratitude."

43. Cf. AB to Herman Scheffauer, 27 Mar. 1903 (*MMM* 100–101): "I should have written you before, but have been in New York, returning only Wednesday. In that city of the giants one cannot write letters. I hate the place—that is, I should hate to live there—but I admire and wonder. Really it is amazing; everything on so colossal a scale. You must not fail to pass a week or two in New York on your way—here. The architecture may not please you; it doesn't please me. It only stuns me. In calling it a city of giants I unintentionally expressed the feeling it gives me. But where are the giants? Alas! it is infested by pigmies, or at least the giants remaining are seen only away up in the sky rearing new structures for their masters,

the pigmies. They look like ants, these titans up there, but of course one knows they are a hundred feet in stature. Even so I think the gods must come down from Olympus to take a hand in the work, especially in that of bridge-building. O yes, you must see New York, preferably under my guidance."

44. In German, *fledermaus* means "bat." In other words, bats in his belfry.

45. See "Prattle," *E* (26 Feb. 1888): 4: "The argument against capital punishment may start how it will, but at the last it commonly rests itself upon the postulate that it is better that ninety-nine guilty men escape than that one innocent man should be punished. This obviously has no more to do with hanging than with any other punishment. Whether it *is* better depends on what is meant by it. It is better for the ninety-nine escapers; it is worse for everybody else. The loss that the State, community, society sustains in the death of an innocent man is insignificant—particularly the kind of innocent man that is likely to be accused and convicted of murder. We lose such men by death every day and hour. But the escape of ninety-nine murderers is a very serious matter indeed. The frosty truth of it is that, so far as the public interest is concerned, it would pay to hang every actual murderer, even if we had to hang an innocent man alongside of him. If ever we have to do that we can lighten our loss by taking the County Assessor."

46. The Populist is associated with Kansas because this political party had been organized in the late 1880s by farmers in the Midwest and Far West. Cf. *DD*: "POPULIST, *n*. A fossil patriot of the early agricultural period, found in the old red soapstone underlying Kansas; characterized by an uncommon spread of ear, which some naturalists contend gave him the power of flight, though Professors Morse and Whitney, pursuing independent lines of thought, have ingeniously pointed out that had he possessed it he would have gone elsewhere. In the picturesque speech of his period, some fragments of which have come down to us, he was known as 'The Matter with Kansas.'"

47. "Drummers" was the term used at this time for traveling salesmen.

48. AB wrote often about this phenomenon. Cf. "The Town Crier," *Fi*, no. 408 (28 June 1873): 5, listing some of things that AB admits not knowing: "I don't know why a jackass raises his tail when he brays."

49. An adaptation of the quotation "beyond the dreams of avarice." See "My Favorite Murder," p. 618 note 4.

50. The object of attack appears to be William McKinley (1843–1901), who during his years as a U.S. representative from Ohio (1877–91) was the leading proponent of tariff protection. AB's words (written in 1888) were prophetic, as McKinley's name was attached to the tariff act of 1890 and he continued to pursue the policy during his presidency (1897–1901).

. 51. The references are to a variety of judicial and legislative branches of the government: "Supreme Council" = U.S. Congress; "Subordinate Council" = state legislatures; "Great Court" = Supreme Court; "Minor Great Court" = state supreme courts.

52. "Our entire system of laws . . . [is] so complicated and contradictory that a judge simply does as he pleases, subject only to the custom of giving for his action reasons that at his option may or may not be derived from the statute. He may sternly affirm that he sits there to interpret the law as he finds it, not to make it accord with his personal notions of right and justice. Or he may declare that it could never have been the Legislature's intention to do wrong, and so, shielded by the useful phrase *contra bonos mores* [contrary to good morals], pronounce that illegal which he chooses to consider inexpedient. Or he may be guided by either of any two inconsistent precedents, as best suits his purpose. Or he may throw aside both statute and

precedent, disregard good morals, and justify the judgment that he wishes to deliver by what other lawyers have written in books, and still others, without anybody's authority, have chosen to accept as a part of the law." AB, [Editorial], *W,* no. 397 (8 Mar. 1884): 4; reprinted in *The Shadow on the Dial,* ed. S. O. Howes (San Francisco: A. M. Robertson, 1909), 65.

53. AB frequently alludes in his writings to the notion of deciding legal cases (or making any important decision) by a throw of the dice, in the manner of the corrupt judge Bridoye (Bridlegoose) in François Rabelais's *Gargantua et Pantagruel.* Cf. *DD*: "APPEAL, *v. t.* In law, to put the dice into the box for another throw"; and "RECOUNT, *n.* In American politics, another throw of the dice, accorded to the player against whom they are loaded."

54. "As long as there exists the right of appeal there is a chance of acquittal. Otherwise the right of appeal would be a sham and an insult. . . . So long as acquittal may ensue guilt is not established. Why, then, are men sentenced before they are proved guilty? Why are they punished in the middle of proceedings against them?" AB, [Editorial], *W,* no. 397 (8 Mar. 1884): 4; reprinted in *The Shadow on the Dial,* 64.

A LEAF BLOWN
IN FROM DAYS TO BE

The Future Historian set his psychograph on the table before him, clasped the band of the transmitting wire about his head, lay back in his easy-chair and closed his eyes. The record, of which ten thousand copies were automatically delivered, follows.

"In the year 1909, as the ancient Americans reckoned time, President Thaddeus Rosenfelt was for some offense not now known banished from his country and sent under heavy guard to Kalamazoo,[1] an African penal colony noted for the number and ferocity of its tigers. To these he was thrown by his keepers, as was secretly commanded by Congress, sitting as a high court of impeachment and conviction. But from a contemporaneous chronicle by Wee Chandler[2] (whose works are now in the imperial library of Timbuctoo) it appears that the tigers would not eat him. On the contrary, he ate them, 'a marked instance,' says another writer of the period, 'of interposition by an overruling Providence.'[3]

"Awed by this obvious miracle, the fallen President's keepers renounced the faith of their fathers and worshiped him as a deity. Not only so, but by force and arms they set up for him a temporal sovereignty which he administered from an ancient palace known as the Bleak House. He bore the title of It, a word signifying Me. The meaning of Me is unknown.

"In subduing the natives, who, according to Herodotus the Tetrarch, were known as Gringos, Rosenfelt came into conflict with many powerful kings, chief of whom was Rhi Nosey Rose, who could summon fifty thousand warriors by a blast upon his horn.[4] Allied with this potentate was the scarcely less powerful High Potamus,[5] of Riparia.[6] (Riparia was a Theocracy; the word potamus appears to have meant priest, and probably alluded to the 'pot' in which hierarchs of another faith were purged of their error by boiling.)

"Contemporary accounts of military operations incident to the conquest have not come down to us. It is known, however, that Rosenfelt, armed with a big sticker, penetrated to the interior of Kankakee[7] and fought the fierce battle of Waterloo, in which the Gringo power was disastrously overthrown by the leader's lone charge up the hill of San Juan Smith. With that memorable feat African independence ceased to exist: the entire continent came under the sway of Bueno Gumbo, 'the man who ate tigers.'

"Among the spoils of war was an almost incalculable number of domestic animals: the gorilla (*Lignifer docilis*),[8] the elephantom, the long-necked graft (*Latro circumspector*),[9] the hobby horse, the teddibear,[10] the skunk (*Curio flabbergastor*),[11] the three-legged ophecleide,[12] the gargoyle, the lion (*Leo arator*),[13] used by the natives in plowing corn, the aeroplane and many other species now long extinct. So great was the multitude of these animals that the task of slaughtering them in order to sell their bones to Smith's Onion Institution for fertilizing was one of extreme difficulty. It was proposed by Nairoba (or Niobe),[14] a friendly chief, that they be shot, but no one would undertake the work but Rosenfelt himself, and he was unacquainted with the use of firearms, having always in his native land hunted with his bare hands, making his kills by a cruel process known as the Presidential massage. The animals were finally chloroformed and shipped to the port of Hohokus,[15] where they were admitted duty free as works of fiction.

"Weeping freely because there were no more worlds to conquer (it was not then known that Arkansas had not been brought under the sway of the Whites) the victor resolved to invade his own country and carry away the Presidential Chair which he had once occupied, and which was then considered the most precious object existing since the Golden Fleece and the Holy Grail.

"Placing his son Kismet[16] on the throne, he gathered a great army of Blacks, and traveling incognito under the name of 'Stanley,' reached the western boundary of his new realm amid the acclamation of his troops, who shouted, 'Thalassa, thalassa!' that being their name for the river Rubicon, separating Africa from America.[17] There at the island of Elba he crossed on a secret bridge and was received with effusion by the populace, by whose spokesmen, Lord Gifford of Pinchot, he was thrice offered a kingly crown, which, according to Shakesporr, an obscure chronicler of the time, he did thrice refuse.[18] This occurred in the reign of William the Fat, whom as an afterthought he deposed and bastinadoed.[19]

"Firmly seated in the Presidential Chair (which had itself been firmly reseated for William) Rosenfelt resolved to remain in the land that loved him for the ructions he had made. By way of assuring the peace, he proceeded to destroy a colony of Ananiasites[20] who had fortified themselves in the fastnesses of the Rocky Mountains, and then he marched against the Nacherfaquers,[21] a formidable tribe of the Bostonese hinterland. Afterwards he subdued and sold into slavery a troublesome people known as Democrats, who were taken to Lincoln, Nebraska, loaded with chains. The name of the purchaser is unknown.

"From this time on, the career of this remarkable personality is lost in the mists of antiquity. Some say that the earth opened and swallowed him; others that he wrote a

A LEAF BLOWN IN FROM DAYS TO BE

book; and in an extant fragment of an ancient poem he is represented as chained to a rock in a caucus, with 'vultures' (epicures) eating his liver.[22] Whatever may have been the manner of his second removal from office, he is now, doubtless, as dead as the vivacity of his disposition permits."

TT 63, no. 11 (17 Mar. 1910): 21.

NOTES

Another unflattering satire on Theodore Roosevelt. As usual the Future Historian creates a confused account from misunderstood fragments of miscellaneous sources.

1. Kalamazoo is a city in Michigan, the seat of Kalamazoo County in the southwestern part of the state.
2. AB refers to William E[aton] Chandler (1835–1917), secretary of the navy (1882–85) and Republican U.S. senator from New Hampshire (1887–1901), who, although supporting Theodore Roosevelt in the presidential campaign of 1904, later fell out with him and opposed his independent candidacy in 1912.
3. AB appears to allude to Joel Chandler Harris (1848–1908), whose *Uncle Remus: His Songs and His Sayings* (1880) is an American children's classic of dialect literature. AB also alludes to the tale of Little Black Sambo (referred to below as "Bueno Gumbo"), who tricked the tigers that pursued him into chasing themselves, thereby turning themselves into butter, which he and his family then ate. The book *Little Black Sambo* (1899) was written by Helen Bannerman, a Scottish woman, and takes place in India. Sambo, an Indian boy, appears African in the book's illustrations.
4. In AB's Little Johnny sketches, the rhinoceros is frequently called the "rhi nosey rose."
5. In AB's Little Johnny sketches, AB frequently referred to the hippopotamus as "hi potamus."
6. "Riparian" means of or relating to the banks of a natural course of a river.
7. Kankakee is a city in Illinois, the seat of Kankakee County, in the northeastern part of the state.
8. AB's mock Latin means "docile wood-carrier."
9. AB's mock Latin means "circumspect thief." In his "Little Johnny" sketches, AB sometimes calls the giraffe the "giraft."
10. The teddy bear was in fact named after Theodore Roosevelt.
11. AB's mock Latin means "flabbergasting curiosity." AB used the name *Flashawful flabbergastor* in *DD,* s.v. "GUNPOWDER."
12. An "ophicleide" is a brass wind instrument whose long tube is bent double.
13. AB's mock Latin means "lion who uses a plow."
14. A play on Nairobi, the capital of Kenya, and Niobe of Greek mythology, daughter of Tantalus. According to the *Iliad,* as punishment for her pride, Apollo killed all her sons and Artemis killed all her daughters.
15. See "Ashes of the Beacon," p. 1086 note 28.
16. AB alludes to Roosevelt's son Kermit (1889–1943).
17. "Stanley" is an allusion to Sir Henry Morton Stanley; see "Dr. Deadwood, I Presume," p. 118 note 2. For "Thalassa, thalassa!" see "A Mirage in Arizona," p. 426 note 4. The Rubicon is the small river outside Rome that Julius Caesar crossed with his army on 10 January 49 B.C.E., thereby initiating the civil war that eventually ended the Roman republic.

18. Elba is the island off the west coast of Italy where Napoleon was exiled from 3 May 1814 to 26 February 1815. Gifford Pinchot (1865–1946) headed the U.S. Forest Service from 1898 to 1910. He was a close friend of Roosevelt. Mark Antony is reported to have attempted several times to place a diadem or crown on Julius Caesar's head during a festival of the Lupercalia on 15 February 44 B.C.E. See Suetonius, *Divus Julius,* 79.2. Suetonius does not specify the number of times Antony made the gesture, writing only *saepius* (frequently); but it became customary in antiquity to claim that the gesture was made three times (cf. Plutarch, *Caesar,* 61.3–4). Shakespeare follows this tradition in *Julius Caesar* 1.2.250f.

19. An allusion to William Howard Taft (1857–1930), twenty-seventh president of the United States (1909–13) who, at three hundred pounds, was the country's heaviest president.

20. For Ananias, see "An Ancient Hunter," p. 1057 note 11.

21. Theodore Roosevelt coined the term "nature faker" in reference to the animal stories of naturalist William J. Long (1867–1952), which he considered unrealistic and scientifically inaccurate. In the article "Nature Fakirs [*sic*]" (*Everybody's Magazine,* Sept. 1907), Roosevelt wrote: "The modern 'nature-faker' is . . . an object of derision to every scientist worthy of the name, to every real lover of the wilderness, to every faunal naturalist, to every true hunter or nature-lover. But it is evident that he completely deceives many good people who are wholly ignorant of wild life. Sometimes he draws on his own imagination for his fictions; sometimes he gets them second-hand from irresponsible guides or trappers or Indians." AB refers to "nature fakers" in "Small Contributions" (*Co,* Jan. 1908), "Little Johnny on the Dog" (*Co,* Apr. 1909), and "Little Johnny, the Nature Faker" (MS, BL).

22. This legend in the life of the Titan Prometheus can be found, inter alia, in Aeschylus' *Prometheus Bound* (c. 460 B.C.E.). AB equates the vultures who pecked at Prometheus' liver with epicures, who would delight in such a delicacy as a liver pâté.

APPENDIX A

VARIANT TEXTS

Beyond merely tightening up and polishing the tales he republished in book form, Bierce occasionally made significant changes in the texts. Rather than just republishing the latest versions, or the versions we prefer, we here reprint the few texts that differ significantly from those in the main body of this edition so that interested readers might see exactly what Bierce did when he made major revisions.

Although only five years separate the publication of "The *Jeannette* and the *Corwin*" and "The Man Overboard" (1876), it is possible to see how quickly Bierce improved in style. Both versions of the story are deliberately ridiculous, but the later one cuts back on the self-indulgent wit, tightens up the action, and gains in topicality as well as focus by addressing the subject of the search for a missing Arctic exploration ship, the *Jeannette*.

The revised versions of "Bodies of the Dead" radically change the original narrative by excluding some sketches in it, making it somewhat shorter; dividing its unbroken sequence of narrative into five sketches, beginning with "Granny Magone" and ending with "A Creature of Habit," each with its own subtitle, and changing the order of their appearance. "Present at a Hanging" and "A Fruitless Assignment" are similarly extracted from "Hither from Hades," which like the previous original is longer, contains more sketches, is unbroken, and is arranged differently. "The Isle of Pines" and "A Cold Greeting" are extracts and adaptations from "Behind the Veil" and repeat the above pattern. The same pattern applies to the next three sketches, "The Difficulty of Crossing a Field," "An Unfinished Race," and "Charles Ashmore's Trail," all derived from "Whither," the last sketch especially modified in substance from the original. "The Spook House" and "A Doppelganger" follow the text of "Two Haunted Houses" more closely, but the format is changed. Why Bierce selected only extracts from the longer originals is not known, but even more interesting is the question of why he changed the text. The fact that he treated its narratives as literary material strongly implies that, knowing that they were not true, he felt himself at liberty to alter their substance to make them more readable.

THE *JEANNETTE* AND
THE *CORWIN*

ADAPTED FROM THE ENGLISH OF DOD GRILE

I.

The *Jeannette* was drifting rapidly upon an ice-floe which appeared to extend an unreasonable distance to the right and left without a break, and I was reading Macaulay's "Naseby Fight" to the man at the wheel, when Lieutenant De Long poked his head above deck and asked where we were. Pausing in my reading, I informed him that we had got as far as the disastrous repulse of Prince Rupert's cavalry, and that if he would have the goodness not to interrupt, we should soon be making it awkward for the wounded, and he might bear a hand at the pockets of the slain. Just then the *Jeannette* struck heavily and went down with all hands.

Summoning another ship, I stepped aboard and gave directions to be taken to 798 Valencia street,[1] where I have an aunt. The ship, I learned, was the *Corwin*, commanded by Captain Hooper. Approaching this officer, I introduced myself as a well-known writer for the San Francisco newspapers, and ordered a dry Macaulay from the ship's stores. Obtaining this, I went to the man at the wheel and resumed the reading of "Naseby Fight." Captain Hooper was the first to succumb, but in a few minutes all the crew were snoring peacefully in unconsidered attitudes about the deck. Suddenly the lookout man, perched on the supreme extremity of the mainmast and consuming a luncheon of cold sausage, began an apparently preconcerted series of extraordinary and indescribable noises. He coughed, sneezed and barked simultaneously; bleated in one breath and cackled in the next; sputteringly shrieked and chatteringly squealed, with a thorough-bass of suffocated roars. There were desultory explosions, tapering off in long wails half smothered in unintelligible small-talk. He wheezed, whistled and trumpeted; began to sharp, and, thinking better of it, flatted; neighed like a horse and then thundered like a drum! Through it all he executed with one hand a series of incomprehensible gesticulations while clutching his throat with the other. Presently he gave it up and silently descended to the deck.

1142

By this time all were awake, and no sooner had the man set foot among us than he was assailed with a tempest of questions which, had they been visible, would have resembled a flight of pigeons. He made no reply, even by a look, but passed through our enclosing ranks with a defiant step and a grim set of the jaw like one repressing an ambitious dinner or ignoring a venomous toothache. Passing down the companion-way, the patient sought the surgeon's cabin, with the whole ship's company at his heels. The surgeon was fast asleep, the larklike performance at the masthead having been inaudible between decks, and while some of us held a whisky bottle to the medical nose to apprise the medical intelligence of the demand upon it, the patient seated himself in statuesque silence. By this time his pallor had given place to a fervent crimson, which visibly deepened into royal purple and was ultimately superseded by a clouded blue, shot through with opalescent gleams and smitten with variable dashes of black. The face was swollen and shapeless, the neck puffy. The eyes protruded like the pegs of a hat-rack.

After the surgeon had mixed himself a toddy, he examined the patient, pronouncing it a perfectly lovely case of suffocation, and soon extracted a sausage of the size, figure and general bearing of a banana. The operation had been performed amid a breathless silence, but the moment it was concluded the patient, whose head and neck had visibly collapsed, sprang to his feet and shouted:

"Man overboard!"

There was a general stampede to the upper deck and everybody flung something over the ship's side—a life-belt, a coil of rope, a crowbar, a pocket handkerchief—anything which it was thought might be useful to a drowning man who had followed the vessel during the hour that had elapsed since the overture at the masthead. Axes were brought out and in a few moments the ship was utterly dismantled; everything had gone overboard except the largest anchor (the right bower, in nautical phrase), which, having fouled its cable, could not be renounced. There was nothing more to do, but the Chaplain explained that if the drowning man did not arrive by noon the next day, he should stand at the stern and read the burial service.

Next morning, while we were drifting helplessly at the mercy of the waves, it occurred to some one to inquire who had fallen overboard, and Captain Hooper mustered all hands for roll-call, when it appeared that no one was missing. Each man on board was then separately sworn, with the same result. In deep disgust, the Captain retired to his cabin, saying he would have nothing more to do with us, but expressed a hope that for the purpose of having everything duly recorded in the ship's log, we would apprise him of any action which in the peculiar difficulties and necessities of our position we might deem it advisable to take, and of any discoveries that we might have the happiness of making.

It was at this time that I felt inspired with one of those magnificent ideas that come to most men but once in their lives, and to some not at all. Hastily convening the crew and passengers, I mounted the capstan and addressed them thus:

"Gentlemen, there has been a little mistake. In a sudden gust of pity, begotten of a false report, we have made a wreck of this good ship *Corwin* in the middle of the Arctic ocean. In our hasty fervor we have made rather free with the property of the United States. For this we shall undoubtedly be called to account the moment we drop anchor at 798 Valencia street, where I have an aunt. It would add strength to our defense in the United States courts if we were able to show that while heeding the sacred dictates of humanity we had acted with some small degree of common sense. We ought to be able to show, for example, that there really was a man overboard who might have been temporarily sustained and comforted by the buoyant and other articles that we so lavishly dispensed. Gentlemen, I have the honor to propose that we throw a man overboard."

The effect was electrical; the motion was carried by acclamation, and a unanimous rush was made at *me*. Captain Hooper came up from below and in a moment had twisted the machinery of the engine he called his hand into the hair of my head, depressing that globe to such an extent that I lay down on the deck rather than maintain a less graceful attitude. The Captain immediately started to the lee bulwarks and I civilly followed, the connection between us being preserved without important alteration. Arrived at the ship's side, I thought it advisable in the interest of peace and quiet to balance myself across the gunwale a moment to hear the cheering, and then I took leave of the *Corwin* and her gallant crew with many expressions of sincere regret which might have been heard at a considerable distance.

II.

Having severed my connection with the *Corwin* expedition I was afterward unable to ascertain her fate, but have lately come across some loose leaves from her log, found floating in the Creek over at East Oakland. I append a few extracts:

June 3.—Heavy gale. Ship laboring a good deal, owing to lack of top-hamper, everything of that kind having been cut away to succor Mr. Dod Grile, who accidentally fell overboard while fishing from the bowsprit. Weather flagrant.

June 10.—No news from Dod Grile. Discovered Wrangel Island and served notice of eviction on old Wrangel. Remained on the Island several days, taking possession and re-rigging ship. The popular lessee of the Grand Central Hotel at Wrangelville deserves great credit for the hospitable manner in which he entertained the ship's officers. Weather ludicrous.

June 20.—Sailed to Melville Bay. Emilie and her troupe were absent, playing an engagement at Petropaulovski, but Captain Hooper slept in her bed. Weather tormenting.

July 4.—Landed at the Farallone Islands, which in honor of the day we renamed Independence Land. Laid in a supply of gulls' eggs and a dog. Weather iniquitous.

July 30.—Stood boldly out to sea, passing in the night many icebergs covered with walruses, Esquimaux, polar bears and advertisements. Took observation and found our latitude was higher than anything and further west from Greenwich. Weather insulting.

August 26.—Found sleeping whale. Took possession in name of the United States and built a cairn. Weather depraved.

September 1.—Sighted Goat Island, Point San Quentin bearing galley-west-and-crooked. Great deal of pack ice over in the Oakland factory. Ship closely beset by natives of Berkeley with relics of Sir John Franklin[2] for sale. Weather hel...

Here the record abruptly ends, leaving the subsequent fate of Captain Hooper and his devoted band of heroes a matter of mournful conjecture.

III.

Rising on an uncommonly high swell, after detaching myself from the *Corwin* expedition, I swept the horizon with my partially submerged eye to see if I could get the bearings of 798 Valencia street, where I have an aunt. I discerned in the direction whence the ship had come, a vast quantity of wreckage. In an hour or two it had overtaken me and I perceived it to be the top-hamper, cargo and other portable belongings of the *Corwin*—the things which we had eschewed under a misapprehension. The different articles had been carefully compiled into a coherent scheme covering a vast area, and were firmly lashed together. I boarded this flotilla as it approached and walked directly across it. There I had something of a surprise. Swimming in the wake of the raft, which with one hand he was urging through the water, while in the other he held the latest number of the New York *Herald*,[3] in which he was deeply absorbed, was Lieutenant De Long, of the late *Jeannette*.

I nodded to the brave mariner, and seating myself on a spar, asked him if he would like to hear me recite some verses called "Naseby Fight."

"No," he said, glancing up from his newspaper; "no, Dod Grile, I've done with you forever. When you sank the *Jeannette* you probably thought you had made an end of me. It was good of you, but I came to the surface and followed the other ship. It was I whom the sailor saw from the masthead; it was for me all these things were cut away and chucked overboard. I made 'em into a raft, as you see. It affords me pleasure to be the means of saving your worthless life, but the moment we reach San Francisco our paths must diverge. You will remember that in the very first sentence of this story you began without provocation to drive the *Jeannette* upon an ice floe."

I was compelled to admit that this was so, and Lieutenant De Long, after giving the raft a vigorous push or two, resumed his reproaches:

"Before you had written a half column you sent her to the bottom with me and all my crew, while *you* escaped in the *Corwin*."

"That is true," I replied; "I cannot deny that the facts are correctly related."

"And in a recent issue of the *Wasp,*" he continued with pitiless persistence, "you took me and my mates to the North Pole and left us frozen dead in the ice like flies preserved in amber. But you did not leave yourself there—*you* escaped."[4]

"Really, Lieutenant," said I, "your memory is wonderfully accurate, considering the unusual hardships you have unhappily had to undergo."

"And a long time before that," he continued, after a long pause, more for the purpose, apparently, of conning his memory that in order to listen to my praise of it, "a long time before *that,* you—yes, you—see here, I don't read the *Argonaut,* but I have been told that in writing for that paper you once sent me to the bottom, drowned in a whale-boat.[5] May I ask if I have been misinformed?"

I could not say he had been misinformed.

"You escaped on that occasion, I think."

It was true. I endeavored to explain to him that, being commonly the hero of my own stories, I *do* usually manage to live through one, in order to figure to advantage in the next. It was, I assured him, a literary necessity. He shook his head.

"No," he said, "it's cowardly and unfair; that's the way *I* look at it."

Suddenly an effulgent idea began to dawn upon me, and I let it have its way until my mind was perfectly luminous. Then I rose from my seat on the spar, and, frowning down into the upturned face of my accuser, spoke in severe and rasping accents thus:

"Lieutenant De Long, in the various perils that you and I have encountered together, in both the *Wasp* and *Argonaut,* if I have always escaped and you have uniformly perished; if, for example, I drowned you in a whale-boat, and afterwards froze you to death at the North Pole, pray have the goodness to tell me whom I have now the honor to address."

It was a blow to the poor man; never was any one so disconcerted by superior logic. Casting aside his newspaper and letting go the raft, he put up his two hands and began absently to scratch his head and think. And, scratching his head and thinking, he sank forever out of sight. I shed a few natural tears for the fate of one so young, so brave, so noble, and then I—escaped.

W, no. 282 (23 Dec. 1881): 413 (as by "B.").

NOTES

The story, an extensive revision of "The Man Overboard" (p. 367), is a take-off of the events surrounding the Arctic expedition of the *Jeannette,* commanded by Lt. George W. De Long of the U.S. Navy. De Long, conjecturing the existence of an overland route to the North Pole, left San Francisco on 8 July 1879, but by September his ship had become locked in pack ice near Wrangel Island, in the East Siberian Sea. It sank on 13 June 1881. Meanwhile, the crew made its way in boats to the Lena River delta on the north coast of Siberia; they died in October and were found by a rescue party the next spring. In June 1880 the revenue cutter the *Thomas L. Corwin,* commanded by Capt. Charles Hooper, entered Alaskan waters in search of the *Jeannette.* It approached Wrangel Island but did not sight *Jeannette.* See, in general, Leonard F. Guttrige, *Icebound: The* Jeannette *Expedition's Quest for the North Pole* (Annapolis: Naval Institute Press, 1986). AB wrote his story before the crew's fate had been ascertained.

1. Valencia Street proceeds south off Market Street in downtown San Francisco.
2. For Franklin see "The Captain of the *Camel*," p. 366 note 3.
3. The *Jeannette* expedition had been financed by James Gordon Bennett Jr., publisher of the *New York Herald*.
4. The allusion appears to be to "The Captain of the *Camel*," but it never appeared in *W.*
5. "A Shipwreckollection" (p. 318).

BODIES OF THE DEAD

GRANNY MAGONE

About ten miles to the southeast of Whitesburg, Kentucky, in a little "cove" of the Cumberland mountains, lived for many years an old woman named Sarah (or Mary) Magone. Her house, built of logs and containing only two rooms, was a mile and a half distant from any other, in the wildest part of the "cove," surrounded by forest except on one side, where a little field, or "patch," of about a half-acre served her for a vegetable garden. How she subsisted nobody exactly knew; she was reputed to be a miser with a concealed horde; she certainly paid for what few articles she procured on her rare visits to the village store. Many of her ignorant neighbors believed her to be a witch, or thought, at least, that she possessed some kind of supernatural powers. In November, 1881, she died and, fortunately enough, the body was found while yet warm by a passing hunter, who locked the door of the cabin and conveyed the news to the nearest settlement.

Several persons living in the vicinity at once went to the cabin to prepare for her burial; others were to follow the next day with a coffin and whatever else was needful. Among those who first went was the Rev. Elias Atney, a Methodist minister of Whitesburg, who happened to be in the neighborhood visiting a relative. He was to conduct the funeral services on the following day. Mr. Atney is, or was, well known in Whitesburg and all that country as a good and pious man of birth and education. He was closely related to the Marshalls and several other families of distinction. It is from him that the particulars here related were learned; and the account is confirmed by the affidavits of John Hershaw, William C. Wrightman and Catharine Doub, residents of the vicinity and eye-witnesses.

The body of "Granny" Magone had been "laid out" on a wide plank supported by two chairs at the end of the principal room, opposite the fireplace, and the persons mentioned were acting as "watchers," according to the local custom. A bright fire on the hearth lighted one end of the room brilliantly, the other dimly. The watchers sat about the fire, talking in subdued tones, when a sudden noise in the direction of the corpse caused them all to turn and look. In a black shadow near the body, they saw two glowing eyes, staring fixedly; and before they could do more than rise, uttering exclamations of alarm, a large black cat leaped upon the body and fastened its teeth into the cloth covering the face. Instantly the right hand of the dead woman was violently raised from the side, seized the cat and hurled it against the wall, whence it fell to the floor, then dashed wildly through an open window into the outer darkness and was seen no more.

Greatly horrified, the watchers stood a moment speechless; but finally, with returning courage, approached the body. The face-cloth lay upon the floor; the cheek was terribly torn; the right arm hung stiffly over the side of the plank. There was not a sign of life. They chafed the forehead, the withered cheeks, neck. They carried the body to the heat of the fire and worked upon it for hours: all in vain. But the funeral was postponed until the fourth day brought unmistakable evidence of dissolution and poor Granny was buried.

"Ah, but your eyes deceived you," said he to whom the reverend gentleman related the occurrence. "The arm was disturbed by the efforts of the cat, which, taking sudden fright, leaped blindly against the wall."

"No," he answered, "the clenched right hand, with its long nails, was full of black fur."

A LIGHT SLEEPER

John Hoskin, living in San Francisco, had a beautiful wife, to whom he was devotedly attached. In the spring of 1871 Mrs. Hoskin went East to visit her relations in Springfield, Illinois, where, a week after her arrival, she suddenly died of some disease of the heart; at least the physician said so. Mr. Hoskin was at once apprised of his loss, by telegraph, and he directed that the body be sent to San Francisco.

On arrival there the metallic case containing the remains was opened. The body was lying on the right side, the right hand under the cheek, the other on the breast. The posture was the natural one of a sleeping child, and in a letter to the deceased lady's father, Mr. Martin L. Whitney of Springfield, Mr. Hoskin expressed a grateful sense of the thoughtfulness that had so composed the remains as to soften the suggestion of death. To his surprise he learned from the father that nothing of the kind had been done: the body had been put in the casket in the customary way, lying on the back, with the arms extended along the sides. In the meantime the casket had been deposited in the receiving vault at Laurel Hill Cemetery, awaiting the completion of a tomb.

Greatly disquieted by this revelation, Hoskin did not at once reflect that the easy and natural posture and placid expression precluded the idea of suspended animation, subsequent revival and eventual death by suffocation. He insisted that his wife had been buried alive through medical incompetency and heedless haste. Under the influence of this feeling he wrote to Mr. Whitney again, expressing in passionate terms his horror and renewed grief. Some days afterward, someone having suggested that the casket had been opened *en route,* probably in the hope of plunder, and pointing out the impossibility of the change having occurred in the straitened space of the confining metal, it was resolved to reopen it.

Removal of the lid disclosed a new horror: the body now lay upon its *left* side. The position was cramped and to a living person would have been uncomfortable. The face wore an expression of pain. Some costly rings on the fingers were undisturbed. Overcome by his emotions, to which was now added a sharp if mistaken remorse, Mr. Hoskin lost his reason, dying years afterward in the asylum at Stockton.

A physician having been summoned to assist in clearing up the mystery viewed the body of the dead woman, pronounced life obviously extinct and ordered the casket closed for the third and last time. "Obviously extinct," indeed: the corpse had, in fact, been embalmed at Springfield.

THE MYSTERY OF CHARLES FARQUHARSON

One night in the summer of 1843 William Hayner Gordon, of Philadelphia, lay in his bed reading Goldsmith's "Traveler," by the light of a candle. It was about eleven o'clock. The room was in the third story of the house and had two windows looking out upon Chestnut Street; there was no balcony, nothing below the windows but other windows in a smooth brick wall.

Becoming drowsy, Gordon laid away his book, extinguished his candle and composed himself to sleep. A moment later (as he afterward averred) he remembered that he had neglected to place his watch within reach, and rose in the dark to get it from the pocket of his waistcoat, which he had hung on the back of a chair on the opposite side of the room, near one of the windows. In crossing, his foot came into contact with some heavy object and he was thrown to the floor. Rising, he struck a match and lighted his candle. In the center of the room lay the dead body of a man!

Gordon was no coward, as he afterward proved by his gallant death upon the enemy's parapet at Chapultepec, but this strange apparition of a human corpse where but a moment before, as he believed, there had been nothing was too much for his nerves and he cried aloud. Henri Granier, who occupied an adjoining room, but had not retired, came instantly to Gordon's door and attempted to enter. The door being bolted and Gordon too greatly agitated to open it Granier burst in.

Gordon was taken into custody and an inquest held, but what has been related was all that could be ascertained. The most diligent efforts by the police and the press failed to identify the dead. Physicians testifying at the inquest agreed that death had occurred but a few hours before the discovery, but none was able to divine the cause; all the organs of the body were in an apparently healthy condition; there were no traces of either violence or poison.

Eight or ten months later Gordon received a letter from Charles Richter in Bombay, relating the death in that city of Charles Farquharson, whom both Gordon and Richter had known when all were boys. Enclosed in the letter was a daguerreotype of the deceased, found among his effects. As nearly as the living can look like the dead it was an exact likeness of the mysterious body found in Gordon's bedroom, and it was with a strange feeling that Gordon observed that the death, making allowance for the difference of time, was said to have occurred on the night of the adventure. He wrote for further particulars, with especial reference to what disposition had been made of Farquharson's body.

"You know he turned Parsee," wrote Richter in reply; "so his naked remains were exposed on the grating of the Tower of Silence, as those of all good Parsees are. I saw the buzzards fighting for them and gorging themselves helpless on his fragments."

On some pretense Gordon and his friends obtained authority to open the dead man's grave. The coffin had evidently not been disturbed. They unscrewed the lid. The shroud was a trifle mouldy. There was no body, nor any vestige of one.

"DEAD AND GONE"

On the morning of the 14th day of August, 1872, George J. Reid, a young man of twenty-one years, living in Xenia, Ohio, fell while walking across the dining room in his father's house.

The family consisted of his father, mother, two sisters and a cousin, a boy of fifteen. All were present at the breakfast table. George entered the room, but instead of taking his accustomed seat near the door by which he had entered, passed it and went obliquely toward one of the windows—with what purpose no one knows. He had passed the table but a few steps when he fell heavily to the floor and did not again breathe. The body was carried into a bedroom and, after vain efforts at resuscitation by the stricken family, left lying on the bed with composed limbs and covered face.

In the meantime the boy had been hastily dispatched for a doctor, who arrived some twenty minutes after the death. He afterward remembered as an uncommon circumstance that when he arrived the weeping relatives—father, mother and two sisters—were all in the room out of which the bedroom door opened. This door was closed; the bedroom had no other. It was at once opened by the father of the deceased, and as the physician passed through it he observed the dead man's clothing lying in a heap on the floor. He saw, too, the outlines of the body under the sheet that had been thrown over it; the profile was plainly discernible under the face-cloth, clear-cut and sharp, as profiles of the dead seem always to be. He approached and lifted the cloth. Nothing was there. He pulled away the sheet. Nothing.

The family had followed him into the room. At this astonishing discovery—if so it may be called—they looked at one another, at the physician, at the bed, in speechless amazement, forgetting to weep. A moment later the three ladies required the physician's care. The father's condition was but little better; he stood in a stupor, muttering inarticulately and staring like an idiot.

Having restored the ladies to a sense of their surroundings the physician went to the window—the only one the room had, opening upon a garden. It was locked on the inside with the usual fastening attached to the bottom bar of the upper sash and engaging with the lower.

No inquest was held—there was nothing to hold it on; but the physician and many others who were curious as to this occurrence made a searching investigation into all the circumstances; all without result. George Reid was "dead and gone," and that is all that is known to this day.

A COLD NIGHT

The first day's battle at Stone River had been fought, resulting in disaster to the Federal army, which had been driven from its original ground at every point but its extreme left. The weary troops at this point lay behind a railway embankment to which they had retired, and which had served them during the last hours of the fight as a breastwork to repel repeated charges of the enemy. Behind the line the ground was open and rocky. Great bowlders lay about everywhere, and among them lay many of the Federal dead, where they had been carried out of the way. Before the embankment the dead of both armies lay more thickly, but they had not been disturbed.

Among those in the bowlders lay one whom nobody seemed to know—a sergeant, shot directly in the center of the forehead. One of our surgeons, from idle curiosity, or possibly with a view to the amusement of a group of officers during a lull in the engagement (we needed something to divert our minds) had pushed his probe clean through the head. The body lay on its back, its chin in the air, and with straightened limbs, as rigid as steel; frost on its white face and in its beard and hair. Some Christian soul had covered it with a blanket, but when the night became pretty sharp a companion of the writer removed this and we lay beneath it ourselves.

With the exception of our pickets, who had been posted well out in front of the embankment, every man lay silent. Conversation was forbidden; to have made a fire, or even struck a match to light a pipe, would have been a grave offense. Stamping horses, moaning wounded—everything that made a noise had been sent to the rear; the silence was absolute. Those whom the chill prevented from sleeping nevertheless reclined as they shivered, or sat with their heads on their arms, suffering but making no sign. Everyone had lost friends and all expected death on the morrow. These matters are mentioned to show the improbability of any one going about during those solemn hours to commit a ghastly practical joke.

When the dawn broke the sky was still clear. "We shall have a warm day," the writer's companion said, as we rose in the gray light; "let's give back the poor devil his blanket."

The sergeant's body lay in the same place, two yards away. But not in the same attitude. It was upon its right side. The knees were drawn up nearly to the breast, both hands were thrust to the wrist between the buttons of the jacket, the collar of which was turned up, concealing the ears. The shoulders were elevated, the head was retracted, the chin rested on the collar-bone. The posture was that of one suffering from exposure. But for what had been previously observed—the ghastly evidence of the bullet-hole—one might have thought the man had died of cold.

A CREATURE OF HABIT

At Hawley's Bar, a mining camp near Virginia City, Montana, a gambler named Henry Graham, but commonly known as "Gray Hank," met a miner named Dreyfuss one day, with whom he had had a dispute the night before, about a game of cards, and asked him into a barroom to have a drink. The unfortunate miner, taking this as an overture of peace, gladly accepted. They stood at the counter, and while Dreyfuss was in the act of drinking Graham shot him dead.

Within an hour of the murder Graham was in the hands of the vigilantes, and that evening at sunset, after a fair if informal trial, he was hanged to the limb of a tree which grew upon a little eminence within sight of the camp. The original intention had been to "string him up," as is customary in such affairs; and with a view to that operation the long rope had been thrown over the limb, while a dozen pairs of hands were ready to hoist him. For some reason this plan was abandoned; the free end of the rope was made fast to a bush and the victim compelled to stand on the back of a horse, which at the cut of a whip sprang from under him, leaving him swinging. When steadied, his feet were about eighteen inches from the earth.

The body remained suspended for exactly half an hour, the greater part of the crowd remaining about it: then the "judge" ordered it taken down. The rope was untied from the bush and two men stood by to lower away. The moment the feet came squarely upon the ground the men engaged in lowering, thinking doubtless that those standing about the body had hold of it to support it, let go the rope. The body at once ran quickly forward toward the main part of the crowd, the rope paying out as it went. The head rolled from side to side, the eyes and tongue protruding, the face purple, the lips covered with bloody froth. With cries of horror the crowd ran hither and thither, stumbling, falling over one another, cursing. In and out among them—over the fallen, coming into collision with others, the horrible dead man pranced, his feet lifted so high at each step that his knees struck his breast, his tongue swinging like that of a panting dog, the foam flying in flakes from his swollen lips. The deepening twilight added its terror to the scene and men fled from the spot, not daring to look behind.

Straight into this confusion from the outskirts of the crowd walked with rapid steps the tall figure of a man whom all who saw instantly recognized as a master spirit. This was Dr. Arnold Spier, who with two other physicians had pronounced the man dead and had been retiring to the camp. He moved as directly toward the dead man as the now somewhat less rapid and erratic movements of the latter would permit, and seized him in his arms. Encouraged by this a score of men sprang shouting to the free end of the rope, which had not been drawn entirely over the limb, and laid hold of it, intending to make a finish of their work. They ran with it toward the bush to which it had been fastened, but there was no resistance; the physician had cut it from the murderer's neck. In a moment the body was lying on its back, with composed limbs and face upturned to the kindling stars, in the motionless rigidity appropriate to death. The hanging had been done well enough—the neck was broken.

"The dead are creatures of habit," said Dr. Spier. "A corpse which when on its feet will walk and run will lie still when placed on its back."

E (22 Apr. 1888): 9 (as "Bodies of the Dead: Some Authentic Accounts of Their Seeming Caprices"); *E* (29 Apr. 1888): 9 (as "Bodies of the Dead: Additional Instances of Physical Activity After Death"); *CSTB* 293–308; **revised version of *CSTB* in MS copy of *CW* 3 (HL).** "'Dead and Gone,'" reprinted in *Short Stories* 1, no. 1 (June–July 1890): 59.

PRESENT AT A HANGING

An old man named Daniel Baker, living near Lebanon, Iowa, was suspected by his neighbors of having murdered a peddler who had obtained permission to pass the night at his house. This was in 1853, when peddling was more common in the Western country than it is now, and was attended with considerable danger. The peddler with his pack traversed the country by all manner of lonely roads, and was compelled to rely upon the country people for hospitality. This brought him into relation with queer characters, some of whom were not altogether scrupulous in their methods of making a living, murder being an acceptable means to that end. It occasionally occurred that a peddler with diminished pack and swollen purse would be traced to the lonely dwelling of some rough character and never could be traced beyond. This was so in the case of "old man Baker," as he was always called. (Such names are given in the western "settlements" only to elderly persons who are not esteemed; to the general disrepute of social unworth is affixed the special reproach of age.) A peddler came to his house and none went way—that is all that anybody knew.

Seven years later the Rev. Mr. Cummings, a Baptist minister well known in that part of the country, was driving by Baker's farm one night. It was not very dark: there was a bit of moon somewhere above the light veil of mist that lay along the earth. Mr. Cummings, who was at all times a cheerful person, was whistling a tune, which he would occasionally interrupt to speak a word of friendly encouragement to his horse. As he came to a little bridge across a dry ravine he saw the figure of a man standing upon it, clearly outlined against the gray background of a misty forest. The man had something strapped on his back and carried a heavy stick—obviously an itinerant peddler. His attitude had in it a suggestion of abstraction, like that of a sleepwalker. Mr. Cummings reined in his horse when he arrived in front of him, gave him a pleasant salutation and invited him to a seat in the vehicle—"if you are going my way," he added. The man raised his head, looked him full in the face, but neither answered nor made any further movement. The minister, with good-natured persistence, repeated his invitation. At this the man threw his right hand forward from his side and pointed downward as he stood on the extreme edge of the bridge. Mr. Cummings looked past him, over into the ravine, saw nothing unusual and withdrew his eyes to address the man again. He had disappeared. The horse, which all this time had been uncommonly restless, gave at the same moment a snort of terror and started to run away. Before he had regained control of the animal the minister was at the crest of the hill a hundred yards along. He looked back and saw the figure again, at the same place and in the same attitude as when he had first observed it. Then for the first time he was conscious of a sense of the supernatural and drove home as rapidly as his willing horse would go.

On arriving home he related his adventure to his family, and early the next morning, accompanied by two neighbors, John White Corwell and Abner Raiser, returned to the spot. They found the body of old man Baker hanging by the neck from one of the beams of the bridge, immediately beneath the spot where the apparition had stood. A thick coating of dust, slightly dampened by the mist, covered the floor of the bridge, but the only footprints were those of Mr. Cummings' horse.

In taking down the body the men disturbed the loose, friable earth of the slope below it, disclosing human bones already nearly uncovered by the action of water and frost. They were identified as those of the lost peddler. At the double inquest the coroner's jury found that Daniel Baker died of his own hand while suffering from temporary insanity, and that Samuel Morritz was murdered by some person or persons to the jury unknown.

E (24 June 1888): 11 (in "Hither from Hades"); *CW* 3.327–30.

A FRUITLESS ASSIGNMENT

Henry Saylor, who was killed in Covington, in a quarrel with Antonio Finch, was a reporter on the Cincinnati *Commercial*. In the year 1859 a vacant dwelling in Vine street, in Cincinnati, became the center of a local excitement because of the strange sights and sounds said to be observed in it nightly. According to the testimony of many reputable residents of the vicinity these were inconsistent with any other hypothesis than that the house was haunted. Figures with something singularly unfamiliar about them were seen by crowds on the sidewalk to pass in and out. No one could say just where they appeared upon the open lawn on their way to the front door by which they entered, nor at exactly what point they vanished as they came out; or, rather, while each spectator was positive enough about these matters, no two agreed. They were all similarly at variance in their descriptions of the figures themselves. Some of the bolder of the curious throng ventured on several evenings to stand upon the doorsteps to intercept them, or failing in this, get a nearer look at them. These courageous men, it was said, were unable to force the door by their united strength, and always were hurled from the steps by some invisible agency and severely injured; the door immediately afterward opening, apparently of its own volition, to admit or free some ghostly guest. The dwelling was known as the Roscoe house, a family of that name having lived there for some years, and then, one by one, disappeared, the last to leave being an old woman. Stories of foul play and successive murders had always been rife, but never were authenticated.

One day during the prevalence of the excitement Saylor presented himself at the office of the *Commercial* for orders. He received a note from the city editor which read as follows: "Go and pass the night alone in the haunted house in Vine street and if anything occurs worth while make two columns." Saylor obeyed his superior; he could not afford to lose his position on the paper.

Apprising the police of his intention, he effected an entrance through a rear window before dark, walked through the deserted rooms, bare of furniture, dusty and desolate, and seating himself at last in the parlor on an old sofa which he had dragged in from another room watched the deepening of the gloom as night came on. Before it was altogether dark the curious crowd had collected in the street, silent, as a rule, and expectant, with here and there a scoffer uttering his incredulity and courage with scornful remarks or ribald cries. None knew of the anxious watcher inside. He feared to make a light; the uncurtained windows would have betrayed his presence, subjecting him to insult, possibly to injury. Moreover, he was too conscientious to do anything to enfeeble his impressions and unwilling to alter any of the customary conditions under which the manifestations were said to occur.

It was now dark outside, but light from the street faintly illuminated the part of the room that he was in. He had set open every door in the whole interior, above and below, but all the outer ones were locked and bolted. Sudden exclamations from the crowd caused him to spring to the window and look out. He saw the figure of a man moving rapidly across the lawn toward the building—saw it ascend the steps; then a projection of the wall concealed it. There was a noise as of the opening and closing of the hall door; he heard quick, heavy footsteps along the passage—heard them ascend the stairs—heard them on the uncarpeted floor of the chamber immediately overhead.

Saylor promptly drew his pistol, and groping his way up the stairs entered the chamber, dimly lighted from the street. No one was there. He heard footsteps in an adjoining room and entered that. It was dark and silent. He struck his foot against some object on the floor, knelt by it, passed his hand over it. It was a human head— that of a woman. Lifting it by the hair this iron-nerved man returned to the half-lighted room below, carried it near the window and attentively examined it. While so engaged he was half conscious of the rapid opening and closing of the outer door, of footfalls sounding all about him. He raised his eyes from the ghastly object of his attention and saw himself the center of a crowd of men and women dimly seen; the room was thronged with them. He thought the people had broken in.

"Ladies and gentlemen," he said, coolly, "you see me under suspicious circumstances, but——" his voice was drowned in peals of laughter—such laughter as is heard in asylums for the insane. The persons about him pointed at the object in his hand and their merriment increased as he dropped it and it went rolling among their feet. They danced about it with gestures grotesque and attitudes obscene and indescribable. They struck it with their feet, urging it about the room from wall to wall; pushed and overthrew one another in their struggles to kick it; cursed and screamed and sang snatches of ribald songs as the battered head bounded about the room as if in terror and trying to escape. At last it shot out of the door into the hall, followed by all, with tumultuous haste. That moment the door closed with a sharp concussion. Saylor was alone, in dead silence.

Carefully putting away his pistol, which all the time he had held in his hand, he went to a window and looked out. The street was deserted and silent; the lamps were extinguished; the roofs and chimneys of the houses were sharply outlined against the dawn-light in the east. He left the house, the door yielding easily to his hand, and walked to the *Commercial* office. The city editor was still in his office—asleep. Saylor waked him and said: "I have been at the haunted house."

The editor stared blankly as if not wholly awake. "Good God!" he cried, "are you Saylor?"

"Yes—why not?"

The editor made no answer, but continued staring.

"I passed the night there—it seems," said Saylor.

"They say that things were uncommonly quiet out there," the editor said, trifling with a paper-weight upon which he had dropped his eyes, "did anything occur?"

"Nothing whatever."

E (24 June 1888): 11 (in "Hither from Hades"); *CSTB* 280–84; ***CW* 3.377–82**.

THE ISLE OF PINES

For many years there lived near the town of Gallipolis, Ohio, an old man named Herman Deluse. Very little was known of his history, for he would neither speak of it himself nor suffer others. It was a common belief among his neighbors that he had been a pirate—if upon any better evidence than his collection of boarding pikes, cutlasses and ancient flintlock pistols, no one knew. He lived entirely alone in a small house of four rooms, falling rapidly into decay and never repaired further than was required by the weather. It stood on a slight elevation in the midst of a large, stony field overgrown with brambles, and cultivated in patches and only in the most primitive way. It was his only visible property, but could hardly have yielded him a living, simple and few as were his wants. He seemed always to have ready money, and paid cash for all his purchases at the village stores roundabout, seldom buying more than two or three items at the same place until after the lapse of a considerable time. He got no commendation, however, for this equitable distribution of his patronage; people were disposed to regard it as an ineffectual attempt to conceal his possession of so much money. That he had great hoards of ill-gotten gold buried somewhere about is tumbledown dwelling was not reasonably to be doubted by any honest soul conversant with the facts of local tradition and gifted with a sense of the fitness of things.

On the 9th of November, 1867, the old man died; at least his dead body was discovered on the 10th, and physicians testified that death had occurred about twenty-four hours previously—precisely how, they were unable to say; for the *post-mortem* examination showed every organ to be absolutely healthy, with no indication of disorder or violence. According to them, death must have taken place about noonday, yet the body was found in bed. The verdict of the coroner's jury was that he "came to his death by a visitation of God." The body was buried and the public administrator took charge of the estate.

A rigorous search disclosed nothing more than was already known about the dead man, and much patient excavation here and there about the premises by thoughtful and thrifty neighbors went unrewarded. The administrator locked up the house against the time when the property, real and personal, should be sold by law with a view to defraying, partly, the expenses of the sale.

The night of November 20 was boisterous. A furious gale stormed across the country, scourging it with desolating drifts of sleet. Great trees were torn from the earth and hurled across the roads. So wild a night had never been known in all that region, but toward morning the storm had blown itself out of breath and day dawned bright and clear. At about eight o'clock that morning the Rev. Henry Galbraith, a well-known and highly esteemed Lutheran minister, arrived on foot at his house, a mile and half from the Deluse place. Mr. Galbraith had been for a month in Cincinnati. He had come up the river in a steamboat, and landing at Gallipolis the previous evening had immediately obtained a horse and buggy and set out for home. The violence of the storm had delayed him over night, and in the morning the fallen trees had compelled him to abandon his conveyance and continue his journey afoot.

"But where did you pass the night?" inquired his wife, after he had briefly related his adventure.

"With old Deluse at the 'Isle of Pines,'"* was the laughing reply; "and a glum enough time I had of it. He had no objection to my remaining, but not a word could I get out of him."

Fortunately for the interests of truth there was present at this conversation Mr. Robert Mosely Maren, a lawyer and *littérateur* of Columbus, the same who wrote the delightful "Mellowcraft Papers." Noting, but apparently not sharing, the astonishment caused by Mr. Galbraith's answer this ready-witted person checked by a gesture the exclamations that would naturally have followed, and tranquilly inquired: "How came you to go in there?"

This is Mr. Maren's version of Mr. Galbraith's reply:

"I saw a light moving about the house, and being nearly blinded by the sleet, and half frozen besides, drove in at the gate and put up my horse in the old rail stable, where it is now. I then rapped at the door, and getting no invitation went in without one. The room was dark, but having matches I found a candle and lit it. I tried to enter the adjoining room, but the door was fast, and although I heard the old man's heavy footsteps in there he made no response to my calls. There was no fire on the hearth, so I made one and laying [*sic*][1] down before it with my overcoat under my head, prepared myself for sleep. Pretty soon the door that I had tried silently opened and the old man came in, carrying a candle. I spoke to him pleasantly, apologizing for my intrusion, but he took no notice of me. He seemed to be searching for something, though his eyes

* The Isle of Pines was once a famous rendezvous of pirates.

APPENDIX A

were unmoved in their sockets. I wonder if he ever walks in his sleep. He took a circuit a part of the way round the room, and went out the same way he had come in. Twice more before I slept he came back into the room, acting precisely the same way, and departing as at first. In the intervals I heard him tramping all over the house, his footsteps distinctly audible in the pauses of the storm. When I woke in the morning he had already gone out."

Mr. Maren attempted some further questioning, but was unable longer to restrain the family's tongues; the story of Deluse's death and burial came out, greatly to the good minister's astonishment.

"The explanation of your adventure is very simple," said Mr. Maren. "I don't believe old Deluse walks in his sleep—not in his present one; but you evidently dream in yours."

And to this view of the matter Mr. Galbraith was compelled reluctantly to assent.

Nevertheless, a late hour of the next night found these two gentlemen, accompanied by a son of the minister, in the road in front of the old Deluse house. There was a light inside; it appeared now at one window and now at another. The three men advanced to the door. Just as they reached it there came from the interior a confusion of the most appalling sounds—the clash of weapons, steel against steel, sharp explosions as of firearms, shrieks of women, groans and the curses of men in combat! The investigators stood a moment, irresolute, frightened. Then Mr. Galbraith tried the door. It was fast. But the minister was a man of courage, a man, moreover, of Herculean strength. He retired a pace or two and rushed against the door, striking it with his right shoulder and bursting it from the frame with a loud crash. In a moment the three were inside. Darkness and silence! The only sound was the beating of their hearts.

Mr. Maren had provided himself with matches and a candle. With some difficulty, begotten of his excitement, he made a light, and they proceeded to explore the place, passing from room to room. Everything was in orderly arrangement, as it had been left by the sheriff; nothing had been disturbed. A light coating of dust was everywhere. A back door was partly open, as if by neglect, and their first thought was that the authors of the awful revelry might have escaped. The door was opened, and the light of the candle shone through upon the ground. The expiring effort of the previous night's storm had been a light fall of snow; there were no footprints; the white surface was unbroken. They closed the door and entered the last room of the four that the house contained—that farthest from the road, in an angle of the building. Here the candle in Mr. Maren's hand was suddenly extinguished as by a draught of air. Almost immediately followed the sound of a heavy fall. When the candle had been hastily relighted young Mr. Galbraith was seen prostrate on the floor at a little distance from the others. He was dead. In one hand the body grasped a heavy sack of coins, which later examination showed to be all of old Spanish mintage. Directly over the body as it lay, a board had been torn from its fastenings in the wall, and from the cavity so disclosed it was evident that the bag had been taken.

Another inquest was held: another *post-mortem* examination failed to reveal a probable cause of death. Another verdict of "the visitation of God" left all at liberty to form their own conclusions. Mr. Maren contended that the young man died of excitement.

E (26 Aug. 1888): 9 (in "Behind the Veil"); *CSTB* 273–79; **CW 3.369–76.**

NOTE

1. The bracketed comment here (and in "The Difficulty in Crossing a Field," p. 1166) is by AB.

A COLD GREETING

This is a story by the late Benson Foley of San Francisco:

"In the summer of 1881 I met a man named James H. Conway, a resident of Franklin, Tennessee. He was visiting San Francisco for his health, deluded man, and brought me a note of introduction from Mr. Lawrence Barting. I had known Barting as a captain in the Federal army during the civil war. At its close he had settled in Franklin, and in time became, I had reason to think, somewhat prominent as a lawyer. Barting had always seemed to me an honorable and truthful man, and the warm friendship which he expressed in his note for Mr. Conway was to me sufficient evidence that the latter was in every way worthy of my confidence and esteem. At dinner one day Conway told me that it had been solemnly agreed between him and Barting that the one who died first should, if possible, communicate with the other from beyond the grave, in some unmistakable way—just how, they had left (wisely, it seemed to me) to be decided by the deceased, according to the opportunities that his altered circumstances might present.

"A few weeks after the conversation in which Mr. Conway spoke of this agreement, I met him one day, walking slowly down Montgomery street, apparently, from his abstracted air, in deep thought. He greeted me coldly with merely a movement of the head and passed on, leaving me standing on the walk, with half-proffered hand, surprised and naturally somewhat piqued. The next day I met him again in the office of the Palace Hotel, and seeing him about to repeat the disagreeable performance of the day before, intercepted him in a doorway, with a friendly salutation, and bluntly requested an explanation of his altered manner. He hesitated a moment; then, looking me frankly in the eyes, said:

"'I do not think, Mr. Foley, that I have any longer a claim to your friendship, since Mr. Barting appears to have withdrawn his own from me—for what reason, I protest I do not know. If he has not already informed you he probably will do so.'

"'But,' I replied, 'I have not heard from Mr. Barting.'

"'Heard from him!' he repeated, with apparent surprise. 'Why, he is here. I met him yesterday ten minutes before meeting you. I gave you exactly the same greeting that he gave me. I met him again not a quarter of an hour ago, and the manner was precisely the same: he merely bowed and passed on. I shall not soon forget your civility to me. Good morning, or—as it may please you—farewell.'

"All this seemed to me singularly considerate and delicate behavior on the part of Mr. Conway.

"As dramatic situations and literary effects are foreign to my purpose I will explain at once that Mr. Barting was dead. He had died in Nashville four days before this conversation. Calling on Mr. Conway, I apprised him of our friend's death, showing him the letters announcing it. He was visibly affected in a way that forbade me to entertain a doubt of his sincerity.

"'It seems incredible,' he said, after a period of reflection. 'I suppose I must have mistaken another man for Barting, and that man's cold greeting was merely a stranger's civil acknowledgment of my own. I remember, indeed, that he lacked Barting's mustache.'"

"'Doubtless it was another man,' I assented; and the subject was never afterward mentioned between us. But I had in my pocket a photograph of Barting, which had been inclosed in the letter from his widow. It had been taken a week before his death, and was without a mustache."

E (26 Aug. 1888): 9 (in "Behind the Veil"); *CW* 3.331–34.

THE DIFFICULTY OF CROSSING A FIELD

One morning in July, 1854, a planter named Williamson, living six miles from Selma, Alabama, was sitting with his wife and a child on the veranda of his dwelling. Immediately in front of the house was a lawn, perhaps fifty yards in extent between the house and public road, or, as it was called, the "pike." Beyond this road lay a close-cropped pasture of some ten acres, level and without a tree, rock or any natural or artificial object on its surface. At the time there was not even a domestic animal in the field. In another field, beyond the pasture, a dozen slaves were at work under an overseer.

Throwing away the stump of a cigar, the planter rose, saying: "I forgot to tell Andrew about those horses." Andrew was the overseer.

Williamson strolled leisurely down the gravel walk, plucking a flower as he went, passed across the road and into the pasture, pausing a moment as he closed the gate leading into it, to greet a passing neighbor, Armour Wren, who lived on an adjoining plantation. Mr. Wren was in an open carriage with his son James, a lad of thirteen. When he had driven some two hundred yards from the point of meeting, Mr. Wren said to his son: "I forgot to tell Mr. Williamson about those horses."

Mr. Wren had sold to Mr. Williamson some horses, which were to have been sent for that day, but for some reason not now remembered it would be inconvenient to deliver them until the morrow. The coachman was directed to drive back, and as the vehicle turned Williamson was seen by all three, walking leisurely across the pasture. At that moment one of the coach horses stumbled and came near falling. It had no more than fairly recovered itself when James Wren cried: "Why, father, what has become of Mr. Williamson?"

It is not the purpose of this narrative to answer that question.

Mr. Wren's strange account of the matter, given under oath in the course of legal proceedings relating to the Williamson estate, here follows:

"My son's exclamation caused me to look toward the spot where I had seen the deceased [*sic*] an instant before, but he was not there, nor was he anywhere visible. I cannot say that at the moment I was greatly startled, or realized the gravity of the occurrence, though I thought it singular. My son, however, was greatly astonished and kept repeating his question in different forms until we arrived at the gate. My black boy Sam was similarly affected, even in a greater degree, but I reckon more by my son's manner than by anything he had himself observed. [This sentence in the testimony was stricken out.] As we got out of the carriage at the gate of the field, and while Sam was hanging [*sic*] the team to the fence, Mrs. Williamson, with her child in her arms and followed by several servants, came running down the walk in great excitement, crying: 'He is gone, he is gone! O God! what an awful thing!' and many other such exclamations, which I do not distinctly recollect. I got from them the impression that they related to something more than the mere disappearance of her husband, even if that had occurred before her eyes. Her manner was wild, but not more so, I think, than was natural under the circumstances. I have no reason to think she had at that time lost her mind. I have never since seen nor heard of Mr. Williamson."

This testimony, as might have been expected, was corroborated in almost every particular by the only other eye-witness (if that is a proper term)—the lad James. Mrs. Williamson had lost her reason and the servants were, of course, not competent to testify. The boy James Wren had declared at first that he *saw* the disappearance, but there is nothing of this in his testimony given in court. None of the field hands working in the field to which Williamson was going had seen him at all, and the most rigorous search of the entire plantation and adjoining country failed to supply a clew. The most monstrous and grotesque fictions, originating with the blacks, were current in that part of the State for many years, and probably are to this day; but what has been here related is all that is certainly known of the matter. The courts decided that Williamson was dead, and his estate was distributed according to law.

E (14 Oct. 1888): 9 (in "Whither?"); *CSTB* 309–12; **CW 3.415–18**.

AN UNFINISHED RACE

James Burne Worson was a shoemaker who lived in Leamington, Warwickshire, England. He had a little shop in one of the by-ways leading off the road to Warwick. In his humble sphere he was esteemed an honest man, although like many of his class in English towns he was somewhat addicted to drink. When in liquor he would make foolish wagers. On one of these too frequent occasions he was boasting of his prowess as a pedestrian and athlete, and the outcome was a match against nature. For a stake of one sovereign he undertook to run all the way to Coventry and back, a distance of something more than forty miles. This was on the 3d day of September in 1873. He set out at once, the man with whom he had made the bet—whose name is not remembered—accompanied by Barham Wise, a linen draper, and Hamerson Burns, a photographer, I think, following in a light cart or wagon.

For several miles Worson went on very well, at an easy gait, without apparent fatigue, for he had really great powers of endurance and was not sufficiently intoxicated to enfeeble them. The three men in the wagon kept a short distance in the rear, giving him occasional friendly "chaff" or encouragement, as the spirit moved them. Suddenly—in the very middle of the roadway, not a dozen yards from them, and with their eyes full upon him—the man seemed to stumble, pitched headlong forward, uttered a terrible cry and vanished! He did not fall to the earth—he vanished before touching it. No trace of him was ever discovered.

After remaining at and about the spot for some time, with aimless irresolution, the three men returned to Leamington, told their astonishing story and were afterward taken into custody. But they were of good standing, had always been considered truthful, were sober at the time of the occurrence, and nothing ever transpired to discredit their sworn account of their extraordinary adventure, concerning the truth of which, nevertheless, public opinion was divided, throughout the United Kingdom. If they had something to conceal, their choice of means is certainly one of the most amazing ever made by sane human beings.

E (14 Oct. 1888): 9 (in "Whither?"); *CSTB* 313–14; ***CW*** **3.419–20**.

CHARLES ASHMORE'S TRAIL

The family of Christian Ashmore consisted of his wife, his mother, two grown daughters and a son of sixteen years. They lived in Troy, New York, were well-to-do, respectable persons and had many friends, some of whom, reading these lines, will doubtless learn for the first time the extraordinary fate of the young man. From Troy the Ashmores moved in 1871 or 1872 to Richmond, Indiana, and a year or two later to the vicinity of Quincy, Illinois, where Mr. Ashmore bought a farm and lived on it. At some little distance from the farmhouse was a spring with a constant flow of clear, cold water, whence the family derived its supply for domestic use at all seasons.

On the evening of the 9th of November in 1878, at about nine o'clock, young Charles Ashmore left the family circle about the hearth, took a tin bucket and started toward the spring. As he did not return, the family became uneasy, and going to the door by which he had left the house, his father called without receiving an answer. He then lighted a lantern and with the eldest daughter, Martha, who insisted on accompanying him, went in search. A light snow had fallen, obliterating the path, but making the young man's trail conspicuous; each footprint was plainly defined. After going a little more than half-way—perhaps seventy-five yards—the father, who was in advance, halted, and elevating his lantern stood peering intently into the darkness ahead.

"What is the matter, father?" the girl asked.

This was the matter: the trail of the young man had abruptly ended, and all beyond was smooth, unbroken snow. The last footprints were as conspicuous as any in the line; the very nail-marks were distinctly visible. Mr. Ashmore looked upward, shading his eyes with his hat held between them and the lantern. The stars were shining; there was not a cloud in the sky; he was denied the explanation which had suggested itself, doubtful as it would have been—a new snowfall with a limit so plainly defined. Taking a wide circuit round the ultimate tracks, so as to leave them undisturbed for further examination, the man proceeded to the spring, the girl following, weak and terrified. Neither had spoken a word of what both had observed. The spring was covered with ice, hours old.

Returning to the house they noted the appearance of the snow on both sides of the trail its entire length. No tracks led away from it.

The morning light showed nothing more. Smooth, spotless, unbroken, the shallow snow lay everywhere.

Four days later the grief-stricken mother herself went to the spring for water. She came back and related that in passing the spot where the footprints had ended she had heard the voice of her son and had been eagerly calling to him, wandering about the place, as she had fancied the voice to be now in one direction, now in another, until she was exhausted with fatigue and emotion. Questioned as to what the voice had said, she was unable to tell, yet averred that the words were perfectly distinct. In a moment the entire family was at the place, but nothing was heard, and the voice was believed to be an hallucination caused by the mother's great anxiety and her disordered nerves. But for months afterward, at irregular intervals of a few days, the voice was heard by the several members of the family, and by others. All declared it unmistakably the voice of Charles Ashmore; all agreed that it seemed to come from a great distance, faintly, yet with entire distinctness of articulation; yet none could determine its direction, nor repeat its words. The intervals of silence grew longer and longer, the voice fainter and farther, and by midsummer it was heard no more.

If anybody knows the fate of Charles Ashmore it is probably his mother. She is dead.

E (14 Oct. 1888): 9 (in "Whither?"); CSTB 315–20; *CW* 3.421–24.

THE SPOOK HOUSE

On the road leading north form Manchester, in eastern Kentucky, to Booneville, twenty miles away, stood, in 1862, a wooden plantation house of a somewhat better quality than most of the dwellings in that region. The house was destroyed by fire in the year following—probably by some stragglers from the retreating column of General George W. Morgan, when he was driven from Cumberland Gap to the Ohio river by General Kirby Smith. At the time of its destruction, it had for four or five years been vacant. The fields about it were overgrown with brambles, the fences gone, even the few negro quarters, and outhouses generally, fallen partly into ruin by neglect and pillage; for the negroes and poor whites of the vicinity found in the building and fences an abundant supply of fuel, of which they availed themselves without hesitation, openly and by daylight. By daylight alone; after nightfall no human being except passing strangers ever went near the place.

It was known as the "Spook House." That it was tenanted by evil spirits, visible, audible and active, no one in all that region doubted any more than he doubted what he was told of Sundays by the traveling preacher. Its owner's opinion of the matter was unknown; he and his family had disappeared one night and no trace of them had ever been found. They left everything—household goods, clothing, provisions, the horses in the stable, the cows in the field, the negroes in the quarters—all as it stood; nothing was missing—except a man, a woman, three girls, a boy and a babe! It was not altogether surprising that a plantation where seven human beings could be simultaneously effaced and nobody the wiser should be under some suspicion.

One night in June, 1859, two citizens of Frankfort, Col. J. C. McArdle, a lawyer, and Judge Myron Veigh, of the State Militia, were driving from Booneville to Manchester. Their business was so important that they decided to push on, despite the darkness and the mutterings of an approaching storm, which eventually broke upon them just as they arrived opposite the "Spook House." The lightning was so incessant that they easily found their way through the gateway and into a shed, where they hitched and unharnessed their team. They then went to the house, through the rain, and knocked at all the doors without getting any response. Attributing this to the continuous uproar of the thunder they pushed at one of the doors, which yielded. They entered without further ceremony and closed the door. That instant they were in darkness and silence. Not a gleam of the lightning's unceasing blaze penetrated the windows or crevices; not a whisper of the awful tumult without reached them there. It was as if they had suddenly been stricken blind and deaf, and McArdle afterward said that for a moment he believed himself to have been killed by a stroke of lightning as he crossed the threshold. The rest of this adventure can as well be related in his own words, from the Frankfort *Advocate* of August 6, 1876:

"When I had somewhat recovered from the dazing effect of the transition from uproar to silence, my first impulse was to reopen the door which I had closed, and from the knob of which I was not conscious of having removed my hand; I felt it distinctly, still in the clasp of my fingers. My notion was to ascertain by stepping again into the storm whether I had been deprived of sight and hearing. I turned the doorknob and pulled open the door. It led into another room!

"This apartment was suffused with a faint greenish light, the source of which I could not determine, making everything distinctly visible, though nothing was sharply defined. Everything, I say, but in truth the only objects within the blank stone walls of that room were human corpses. In number they were perhaps eight or ten—it may well be understood that I did not truly count them. They were of different ages, or rather sizes, from infancy up, and of both sexes. All were prostrate on the floor, except one, apparently a young woman, who sat up, her back supported by an angle of the wall. A babe was clasped in the arms of another and older woman. A half-grown lad lay face downward across the legs of a full-bearded man. One or two were nearly naked, and the hand of a young girl held the fragment of a gown which she had torn open at the breast. The bodies were in various stages of decay, all greatly shrunken in face and figure. Some were but little more than skeletons.

"While I stood stupefied with horror by this ghastly spectacle and still holding open the door, by some unaccountable perversity my attention was diverted from the shocking scene and concerned itself with trifles and details. Perhaps my mind, with an instinct of self-preservation, sought relief in matters which would relax its dangerous tension. Among other things, I observed that the door that I was holding open was of heavy iron plates, riveted. Equidistant from one another and from the top and bottom, three strong bolts protruded from the beveled edge. I turned the knob and they were retracted flush with the edge; released it, and they shot out. It was a spring lock. On the inside there was no knob, nor any kind of projection—a smooth surface of iron.

"While noting these things with an interest and attention which it now astonishes me to recall I felt myself thrust aside, and Judge Veigh, whom in the intensity and vicissitudes of my feelings I had altogether forgotten, pushed by me into the room. 'For God's sake,' I cried, 'do not go in there! Let us get out of this dreadful place!'

"He gave no heed to my entreaties, but (as fearless a gentleman as lived in all the South) walked quickly to the center of the room, knelt beside one of the bodies for a closer examination and tenderly raised its blackened and shriveled head in his hands. A strong disagreeable odor came through the doorway, completely overpowering me. My senses reeled; I felt myself falling, and in clutching at the edge of the door for support pushed it shut with a sharp click!

"I remember no more: six weeks later I recovered my reason in a hotel at Manchester, whither I had been taken by strangers the next day. For all these weeks I had suffered from a nervous fever, attended with constant delirium. I had been found lying in the road several miles away from the house; but how I had escaped from it to get there I never knew. On recovery, or as soon as my physicians permitted me to talk, I inquired the fate of Judge Veigh, whom (to quiet me, as I now know) they represented as well and at home.

"No one believed a word of my story, and who can wonder? And who can imagine my grief when, arriving at my home in Frankfort two months later, I learned that Judge Veigh had never been heard of since that night? I then regretted bitterly the pride which since the first few days after the recovery of my reason had forbidden me to repeat my discredited story and insist upon its truth.

"With all that afterward occurred—the examination of the house; the failure to find any room corresponding to that which I have described; the attempt to have me adjudged insane, and my triumph over my accusers—the readers of the *Advocate* are familiar. After all these years I am still confident that excavations which I have neither the legal right to undertake nor the wealth to make would disclose the secret of the disappearance of my unhappy friend, and possibly of the former occupants and owners of the deserted and now destroyed house. I do not despair of yet bringing about such a search, and it is a source of deep grief to me that it has been delayed by the undeserved hostility and unwise incredulity of the family and friends of the late Judge Veigh."

Colonel McArdle died in Frankfort on the thirteenth day of December, in the year 1879.

E (7 July 1889): 9 (in "Two Haunted Houses"); *CW* 3.393–99.

A DOPPELGANGER

John Easton Lord, of Coopertown, Pennsylvania, sold his house and lot in that town to William Burrill and moved with his family to the suburbs of Pittsburg. The Burrill family occupied the Coopertown house for nearly four years, then abandoned it—being unable to resell it—and occupied another, a half-mile away, which at first they rented and afterward bought. Here the widow of William Burrill and one maiden daughter were living as lately as 1884.

At that time the old Lord dwelling, which had stood tenantless for years, had just been demolished, with many others, to make room for a new street. It had long had an uncanny reputation as a "haunted house," and although the skeptics were many, and repeated investigations had been made of the supernatural phenomena said to occur nightly within its walls, it was noticeable that even the most incredulous always spoke of them with gravity and no one in Coopertown attempted to discredit them by ridicule. The subject was universally regarded as worthy of serious discussion. There was reason enough; one of the dismal traditions of the house—namely that no one could remain alone in it over night and keep both life and reason—had been twice confirmed in the most authenticating way. One hardy investigator had been found in the morning dead, without a wound or assignable cause, and another person—a tramp who in all unconsciousness of the dwelling's history had stolen a lodging there—had rushed out at the gray of the morning incurably mad. That the house was haunted was open to honest doubt, but these somber passages in its annals had at least invested that proposition with a certain dignity which made it immune to ridicule.

The manifestations, it appears, began on the 20th day of June, 1872, somewhat more than three years after the Burrill family moved into the house. On the evening of that day, at about 7 o'clock, while the family were sitting on the veranda after dinner, John Easton Lord, the former owner, came in at the gate, ascended the steps of the veranda and passing directly between Mr. and Mrs. Burrill entered the house by the hall door. Mr. Burrill had risen to greet him, but the proffered hand had remained unheeded. By not so much as a look had Lord recognized any member of the family, to all of whom he was well known. He was immediately followed into the house by Burrill and his son Parker, whose astonishment was great indeed at not finding their visitor. The only door by which he could have left the house was found securely locked, with the key inside, and all the windows were fastened excepting those opening on the veranda. A search of the entire house resulted in nothing. Lord had not been seen by anybody else in town, and the incident was without an explanation. A letter to Pittsburg brought out the fact in reply that on the day of its occurrence John Easton Lord had been seven weeks dead.

From this time forward, until they left the house months afterward, the Burrill family appear to have suffered annoyance and alarm from what were affirmed to be supernatural manifestations. The character of these is inexactly known; with a view to damaging their property as little as possible, all the members of the family preserved a discreet silence; but the most extravagant tales were bruited about, orally and through the local newspapers. It is needless to repeat them here: they were of the kind usually related of houses said to be "haunted." By the time the property had been condemned for a public use, appraised and paid for, Mr. Burrill was dead, and the family scattered in distant parts of the country—all except the widow, who was in her dotage, and one elderly maiden daughter whose austere silence on this subject was infrangible. There is ample and credible testimony, popular and professional, that when the family moved out of the house all were suffering acutely from insomnia and nervous prostration— from which, indeed, the youngest, a girl of seventeen, eventually died.

From voluminous notes of an investigation made by a competent inquirer in 1884 it is found that all, or nearly all, of the least incredible accounts of supernatural occurrences in and about the Lord house relate to the visible apparition of the late John Easton Lord. Most of the testimony as to that element has in it something approaching trustworthiness. If anything at all "out of the common" ever took place there, something which many cool-headed witnesses took to be the ghost of Lord habitually showed itself about the premises by night and sometimes by day. It was considered a malign spirit although in life Lord had been of a singularly amiable disposition.

E (7 July 1889): 9 (in "Two Haunted Houses"); **revised clipping (VA)**.

APPENDIX B

BIERCE ON HIS FICTION

Bierce was not above applying some fiction to his prefaces. The most famous one, that to *Tales of Soldiers and Civilians*, if not actually untrue, certainly strains credulity. In two of the other prefaces he also uses quaint and very ornate language quite unlike the styles of either his stories or his journalism to cloud the fact that he is distancing himself from the position that his narratives are fictitious.

The most extensive and, beyond question, the most important trove of information about Bierce is in the presently uncollected journalism of his lifetime—more than forty years' worth of fascinating columns. A great deal of material of autobiographical value occurs in them, as well as the three selections of comments from "Prattle" that respond to reviews of *Tales of Soldiers and Civilians* and of individual stories. Bierce knew enough not to get too specific about his stories in his journalistic columns and supply anything approaching an official interpretation; still, even in responding indirectly to some comments he does give away clues about what he thinks that most readers will find interesting.

PREFACE TO *TALES OF SOLDIERS AND CIVILIANS*

Denied existence by the chief publishing houses of the country,[1] this book owes itself to Mr. E. L. G. STEELE,[2] merchant, of this city. In attesting Mr. STEELE'S faith in his judgment and his friend, it will serve its author's main and best ambition.

A. B.

SAN FRANCISCO, Sept 4, 1891.

TSC [3].

NOTES

1. There is reason to doubt the accuracy of this statement. No evidence exists to support it, and inasmuch as three of its stories were published in 1891, the year the book went to the press, there does not seem to have been sufficient time for AB to have sent it to many publishers.
2. E. L. G. Steele (d. 1894) was a wealthy San Francisco businessman and head of C. Adolphe Low and Company, Importers. AB had been in touch with him since at least 1883.

PREFACE TO *IN THE MIDST OF LIFE*

In reissuing this book, with considerable alterations and additions, it has been thought expedient, for uniformity, to give it the title under which it was published in London and Leipzig.[1] The merely descriptive name of the original American edition (published by the late E. L. G. Steele) is retained as a sub-title in order to prevent misunderstandings by purchasers—if the book be so fortunate as to have any.

A. B.

IML iii.

NOTES

1. *TSC* had been published in London (Chatto & Windus, 1892) and Leipzig (Tauchnitz, 1892) as *In the Midst of Life* (a phrase deriving from the *Book of Common Prayer*: "In the midst of life we are in death").

PREFACE *TO BUBBLES LIKE US* *[CAN SUCH THINGS BE?]*

The contents of this book are stories of various kinds: they cover, in character, a pretty wide field. Many of them are military—tales of the civil war, in which the author served throughout. Many of these are tragic, a few "humorous," according to the author's somewhat grim notion of humor; a conception in which levity is not altogether incompatible with lurid glimpses of "the Reaper whose name is Death."[1]

In the non-military tales also the tragic note is dominant. They have to do mostly with the supernatural, and in a way that makes small allowance for weak nerves. They are not recommended for nocturnal reading in an abandoned house, by the light of a tallow candle, though in one of his best-known stories the author, through the mouth of his hero, has expounded his belief that the reader of a "ghost story" owes it to the writer to put himself under such conditions of environment as to give full effect to the uncanny spirit of the tale.[2]

In the latter part of the book, under the headings "Some Haunted Houses," "Bodies of the Dead" and "Mysterious Disappearances," are related with the utmost particularity, with names, dates and places, some certainly very extraordinary occurrences. Concerning these the author, in his real or assumed character of compiler, says, with apparent candor:

"My peculiar relation to the author of the following uncommon narratives is such that I must ask the reader to overlook the absence of all explanation of how they came into my possession. Withal, my knowledge of him is so meager that I would rather not undertake to say if he was himself persuaded of the truth of what he relates; certainly such inquiries as I have thought it worth while to set about have not in every instance tended to confirmation of the statements made. Yet his style, devoid alike of artifice and art, almost baldly simple and direct, seems hardly compatible with the disingenuousness of a merely literary intention; one would call it the manner of one more concerned for the fruits of research than for the flowers of expression."

TMS (BL).

NOTES

A preface written for Walter Neale's proposed reprint of *CSTB* (see below), which AB wished to retitle *Bubbles Like Us* (a phrase derived from *The Rubaiyat of Omar Khayyam*, translated by Edward FitzGerald [1859], stanza 46); see AB to Myles Walsh, 21 September 1902 (MS, Univ. of Cincinnati). In the end, this preface was not used and the book was not retitled; instead, a very brief preface was inserted into the 1903 reprint.

1. Longfellow, "The Reaper and the Flowers" (1839), l. 1 ("a" for "the" in Longfellow).
2. "The Suitable Surroundings" (p. 677).

PREFACE TO *CAN SUCH THINGS BE?*

Of some of the tales in this new and authorized edition the author wishes to explain that their appearance in other forms since the original edition of 1893 has been without his knowledge or assent.

A. B.

Washington, D. C.,
February 10, 1903.

Can Such Things Be? (Washington, DC: Neale Publishing Co., 1903), [i].

[PREFATORY NOTE TO "THE WAYS OF GHOSTS"]

My peculiar relation to the writer of the following narratives is such that I must ask the reader to overlook the absence of explanation as to how they came into my possession. Withal, my knowledge of him is so meager that I should rather not undertake to say if he were himself persuaded of the truth of what he relates; certainly such inquiries as I have thought it worth while to set about have not in every instance tended to confirmation of the statements made. Yet his style, for the most part devoid alike of artifice and art, almost baldly simple and direct, seems hardly compatible with the disingenuousness of a merely literary intention; one would call it the manner of one more concerned for the fruits of research than for the flowers of expression. In transcribing his notes and fortifying their claim to attention by giving them something of an orderly arrangement, I have conscientiously refrained from embellishing them with such small ornaments of diction as I may have felt myself able to bestow, which would not only have been impertinent, even if pleasing, but would have given me a somewhat closer relation to the work than I should care to have and to avow.—A. B.

CW 3.[326].

[ON *TALES OF SOLDIERS AND CIVILIANS*]

Having in the beginning of this screed made certain strolling comments on the Author as I know him, I am minded fairwise to say something of the Critic; for the two go together, like hare and hound, author a little ahead. The immemorial quarrel between them is comparable to nothing but the permanent misunderstanding between the driver of a stage-coach and the off wheeler. The driver has really nothing against that animal; its only sin is accessibility to the lash. And the driver is himself not at all bad; he is severely addicted to the whip-habit, and the awful imprecations accompanying his blows are produced by some kind of reflex action, without his connivance. The book reviewer, too, is commonly a very good fellow and would not willingly hurt a fly; and if he pile his immediate circumference with tumuli of dead the fault is attributable rather to opportunity than to a bad heart. Who is proof against opportunity?—it tempts us and we fall as fall the early pious in the bud and promise of their bloom. But as there are honest publishers, there are wicked critics— critics whose hearts are nests of naughtinesses, and who but open their minds to let out and in the evil beasts infesting them. Such a one I know, and I have it in purpose to expose the wretch to public reprobation and deprive him even of his own esteem as an undetected rogue.[1]

The fellow reviews books in the New York *Sun.* That journal is said to be regarded as "high authority" in matters literary, mainly because of this chap's works. I'm told that his name is Hazeltine, but of that I'm not sure. A few months ago I had the hardihood to utter upon an unoffending world a book of tales, which the critics generally have received with surprising favor. But this *Sun*-dog!—he got hold of it (it was not sent him) and chewed it into small wads. As he was not invited to the feast I won't have things left in that condition without exerting the flexors and extensors of my red right leg—no, indeed. He says:

> The opening tale, 'A Horseman' in the sky is the worst in the book so far as illusion is concerned. We will venture to say that no such erroneous impression could have been produced in the Federal army, or in any portion of it, as the author here alleges. We are certain that the horseman in the sky was never mistaken for a repetition of the Apocalyptical vision, but was only regarded as a Confederate General and his horse descending a precipice in obedience to the laws of gravitation, as the facts warranted.

Now, the author alleged nothing of the kind—yes, something of the kind, but mark the difference in degree. The only "Federal army" or "portion of it" that saw the horseman in the sky was a single man, who saw him for one instant and for that instant half believed it an Apocalyptic vision. The exact words of the yarn are:

> Filled with amazement and terror by this apparition of a horseman in the sky— half-believing himself the chosen scribe of some new Apocalypse, the officer was overcome by the intensity of his emotions.

A moment afterward he was searching for the "vision's" body, among the trees. If the critic's comments on that insignificant passage do not rise to the dignity of virtual lying of a pretty lofty sort there are no pigs.

He goes on to say:

> Nor does there seem to us to be the appearance of truth or reason in some of the other tales. * * * If the San Francisco physicians had got an ordinary undertaker to sit up with their dead man matters would have gone on with the utmost felicity; and if the officer in charge of the battery at Coulter's Notch had publicly explained the circumstances, we feel quite sure that he could have avoided the unpleasant duty of shooting cannon balls at his wife and child.[2]

O what a thing it is to be an ass! No doubt the undertaker might do a number of things "with the utmost felicity," but my story was about a man unaccustomed to the society of the dead, who heard the corpse walking softly toward him in the darkness. If his death from fright lacks "the appearance of truth and reason," it can hardly be because an undertaker might have been braver. I will cheerfully confess that if my story had been different from what it was it might have been worse than it is. Regarding the officer at Coulter's Notch, I will confess, too, the probable efficacy of a "public explanation," whatever that might be in an army, though military subordination is not favorable to it. Unfortunately, though, for the relevancy of the suggestion I had chosen to write of an officer whose pride and sense of duty forbade him to explain. On the whole, I am of the conviction that my critic was at his best at first; he shines with a brighter splendor as a liar than as a fool, though in either character I should suppose he might cause a good deal of trouble to the fire department.

From "Prattle," *E* (26 June 1892): 6.

NOTES

1. The reference is to an unsigned review of *TSC* in the *New York Sun* (12 Mar. 1892): 7. It is probably by M. W. Hazeltine, the *Sun*'s staff reviewer.
2. The references are to "A Watcher by the Dead" (p. 697) and "The Affair at Coulter's Notch" (p. 684).

Among examples of "literary criticism" which I joy to collect for no better reason than that they relate to my books are some in which I cannot fail to discern the hand of a frowning Providence put forth to humble my proud spirit. Beneath the following, from "Life,"[1] I bend my corrigible neck like a rose detected in an attempt to associate with cabbages:

> "The younger American writers are doing some very artistic killing in their stories. Stephen Crane, Robert W. Chambers, Ambrose Bierce, E. W. Thomson, Owen Wister and Richard Harding Davis[2] have all tried their hands at blood-spilling with the accessories of war. They are clever young men who never smelt powder burnt in battle, but they have a certain realistic faculty of making the reader see what they have only imagined. Whether Kipling started them on their career of revolution and slaughter, or whether it was something in the air that struck them all about the same time, is not quite clear." Etc.

To which I venture to add, in corroboration, the facts following: (1) I am an older man than any young man in America. (2) The fragrance of "powder burnt in battle" has many times reminded me of my preference for that of roasted critic. (3) The stories that this gentleman had in mind were published (and reviewed in more than four hundred of the magazines and newspapers of this country and Europe)[3] before Mr. Kipling had been heard of outside the editorial rooms of "The Mulligachutney Bango."[4] If my esteemed reviewer will add these facts to his esteemed review he will enhance its value by as much as two cents.

By the way, it commonly occurs that in my poor little battle-yarns the incidents that come in for special reprobation by the critics as "improbable" and even "impossible" are transcripts from memory—things that actually occurred before my eyes. In mentioning a certain story of mine the curio that "censures letters" in "Life" supplies an added instance:

> "It is a great thing to watch the 'Son of the Gods' ride out to his sure death like a stage hero. It is magnificent, but it is not war."

Well, I saw that thing done, just as related. True, the "Son" escaped whole, but he "rode out" all right, and if matters had been as we all believed them to be, and as he thought them himself, he would have been shot to rags.[5]

Let me not be unfair. My critic's civilian training has led him into the lamentable error of censuring me, but with reference to the other story-tellers whom he names his reprehension is singularly intelligent—he could not have overdamned them if he had tried. This admission, I take it, is commendably just. 'Egad, it is magnanimous!

From "Prattle," *E* (1 Mar. 1897): 6.

APPENDIX B

NOTES

1. The article, entitled "A Cry for Peace in Fable-Land" and signed "Dorch," appeared in *Life,* no. 739 (18 Feb. 1897): 128.
2. The references are to Stephen Crane (1871–1900), author of *The Red Badge of Courage* (1895); Robert W. Chambers (1865–1933), popular novelist and author of *The Red Republic* (1895), a historical novel about the Franco-Prussian War; E. W. Thomson (1849–1924), who served in the Federal army during the Civil War and wrote *Old Man Savarin and Other Stories* (1895), which contains several war stories; Owen Wister (1860–1938), best known for the Western novel *The Virginian* (1902) but also the author of *Red Men and White* (1895), stories about battles between Native Americans and whites; and Richard Harding Davis (1864–1916), prolific and popular novelist and author of *Soldiers of Fortune* (1897), about a war in a fictitious South American country.
3. AB's scrapbooks of hundreds of reviews of *TSC* (mostly in newspapers) survive in VA and the Library of Congress.
4. Fictitious, but an allusion to Kipling's early editorial work for several papers in India, including the *Civil and Military Gazette* and the *Pioneer Mail.*
5. It is possible that AB is here referring to himself. He told of an episode during the Civil War in which he rode ahead of a Union column, in order to draw the Confederate fire. See "Prattle," *W,* no. 363 (14 July 1883): 5.

[ON "THE DAMNED THING"]

A person who, for aught I know, may represent a considerable class of readers fiercely accuses me of having, in a story entitled "The Damned Thing," plagiarized from a story by Fitz-James O'Brien entitled "What Was It?"[1] If I know anything of the unwritten laws of literature my accuser is as wrong in matter as in manner; anyhow I should not like to be thought unwilling to give all possible publicity to the charge. I will waive whatever advantage may accrue from affirming that in writing my story I did not even think of O'Brien's (for that I cannot prove) and proceed to point out what I deem essential differences in the sole incident upon which the charge is based. In O'Brien's story a man is attacked by, and overcomes, a supernatural and impossible being, invisible because transparent; in mine a man is attacked and killed by a wild animal that cannot be seen because, although opaque, like other animals, it is of an invisible color. The one story is devoid of basis in life or fact—though none the worse for that; the other is such a transcript from nature as no prior play of another's imagination can deprive one of the right to make. That there are colors invisible to the human eye is a fact attested by science; that there are animals and other things having them, wholly or in part, I have the strongest reasons to believe, and do believe. Indeed, my story was suggested by a rather disquieting personal experience while gunning. I am convinced that in daylight and on an open plain I stood in the immediate presence of a wild beast invisible to me but sufficiently conspicuous to my dog, and sufficiently formidable, to frighten it exceedingly.

"Invisible" is, of course, hardly the word to use of an opaque body, which must necessarily obscure, or blot out, its background, and, that being favorable, and the body at rest, reveal its outline to the eye. The color only is really invisible, but we have no word for the strange effect. In my story the obscuration of the animal's background is several times distinctly pointed out. In order that any curious reader may judge for himself I may add that my story appeared in the last Christmas number of the New York *Town Topics,* and that I wish it were as good as the tale with which it is ignorantly "paralleled."

If my critic were not, through his ignorance and ill-manners, so impossible a controversialist I should like to ask him this: Suppose I write a yarn about a lunatic or somnambulist with a stony stare and a long white robe, which may be a bedgown. Now *ghosts* of that sort have walked the ways of literature from the dawn of letters. Am I therefore a plagiarist? Nay, of the hundreds of authors who have used the lithoptic spook, noctivagant in a white habiliment, are all thieves but the long-dead and let us hope well-damned first? If not, *why* not? His conception was original and very striking; if the second man had no title to it, by what title is it held by the chap at the hither end of the long illustrious line? How frequently must a theft be committed before the thing stolen belongs to everybody? Not all these doubts are relevant to the case at bar; their purpose here is to show that questions raised by literary resemblances are not necessarily distinguished by that admirable simplicity which alone should commend them to the stamping critic

> endowed
> With a chest-note loud
> And a special kind of ear.[2]

If it is really desirable to charge me with plagiarism why does not some ingenious gentleman state that the title of my latest book of stories, "Can Such Things Be?"—published last autumn by the Cassell Publishing Co., New York—is identical with that of a romance by Mr. Keith Fleming, published by Geo. Routledge & Sons, London, in 1889?[3] When that accusation is definitively made in print by some one of sufficient note or civility to command consideration I may have something to say in explanation. In the mean time it strikes me as rather hard that my enemies are so ignorant or slothful that I am compelled to point out my own depravity. As Col. John P. Irish, P. O. 8,[4] is now enjoying a felicitous distinction as an authority in letters, I beg leave to invite his attention to the coat-tail that I am dragging within a pace of his toes.

From "Prattle," *E* (27 May 1894): 6.

NOTES

1. Fitz-James O'Brien (1828–62), "What Was It?" (*Harper's,* Mar. 1859; reprinted in O'Brien's *Stories and Poems* [1881] and many subsequent collections). O'Brien, born in Ireland but living in the United States since at least 1852, fought in the Civil War on the Federal side. He was wounded on 26 February 1862 and died on 6 October of that year.
2. Unidentified.

APPENDIX B

3. Keith Fleming, *"Can Such Things Be?"; or, The Weird of the Beresfords* (London: Routledge, 1889).
4. John P. Irish (1843–1923), editor of the *Oakland Times* and *Alta California*. "P. O. 8" refers to Charles E. Boles (1830?–1917), a stagecoach robber known as Black Bart, who sometimes left poems at the scene of his crimes signed "Black Bart, the Po-8 [poet]." See AB's poem, "'Black Bart, Po8'" (1888; *CW* 5.136–38). The printed text here reads "P. O. S.," an apparent error.

APPENDIX C

SUPPLEMENTARY TEXTS

Some of Bierce's writings balance on the fine line between tales and essays. Insofar as he uses fictional elements, or has obviously embellished with literary treatment an item that might have a kernel of fact, we have been inclined to include them here for the insights they might provide into his thought and art. "Before the Mirror" is the title we have offered for an otherwise untitled piece that first appeared in his column in *NL* (29 April 1871) and was subsequently reprinted in *FD* (1873). Despite its early date of composition it is unusually powerful and shocking, and despite its seemingly mocking tone it depicts a genuinely tragic situation that must have affected Bierce, for it was not his wont to ridicule true victims of nature, society, or circumstances.

"The Evolution of a Story" is intended as an essay on how *not* to write stories, but besides revealing something about Bierce's sense of structure, it also works as an amusing tale in its own right. Because Bierce wrote so many tales of the supernatural, it is well to know that he did not believe in ghosts. Toward the end of his career, he did suggest in a few late stories that there might be some legitimacy in paranormal phenomena, but the conditions for that legitimacy were closely circumscribed; he did not take seriously most reports of uncanny incidents or disappearances. "A Ghost in the Unmaking" and "The Clothing of Ghosts," two essays from his prime and his late periods, respectively, make his position clear.

Inasmuch as entire pieces in the subgenre of Future Historian predictions have been included in the main body of this edition, several paragraphs in the same subgenre are included in this section as "Annals of the Future Historian." The first dates to 1869, apparently marking the birth of the idea; the rest to the early twentieth century. The range of topics covered by this subgenre speaks to Bierce's fondness for its possibilities.

Bierce essentially stopped writing in 1909; "A Leaf Blown In from Days to Be" dating to 1910 appears to have been his last fictional venture. Additional stories of his may yet turn up; two stories in this collection are undated and unprovenanced items found as clippings in an archive. On the basis of internal evidence, it appears that they were written in the 1880s or 1890s, his best years. "An Untitled Tale" appears to have been printed in a newspaper and refers to itself in its original form as an "article," although it is clearly a narrative and a hoax. It is an accomplished work in its own right. "Alasper" is unfinished, but enough of it remains to establish it as an allegory.

TEXTS BY BIERCE

[BEFORE THE MIRROR]

A young woman stood before the mirror with a razor. Pensively she twirled the unaccustomed instrument in her jewelled fingers, fancying her smooth cheek clothed with a manly beard. In imagination she saw her pouting lips shaded by the curl of a dark moustache, and her eyes drew dim with tears that it was not, never could be, so. And the mirrored image wept back at her a silent sob, the echo of her grief.

"Ah," she sighed, "why did not God make me a man? Must I still drag out this hateful, whiskerless existence?"

The girlish tears welled up again and overran her eyes. Thoughtfully she crossed her right hand over to her left ear; carefully but timidly she placed the keen, cold edge of the steel against the smooth alabaster neck, twisted the fingers of her other hand into her long back hair, drew back her head and ripped away. There was an apparition in that mirror as of a ripe watermelon opening its mouth to address a public meeting; there were the thud and jar of a sudden sitting down; and when the old lady came in from frying doughnuts in the adjoining room she found something that seemed to interest her—something still and warm and wet—something kind of doubled up.

Ah! poor old wretch! your doughnuts shall sizzle and sputter and swim unheeded in their grease; but the beardless jaw that should have wagged filially to chew them is dropped in death; the stomach which they should have distended is crinkled and dry for ever!

From TC, *NL* 21, no. 13 (29 Apr. 1871): 9 (unsigned); **FD** 120–21.

THE EVOLUTION OF A STORY

On a calm evening in the early summer, a young girl stood leaning carelessly against a donkey at the top of Plum Hill, daintily but with considerable skill destroying a biscuit

1190

by mastication's artful aid. The sun had been for some time behind the sea, but the conscious West was still suffused with a faint ruddiness, like the reflection from an army of boiled lobsters marching below the horizon for a flank attack upon the stomach of Boston.

Slowly and silently the ruby legion held its way. Not a word was spoken; commands given by the general were passed from mouth to mouth, like a single bit of chewing gum amongst the seven children immortalized by Edward Bok,[1] who was more than usually active this evening, if that were possible.

And it was possible; in no spirit of bravado, but with firm reliance on the *blanc mange* he had eaten for dinner, and which was even now shaping itself into exquisite fancies in the laboratory of his genius, the great editor had resolved to reach a higher excellence, or perish in the attempt, as the tree frog, baffled by the smooth bark of the beech, falls exhausted into the spanning jaws of the serpent biding his time below.

Having swallowed the frog, the reptile turned to go away, and by a sinuous course soon reached the highway. Here he stood up and looked about him. There was no living thing in sight. To the right hand and the left the dusty white road stretched away without a break in its dreary, mathematical sameness. Beyond a belt of pines on the opposite side rose a barren, rounded hilltop, resembling the bald crown of a game keeper thrust upward from behind a hedge to offer a shining mark for the poacher.

Grimly the poacher raised and sighted his gun, charged with a double quantity of heavy slugs. There was a moment of silence—a silence so profound, so deathlike in its intensity, that a keen ear might have heard the spanking of an infant in a distant village.

This infant had come, no one knew whence. The story went that it had tramped into town one cold morning, with its cradle slung across its back, and after being refused admittance to the hotel, had gone quietly to the back door and lain down, having first written and pinned to its gown the following placard: "This unfortunate child is the natural son of a foreign prince, who until he shall succeed to the throne of his ancestors begs that the illustrious waif may be tenderly cared for. His Royal Highness cannot say how long his own worthless father may continue to disgrace the realm, but hopes not long. At the end of that time, his Royal Highness will appear to the child's astonished benefactor, crusted as thickly with gems as a toad with warts."

These troublesome excrescences had given the poor toad much pain. Everything that science had devised, and skill applied, had been a mere waste of money; and now at the age of four hundred years, with life just opening before him, with other toads reveling about him in all the jump-up-and-come-down-hardness of their hearts he was compelled to drag himself nervelessly through existence, with no more hope of happiness than a piano has of marriage.

It was not a nice piano; the keys were warped, the mainspring was relaxed, the cogwheels would not have anything to do with one another, and the pendulum would swing only one way. Altogether a disreputable and ridiculous old instrument. But such as it was, it had stood in that dim old attic, man and boy, for more than thirty years. Its very infirmities, by exciting pity, had preserved it; not one of the family would have laid an ax at the root of that piano for as much gold as could be drawn by a team of the strongest horses.

Of these rare and valuable animals we shall speak in our next chapter.

F 19 (24 Jan. 1874): 35 (as "A Novel"; unsigned); *W,* no. 241 (12 Mar. 1881): 170 (as "A Novel"; unsigned); *CW* 12.398–401.

NOTES

AB was a strong believer in logical reasoning and organization. This sketch underlines the perils, and thus ridicules the use, of chain-of-association as an organizing principle.

1. For Edward W. Bok see "Ashes of the Beacon," p. 1086 note 25. In earlier versions of the story, the text read "the poet" *(F)* and "Hector Stuart" *(W)*. Hector A. Stuart was a poetaster in San Francisco whom AB repeatedly lampooned.

A GHOST IN THE UNMAKING

Belief in ghosts is natural, general and comforting. In many minds it is cherished as a good working substitute for religion; in others it appears to take the place of morality. It is rather more convenient than either, for it may be disavowed and even reviled without exposing oneself to suspicion and reproach. As an intellectual conviction it is, in fact, not a very common phenomenon among people of thought and education; nevertheless the number of civilized and enlightened human beings who can pass through a graveyard at midnight without whistling is not notably greater than the number who are unable to whistle.

It may be noted here as a distinction with a difference that belief in ghosts is not the same thing as faith in them. Many men believe in the adversary of souls, but comparatively few, and they not among our best citizens, have any faith in him. Similarly, the belief in ghosts has reference only to their existence, not to their virtues. They are, indeed, commonly thought to harbor the most evil designs against the continuity of peaceful thoughts and the integrity of sleep. Their malevolence has in it a random and wanton quality which invests it with a peculiarly lively interest: there is no calculating upon whom it will fall: the just and the unjust alike are embraced in its baleful jurisdiction and subjected to the humiliating indignity of displaying the white feather. And this leads us directly back to the incident by which these remarks had the honor to be suggested.

A woman living near Sedalia, Missouri, who had recently been married alive to a widower, was passing along a "lonely road" which had been thoughtfully laid out near her residence. It was late in the evening, and the lady was, naturally, somewhat apprehensive in a land known to be infested by Missourians of the deepest dye. She was, therefore, not in a suitable frame of mind for an interview with an inhabitant of the other world, and it was with no slight trepidation that she suddenly discovered in the gloom a tall figure, clad all in white, standing silent and menacing in the road before her. She endeavored to fly, but terror fastened her feet to the earth; to shriek, but her lungs refused their office—the first time that an office was ever refused in that sovereign commonwealth. In short, to use a neat and graphic locution of the vicinity, she was utterly "guv out." The ghost was tremendously successful. Unluckily it could not hold its ghost of a tongue, and that spectral organ could accomplish feats of speech intelligible to ears still in the flesh. The apparition advanced upon its helpless victim and said in hollow accents: "I am the spirit of your husband's first wife: beware, beware!"

Nothing could have been more imprudent. The cowering lady effected a vertical attitude, grew tall and visibly expanded. Her terror gave place to an intrepidity of the most military character, and she moved at once to the attack. A moment later all that was mortal of that immortal part, divested of its funereal habiliments, hair, teeth and whatever was removable—battered, lacerated, gory and unconscious—lay by the road-side awaiting identification. When the husband arrived upon the scene with a horrible misgiving and a lantern, his worst fears were not realized; the grave had bravely held its own; the object by the roadside was what was left of his deceased wife's sister. On learning that her victim was not what she had incautiously represented herself to be, the victorious lady expressed the deepest regret.

Such incidents as this go far to account for that strong current of human testimony to the existence of ghosts, which Dr. Johnson found running through all the ages,[1] and at the same time throw a new and significant light upon Heine's suggestion that ghosts are as much afraid of us as we of them.[2] It would appear that some of the less judicious of them have pretty good reason.

E (25 Dec. 1887): 4 (unsigned; as "Concerning Ghosts"); *CW* **11.368–71**.

NOTES

1. James Boswell quotes Samuel Johnson as saying, "It is wonderful that five thousand years have now elapsed since the creation of the world, and still it is undecided whether or not there has ever been an instance of the spirit of any person appearing after death. All argument is against it; but all belief is for it." Boswell, *Life of Johnson* (1791), s.d. 3 Apr. 1778.
2. AB reports this comment frequently; cf. *DD*: "GHOST, *n*. . . . Accounting for the uncommon behavior of ghosts, Heine mentions somebody's ingenious theory to the effect that they are as much afraid of us as we are of them." The source of AB's information on this point has not been identified.

THE CLOTHING OF GHOSTS

Belief in ghosts and apparitions is general, almost universal; possibly it is shared by the ghosts themselves. We are told that this wide distribution of the faith and its persistence through the ages are powerful evidences of its truth. As to that, I do not remember to have heard the basis of that argument frankly stated; it can be nothing else than that whatever is generally and long believed is true, for of course there can be nothing in the particular belief under consideration making it peculiarly demonstrable by counting noses. The world has more Buddhists than Christians. Is Buddhism therefore the truer religion? Before the day of Galileo there was a general though not quite universal conviction that the earth was a motionless body, the sun passing around it daily. That was a matter in which "the united testimony of mankind" ought to have counted for more than it should in the matter of ghosts, for all can observe the earth and sun, but not many profess to see ghosts, and no one holds that the circumstances in which they are seen are favorable to the calm and critical observation. Ghosts are notoriously addicted to the habit of evasion; Heine says that is because they are afraid of us. "The united testimony of mankind" has a notable knack at establishing only one thing—the incredibility of the witnesses.

If the ghosts care to prove their existence as objective phenomena they are unfortunate in always discovering themselves to inaccurate observers, to say nothing of the bad luck of frightening them into fits. That the seers of ghosts are inaccurate observers, and therefore incredible witnesses, is clear from their own stories. Who ever heard of a naked ghost? The apparition always is said to present himself (as he certainly should) properly clothed, either "in his habit as he lived"[1] or in the apparel of the grave. Herein the witness must be at fault: whatever power of apparition after dissolution may inhere in mortal flesh and blood, we can hardly be expected to believe that cotton, silk, wool and linen have the same mysterious gift. If textile fabrics had that property they would sometimes manifest it independently, one would think—would "materialize" visibly without a ghost inside, a greatly simpler apparition than "the grin without the cat."

Ask any proponent of ghosts if he thinks that the products of the loom can "revisit the glimpses of the moon"[2] after they have duly decayed, or, while still with us, can show themselves in a place where they are not. If he have no suspicion, poor man, of the trap set for him, he will pronounce the thing impossible and absurd, thereby condemning himself out of his own mouth; for assuredly such powers in these material things are necessary to the garmenting of spooks.

Now, by the law *falsus in uno falsus in omnibus*[3] we are compelled to reject all the ghost stories that have ever been seriously told. If the observer (let him be credited with the best intentions) has observed so badly as to think he saw what he did not see, and could not have seen, in one particular, to what credence is he entitled with regard to another? His error in the matter of the "long white robe" or other garment where no long white robe or other garment could be puts him out of court altogether. Resurrection of woolen, linen, silk, fur, lace, feathers, hooks and eyes, hatpins and the like—well, really, that is going too far.

No, we draw the line at clothing. The materialized spook appealing to our senses for recognition of his ghostly character must authenticate himself otherwise than by familiar and remembered habiliments. He must be credentialed by nudity—and that regardless of temperature or who may happen to be present. Nay, it is to be feared that he must eschew his hair, as well as his habiliments, and "swim into our ken"[4] utterly bald; for the scientists tell us with becoming solemnity that hair is a purely vegetable growth and no essential part of us. If he deem these to be hard conditions he is at liberty to remain on his reservation and try to endow us with a terrifying sense of himself by other means.

In brief, the conditions under which the ghost must appear in order to command the faith of an enlightened world are so onerous that he may prefer to remain away—to the unspeakable impoverishment of letters and art.

NYA (3 May 1902): 8; *E* (8 May 1902):14; *CW* **9.117–20**.

NOTES

1. Shakespeare, *Hamlet,* 3.4.135.
2. Shakespeare, *Hamlet,* 1.4.52–53: "That thou, dead corse, again in complete steel, / Revisits thus the glimpses of the moon."
3. "False in one [thing], false in all."
4. Keats, "On First Looking into Chapman's Homer" (1816), l. 10: "When a new planet swims into his ken."

A SCREED OF THE FUTURE HISTORIAN

The year 1903, as the ancient Americans reckoned time, was a memorable one in the annals of that strange and unfortunate people. In the latter part of that year Señor Tomas Lupton, a famous Spanish pirate, inspired partly by revenge for the wrongs of his country and partly by greed of gain, sailed into the port of New York with a fleet of warships and attacked the American vessels lying at anchor there, each held by a sand hook of such enormous dimensions that the resulting engagement took its name from them. That inaccurate historian, Dumbleshaw, endeavors to show that he had made a previous attack of the same kind at the same place, but the evidence adduced is unworthy of attention. The result of the battle was disastrous to the Americans, and Señor Tomas sailed away with immense booty, including what was known as "America's Cup," an enormous flagon of pure gold, having a capacity of 907 smackims of Bourbon wine and supposed to symbolize the national supremacy in the matter of drink.

The calamity seems to have driven the losers wild. In the recriminations that ensued the army and navy, both severely blamed by the people, became involved, each accusing the other of delinquent courage and imperfect vigilance. The Secretary of War was compelled to retire from office and Admiral Langley, commanding a fleet on the lower Potomac, a confluent of the Mississoppy, drowned himself in the most spectacular manner while flying from his accusers.[1]

In an astonishingly brief time the dissension reached the dimensions of actual warfare between the army on one side and the navy on the other. The Democratic party, an organization of patriotic civilians, took up arms against both, while the Republicans and Sinners, an association of persons in authority, k[nowing that they were] outnumbered, retired to [. . .] fortified them with cann[on . . . de]clare themselves favorable [. . .] and the spoils.

During the dark of the [. . .] Atlantic squadron, consisting [. . .] of the line, commanded by [. . .] sailed out of Hohokus h[arbor[2] . . .] and moved upon Sportland [. . .] on the coast of the Stat[en Is]land. As soon as the mo[. . .]tected all the land forces [. . . Gen]eral Corbin[3] being ill, were [. . .] toward the same place. T[. . . Com]mander-in-Chief, General M[iles,[4] whom the] President had cast into p[rison . . .] with chains, was released [. . . and re]stored to power. Comma[nd . . . of re]serves was conferred upon [. . .] Smith (retired) and orders [. . .] if Admiral Schley,[5] a well-k[nown pirate of] the Spanish main, acting [. . .] should be taken no quarter [should be] given him. All these prep[arations were] made by the President, who [. . . dis]tinguished solder, naturally [. . .] army. Unfortunately his na[. . . de]scended to us.

The fighting was terrible! [In those bar]barous times human life [was so] cheap that historians of the [period kept] no record of the number s[lain. From] an ancient manuscript attr[ibuted to an] Ordnance Officer of the la[. . . we] learn that the consumption [of ammuni]tion was no less than 7,000 [. . .] gunpowder, and that the co[. . .] and shell expended on bo[. . .] 6,439 "orphannuals." (The [orphannual] as a unit of value appears to [belong to a] later date. It was the cost [of feeding] one orphan one year.) Th[e entire A]tlantic Squadron was totally [destroyed, and] the rest of the navy soon [surren]dered, excepting a fleet on [. . .] commanded by Rear-Admiral [. . .] illustrious warrior attempted [. . .] the island of Guam, but b[. . .] by the village schoolmaster, [. . .] vessels on the high seas, an[d . . . en]deavor to reach Japan afoot [. . . unfor]tunately drowned.

NYA (3 Sept. 1903): 16.

NOTES

All copies of *NYA* consulted for this piece were defective, so the editors have attempted to restore the text with reasonable conjectures (in brackets) wherever possible. The mutilated text ironically reinforces the impression AB was trying to project, of how imperfectly future historians may piece together current events from surviving scraps of records. In this case, the Future Historian misunderstood that Sir Thomas Lipton, the wealthy English tea merchant and yachting enthusiast, lost a sailing competition off Sandy Hook, New Jersey, for the America's Cup. The Historian then blended distorted fragments of records relating to other events into a confused narrative, and even erroneously believed the Potomac River to be a tributary of the Mississippi.

1. The secretary of war under McKinley and Theodore Roosevelt was Elihu Root (1899–1903); he resigned in August 1903 because of failing health and his wife's wishes. He was not well liked by AB, as evidenced by the quatrain "Elihu Root" (*CW* 4.361):

Stoop to a dirty trick or low misdeed?
What, bend him from his moral skies to it?
No, no, not he! To serve his nature's need
He may upon occasion rise to it.

"Admiral Langley" likely refers to Samuel Pierpont Langley (1834–1906), American aeronautics pioneer who built the first heavier-than-air flying machine to achieve sustained flight. AB wrote on several occasions about Langley's failed experiments; see the essay "The Man and the Bird," *NYA* (11 Dec. 1902): 14; *E* (27 Dec. 1902): 12.

2. Ho-Ho-Kus, N.J. (see "Ashes of the Beacon," p. 1086 note 28), is inland and has no harbor. AB is deliberately confusing it with Hoboken, N.J., then a major port in the New York city region.

3. Gen. Henry Clark Corbin (1842–1909), adjutant general of the U.S. army during the Spanish-American War.

4. Nelson Appleton Miles (1839–1925), a leading American soldier of the later nineteenth century, appointed by Grover Cleveland commanding general of the U.S. army. He later fell out with the administrations of the Republicans William McKinley and Theodore Roosevelt and was forced to retire in 1903.

5. Adm. Winfield Scott Schley (1839–1911) evoked controversy by an unusual naval maneuver during the blockade of Cuba in the Spanish-American War; the controversy over it lasted for years. AB generally took the side of his opponent, Adm. William T. Sampson, and wrote numerous lampoons of Schley—e.g., "The Unadmirable Admiral," *NYJ* (2 Aug. 1901): 12; *E* (6 Aug. 1901): 12.

[ANNALS OF THE FUTURE HISTORIAN]
[Anglo-Saxon Enlightenment]

The last official act of Mr. Gathorne Hardy[1] was to receive at the Home Office a deputation from the Church and State Defense Society. An address was presented to the right hon. gentleman, containing more than 350,000 signatures, with a request that he would lay it before her Majesty. This, Mr. Hardy promised to do.—*Court Journal.*

[NOTE BY A FUTURE HISTORIAN.—In the latter part of the year 1868 it was a common boast of the people then living, and especially of that race known as the Anglo-Saxon (this was anterior to the general fusion of races and nationalities) that theirs was an age of pre-eminent civilization and enlightenment. They kept repeating this over, parrot-like, after one another, until they finally came to believe it themselves. And yet the recent exhuming of certain ancient documents of the period puts it beyond the possibility of a doubt that there were at that time at least three hundred and fifty thousand persons in England alone who believed that a certain religion then existing should be supported by government. Truly these ancients needed light.

From TC, *NL*, 18, no. 51 (16 Jan. 1869): 9 (unsigned).

NOTE

1. Gathorne Gathorne-Hardy, first earl of Cranbrook (1814–1906), Home Secretary (1867–68) and a vigorous champion of the Church of England.

[The Fall of Christian Civilization]

"It is interesting to observe," wrote the Future Historian, his toes flying rapidly across his paper, "what an apparently trivial cause brought about the downfall of what is commonly known as the 'Christian civilization'—in reality its essential and characteristic feature was not Christianity, but the Pink Shirt. Many pious persons have professed to see in the extinction of the blood-thirsty heathens of that ancient regime a signal instance of divine justice. Certain it is that in their zeal to destroy one another they evolved a malefic agency which, directly and indirectly, destroyed them all; but whether or not that beneficent result was due to the will of Buddha it is not given to mortals to know. At a time shortly anterior to the reign of the first American Kings all the great pink-shirted nations began to experiment with smokeless and noiseless gunpowder. (Gunpowder was a liquid explosive which the ancients used in tubes to kill one another, as we, to destroy the irritating nightingale, use crystallized thunder.) In about three jowyows after they began their experiments they succeeded in making a gunpowder whose explosion was absolutely silent and invisible, and used it in 'war' with great satisfaction. But they very soon learned that it could be used in private assassination, and with almost perfect immunity from detection. Men and women began to fall dead in the streets, slain from behind window shutters, along highways bordered with bushes, in theatres and churches and all manner of public assemblies. Statesmen addressing Senates and demagogues haranguing the people would pitch forward and give up the ghost, the only thing they had ever been known to give up. By use of a short tube a villain could mingle in a crowd and slaughter a half-dozen victims without removing his hand from his pocket. Everywhere was sudden death; no one who had an enemy was safe, and the passion for killing wantonly so infected all classes, particularly the women, that eventually nobody dared go out of doors until necessity compelled. The courts were powerless. Not only could they seldom procure evidence to convict, but few judges lived to finish a trial. Finally all took to the woods, no one daring to meet another. Civilization is gregarious; isolation is barbarism. In two or three generations the world was a wilderness sparsely infested by naked savages, mostly cannibals and Republicans. And such was the state of affairs when our hardy forefathers alighted at Topeka."

From "The Passing Show," *NYJ* (18 Feb. 1900): 26; *E* (**18 Feb. 1900): 26.**

NOTE

This item discusses the invention of a smokeless and noiseless gunpowder. For further reflections on this theme see "The Dispersal."

[On the Canal]

Taking a new pen and placing it between the fifth and sixth toes of his left foot, according to the fashion of his time, the Future Historian wrote as follows:

During what were known as the "nineteenth" and "twentieth" centuries (for what reason is not now even conjectured) the middle part of our continent was inhabited by a people calling themselves Amorigans. They appear to have consisted of four great tribes: In the East the Smugwumps, in the North the Pewks, in the South the Coons, and in the West the Galoots.[1] The seat of government (Throne) was at Laundryton,[2] which is believed to have been situated at the confluence of the Jojuk and Gwap Rivers—then known as the Potstomach and Mishashippy. Here their national parliament met and for more than fifty years discussed nothing but the making of a canal through the Republic of Niggerawgua, which lay to the southward. Many parties of surveyors, engineers and statesmen were sent at enormous expense to select a route, survey it and estimate the cost of the canal. Several treaties were made with other nations that lived on the other side of the world and having no rights in the matter would make any treaty desired if it cost them nothing and gave them some share in the ownership. Dumbleshaw, an historian of the period, quoted in one of the sacred books of the prophet Mark Twain, says that a new treaty was negotiated every full moon and amended every foggy morning. At one time the disputes about the canal caused a great civil war in which the Coons were beaten by the Smugwumps and the Pewks, and which resulted incidentally in emancipation of all the mules in the country. Finally, during the early part of the "Twentieth" Century, while in both houses of the Potstomach parliament the dispute was at its hottest and no fewer than four commissions were in Niggerawgua re-examining the route, the French, who had long been working at a better place near by, completed their own canal, which was promptly seized by the British, who never permitted a competing one to be made nor an Amorigan to pass through that one. The site of it is not now known.

From "The Passing Show," *E* **(15 Apr. 1900): 27;** *NYJ* (16 Apr. 1900): 8 (as "Ambrose Bierce Says").

NOTES

This item is a satire on the long and seemingly fruitless discussions in Congress, extending back at least to the 1870s, over the viability of an isthmian canal linking the Atlantic and Pacific Oceans. AB supported the construction of a canal in Nicaragua (see "Ambrose Bierce Says: The Nicaragua Canal Is Not Yet Assured," *NYJ* [17 Jan. 1900]: 8). France had attempted in the 1880s to construct a canal in Panama, but the effort collapsed through bad planning and lack of funds. AB's remarks here were probably inspired by President William McKinley's appointment in 1899 of an Isthmian Canal Commission. U.S. work on the Panama Canal did not begin in earnest until 1904.

1. This geographical distinction corresponds roughly to that outlined in "For the Ahkoond."
2. A pun on *Washing*ton.

[The Minister's Death]

The Future Historian had been out all night dallying unwisely with the gin rickey of his period and was indisposed. He sat a long time at his work, evolving nothing worthy of his genius; then as the electrical whistle in a neighboring church pealed the hour of forty-nine his dead faculties revived and he wrote rapidly as follows:

It was a solemn and painful scene. The unhappy Minister had asked that he might die in his robes of state, and he was led to execution clad in the barbarous magnificence of his time, his country and his office. His appearance was in strong contrast with that of the President, who wore what one of the poets of the period has graphically if not now altogether intelligibly described as "a long-tailed coat all buttoned down before." As commander-in-chief of the American army he was attended by a glittering retinue, led by a dashing young officer of uncertain rank named Miles or Mills.[1] As the doomed Chinaman had committed no crime but that of incessant garrulity he was spared other indignity than the necessary binding of his hands, though the obvious suggestion had been made by a mean-spirited writer that a more appropriate and needful precaution would be the tying of his tongue. In his character of hostage the illustrious diplomat was accorded every immunity and mark of respect that was consistent with the right of the populace to pelt him with stones and the duty of the soldiers to shoot him.

At this point the narrative inaccountably merged into a subtle dissertation on what was once known as "international law," but is now ascertained to have been the fantastic invention of a lunatic, the discredit of whose birth is now disclaimed by seven cities.[2] This dissertation now fills seven octavo volumes. The narrative of the execution was then resumed in too horrible detail to be repeated here. It concluded as follows:

As the troops and people marched past the mangled body they seem to have experienced a revulsion of feeling. Many who had known the unfortunate man in life and had won money from him at a game of chance called poker, even some of those who had thrown stones at him as he went to his death turned away their heads and sighed heavily. The President himself was visibly affected. His retinue glittered sympathetically and the dashing young officer mentioned as its commander stood gloomily apart, silently dashing, in profound dejection. Thus perished, in atonement for the crimes of his government and people, an illustrious man and beloved servant of the Daughter of Heaven. The City of Washington is no more. Its site is unknown. The people of whose ancestors it was the capital are naked savages without a tribal designation. But history has forever embalmed the name and fame of Wu Ting Fang, inventor and expounder of the State of Peace attended with Appalling Casualties.

From "The Passing Show," *NYJ* (1 July 1900): 34; *E* **(1 July 1900): 14**.

NOTES

This item deals with Wu Ting Fang, Chinese minister to the United States, who in late June 1900 had asked the United States for an armistice during the Boxer Rebellion. (U.S. troops had been sent to China to protect American missionaries and other foreigners from attacks by the Chinese.) AB had recommended that Wu himself be held hostage until the Americans' safety was assured. See "Ambrose Bierce Says: We Should Hold Wu Ting Fang as a Hostage," *NYJ* (21 June 1900): 8; *E* (23 June 1900): 6 (as "We Should Hold Minister Wu Ting Fang as a Hostage").

1. A reference to Gen. Nelson Appleton Miles (1839–1925), who since 1895 had been commander-in-chief of the U.S. army. In July 1900 (after AB wrote this story), Miles

requested permission to lead a large force of troops to China to raise the Boxers' siege of Peking, but Secretary of War Elihu Root sent a smaller force as part of the International Relief Force, which lifted the siege in August.

2. See "John Smith, Liberator," p. 165 note 4.

[The Republic of Panama]

"In the month of February of the year 1904, as for some reason not now understood the Americans reckoned time," wrote the Future Historian, "the Senate passed the last of a series of resolutions commanding the President to transmit to that august body forthwith all the information remaining in his possession relating to the rise of the new republic of Panama and his recognition of it as a treaty-making power. It was commonly believed that the secession of this Colombian province and its erection into an independent State had been brought about by an unlawful conspiracy in which he was deeply involved, if not the actual instigator. The resolution, drawn in the most peremptory terms, passed with only three dissenting votes—those of Senators Hoar, Morgan and Gorman[1]—and was at once sent by a special messenger to the White Palace, the Senate refusing to adjourn until a reply should be received. After a wait of two hours, during which the excited populace poured into the galleries, thronged the corridors of the entire Capitol and swarmed in immeasurable multitudes about the statue of Adam, near the east front, the messenger returned and delivered the President's reply. The seals were broken in profound silence and the message read. To the amazement of both Senate and people it was found to consist of only three words—'I will not!' Of the momentous events that ensu. . . . . . ." Here the Future Historian, overcome by the magnitude of his subject, broke off and took to his bed. Alas, that so brilliant a narrative must remain forever incomplete—that so stupendous events must belong eternally to the realm of conjecture!

From "The Passing Show," *NYA* (7 Feb. 1904): 24; *E* **(21 Feb. 1904): 44**.

NOTES

This extract deals again with the Panama Canal, although the situation surrounding the canal was now very different. As a result of Colombia's rejection of the Hay-Pauncefote Treaty, in which Great Britain yielded its interests in a Panama canal to the United States, revolutionaries in Panama (then a Colombian colony) rose in rebellion, declaring independence on 3 November 1903. The rebellion was covertly aided by the United States, which recognized the new state on 6 November. On 18 November the Hay-Bunau-Varilla Treaty was negotiated, giving the United States full control of a ten-mile canal zone. The treaty was formally ratified on 26 February 1904.

1. George Frisbie Hoar (1826–1904), senator (Republican) from Massachusetts (1877–1904); John Tyler Morgan (1824–1907), senator (Democrat) from Alabama (1877–1907); Arthur Pue Gorman (1837–1906), senator (Democrat) from Maryland (1881–99, 1903–6).

[The Second American Invasion of China]

Following is an extract from "The Second American Invasion of China," by the Future Historian:

"To what extent the disasters to the American arms in the bloody campaign of 1907 were justly attributable to the general staff of the army may never accurately be known. The severest critic of the general staff was Senator Hale of Maine, who at all times and with considerable eloquence bitterly averred a criminal lack of foresight and preparation. Hostilities, he declared, had been obviously inevitable for many months before the dispatch of the army of invasion on its punitive mission, yet no proper study of the theatre of war had been made and no systematic and coherent plan of operation devised. So violent were this great statesman's denunciations of the general staff for apathy and procrastination, that he was put in irons and removed from the Senate chamber to an asylum for the insane, where he rose to great eminence."

From "The Views of One," *NYA* (12 Mar. 1906): 16; *E* **(17 Mar. 1906): 20.**

NOTE

This item deals with the possibility of a conflict between the United States and China. In mid-February 1906, the War Department was contemplating sending troops to the Philippines as part of a plan to invade the Chinese mainland during the summer in order to forestall an uprising of Chinese natives against the many Americans and other foreigners in the country. The plan was vigorously opposed by Eugene Hale (1836–1918), U.S. senator from Maine (1881–1911), who, although a Republican, had repeatedly condemned the military actions of the McKinley and Roosevelt administrations, including the Spanish-American War and the Philippine War. AB's reference to a "second" invasion of China alludes to the Boxer Rebellion of 1900, in which the United States and several European nations sent troops to quell a nationalist uprising in China.

AN UNTITLED TALE

As I have never talked with any one on the subject-matter of this story, nor in my small reading come upon anything treating of it in such a way as to enlighten my ignorance, I do not know if the experiences—to call them so—that I am about to relate are, in their nature, individual or general. It seems to me more probable that what occurs in my own intellectual area—and conceptions of the kind herein to be described with such lucidity as my unpracticed pen may be able to achieve are, I take it, a kind of events—occurs equally in the mental domain of another. If so, it may afford the reader a momentary gratification to recognize some of his own familiar experiences of the mind; if not, my report may be acceptable because of the novelty of what is reported. In any case I hope he will have the civility to read to the end, for it is disagreeable to me to think that for lack of knowledge how to impart my thoughts in the best way, I may fail of persuading him that they are worth imparting; for as Scaliger[1] justly remarks, he that will take what we wish to give may do with it afterward what he will, but for him who will not accept there is no forgiveness, even though he had no need.

I must tell you, then, that it not infrequently happens that abruptly in the midst of whatever occupation I am engaged in, and altogether without warning, my entire actual environment—fields, woods, houses, hills, the sea—men, women and beasts—the room in which I am sitting, the shop on whose deck I stand, the horse I ride—everything seems to shift with an awful, visible motion toward my left. I cannot describe to you the horror of this phenomenon—a horror that is rather augmented than softened by repetition. It is as if the earth, struck by some greater orb, had been urged by the monstrous impact and was flying from beneath my feet to leave me helpless and forgotten in space. Then ensues an interval of darkness—perhaps unconsciousness; I cannot say—accompanied by a low and not unmusical humming—in what direction it is impossible to know; and this gradually increases in volume, giving a sense of approach. As it grows louder I note with alarm the recurrence of an occasional emphasis—a periodical *thickening* of the sound, if I may say so—a slow, muffled throbbing, like the thunder of great guns at a distance, heard through the song of the sea: the pulse of a fevered world. As the murmur rises to a roar these great pulsations increase in definition, loudness and rapidity until they swallow up all other sound and become inconceivably terrifying. I have a feeling that this dreadful noise, in which a drum-roll of thunder-claps would be unheard, is sentient: it is an intelligence, but pitiless and deaf to supplication. The thought, indeed, of propitiating this vast malevolence never occurs to me: I would be as likely to beseech an approaching planet, whose visibly expanding sphere already had filled half the sky. This hideous uproar is a being—a something ranging through chaos with a fell purpose, the nature of which none may divine. It has its will of the universe, if universe remain. In the presence of this soulless and unspeakable Thing—abandoned, cut off and exposed for annihilation—forgotten of God and the angels—my beautiful green earth with all its load of life gone I know not whither, and none knowing of my plight, terror at last gives way to self-pity and I lament my melancholy fate with sobs and tears. Suddenly falls a dead silence—a silence which seems to smite me, and I shriek from the shock.

I am now conscious of a faint and inconceivably distant light, which, without approaching, grows from a mere luminous point to a broad and gracious resplendence pervading and suffusing—what?

I am trying to relate these events as they commonly occur; sometimes there is a variation, but in the main the foregoing is as plain and intelligible an account as I am able to give up to this point. Here I must beg the reader's indulgence. The place in which I find myself when this revealing light is full and perfect, the objects by which I am surrounded, their changes and activities—all this I must pass over, for it is all nameless in any human tongue. Nothing that anywhere meets the eye has its type or likeness in our real world—if, indeed, our world is real. Not even in dreams has mortal man ever seen such shapes or heard such sounds as now ensue. For dreams are but

APPENDIX C

torn scraps of memories, fortuitously placed together in a patternless design by the blind workman Chance; but of such things as these the memory has no store. I can only say that here, at this stage of my unwilling journey into the Unknown, are things unthinkable and forbidden to be.

As they are themselves, so is their effect upon the mind: indescribable. They inspire me with the most intense and vivid emotions, which even in recalling I again experience, but for which I can find no names to describe and no language to impart. Neither love, nor hate, nor hope, nor fear, nor grief, nor joy, nor any feeling that is known to my normal consciousness do I experience in that unfamiliar world; yet its phenomena so powerfully affect me that I do not know if I have ever been so moved by anything in this actual world. As they develop successively before my discernment—for nothing there occurs simultaneously—my feelings overcome me. I call aloud and run about with waving arms till I fall from exhaustion.

The light grows dim and shrinks to a shining point; the darkness comes and with it the poignant silence, and I shriek. Again, with the suddenness of its cessation, the monstrous uproar begins, and as I lament my unhappy fate exposed to its pitiless malevolence it dies away to a pleasant murmur and ceases. Then dawns another light—the light of the blessed sun—and back from the invisible, with a mighty motion from left to right, swings into view that earthly scene which had shifted from before my eyes. In short, I return to my own world by the same route that I took in leaving it, passing through the same stages of pain, sorrow and terror.

Conceiving that the subjection to these awful experiences is a common inheritance of woe—though doubtless the experiences themselves are widely various, and no two have the same—I have thought it well to solicit hereby a comparison of notes, so to speak, and hope that others may relate their stories with as great particularity as I have done, and with a better skill in the use of the pen.

With a view to better light upon these obscure mental phenomena, I venture to submit the following evidence as to their duration, in my own case. On one occasion, when they had been recurring with unusual frequency and vividness, I was in conversation with the Superintendent, whom it pleases, good man, to take a friendly interest in me and my affairs.

"Where," said he, "did you procure the—"

At that instant the blank wall of my apartment, the floor at its base, my furniture and the Superintendent himself, made a great lurch to the left and vanished. The other frightful incidents ensued; I visited again the unthinkable world, and again returned to this—or rather it returned to me. The Superintendent had not left me; he looked at me gravely and said: "Dope."

A long time must have elapsed for his mind to have strayed so far from the question which he had been about to ask me.

Unidentified newspaper clipping (BL), revised by AB.

NOTES

This story shows signs of having been written during AB's prime years, the 1880s or early 1890s. It is playful, clearly in the tradition of Poe, and a hoax. As often occurs in Poe's stories, and frequently in AB's, the narrator seems cultured and sensitive, but is seriously unreliable. Not until the very end, when he mentions the superintendent, is it apparent that the narrator is probably in a mental institution. He does not realize that the interruption in the superintendent's question, which he believes is a long, involved, and sensational event on a cosmic scale, takes no more time than the normal pause between one word and another, and does not even break the question, which is where he got his dope. Readers, therefore, are unlikely to realize until the last two sentences that they have been tricked into taking seriously the bizarre hallucinations of someone, possibly a drug addict, who is institutionalized.

1. AB probably refers to Joseph Justus Scaliger (1540–1609), the greatest classical scholar of the later sixteenth century, although his father, Julius Caesar Scaliger (1484–1558), was also a well-known scholar. The quotation has not been identified. Cf. "A Correction," *F* (11 July 1874): 17: "as Scaliger has remarked, the joy of penitence is embittered by the grief of restitution."

ALASPER

Alasper was the son of humble and pious parents in the little village of   on the great plains of   . There all Alasper[']s forefathers had dwelt since the creation [of] the world[,] as was attested by many a headstone in the village burial ground, upon which their names could be scarcely deciphered; and that was true of all the inhabitants of   . Their only knowledge of other places came from the lips of merchants[,] camel drivers and pilgrims of the faith; and these were few and taciturn. The good people of   were the wisest of mankind; they loved their gods and in the service of the temple and the celebration of their simple religious festivals found abundant satisfaction of the higher needs to which their daily toil did not minister. "Blessed is the man," they said, for so their good priests had taught them, "who is content with what the gods bestow nor seeks by the wickedness of travel to enlarge his possessions and contract his mind." The gods heard and repaid their piety a harvest every year.

But Alasper was different. He loved his parents and his brothers and sisters but for his forefathers and his neighbors he cared little. Their faith he shared but their wisdom had no place in his mind and heart. He longed to see the world that lay a day's journey beyond the Hills of the Setting Sun and which was many a day[']s journey in breadth[,] embracing the City of Gold of which a garrulous camel driver had told him. The camel driver had himself seen it from afar[,] its domes and minarets glittering in the sky. In that city dwelt great kings and queens clad in garments purple and white and so rich they were that they had elephants to ride on and the elephants themselves wore jewels. In that city none toiled but passed their lives in feasting and song and dancing to the music of instruments. None who entered it ever returned—why should they?

So [with?] the City of Gold ever in mind Alasper fell into dejection utterly because he knew not in what direction it lay nor how [far?] away it was. Moreover there was his duty to his father and brothers for his father was old and his brothers were young. Without his own strong hands the ancestral field would be tilled in a way to displease the gods who would punish with a niggard harvest. Yet his discontent would not leave him. By day he could think coherently of nothing but the City of Gold and by night it blazed and sparkled in his dreams. (contrast)[1] He grew moody and morose[,] performed his daily toil with a heedless hand[,] shunned his brothers and friends and absented himself from the even song when _____[2] made melodious profession of its gratitude to the god of the harvest. And at last with no word of farewell he set out with staff and scrip in quest of the City of Gold.

Crossing the Hills of the Setting sun [*sic*] he held his way to-West with a stout heart, and at the close of day found himself in an unfamiliar land which he doubted not lay well forward toward the center of the world. Some familiar berries supplied him with a sufficient meal and lying down beside a rock warmed by the sun he slept away the night too weary for dreams. <He was roused by a touch upon his forehead and sprang to his feet in alarm. The sun>[3]

AMS (BL).

NOTES

Another undated tale, this ambitious but unfinished story also suggests composition during AB's prime years. Bearing some resemblance in style to "Haïta the Shepherd," it seems to be an allegory along the line of Samuel Johnson's *The History of Rasselas, Prince of Abyssinia* (1759). In that story, an unhappy prince escapes the Happy Valley, where every wish is gratified, in order to learn about the world. In this, a youth leaves his happy home for the City of Gold, where everyone feasted and made merry, and none toiled. Anyone who has read much of AB can be confident that in what followed Alasper would experience deception.

1. The significance of this word (inserted into the text with a caret) is unclear.
2. The underscore is AB's, presumably indicating that he had not decided upon the name of the fictitious village that serves as the setting of the tale (see the first sentence of the text for a similar gap).
3. The sentence in carets has been crossed out in the text. It appears at the very end of the last page of the manuscript. Presumably AB wrote at least another sheet of text, but perhaps decided to omit it and resume the text at this point, but never did so.

TEXTS BY OTHERS

One of the most fascinating conjectures about Bierce's stories is where he got the ideas for them. Many of them do have some basis in his personal experience but only recently has evidence surfaced that the stories of others might have constituted the seed of at least a few of his tales. Two such tales are reprinted here because of their difficulty of access. "The Fortune of War," a reprinted anecdote in *E* (23 October 1887), preceded "The Affair at Coulter's Notch" by two full years. The similarity of the two plots is so great that it is difficult to believe it accidental.

"A Strange Adventure," by W. C. Morrow, a San Francisco author of short stories and a personal friend of Bierce, appeared in *Wa* on 7 March 1891, but was datelined 1 March. On 15 March, Bierce published his lighthearted romance "An Heiress from Redhorse" (later retitled "A Lady from Redhorse") in *E*. Both stories deal with mistaken identities, take place in seaside hotels, and feature beautiful and impressionable young ladies who fall hopelessly in love with handsome and somewhat mysterious men with personalities that were awesome yet attractive. Again, it is difficult to believe that the points of similarity and the closeness of dates are only accidental. Just as Morrow's story good-naturedly ribs Bierce, "An Heiress from Redhorse" appears to have been the prompt response in kind it inspired, wryly countering Morrow's plot with a variation: when the heiress learns that the "divinity" she worships is only a human after all, she remains in love with him. Inasmuch as "An Heiress from Redhorse" seems so unlike most of Bierce's other stories, "A Strange Adventure" is valuable not only for evoking that charming tale, but also for supplying the occasion to reveal that Bierce could enjoy a joke and had a side that was light, gentle, and humorous.

THE FORTUNE OF WAR

How a French Gunner Was Made to Wreck His Home.
[Youth's Companion.]

The story is told in a French newspaper of Pierre Barlat, an humble laborer, who lived at Sevres, near Paris, with his wife Jeanne and their three children. Industrious, frugal, knowing nothing of the wine shop, Pierre saved his spare money, working harder and harder, and at last bought the tiny cottage in which he and his wife lived. It was a tiny cottage indeed; built of stones, however, with tiled roof, standing amidst shrubs and covered with clematis, it always attracted the eye of the traveler on the left as he crossed the Sevres bridge. Pierre and Jeanne scrimped and saved until the little cottage was paid for, and made a feast when it was all done to celebrate their ownership. A landed proprietor, to be sure, does not mind an occasional expenditure to entertain his friends.

All this Pierre and Jeanne had accomplished just before the war of 1870 with Germany broke out. The conscription fell upon Pierre, who, moreover, was an old soldier and belonged to the reserves. A gunner he had been, famous for his skill in hitting a mark with a shell.

Sevres had fallen into the hands of the Germans, but the French guns were pounding away at them from the fort on Mont Valerien. Pierre Barlat was a gunner at that fort, and was standing one wintry day by his gun, when General Noel, the commander, came up and leveled his field-glass at the Sevres bridge.

"Gunner!" said he sharply, without looking at Pierre.

"General?" said Pierre, respectfully, giving the military salute.

"Do you see the Sevres bridge over there?"

"I see it very well, sir."

"And that little shanty there, in a thicket of shrubs, at the left."

"I see it, sir," said Pierre, turning pale.

"It's a nest of Prussians. Try it with a shell, my man."

Pierre turned paler still, and, in spite of the cold wind that made the officers shiver in their great coats, one might have seen big drops of sweat standing on his forehead; but nobody noticed the gunner's emotion. He sighted his piece deliberately, carefully—then fired it.

The officers, with their glasses, marked the effect of the shot after the smoke had cleared away.

"Well hit, my man! well hit!" exclaimed the General, looking at Pierre, with a smile. "The cottage couldn't have been very solid. It is completely smashed now."

He was surprised to see a great tear running down each of the gunner's checks.

"What's the matter, man?" the General asked rather roughly.

"Pardon me, General," said Pierre, recovering himself. "It was my house; everything I had in the world!"

E (23 Oct. 1887): 9.

APPENDIX C

A STRANGE ADVENTURE
by W. C. Morrow

(As Mr. Ambrose Bierce has suffered much annoyance lately from rumors connecting him with a certain peculiar happening of which I have full knowledge, he has urged me to publish the facts. This I finally have consented to do, but it is only a strong sense of justice to him that impels me to thrust my personal affairs on the public; and as for the extraordinary light in which this relation may place me, I fear nothing from the opinion of my friends, and am not concerned with that of strangers.)

———

Not long ago I met Mr. Bierce on the street and asked him to go with me to the Cliff House.[1] He assented. We took a car, and at the terminus of the cable we seated ourselves in one of the open cars of the steam road. Facing us, two or three seats away, were two women, evidently mother and daughter, both well-dressed and in appearance ladylike. The younger woman was an exceedingly pretty girl of about nineteen years. She was a brunette, with an uncontrollable mass of black hair, splendid black eyes, rosy cheeks, a delicious mouth, and a tempting neck, the better displayed by a collarless gown. She was dressed in black, and wore a very handsome broad-brimmed black hat with rich ostrich feathers. Her sealskin coat was open. We could not help noticing so beautiful, healthy and radiant a creature, in whom all the very richest treasures of feminine youth were entrancingly invested, but she did not deign even to look at us.

We were soon talking, almost forgetting the radiant Presence; but, suddenly, we became aware that they were talking about us, that is to say, they were using our names with perfect freedom, and yet were not regarding us at all. Without being conscious of our rudeness, we ceased talking for a moment, and listened. The two women handled our names pretty freely, but we did not clearly hear their remarks. I had an idea that they were saying uncomplimentary things about us. I am very certain that the mother said something savage about Bierce.

We had not noticed a man sitting near; but at once, while the ladies were talking and we were unconsciously listening, he attracted our attention by his uneasy manner. Then, as the train halted at a station, and the words of our judges became distinct, he evidently could control his impatience no longer, for he crossed over to the ladies, and, bending over them, whispered something to them. Both were shocked with surprise, and both looked quickly at us, the elder woman paling a little, the younger blushing crimson. It was clear that the man had told them we were the persons whom they were discussing. They remained in silent embarrassment some time, and we, pretending to have noticed nothing, enjoyed the little comedy.

Before the train arrived at the final station a curious thing happened. I chanced to look at the girl, and discovered her gazing steadily at me, a queer expression on her face. Her eyes dropped upon encountering my glance, and her face became rosy. This was both puzzling and interesting. After a time I found her again regarding me steadily, but this time she had more courage, and she held her ground. Her look was so direct and intent that it embarrassed me, and it was my turn to be looked out of countenance. Evidently this was fine entertainment for the girl.

The train stopped, and Bierce and I walked down to the Cliff House, the ladies following. We went upon the upper veranda and sat down to enjoy the breeze and the wide ocean and the ships with their sails of cream or gray color and their tall masts leaning from the wind. It was a noble, luxurious day. The seals floundered awkwardly on the rocks; and small rainbows, quickly vanishing, tipped the white spray with a band of soft color.

I hardly know why it is that I was not surprised when the two ladies also came upon the veranda and sat down, not far from us, to enjoy the matchless charms of the ocean. None other was present. The girl was seated in such a way that she faced me, Bierce having his back toward her. Soon again my glance encountered that look of hers that might have meant so much to many another man. I will not say what I thought it meant to me; but certain it is that it filled me with a strange sensation of disquiet and longing, and made me wonder at the cause of this throwing open of a gate of paradise. It is at such times that a man feels within him a heavy tugging at the bonds with which conventionality binds us all. My sensations were painful but delicious; and through the darkness which fell upon me, shone the heavenly light of two beautiful liquid eyes that flashed both a challenge and an invitation.

Did Bierce notice that there was anything wrong with me? Certainly I tried not to let him see it. I know now that I must have bored him with remarks about little Johnny, and Misses Doppy (wich has the red hed), and the rascal old old uncle (wich had been in Injy and everywhere) and Bildad (that's the new dog),[2] and the Devil's Dictionary, and the whimsical nonsense of Dod Grile, and the fables, and My Favorite Murder, and things like that.

My senses became more and more turbulent, for there was riot within me. My heart went at a furious pace, and the breakers sounded dull and distant. I called myself a fool, a fool, a fool, a staring madman. Was the big world become so small that there was room in it for but two? Was the light of the sun so waned that it dimmed in the effulgence that swept from two matchless eyes? Had not my heart more sober work to do than run a mad race with the devil? But I was torn all at large from my old anchorage in common sense, and the waves dashed not more madly on the rocks than did I on my ruthless environment.

I hardly know how it all happened, but before I understood it the Radiance had arisen, and, behind her mother's chair, had made a sign that might have meant nothing, that might have meant everything; but a slight returning sign from me, given wholly without volition, brought a flush into the winsome face, and then a strange look of fright and a painful pallor. She said something to her mother, and left the place.

Soon afterward one of the waiters, having a quizzical look and a peculiar smile on his face, came out, and in tones loud enough for us to hear, said that the young lady had just been taken into the carriage of some passing friends, and had gone to the city, and hoped her mother would overlook the unceremonious departure and go home without her. The elderly woman looked a little surprised and more annoyed, but without long delay she left, and Bierce and I were alone on the veranda.

Am I expected to confess all my meanness? Well, perhaps, after all, Bierce might be willing to go back to the city without me. But I am always so slow and stupid, and then, I had invited him to come with me to this place! If I had not been so blind and raging I might have seen a queer look in his face. The irksomeness of the situation became unbearable. Finally Bierce, with that queer look, half annoyance and half mischief, remarked:

"Shall we go? I have an appointment for twelve o'clock, and it is now twenty minutes past eleven."

"Really," I replied, trying to yawn and look drowsy, "It is so delightful out here that I feel an almost irresistible inclination to lie down and sleep."

"Then stay, by all means," he said; and he added with hardly discernible irony, "I trust you will have pleasant dreams." With that he went away.

I wish I could close this painful narrative here where he steps out of sight, but ah, me! his ghost hovers about to the end.

The waiter with the quizzical look—how sharp these scoundrels become—came to me and insinuatingly asked:

"Is there anything you wish, sir?"

I got to my feet again, slipped some money into his prehensile claws, and bade him clear out and not let me see him again. Then with a great show of indifference I sauntered to the parlors, and the wild riot within me increased; hot flames swept over me; fear, eagerness, madness, stirred me to the profoundest depths. No longer had the gentle spicy wind from far Japan a sweetness for me, and the sound of the rumbling breakers was lost.

I entered the main parlor; it was empty. The portières of the little stalls were looped back in decorous fashion—with one exception. To that one I went, and my heart bounded with an activity that was near to strangling me. I arrived at the portière and thrust it aside. Standing there, her wrap thrown aside, was the matchless Radiance of the train and the veranda, waiting for me! Every outline of her fine, dainty figure stood out clearly in the light of the window behind her. A tremulous vibration pervaded her form. Her ripe lips were apart and the intense light which shone from her eyes accentuated the unnatural pallor of her face.

"Well," she gasped, breathlessly, "say that you think I am a bold, shameless, girl!"

"No," I replied; "I see only that you are incomparably beautiful and winsome."

"But this is such an awful thing to do, and you will despise me!"

"Matchless loveliness can make its own laws," I said.

I had dropped the portière behind me. She came quite close to me, and, looking up into my face, all earnestness and timidity and fear, and trembling in every member, she said:

"Ah, but you *will* despise me hereafter—you, the man above all others in the world whose respect and affection I would prize most highly. The mere sound of your voice is the sweetest music in the world to me. I believe there was a holy guidance that brought me face to face with you here—that made me throw aside the modesty of womanhood and dare to bring you here, close to me—close to me, standing here alone with me, looking down into my eyes, holding my hand and filling all my soul with gladness. Here alone with poor ignorant *me*. Think of it! A man of genius, whom people quote, and whom they fear as the Evil One, standing here alone with poor insignificant *me,* and deigning to listen to me! Oh, what a moment is this! You will not despise me, will you? I wanted to have you here alone with me a moment and hear you speak to me, and then I will go and feast on the memory of it all my days. What if women do scold when you rail at them? Even your sneers are precious to me."

"I rail at women? Why—"

"I read everything you publish," she resumed, with the same breathless eagerness. "Oh, the terrible stories yon write, that keep me awake and make me afraid when I am alone! What a master mind to do these things! I have worshiped you so long from a great distance, and you didn't know even that such an insignificant thing as I am existed at all. Now, you will despise me for saying I have worshiped you, but I can't help it; it is the truth. And when your writings don't terrify me they make me laugh. What a funny old man Uncle Ned is, and then there's Misses Doppy, and—"

"Heavens! what—"

"And now," she resumed, with increased excitement, "the supreme happiness of my life has come and I could lie down now and die content; for have I not at last taken Ambrose Bierce to my heart?"

God forgive me! Before I could move a finger the poor girl had thrown her arms around my neck, clasped me close to her breast and pressed her lips to mine.

SAN FRANCISCO, March 1.

Wa 6, no. 44 (7 Mar. 1891): 13.

NOTES

1. See "L. S.," p. 88 note 4.
2. These are characters in AB's "Little Johnny" sketches. Morrow imitates the fractured English of the sketches.

SELECTED TEXTUAL VARIANTS

ABBREVIATIONS

Co   *Cosmopolitan*
CW   *Collected Works* (1909–12)
E   *San Francisco Examiner*
H   AB's MS copy of *CW* 2, 3, 8 (Huntington Library)
I   *In the Midst of Life* (1898)
N   *New York Journal*
U   unidentified newspaper clipping

THE GREAT STRIKE OF 1895

899.1	1895.] 1899. *E*
899.3	last year] 1891 *E*
899.5	hourly.] daily. *E*
899.6	non-union] scab *E*
899.18	non-union] scab *E*
900.11	non-union] scab *E*
900.16	The Mayor] Mayor Eugene Field *E*
900.17	say] ~ (with how much truth is not known) *E*
900.18–19	He . . . Snow."] *om. E*
900.29	independence] liberty *E*
900.33	strike-breaking] scab *E*
901.2	leave] "hegirate" from *E*
	metropolis.] ~.¶ *E*
901.4	strike-breaker] scab *E*
901.9	*Fadder.* ¶] ~.¶ *E*
901.10	Pinkerton spy] scab *E*

901.17	at one time.] in one place. *E*
901.23	Brander] *om. E*
901.27	line.] ~.¶ *E*
901.33	fire.] ~.¶ *E*
902.6	go . . . stage.] start on a lecturing tour. *E*

THE EYES OF THE PANTHER

905.2	ONE . . . INSANE] *om. E*
905.3	Nature] nature *E, I, CW* [cf. 906.38]
906.37	a] two *E, I*
908.1	one] *om. E*
909.10	pressed] passed *E*
909.20	will. ¶] ~.^ *E*
909.34	hand. ¶] ~.^ *E*
910.34	shining eyes!] gleaming eyes. *E*; shining eyes. *I*
911.25	Presently] Suddenly *E, I*
911.26–27	terrible!] horrible! *E, I*
911.30	had been able.] could. *E*
911.31	shining] glowing *E*
912.7	sorrow-seamed] seamed *E, I*

AN AFFAIR OF OUTPOSTS

913.4	war] civil war *E*
913.26	something . . . sleeve] '~ . . . ~' *E, I*
914.5–6	is a . . . way,"] are . . . ways," *E, I*
914.7	do that] commit suicide *E, I*
914.28	said.] ~; "I don't like it." *E, I*
914.32	of her own sins] *om. E, I*
	men] rakes *E*
915.23	them away] away the guns *E*
916.9	streaked] freaked *E*
916.18	his face] he *E, I*
917.3–4	skirmishers,] entire surviving skirmishing line, *E*
917.15	inly] *E, I*; only *CW*
917.28	his] ~ own *E, I*
917.35	austerely] sullenly *E, I*
918.17	In] As *E*
918.25	Only] But *E, I*
919.5	fired] discharged *E, I*
	terrible] horrible *E, I*

919.21	HONOR] LOVE TO ~ *E, I*
919.24	Governor's] Gubernatorial *E*; gubernatorial *I*
919.37–38	faithless . . . betrayer.] deserted mistress. *E, I*
919.40–920.11	An aide-de camp . . . heard. *placed after* "Where . . . bleed." *in E*
920.11	heard.] ~. But Captain Armisted did not hear. *E*
920.12	the Governor . . . carelessly.] he asked. *E*

MOXON'S MASTER

931.2	which] and ~ *E*
931.17	jest;] incivility; *E*
931.22	*I*] I *E*
932.5	sharpest . . . thinkers,] deepest of thinkers and sharpest of observers^ *E*
932.11	unfriendly, perhaps malign.] malign, perhaps malevolent. *E*
932.18	understanding.] ~.¶ *E*
932.28	fateful] uncanny *E*
932.29	friend's] ~ *alma mater,* the *E*
932.33	destiny] fate *E*
932.40	*are*] are *E*
933.7	reason.] thought. *E*
933.11	I was] *om. E*
933.39	seen.] visible. *E*
933.40	right hand,] right, *E*
934.13	But] ~ then *E*
934.24–25	irritated;] ~: *E, CW*
934.28	backward, as in alarm.] backward and grew visibly paler. *E*
935.35	away from me.] out of a window, with his back to me. *E*

AT OLD MAN ECKERT'S

955.2	Marion, in Vermont.] Morton, in Missouri. *E*
955.11	Marion.] Morton. *E*
955.23	important,] credible, *E*
	Marion's] Morton's *E*
956.13	footfalls] unmistakable ~ *E*

A DIAGNOSIS OF DEATH

957.11	"Yes, . . . conveying] "Say, rather, the usual kind of eyes, purveying *N*
957.22	Meridian.] Meridan. *N*
957.22	doctor] physician *N*

958.7   good] absolute *N*
958.15   gave] imparted *N*
958.26   familiar . . . me,] very familiar to me, *N*
958.28   Meridian.] Meridan. *N*
958.32   a man] the figure of ~ *N*
958.38   entrance. ¶] ~.^ *N*
959.7   silent.] ~. The wind had risen and was rattling away at the
             closed shutters just as if this had been a real ghost story. *N*
959.7–8   absently . . . fingers] thoughtfully stirred the coals in the grate. *N*
959.16   him?" ¶] ~?"^ *N*

A VINE ON A HOUSE

984.13–14   cold-mannered] saturnine *Co*
984.14–15   cared to make none.] did not care to. *Co*
984.20   gentle,] well-mannered, *Co*
984.21   she] Mrs. Harding *Co*
985.9   stagnant.] absolutely ~. *Co*
985.10   Presently] Suddenly *Co*
985.23   recalled,] ~ by the writer, *Co*
985.27   wise, it is thought,] wise *Co*
986.6   unite] divide *Co*
986.11   incapable counselors.] counselors who did not know what
             to do. *Co*
986.17   so. ¶] ~.^ *Co*

A MAN WITH TWO LIVES

987.7   eighty-one] nearly a hundred *Co*
987.15   It . . . bowlders,] Flowing out of this was a creek of no consider-
             able size, bordered by cottonwood trees and large bowlders that
             had been *Co*
988.2–3   the limit . . . It] a large spring—the source of the creek. Imme-
             diately beyond was the head of the gulch which I had mistaken
             for a cañon; it *Co*
988.3   breast] surface *Co*
988.4   pen.] trap. *Co*
988.10   a keen] my keenest *Co*
988.29   otherwise,] *OM. Co*
988.40   are.'] ~ and what all this means!' *Co*
989.1   guardhouse] fort *Co*

A WIRELESS MESSAGE

990.7	living] *om. Co*
990.8	whom . . . visiting,] with whom he was living, *Co*
990.15	"lost." ¶] ~.^ *Co*
990.18–19	distinct] distinctly visible *Co*
990.25	surprising;] disquieting; *Co*
991.3	astonished] inexpressibly surprised *Co*
991.5	plainly] distinctly *Co*
991.7	intense,] intenser, *Co*
999.19	visible.] ~. The persisting but ever-fading light served to guide his shaking legs from the spot, in what direction he neither knew nor cared. *Co*
991.28–29	the floor . . . way,] the roof fell in with a loud crash, followed by a blinding light, *Co*
991.29	more. ¶] ~.^ *Co*

AN ARREST

992.1	Brower] Mannering *Co* [*et seq.*]
	of Kentucky] *om. Co*
992.2	county jail] Dunham County jail, in Tennessee, *Co*
992.16	gloom.] ~—evidently posted there to intercept him. *Co*
993.5	submits.] ~ to the inevitable. *Co*
993.9	Burton] John *Co*
993.17	Burton] John *Co*

ONE SUMMER NIGHT

997.25	be. ¶] ~.^ *Co*
998.17	They went] What they did was to pass *Co*
998.19	the obscurity] a corner *Co*

JOHN MORTONSON'S FUNERAL

Footnote om. in Co.

1000.5	ran] rushed frantically *Co*
1000.8	arms] ~, her face assumed a dreadful pallor *Co*
1000.14	concussion. ¶] ~.^ *Co*

STALEY FLEMING'S HALLUCINATION

1001.2	Doctor,"] Halderman," *Co*
1001.7	sometimes only] commonly *Co*

1001.26	I] *I Co*
1002.10	trouble, Dr. Halderman?] trouble? *Co*
1002.17	If] If—if *Co*

A BAFFLED AMBUSCADE

1009.3	Tullahoma.] *Co*, H; Tulahoma. *CW*
	big] *om. Co*
1009.4	River] ~ (Murfreesboro) *Co*
	trouble] "trouble" *Co*
1009.7	good-will.] ~. A true history of those spirited encounters would make an interesting book. *Co*
1009.10	silence.] ~. Conversation was forbidden; arms and accouterments were denied the right to rattle. The horses' trampling was all that could be heard, and the movement was slow in order to have as little as possible of that. It was after midnight and pretty dark, although there was a bit of moon somewhere behind the masses of cloud. *Co* [*moved to 1009.21–25.*]
1009.21–25	Conversation . . . cloud. ¶] *om.* ^ *Co*
1010.8	space . . . away,] space, *Co*
1010.17	light.] ~ and hardly five paces away. *Co*
1010.18	bareheaded.] ~, his face showing a great gout of blood. *Co*
	object] dark ~ *Co*
1010.35	upward,] ~ and defiled with a great gout of blood from *Co*
1010.37	half-hour] quarter-hour *Co*

TWO MILITARY EXECUTIONS

1012.1	big army lay in camp,] army lay at Nashville, *Co*
1012.9	volunteer] *om. Co*
1012.11	Bennett Story] John Bennett *Co*
1012.20	Ben] John *Co*
1012.22	guard-tent . . . occurred,] guard-tent, *Co*
1013.1	Greene] John ~ *Co*
1013.8–9	ever . . . heard] never . . . unheard *Co*
1013.32	"Bennett] "John *Co*
1013.35	Greene] John ~ *Co*
1013.39	"Bennett Story] "John Bennett *Co*
1014.2	was heard,] rang out from the obscurity *Co*
1014.4	through the line,] overhead, *Co*
1014.12	Bennett] John *Co*

THE MOONLIT ROAD

1015.2	JOEL] JOHN *Co*
1015.4	other] of the *Co*
1015.7	demanding] claiming *Co*
1015.10	Joel] my parents, John *Co*
1015.15	shrubbery. ¶] ~.^ *Co*
1015.16	Yale.] ~. ¶ *Co*
1015.20–21	conjecture, . . . these: ¶] conjecture.^ *Co*
1015.24	dawn.] ~. ¶ *Co*
1016.13	taciturn] saturnine *Co*
1016.25	sounds] *Co*, H; sound *CW*
1017.14	enough. The name] enough; it *Co*
1017.19	day, for illustration,] day *Co*
1017.20	in uniform,] similarly clad, *Co*
1017.21	man] chap *Co*
1018.19	distrusted.] suspected. *Co*
1018.29–30	Sometimes . . . being.] *om. Co*
1018.37	darkness of the] *om. Co*
1019.11	aware] conscious *Co*
1019.23	foolish] fool *Co*
1019.29	peaceful] dreamless *Co*
1019.30	indefinable] vague, ~ *Co*
1019.32	husband, Joel Hetman,] husband *Co*
1021.11	I had lingered long] For weeks I had lingered *Co*
1021.21	life. ¶] ~.^ *Co*
1021.37	this Life] the *Co*

THE OTHER LODGERS

1026.3	Breathitt] Brathitt *Co*, H
1026.17	spooky,] uncanny, *Co*
1026.18	Imagine] You can imagine *Co*
1026.19	earnestly] audibly *Co*
1027.1	All the faces were] Every face was *Co*
1027.2–3	in sharp . . . chin.] with a sharp and ghastly definition. The clothing of some was freaked and gouted with blood. *Co*
1027.4	bad] horrible *Co*
1027.14	do you] does this *Co*
1027.19	Unspeakably] Inexpressibly *Co*
1027.25	dare to] *om. Co*

1027.27	Now . . . tenant.] *om. Co*
1027.36	Breathitt] Brathitt *Co*, H
1027.37	comfort.] the Waldorf-Astoria. *Co*

BEYOND THE WALL

1029.16	element] vein *Co*
1030.13	any . . . inhospitality.] it. *Co*
1031.30	*know*] know *Co*
1032.4	box-bordered] *om. Co*
1032.35	character? ¶] ~ ? ^ *Co*
1033.20	reason,] ~ and considerations of worldly expediency, *Co*
1034.25	night, . . . later,] night *Co*

A RESUMED IDENTITY

1036.14	showing] gleaming *Co*
1036.18	dimly] *om. Co*
1037.1	*timbre* and] timbre—of *Co*
1037.8	clearly] *om. Co*
1038.9	into . . . Stone's] the national cemetery on the Stone *Co*
1038.18	a lieutenant,] Lieutenant Bannister, *Co*
1038.26	he added, smiling.] *om. Co.*
1039.29	should] do *Co*
1039.33	stone] *om. Co*
1040.10–11	pool . . . life.] pool. ¶ And within that hospitable wall, among the comrades of his youth, he sleeps no less soundly than they. *Co*

THREE AND ONE ARE ONE

1041.7	severity] austerity *Co*
1041.11	touched] been imparted to *Co*
1041.14	family,] Lassiter ~, *Co*
1042.7	trooper . . . aware.] trooper, serving far away, knew nothing. *Co*
1042.8	a natural] an irrepressible *Co*
1042.10	out] out afoot *Co*; foot *CW* [See AB to Walter Neale, 28 Nov. 1911 (MS, HL).]
1042.17	an ache] a strangling ache *Co*
1042.18	making] appearing to be ~ *Co*
1042.29	east] *om. Co*
1042.30	hearthside, . . . place,] hearthside *Co*
1042.41	Blended . . . the gravel] The gravel walk, blended with its borders, *Co*

1043.1   young] hardy and courageous *Co*
1043.5   half-mile] quarter-mile *Co*
1043.19   All were] They were all *Co*

RISE AND FALL OF THE AËROPLANE

1044.1   appears] [wrote the Future Historian] seems *Co*
            year] ~ 1917—corresponding to our *Co*
1044.2   of travel.] by which the ancients went from where they were to
            where they were not. *Co*
1044.10   348 B. S.;] 1910; *Co*
1044.11   single] ~ international *Co*
1044.12   "History of Invention"] *History of Invention Co, CW*
1044.13   at one time] in 1916 *Co*
            ten] twenty *Co*
1044.24   causes. ¶] ~.^ *Co*
1045.5   in a park] on a roof *Co*
1045.11   reaction] "tired feeling," as it was called, *Co*
1045.12   hastened] intensified *Co*
1045.18   sikliks] prastams *Co*
1045.25   when] ~ in 1918 (B. S. 368) *Co*

THE STRANGER

1047.20   river] *om. Co*
1047.21   Big] the ~ *Co*
1048.16   say: ¶] ~:^ *Co*
1049.31   while.' ¶] ~.'^ *Co*
1049.35   them. ¶] ~.^ *Co*
1049.36–37 William . . . Kent.] William Shaw and George W. Kent. *Co*
1050.29   excited. ¶] ~.^ *Co*
1050.37   swearing, . . . return.] swearing. *Co*
1050.38   said:] ~, ¶ *Co*
1051.1   shot] plugged *Co*

THE DISPERSAL

1052.2   generation is,] generation," wrote the Future Historian, "is *Co*
1052.6   man.] ~! True, he was the logical product of his time and its
            tendencies, and even before his sinister power had begun to
            accomplish the destruction of his race was so illustrious among
            his countrymen that he was known as Maximus—the Greatest.
            As in the instances of all who had previously achieved the lesser

distinction of 'the Great,' his claim to preeminence cannot now be ascertained, but his modern title, 'Maledictus,' is easily understood. *Co*

1052.11   "1813"— . . . been.] 1813. Whatever strain of ancestral cruelty may have deformed his character, it is probable that his malign bent was mostly a racial heritage, for to its invention and operation of devices for destroying life the entire civilization of his period owes its unenviable place in the world's annals. With a now inconceivable perversity, all the American and European nations of the time competed in encouraging, by public honors and material rewards, the making of destructive mechanical devices and chemical compounds, which they spent millions of lives and treasure in testing upon one another. It was inevitable that this terrible infatuation would one day have its logical consequence in something which, like a judgment of the gods, would involve them all in merited ruin. *Co*

1052.12   invention, . . . improvements,] invention *Co*

1052.14   fragmentary . . . period;] such fragmentary chronicles of the period as have come down to us; *Co*

1052.15–16   "Dictionary of Antiquities"] *Dictionary of Antiquities Co, CW*

1052.26   civic] civil *Co*

1053.4   one.] ~; and Socialism, her handmaiden, yielding to the temptation of opportunity, served her mistress, with no franker devotion but superior efficiency, by substituting for the secret ballot the secret bullet. In the temples of religion the *odium theologicum* asserted itself in suppression of heresy by assassination of heretics; animosities of writers and artists found expression in the new criticism; competition in business sought monopoly of life. Government, religion, literature, art, commerce, all became 'perilous trades,' were abandoned in terror, and perished without hope of resurrection. *Co*

1053.8–9   deed. ¶ So] deed. With his hand in his 'pocket' he could stroll listlessly through a crowd, operating the fatal device with immunity from special suspicion. Concealed in the drapery of a window he could safely kill anyone passing by. ¶ "In these awful conditions the foolish belief that detection and punishment of crime are not deterrent was refuted, alas! too late, by a régime of general murder. So *Co*

1053.17   barbarism.] ~ from which they had so slowly and painfully emerged, and their subjugation and virtual extermination by our Polynesian ancestors, with their primitive weapons and genius for 'team-work,' followed as a matter of course. ¶ "The fate of 'the Greatest' is unknown. There is a tradition that while expounding to a committee of Congress the advantages of his silent firearm he was destroyed by a bolt of inaudible lightning. Another relates that he fled to Central America, where he was stricken dumb, and lived for many years, silent, upon a peak in Darien." *Co*

AN ANCIENT HUNTER

1054.2	era,"] era,'" wrote the illustratious Future Historian, *Co*
1054.15	poets] blind poet, Homer Edward Bok *Co*
1055.17	Wheeler Wilcox's] Bok's *Co*
1055.37–38	pioneers and promoters] harbingers *Co*
1056.1	hold] think *Co*
1056.8	the year 254 B. S.] '1923' *Co*

BIBLIOGRAPHY

A. PRIMARY

Can Such Things Be? New York: Cassell Publishing Co., [December] 1893. Washington, DC: Neale Publishing Co., 1903.

Cobwebs from an Empty Skull. London & New York: George Routledge & Sons, 1874, [1878]. London: "Fun" Office, [1884] (as *Cobwebs: Being the Fables of Zambri the Parsee*).

The Collected Fables of Ambrose Bierce. Edited by S. T. Joshi. Columbus: Ohio State Univ. Press, 2000.

The Collected Works of Ambrose Bierce. 12 vols. New York & Washington, DC: Neale Publishing Co., 1909–12. Reprint, New York: Gordian Press, 1966.

The Fall of the Republic and Other Political Satires. Edited by S. T. Joshi and David E. Schultz. Knoxville: Univ. of Tennessee Press, 2000.

The Fiend's Delight. London: John Camden Hotten, [July 1873]. New York: A. L. Luyster, 1873.

A Much Misunderstood Man: Selected Letters of Ambrose Bierce. Edited by S. T. Joshi and David E. Schultz. Columbus: Ohio State Univ. Press, 2003.

Nuggets and Dust Panned Out in California. London: Chato & Windus, [1873].

Phantoms of a Blood-Stained Period: The Complete Civil War Writings of Ambrose Bierce. Edited by Russell Duncan and David J. Klooster. Amherst: Univ. of Massachusetts Press, 2002.

Skepticism and Dissent: Selected Journalism, 1898–1901. Edited by Lawrence I. Berkove. Ann Arbor, MI: Delmas, 1980. Rev. ed., Ann Arbor: UMI Research Press, 1986.

A Son of the Gods and A Horseman in the Sky. San Francisco & New York: Paul Elder & Co., 1907.

A Sole Survivor: Bits of Autobiography. Edited by S. T. Joshi and David E. Schultz. Knoxville: Univ. of Tennessee Press, 1998.

Tales of Soldiers and Civilians. San Francisco: E. L. G. Steele, 1891 [February 1892]. London: Chatto & Windus, 1892 (as *In the Midst of Life*). Rev. ed., New York: G. P. Putnam's Sons, 1898 (as *In the Midst of Life*).

The Unabridged Devil's Dictionary. Edited by David E. Schultz and S. T. Joshi. Athens: Univ. of Georgia Press, 2000.

B. SECONDARY

Aaron, Daniel. "Ambrose Bierce and the American Civil War." In *Uses of Literature,* ed. Monroe Engel, 115–31. Cambridge, MA: Harvard Univ. Press, 1973.

Berkove, Lawrence I. "'Hades in Trouble': A Rediscovered Story by Ambrose Bierce." *American Literary Realism* 25 (1993): 67–84.

———. *A Prescription for Adversity: The Moral Art of Ambrose Bierce.* Columbus: Ohio State Univ. Press, 2002.

———. "'A Strange Adventure': The Story Behind a Bierce Tale." *American Literary Realism* 14 (1981): 70–76.

———. "Two Impossible Dreams: Ambrose Bierce on Utopia and America." *Huntington Library Quarterly* 44 (1981): 283–92.

The Century Dictionary. 12 vols. Edited by William Dwight Whitney, revised by Benjamin E. Smith. New York: Century Co., 1911–13.

Couser, G. Thomas. "Writing the Civil War: Ambrose Bierce's 'Jupiter Doke, Brigadier-General.'" *Studies in American Fiction* 18 (1990): 87–98.

Davidson, Cathy N., ed. *Critical Essays on Ambrose Bierce.* Boston: G. K. Hall, 1982.

———. *The Experimental Fictions of Ambrose Bierce: Structuring the Ineffable.* Lincoln: Univ. of Nebraska Press, 1984.

A Dictionary of American English. 4 vols. Edited by Sir William A. Craigie and James R. Hulbert. Chicago: Univ. of Chicago Press, 1938–44.

Fatout, Paul. *Ambrose Bierce: The Devil's Lexicographer.* Norman: Univ. of Oklahoma Press, 1951.

———. *Ambrose Bierce and the Black Hills.* Norman: Univ. of Oklahoma Press, 1956.

Fry, Carroll L., and Wayne A. Chandler. "An Epiphany at Owl Creek Bridge: Intimations of Immortalities in Ambrose Bierce's Fiction." *Studies in Weird Fiction,* no. 24 (Winter 1999): 8–14.

Gale, Robert L. *An Ambrose Bierce Companion.* Westport, CT: Greenwood Press, 2001.

Grenander, M. E. *Ambrose Bierce.* New York: Twayne, 1971.

———. "Ambrose Bierce, John Camden Hotten, *The Fiend's Delight,* and *Nuggets and Dust." Huntington Library Quarterly* 28 (1965): 353–71.

———. "Bierce's Turn of the Screw: Tales of Ironical Terror." *Western Humanities Review* 11 (1957): 257–64.

Hall, Carroll D. *Bierce and the Poe Hoax.* Introduction by Carey McWilliams. San Francisco: Book Club of California, 1934.

Hoppenstand, Gary. "Ambrose Bierce and the Transformation of the Gothic Tale in the Nineteenth-Century American Periodical." In *Periodical Literature in Nineteenth-Century America,* ed. Kenneth M. Price and Susan Belasco Smith, 220–38. Charlottesville: Univ. Press of Virginia, 1995.

Joshi, S. T. "Ambrose Bierce: Horror as Satire." In *The Weird Tale,* 143–67. Austin: Univ. of Texas Press, 1990.

Joshi, S. T., and David E. Schultz. *Ambrose Bierce: A Bibliography of Primary Sources.* Westport, CT: Greenwood Press, 1999.

Kazin, Alfred. "On Ambrose Bierce and 'Parker Adderson, Philosopher.'" In *The American Short Story,* ed. Calvin Skaggs, 26–35. New York: Dell, 1977.

La Rochefoucauld, François de Marsillac, duc de. *Maxims.* Translation and introduction by I. W. Tancock. Baltimore: Penguin, 1959.

Logan, F. J. "The Wry Seriousness of 'Owl Creek Bridge.'" *American Literary Realism* 10 (1977): 101–13.

Maclean, Robert C. "The Deaths in Ambrose Bierce's 'Halpin Frayser.'" *Papers on Language and Literature* 10 (1974): 394–402.

McWilliams, Carey. *Ambrose Bierce: A Biography.* New York: Albert & Charles Boni, 1929.

Miller, Arthur M. "The Influence of Edgar Allan Poe on Ambrose Bierce." *American Literature* 4 (1932): 130–50.

Morris, Roy, Jr. *Ambrose Bierce: Alone in Bad Company.* New York: Crown, 1995.

Mencken, H. L. "Ambrose Bierce." In *Prejudices: Sixth Series,* 259–65. New York: Knopf, 1927.

Neale, Walter. *Life of Ambrose Bierce.* New York: Neale Publishing Co., 1929.

Oates, Whitney J., ed. *The Stoic and Epicurean Philosophers.* New York: Modern Library, 1957.

Owens, David M. "Bierce and Biography: The Location of Owl Creek Bridge." *American Literary Realism* 26 (Spring 1994): 82–89.

Schaefer, Michael W. *Just What War Is: The Civil War Writings of De Forest and Bierce.* Knoxville: Univ. of Tennessee Press, 1997.

Solomon, Eric. "The Bitterness of Battle: Ambrose Bierce's War Fiction." *Midwest Quarterly* 5 (1964): 147–65.

Starrett, Vincent. *Buried Caesars.* Chicago: Covici-McGee, 1923.

Stein, William Bysshe. "Bierce's 'The Death of Halpin Frayser': The Poetics of Gothic Consciousness." *Emerson Society Quarterly* 18 (Second Quarter 1972): 115–22.

Wilson, Edmund. "Ambrose Bierce on the Owl Creek Bridge." In *Patriotic Gore: Studies in the Literature of the American Civil War,* 617–34. New York: Oxford Univ. Press, 1962.

Wilt, Napier. "Ambrose Bierce and the Civil War." *American Literature* 1 (1929): 260–85.

BIERCE'S CIVIL WAR STORIES ARRANGED CHRONOLOGICALLY

1861

One Kind of Office
The Mocking-Bird
A Horseman in the Sky
A Tough Tussle
Jupiter Doke, Brigadier-General

1862

An Affair of Outposts
An Occurrence at Owl Creek Bridge
The Coup de Grâce

1863

A Baffled Ambuscade
Three and One Are One
The Affair at Coulter's Notch
George Thurston
The Story of a Conscience
Parker Adderson, Philosopher
One Officer, One Man
Chickamauga

1864

Killed at Resaca
One of the Missing
A Son of the Gods
The Major's Tale

1865

The Other Lodgers
A Resumed Identity

ALPHABETICAL LISTING
OF BIERCE'S FICTION

1232

ALPHABETICAL LISTING OF BIERCE'S FICTION

ALPHABETICAL LISTING OF BIERCE'S FICTION

INDEX TO BIERCE'S FICTION

1240

Court of Variable Jurisdiction, 444
Coventry (England), 627, 1167
Covington, Kentucky, 431, 435, 596, 1156
Coyote, California, 613
Coyote County, 751, 752
Crackers, 540
Craven, James, 584
Creede, Alvan, 852–55
Creede, Eddy, 854
Creede, Jane, 853
Cremorne Gardens (London), 314
"Crimean War" (Kinglake). *See Invasion of the Crimea, The*
Crow (Indians), 261
Cubebs, 1054
Cubo, 213
Cumberland Gap, 673, 1171
Cumberland Mountains, 580, 714, 1147
Cummings, Rev. Mr., 595–96, 1154–55
Curtis, Edward, 740
Curtius, Marcus, 326
Cuticura, 741
Cytherea, 1945

D——, Bob, 218–21
Dacier, André, 265
Daedalus, 159
Daily Malefactor, 453
Damascus (Syria), 152
Dampier, Mohun, 1029–35
Dan, 124, 187
Darnell, Mrs., 801
Darwin, Charles, 22, 23
Dave ("The Baffled Asian"), 89
Dave, Lame, 201, 203
David Copperfield (Dickens), 924, 1105
Davidson, Professor (George), 617
Davis, Abner, 48
Davis, Berry, 1047–51
Davis, Richard Harding, 901
Dawson (Yukon Territory), 924
Dead Man's Cave, 530
Dead March (*Saul*), 356
Deadman's Gulch, 282–87
Deadwood, Dr., 118–19
Dean, Ben, 195–96
Debrethin, 559, 1076
Debs, Eugene V., 953
Decline and Fall of the American Republics (Golpek), 1060

Decline and Fall of the American Republics (Mancher), 556
Decline and Fall of the Roman Empire, The (Gibbon), 924, 1105
Deemer, Silas, 851–56
De Long, George W., 1141, 1144–45
Delphi (oracle), 147
Deluse, Herman, 608–10, 1159–62
Dement, Mary Jane, 777–78
Democrats, 20, 70, 113, 190, 270, 277, 425, 432, 520, 740, 752, 1135, 1194
Dempster family, 226–30
Denneker's Meditations, 387, 389, 1002
Dennison, Mr. and Mrs., 173–75
Denver, Colorado, 230, 537, 741
Department of Highways and Cemeteries, 924, 1105
Department of Negotiations with the Enemy, 937
Derby, 311, 349
Desert of Despair, 1120
Deutscherkirche, 146
"Devil's Dream, The," 280
Devonshire (England), 386, 388
Dewey, George, 937–38
Diablo, Monte, 253
Diablo range, 20
Dickens, Charles, 300
Dictionary of Antiquities (Pantin-Gwocx), 1052
Dieppe (Netherlands), 314
Dimshouck, 1045
Diogenes, 314
Distilleryville, Kentucky, 431, 432, 433, 434, 435
Divinia, 393–94
Dixon's River, 204
Djainan, 152–54
Djulya, 152–54
Doane, John, 455
Dobelly IV, 242–45
Doble, Bud, 291
Doble, Captain, 427–29
Dobsho, Thomas, 307–10
Doke, Jabez Leonidas, 432, 433
Doke, Jupiter, 430–36
Dolorous Mountains, 1120
Doman, Dr., 253–55
Doman, Jefferson, 411–19
Domremy, 946
Donelson, James, 567, 568

INDEX TO BIERCE'S FICTION

Gobwottle, Mr., 51–52
God's Location, 411
Gokeetle-guk, 1117
Golampi(an)s, 587–92, 692–96, 1090–94
Golby, Dan, 176–78
Golden Eagle Hotel (Sacramento), 610
Golden Fleece, 1135
Goldsmith, Oliver, 300, 578, 1149
Goliah, 174
Golpek, 1060, 1075
Golunk-Dorstro, 1004, 1070
Gompers, Samuel, 949, 952, 1056
Good Will, 336
Gopher, 29, 35
Gordon, William Hayner, 578–79, 1149–50
Gorgeous Obsequies Guarantee Fraternity, 446
Gorham (soldier), 1013
Gorman, Arthur Pue, 1200
Graffenreid, Anderton, 654–58
Grafton, W. V., 661, 716
Graham, Captain, 717
Graham, Henry, 585, 1152
Grand Army (of the Republic), 558, 953, 1075
Grand Central Hotel, 1143
Grand Combination Circus, 441
Granier, Henri, 578, 1149
Grant, Ulysses S., 113, 706, 790, 914, 1013
Grass Valley, California, 55
Grattan, Caspar, 1017
Graymaulkin, 760
Graymaulkin, University of, 758
Grayrock (soldier), 1013
Grayrock, John, 790–94
Grayrock, William, 793
Grayville, 829–32
Great Britain. *See* England and the English
Great Court, 572, 573, 1123, 1124
Great Lakes, 906
Great Mowbray, 829
Great White Throne Walk, 452
Greece and Greeks, 60, 100, 425, 438, 556, 588, 662, 723, 1054, 1060, 1061, 1079, 1090
Greedy-Gut, 848
Greenbrier, 620
Greene, Bennett Story, 1012–14
Greenton, 800, 802
Greenwich (England), 1144
Grile, Dod, 72, 77–78, 79, 257, 314–16, 332–34, 1141, 1143, 1144

Grile, Gloriana, 72
Gringos, 1134, 1134
Gropilla-Stron, 570, 1121
Gropoppsu, 590
Grossmith, Robert, 746, 747
Gruber, Rev. J., 985
Grumsquutzy, 926–27, 1106–7
Guadalquivir (river), 133
Guam, 1195
Guatimozin, 186
Gufferson, 978, 1059
Guildhall, 125
Guildhall (Bath), 298
Guinea, 364
Gulf (of California), 1048
Gulf of Mexico, 906
Gull, Sir William, 158
Gulliver, 304
Gumammam, 967, 968, 1110
Gumbo, Bueno, 1135
Gump, Claude Reginald, 373
Gunkle, 980
Gunkux, 1060, 1067, 1069, 1073
Gunny, 775–76, 778
Gurney, Moll, 380
Gwap River, 1198
Gynograph, 304

Haberton, Lieutenant, 707–11
Hadeen, Garden of, 9
Hades, 84, 543–54
Haight, Henry Huntly, 11
Haïta, 763–67
Halcrow, Caffal, 667–70
Halcrow, Creede, 667–70
Halderman, Dr., 1002
Hale, Eugene, 1201
Haley, 935
Hali, 457, 804
Halleck, Henry Wager, 915
Halsey, 170–71
Ham, 1041
Hamilton (provost-marshal), 839
Hamlet (Shakespeare), 97
Hampton Rocks, 298
Hang Tree *Herald*, 74
Hank, 70
Hannah (Hanner), 110–11
Hannah, Aunt, 185
Harbin (battle of), 964

Hotbath Meadows, 362
Hottentots, 26
Houghton, Mifflin & Co., 900
Houndsditch (London), 118
House of Indolence, 590, 1092
Howard, Arabella Cliftonbury, 48–49
Howe, Julia Ward, 900
Howells, William Dean, 899
Huggins, Rev. Berosus, 342–44
Hugo, Victor, 133
Hunker, Jacob, 58
Hunker, Jerry, 178
Huns, 33, 965
Hurdy-Gurdy, 409–19
Hurdy Herald, 413
Hutton's, 28
Hyades, 459
Hyatt, Mr., 985
Hyde Park (London), 352
Hymettus, 218
Hymn to the Gone Away, 645

Iago (character in Shakespeare), 96
Iaxon, 978
Icarus, 159
Idaho, 202, 433
Ignotus, St., 362
Illinois, 184, 307, 430, 433, 455, 584, 594, 627,
    987, 1148, 1169
Imperial Austrian Order of Assassins by
    Poison, 761
Independence Land, 1143
India and Indians, 556, 738, 775
Indian Hill, California, 784
Indian Ocean, 1055
Indiana, 79, 578, 627, 1169
Indiana State University, 741
Indians (Native Americans), 13, 25, 170, 178,
    202, 204, 212, 240, 264, 987, 1048, 1049
Infants' Sheltering Home, 801
Infernia, 401–3
Ingalls, General, 558
Inhumio, 453
Injun Creek, 409, 410, 411, 419
Invasion of the Crimea, The (Kinglake), 367
"Invigorating Zephyrs," 326
Inxling, Henry, 266–67
Iodine, Kentucky, 435
Iowa, 179, 1154
Ireland and the Irish, 257, 351, 962, 963, 1060

Irene, 774, 775, 778
Isle of the Happy Change, 968, 1110
Isle of Man, 963
Isle of Pines, 609, 1160
Isthmus (of Panama), 77
Italy and Italians, 253, 759

Jabe, 81
Jabez Jones (ship), 567, 568
Jabsley, Burbank, 751–53
Jack, 360
Jack, Preacher, 362
Jack, Stumpy, 202, 203
Jackass Flat, 207
Jackass Gap, 254
Jackhigh, Colonel, 311
Jackson, Andrew, 220
Jackson brothers, 796
Jake, Clawhammer, 208
Jalap, 138
Jamison, Gus, 202, 203
Japan and Japanese, 14, 559, 588, 965, 1070,
    1077, 1090, 1195
Japy-Djones, 923
Jaralson, Mr., 810–15
Jarette, Mr., 699–705
Jarrett, William, 386–89
Jarvis, Algernon, 289–90
Jarvis, Dr., 578
Jaxon, 1059
Jayhawk, 74, 269, 433, 434, 435, 436, 752
Jeannette (ship), 1141–45
Jefferson, Thomas, 56, 57
Jerusalem (dog), 187–90
Jess, 997–98
Jesus Christ, 13, 93, 602
Jews, 77
Jim ("The Baffled Asian"), 89
Jim ("Making a Clean Breast of It"), 108
Jim, Calamity, 775, 776
Joab, 48–49
Job, Peter, 11
Jobblecopper, 1044
Jobson, Wemyss, 11
Jogogle-Zadester, 922–24, 925, 1104, 1106
John ("The Glad New Year"), 43
John ("The Head of the Family"), 62
John ("The Hypnotist"), 849
John XI, 555
John CLXXVIII, 165

GENERAL INDEX

"Ancient Hunter, An," 974

"Androcles and the Lion," 157

"Annals of the Future Historian," 1187

"Another Thieves' Scheme on the Pacific Coast," 1130n30

Antarctica, 366n3, 366n9

Anti-Philistine, 604, 618, 652, 705, 739, 863

Antony, Mark, 1137n18

Antony and Cleopatra (Shakespeare), 534n4, 1014n1

"Aphorisms of a Late Spring," 1088n44

Apparition of Mrs. Veal, The (Defoe), 676

Aquarium (Brighton), 316n2

Arabian Nights, 97n2, 148n2, 441–42, 586n2, 1040n6

Arctic, 366n3

Arena Publishing Co., 904n17

Argens, Jean-Baptiste de Boyer, marquis, 15

Argonaut, xxvii, 125, 129, 145, 157, 169, 182, 190, 197, 200, 203, 252, 268, 271, 281, 288, 313, 320, 323, 328, 337, 339, 377, 378, 385, 389

Arguelles, Manuel, 939n5

Arica (Peru/Chile), 183n2

Arion, 249n2

Arizona, 1051

"Arizona Mirage, An," 225n4

"Arizonian, The" (Miller), 73n3

"Arrest, An," 975

Ars Poetica (Horace), 268n1

Arthur, Chester Alan, 1130n25

As You Like It (Shakespeare), 454

"Ashes of the Beacon," 566, 948n5, 974, 983, 1008, 1014n2

"Assignment, An," 598

"At Clipper Gap," 691

"At Old Man Eckert's," 898

"At the Close of the Canvass," 742n1

"At the Eckert House," 956

Atlanta Campaign, 1028n2

Atlantic Monthly, 739n4

Auburn, California, 739nn1–2

Augspur, 334n5

Aurelius, Marcus, 503

Axminster (England), 278n2

Aztecs, 186n4

"B., H.," 271

"'Bad Woman, A,'" 400

Badlands, 225n1

"Baffled Ambuscade, A," 975

Bailey, Cyril, 773nn1–2, 1128n10, 1129nn12–13

Balboa, Vasco Nuñez de, 299n1

Baldwin, Thomas, 299n4

Ball, John, 166n11

"Banking at Mexican Hill," 36n1, 222n3

Bannerman, Helen, 1136n3

"Baptism of Dobsho, The," 271n1

Barbary Coast (San Francisco), 743n14

Barber, Henry, 271n1, 310n6

Barstow, George, 17n14

Bartlett, Washington, 743n7

Bastien-Lepage, Jules, 948n9

Bath (England), 160–62, 299n2, 586n1

Bathampton (England), 299n3

Batheaston (England), 161n7

"Battle Hymn of the Republic, The" (Howe), 190n5, 903n6

"Battle of Naseby, The" (Macaulay), 374n1

"Battlefields and Ghosts," 665n1

Baxter, Sam, 183n3

Bayrolles, 460n3

Beauregard, Pierre Gustave Toutant, 733n6

"Beautiful Snow, The" (Watson), 903n9

Beckford, William, 586n2

Beckwourth, James Pierson, 203n1, 264

"Before the Mirror," 1187

Behemoth, 21n7

"Behind the Veil," 630, 1139, 1162, 1164

Bell, Charles J., 1086n24

Bellamy, Edward, 696

Bellevue Hospital (New York), 903n6

Ben-Hur (Wallace), 904n21, 1131n31

Benjamin, Judah P., 437n8

Bennett, James Gordon, Jr., 1146n3

Bergal, 939n5

Berkeley, California, 21n10

Berkove, Lawrence I., xxivn3, xxivn5, 302, 533, 554, 732, 778, 936, 1084

"Between Two Bullets," 604

"Beyond the Wall," 512n4, 976

Bible, 17n10, 17n15, 17n18, 21n11, 36n3, 36n8, 42n5, 49n1, 55n1, 80n2, 94n2, 95n3, 99n3, 105n1, 125, 175n1, 217n5, 221–22, 264n1, 271n3, 281n7, 310n2, 310n5, 313n3, 316n3, 320n2, 345n4, 366n5, 366n8, 374n7, 503, 554nn1–3, 554n5, 554n8, 618n8, 624n4, 653nn5–6, 665n2,

Diablo Range, 21n8

"Diagnosis of Death, A," 898

"Diagnosis of Death, The," 959

Dickens, Charles, 47, 712n12, 743n16

Dickinson, Emily, 16n9

Dictionary of American English, 313n4, 618n3, 803n7

Dictionary of the English Language (Johnson), 161n8

"Difficulty of Crossing a Field, The," 629, 1139

Diogenes, 316n5

Diogenes Laertius, 316n5

Discourse of Natural Bathes and Mineral Waters, A (Jorden), 162n12

"Dispersal, The," 948n5, 975, 1197

"Dog in Ganegwag, The," xxviii, 896, 1127

"Dogs and Hydrophobia," 206n3, 260n1

"Domestic Heat Escape, The," 542n10

Domrémy-la-Pucelle, 948n10

Donnelly, Ignatius, 1053

"Don't Give Up the Ship," 963n1

Doo-sno-swair, 593n1, 1127n2

"Doppelganger, A," 675, 1139

"Dorch," 1183n1

Doré, Gustave, 105n1

Doubleday, Page & Co., 856n1

Dowson, Ernest, 1035n2

Doyle, C. W., 912

"Dr. Deadwood, I Presume," 305n5

"Dramer Brune, Deserter," 718

Dryden, John, 344n1

Dumbleshaw, Potwin, 948n5, 1053n2, 1084n10

Dunciad, The (Pope), 739n5, 1084n2

Dunne, Finley Peter, 1056

Dziemianowicz, Stefan, 630n1

"Early History of Bath, The," 586n1

"Earthquake Items," 24n5

Edison, Thomas Alva, 682n1

Edward (Prince of Wales), 161nn1–2

Edward IV (King of England), 1130n23

Eells, James, 16n9

Egypt and Egyptians, 1131n36

Elba, 1137n18

"Election Day," 742n1

Elegy Written in a Country Churchyard (Gray), 339n1, 385n2, 825n2, 825n4

"Elihu Root," 1195n1

Eliot, George, 936n5

Elizabeth, New Jersey, 419n4

Elkins, Stephen Benton, 1130n30

Emerson, Ralph Waldo, 939n3

Emma Silver Mining Company, 260n2

England and the English, xviii, xix, 4, 5, 7, 16n3, 24n4, 79n1, 120, 160–62, 217n1, 245, 260n2, 299n2, 306n7, 313n2, 352, 377, 426n3, 586n1, 898, 963, 1130n23

Englewood, New Jersey, 948n7, 1130n29

English as She Is Spoke (Fonseca), 939n6

English Bards and Scotch Reviewers (Byron), 512n1, 739n4

Epaminondas, 231n2

Epictetus, 503, 691, 773

Epicurus, 773, 973, 1127, 1128n10, 1129nn12–13

"Epilogue to the Satires" (Pope), 66n1, 161n8

Essay on Man, An (Pope), 566n2

euchre, 313

Evening Sun (New York) 682

Everybody's Magazine, 1008n1

"Evolution of a Story, The," 1187

Examiner (London), 139n4

Excursion, The (Wordsworth), 816n8

"Execution in Batrugia, An," 961, 974, 1127

"Extinction of the Smugwumps, The," 897, 948n5

"Eyes of the Panther, The," 898

"Fables and Anecdotes," 245n3

"Fables of Zambri, the Parsee, The," 582n3, 593n1, 936n1

"Faithful Wife, The," 7

"Faithless Nelly Gray" (Hood), 618n8

"Fall of the Republic, The," xxviii, 705n3, 757n4, 1057n7, 1083, 1087n41

Fall of the Republic and Other Satires, The, 903n12

Falstaff, Sir John, 350n3

"Famous Gilson Bequest, The," 377, 618n3

Fantastic Fables, 593n1, 1127n2

Farewell to Arms, A (Hemingway), 794

Fargo, George, 779n8

Fatout, Paul, 378

Faust (Goethe), 296n1

Federal army, 437n2, 512n2, 533n1, 534n3, 604, 611n4, 665n1, 733n6, 1011n1, 1040n3, 1043n1, 1043n3, 1087n38, 1088n42, 1180, 1181, 1183n2, 1184n1

"Golampians, The," xxviii, 773nn1–2, 1127
Golden Era, 4, 79n1
Goldsmith, Oliver, 15, 566n5, 642n1, 1022n4
"Goldsmith's Friend Abroad Again"
    (Twain), 15
Goliath, 175n1
Gompers, Samuel, 951n3, 1057n18
"Gone Away, The," 647
Good Words, 337n2
Goodman, Joseph Thompson, 268
Goose-Quill 618
Gorman, Arthur Pue, 1200n1
Gourgard, Gaspard, 920n1
Grafton (battle of), 665n1
Grand Army of the Republic, 566n4, 743n4,
    1088n42
Grant, Ulysses S., 113n1, 437n2, 534n3, 711n1,
    742n4, 794n2, 920n3, 1040n4, 1129n21
grapeshot, 733n8
"Grateful Bear, The," 6
Gray, John Chapman, 724n3
Gray, Thomas, 339n1, 385n2, 825n2, 825n4
Great Britain. *See* England and the English
Great English Short-Story Writers, The
    (Dawson-Dawson) 732
Great Northern Railroad, 954n2
"Great Strike of 1895, The," 895
Greece and the Greeks, 268n4, 724n4, 939n4,
    1087n37
Greeley, Horace, 1129n21
Grenander, M. E., xx, xxivn1, 724, 815
Grile, Dod, 160, 190, 200, 252, 260, 281,
    302n2, 316, 334, 344, 366, 374
"Grizzly Papers," 157
Guatimozin, 186n4
Guildhall (Bath), 299n4
Gull, Sir William, 161nn1–2
Gulliver's Travels (Swift), 15, 21n9, 305n4,
    505, 576, 696, 828n4, 895, 924, 1057n6,
    1127, 1128n9, 1131n32, 1131n35, 1131n39
Guttrige, Leonard E., 1146

"Hades in Trouble," 85
Haeckel, Ernest, 1057n9
Haight, Henry Huntly, 16n9
"Haïta the Shepherd," 460n2, 504, 1205
Hale, Eugene, 1201
Hali, 460n1, 815n1
Halleck, Fitz-Greene, 850n2

Halleck, Henry Wager, 920n3
Ham, 1043n2
Hamlet (Shakespeare), 123n5, 139n1, 445n2,
    705n2, 825n1, 1194nn1–2
Hancock, Winfield S., 1129n21
Handel, George Frideric, 357n1
Harbin (China), 965n1
Hardin, Illinois, 310n1
Hardy, Thomas, 897
Harper & Brothers, 902n1
Harris, Joel Chandler, 1136n3
Harrison, Benjamin, 1088n42, 1130n22,
    1130n30
Harrison, Carter, II, 903n9
Harrison, William Henry, 1085n15
Harte, Bret, 4, 36, 90
Harte, Walter Blackburn, 750n4, 904n17
Harun al-Raschid, 441n3
Hastings, Warren, 374n2
Hastur, 460n2, 767n1
"Haunted Valley, The," 5, 241n1, 256, 518, 682
Hawes, Horace, 47n3
Hawthorne, Julian, 724, 778
Hay-Bunau-Varilla Treaty, 1200
Hay-Pauncefote Treaty, 1200
Hayes, Rutherford B., 1129n21
Haymarket riots, 454n1
Hazeltine, M. W., 1181n1
Hazen, William B., xvii, 203n1, 264n2, 512,
    586n5, 1040, 1051
"Head of the Family, The," 6
Hearst, William Randolph, xvii, xviii, 21n1,
    166n8, 501, 511, 944, 973, 975, 1127
Heine, Heinrich, 1193
"Heiress from Redhorse, An," 778
Hemans, Felicia Dorothea, 345n2, 429n2,
    779n5
Hemingway, Ernest, 794
Henley, William Ernest, 1022n6
Henry IV, Part 1 (Shakespeare), 733n4
Henry VI (King of England), 1130n23
Henry rifle, 989n2
Herakles, 1057n14, 1057n16
Herod, King, 268n4, 313n3
Herodotus, 249n2
Higginson, Thomas Wentworth, 903n4
"His Railway," 271n2, 753n3
"His Waterloo," 753
History of Philosophy from Thales to Comte,
    The (Lewes), 936n5

1268

Milton, John, 49n2, 85nn1–2, 105n1, 139n3, 166n6, 231n4, 554, 566n6, 825n2
"Mind-Reading," 850
"Mirage, The," 225n4
Mission San Francisco de Assis (Mission Dolores), 518n5
Mission San Padro y San Pablo, 419n9
Mission Santa Clara, 397n1
Missionary Ridge (battle of), 534n3
Missouri, 750n1
Moby-Dick (Melville), 816n9
"Mocking-Bird, The," 1014n5, 1022n3
"Modest Proposal, A" (Swift), 696
Modocs, 256n7, 288n3, 331n2
Mohammed, 97n1. 268n3
Mombasa (Kenya), 828n3
Monk and the Hangman's Daughter, The (Voss), xxv
Montesquieu, Charles-Louis de Secondat, baron de, 15
Montezuma II, 186n4
Moody, Dwight L., 352n3
Moody, William Vaughn, 817n11
"Moon in Letters, The," 197n3
"Moonlit Road, The," 460n3, 975
Moore, Edward, 618n4
Moore, Thomas, 123n4
Morgan, George Washington, 676n1
Morgan, J. Pierpont, 954n3
Morgan, John Tyler, 1200n1
Mormons, 26n1, 948n3
Morning Post (London), 355n2
Morris, Roy, Jr., 920, 1035
Morrow, W. C., 630n1, 778, 1207
Morryster, 724n1
Morton, Oliver P., 920
Moulton, Louise Chandler, 904n18
"Moxon's Master," 162n9, 898
"Mr. Barcle's Mill," 385n5
"Mr. Hunker's Mourner," 179n5
"Mr. Jim Beckwourth's Adventure," 203n1
"Mr. Mastehad, Journalist," 1088n45
"Mr. Perry Chumly's Eclipse," 323
"Mr. Swiddler's Flip-Flap," 6, 182n1
Much Ado about Nothing (Shakespeare), 76n2
Mud Springs, California, 27n6
Mugwumps, 542n9, 576n2, 1129n19
Mulford, Prentice, 79n1
Münchhausen, Baron, 305n4
Murfreesboro, Tennessee, 1011n1, 1043n1

"My Favorite Murder," 237, 445, 753nn1–2
"My Shipwreck," 389
"Mysterious Disappearances," 1178
"Mystery of Charles Farquharson, The," 581

Nairobi, Kenya, 1136n14
Napier, Sir Robert, 306n7
Napoleon Bonaparte, 165n2, 920n1, 1137n18
Napoleon III (Emperor of France), 165n2
Narrative of Arthur Gordon Pym of Nantucket, The (Poe), 16n4
Narrative of Military Service, A (Hazen), 512
Nash, Richard ("Beau"), 161n8
Nashville, Tennessee, 423n3, 711n4, 1043n3
Nation, Carry, 897, 947
Nation, David, 948n3
Nature, 802n3
"Nature as a Reformer," 950n2
nature faker, 1137n21
"Nautical Novelty, A," 366
Neale, Walter, xxv, 1043n4, 1179
Neale's Monthly 732
"Negligible Tales," xxvii
Nevada, 27n2
"New Bedder, The," 5, 6
New England Magazine, 904n17
New York American, 961, 963, 965, 969, 1083, 1127, 1194, 1195, 1200, 1201
New York City, 1056n2, 1131n43
New York Evening Post, 691
New York Journal, 947, 950, 954, 959, 1197, 1198, 1199
New York Lunatic Asylum, 705n8
New York Public Library, 903n5
New York Sun, 1180
Newcastle, California, 739n1
Newfoundland dogs, 206n3
Nicaragua, 1198
Nicholas Nickleby (Dickens), 743n16
Nigger Tent, California, 618n2
"Night at Moxon's, A," 935
"Night-Doings at 'Deadman's,' The," 385n1
Niobe, 1136n14
"Non Sum Qualis Eram Bonae Sub Regno Cynarae" (Dowson), 1035n2
Norris, Frank, 533
North Beach (San Francisco), 293n3, 518n1
Northumberland, Elizabeth (Seymour) Percy, duchess of, 161n7

phrenology, 115n1
Pickering, Loring, 360n1, 448n2
Pickett, George Edward, 1040n4
Pike's Peak, 541n5
Pilgrim's Progress, The (Bunyan), 105n1
Pinchot, Gifford, 1137n18
Pinkertons, 903n7
Pittsburg(h), Pennsylvania, 80n1
Piute Indians, 803n5
"Pi-Ute Indians of Nevada, The," 803n5
"Plain Language from Truthful James" (Harte), 90
Pleasures of Hope, The (Campbell), 345n3
Plutarch, 1137n18
Podunk, 947, 1053n1
Poe, Edgar Allan, 16n4, 103, 166n9, 350n5, 378, 524n3, 732n12, 762, 850, 998, 1000n1, 1204
Polk, James Knox, 954n7
Pollard, Percival, 903n10
Pope, Alexander, xxi, 66n1, 161n8, 281n5, 566n2, 739n5, 1084n2, 1128n4
Populism, 1132n46
Port Arthur (China), 965, 966n2
Port Royal (battle of), 1040n3
Potawatomi, 958n11
"Practical Joke, A," 711
"Prattle," 16n3, 27n1, 80n1, 136n5, 162n13, 165n3, 194n3, 231n1, 234n1, 344n2, 350n2, 377, 400, 460n3, 501, 502, 503, 541n1, 566, 504, 658, 683n2, 690, 705n6, 718n2, 724n1, 724n5, 742n1, 750n3, 779n2, 817n17, 817n19, 850, 864, 902n1, 921n3, 936n1, 948n6, 973, 1057n5, 1084n5, 1084n12, 1088n45, 1127n4, 1128n7, 1129n20, 1130n22, 1130n26, 1132n45, 1177, 1181, 1182, 1183n5, 1184
"Premature Burial, The" (Poe), 998
"Presence of Mind—A Wonderful Example," 157
"Present at a Hanging," 598, 1139
"Prevention vs. No Cure," 454n1
Principles of Biology, The (Spencer), 936n1
Principles of Psychology, The (Spencer), 936n1
Proctor, Richard Anthony, 1085n13
Prometheus, 1137n22
Proverbial Philosophy (Tupper), 166n7
"Providential Intimation, A," 429n1
Provines, Robert R., 17n11
"Psychological Shipwreck, A," 377, 1003n1

Pullman Company, 954n2
Putnam House (Auburn), 739n2

Quay, Matthew, 954n6
"Queer Story, A," 798
"Questions of Life" (Whittier), 179n1

Rabelais, François, 1133n53
"Rabid Transit," 828
"Race at Left Bower, The," 256n2
"Raging Canal, The," 299
Ralston, William C., 145n1, 293n6, 395n2
Randolph, George Wythe, 437n8
Rape of the Lock, The (Pope), 1128n4
Rapunzel, 125
Raspe, Rudolf Erich, 305n4
Rasselas (Johnson), 696, 1205
"Raven, The" (Poe), 350n5
Read, Opie, 903n11
Readyville, Tennessee, 1011n1
"Real Art of Reading a Ghost Story, The," 682
"Realm of the Unreal, The," 750, 825
"Reper and the Flowers, The" (Longfellow), 1179n1
"Recessional: June 22, 1897" (Kipling), 1040n7
Reed, John, 897
Reese, Michael, 17n9
"Reform School Board, The," 1127n2
Regent's Park (London), 316n1
Reliance (ship), 963
"Reminiscence of Artemus Ward, A" (Twain), 217n4
Republican State Convention, 742
"Requiem: Dedicated to the Memory of the Slain in Battle" (Lunt), 512n3
Restraints on the Alienation of Property (Gray), 724n3
"Resumed Identity, A," 975
Reuter, Paul Julius, 317n8
Reuters, 317n8
"Reversion to Barbarism, The," 1053
"Revision of a Catalogue," 408n1
"Revolt of the Gods, A," 378, 445, 743n6, 762n2
Rich Mountain (battle of), 624n3
Riley, James Whitcomb, 234n1, 750n4

Rime of the Ancient Mariner, The (Coleridge), 817n12, 991n1
Rincon Hill (San Francisco), 512n4
"Rise and Fall of the Aëroplane," 974
"Rise and Fall of the Aeroplane, The," 1045
road agents, 618n3
Rogers, Mary Mabel, 1086n24
Romance, 778
Rome and the Romans, 161n5, 328n1, 352n2, 419n5, 966n5, 1084n6, 1136n17
Romeo and Juliet (Shakespeare), 145n2
Roosevelt, Franklin D., 1056n2
Roosevelt, Kermit, 1136n16
Roosevelt, Theodore, 897, 944, 974–75, 1056, 1136, 1195n1, 1196n4, 1201
Root, Elihu, 1195n1, 1200
Rosecrans, William S., 512n2, 711n5
Ross, James Clark, 366n3
Roughing It (Twain), 299
Rubaiyat of Omar Khayyam, The, 1179
Rubicon (river), 1136n17
Rupert, Prince, 374n1
Russia, 898, 965
Russian Hill (San Francisco), 24n6
Russo-Japanese War, 965–66
Rust, Albert, 624n1

Sacramento, California, 27n6
Sacred Songs and Solos (Moody), 352n3
Sagebrush School, xxiii, 4, 676
Saint Helena, 165n2
Salmasius, Claudius, 166n6
Salmon River, 281n2
Salomon, Edward S., 742n4
Saltus, Edgar, 1127
"Sam Baxter's Eel," 183n3
"Samboles," 26
Sampson, William T., 1196n5
"Samuel Baxter, M.D.," 183n3
San Carlos, California, 426n2
San Francisco, xvii, xviii, 3–4, 16nn6–7, 16n9, 17n14, 24n6, 27n6, 54n1, 61n2, 67n2, 88, 97n4, 145n1, 145nn3–5, 231n7, 278, 292n1, 293n3, 293n6, 360n1, 377, 378, 395n2, 397n1, 400n3, 426n2, 454n2, 503, 512n4, 518n1, 518nn5–6, 739n3, 742n4, 743n14, 815n2, 828n3, 897, 983, 1008, 1086n32, 1087n35, 1145, 1146n1, 1178n2, 1181, 1191n1
San Francisco Bulletin, 16n7, 79n1
San Francisco Call, 448n2, 604
San Francisco Chronicle, 79n1, 419n6
San Francisco Examiner, xvii, xx, 501–2, 511, 518, 524, 533, 541, 554, 566, 576, 581, 586, 592, 598, 604, 611, 618, 624, 629, 635, 642, 647, 652, 658, 664, 670, 675, 676, 682, 690, 696, 705, 711, 718, 724, 732, 739, 750, 773, 778, 783, 794, 798, 802, 816n5, 825, 828, 840, 846, 850, 856, 863, 902, 912, 920, 924, 928, 935, 938, 944, 947, 950, 956, 963, 1085n17, 1127, 1153, 1155, 1162, 1164, 1166, 1168, 1170, 1173, 1175, 1181, 1182, 1184, 1192, 1194, 1197, 1198, 1199, 1200, 1201, 1207, 1208
San Francisco Morning Call, 16n7
San Francisco News Letter, xxvi, 3, 4, 5, 7, 15n1, 15n9, 20, 23, 26, 27n5, 39, 41, 50, 52, 55, 57, 58, 61, 64, 69, 71, 72, 74, 75, 76, 78, 79, 81, 83, 85, 86, 90, 94, 99, 101, 106, 107, 108, 109, 111, 114, 115, 116, 117, 377, 459, 1187, 1189, 1196
San Francisco Sub-Treasury and Mint, 3, 222n1
San Francisco Times, 16n7
San Francisco Vigilance Committee, 256n5
San Rafael, California, 281n1
Sankey, Ira David, 352n3
Satan, 1128n6, 1129n17, 1130n26
Saturday Night Lantern 618
Saturday Review, 355n1
Saul (Handel), 357n1
Sayler's Creek (battle of), 1040n4
Scaliger, Joseph Justus, 1204n1
Scheffauer, Herman, xxi, 1131n43
Schiller, Friedrich von, 1088n44
Schley, Jessie, 1086n23
Schley, Winfield Scott, 1196n5
Schopenhauer, Arthur, 973, 1127, 1128n11, 1129nn14–15
"Science to the Front," 629
Scientific American, 802n3
"Scientific Dream, A," 6
Scotland and the Scots, 352n2
Scott, Sir Walter, 743n8, 841n2
Scott, Winfield, 653n1
"Scrap-Heap, The," 1046n7
"Screed of the Future Historian, A," 948n5
Scudder, Henry Martyn, 16n9
Secret Doctrine, The (Blavatsky), 779n2

1272

Sedalia, Missouri, 1191
Seidlitz powder, 310n4
Selma, Alabama, 172, 630n1
Sentimental Journey through France and Italy, A (Sterne), 120n1
Sepoy Mutiny, 779n3
Seymour, Horatio, 1129n21
Shadow on the Dial, The, 816n5, 1133n54
Shakespeare, William, 49, 76n2, 97n3, 123n5, 139n1, 145n2, 151n3, 165n1, 165n5, 186n2, 217n3, 231nn5–6, 305n1, 350n3, 419n2, 437n6, 445n2, 454, 503, 534n4, 705n2, 705n5, 712n11, 733n4, 743n9, 825n1, 921n6, 1014n1, 1014n4, 1035n6, 1137n18, 1194nn1–2
Sham Castle (Bath), 161n8
Shamrock (ship), 963
Shapes of Clay, 1046n7
"Shellback," 320
Shelley, Percy Bysshe, 20, 460, 897
Sheridan, Philip Henry, 1040n4
Sherman, William Tecumseh, 533n1, 1028n2
Shiloh (battle of), 711n1, 733n6, 794n2, 840, 920n3
"Shipwreckollection, A," 366n1, 374, 1146n5
Short Stories, 182, 581, 618, 664, 670, 696, 705, 1153
Short Story Classics (Patten), 863
Sickler, Eleanor (Vore), 293n5
Sill, Edward Rowland, 576n3
Silverado Squatters, The (Stevenson), 817n13
"Sindbad the Sailor" (*Arabian Nights*), 148n4, 441–42
"Sinful Freak, A," 310
Sioux Indians, 989n1
"Small Contributions," 1025, 1045, 1053, 1056, 1137n21
Smartville, California, 116n1
Smedley, Edward, 733n7
Smith, Edmund Kirby, 676n1
Smith, Joseph, 26n1
Smugwumps, 950
"Snaking," 183n3, 392n2
Society for Psychical Research, 611n2, 1014n6
"Society Notes," 123n2
"Soldiers and Ghosts," 1010, 1014
"Sole Survivor, A," 203n1, 973, 1084n10
"Some Californian Pictures," 408n1
"Some Haunted Houses," 1178

"Some Queer Experiences" (Morrow), 630n1
"Some Thoughts on the Hanging," 1086n24
"Some Uncanny Tales," 986, 989, 991, 993, 998, 1000, 1002
"Some Unusual Adventures," 374
"Son of the Gods, A," xxiv, 504, 1182
Son of the Gods and A Horseman in the Sky, A 664
Songs of the Sierras (Miller), 47n2
Sonora, California, 288n2
"Sons of the Fair Star," xxviii, 696n1, 1127
Southern Pacific Railroad, 16n6
Spain and Spaniards, 135nn2–3, 897, 928, 939, 1131n33
Spanish language, 135n2, 136n7, 136n9
Spanish-American War, 896, 897, 928, 939, 1057n3, 1131nn33–34, 1196n3, 1196n5, 1201
Spencer, Herbert, 161n9, 936n1
"Spook House, The," 675, 1139
Springfield Republican, 26
Stafford House (London), 357n3
"Staley Fleming's Hallucination," 389n1, 975
Stanley, Sir Henry Morton, 120, 1136n17
Stanton, Edwin M., 437n1
Stanton, Elizabeth Cady, 73n1
Starrett, Vincent, 973
Stebbins, Horatio, 16n9
Steele, E. L. G., 1177, 1178n2
Steele, Joel Dorman, 986n2
Steffens, Lincoln, 897
Stein, William Bysshe, 815
Sterling, George, 816n10, 817n18, 856n1, 1000, 1035n1, 1087n35, 1087n37
Sterne, Laurence, 120n1
Stevenson, Robert Louis, 502, 817n13
Stockton, California, 21n8, 518n4
Stoddard, Richard Henry, 902n2
Stoicism, xxi, 503–4, 505, 690–91, 767, 773, 973, 1127
Stone, Andrew Leete, 108n1
Stone & Kimball, 903n12
Stone's River (battle of), 512n2, 1011, 1040
"Story at the Club, A," 739n3
"Story of a Conscience, The," 41n1
"Story of the Bad Little Boy Who Didn't Come to Grief, The" (Twain), 169
"Strange Adventure, A" (Morrow), 778, 1207
"Strange Night-Doings at Deadman's," 288
"Stranger, A," 1051

The Short Fiction of Ambrose Bierce Volume III was designed and typeset on a Macintosh computer system using QuarkXPress software. The body text is set in 9.5/13 Granjon and display type is set in Granjon. This book was designed by Kelly Gray and typeset by Barbara Karwhite and manufactured by Thomson-Shore, Inc.